JACQU
THI

MW00605529

The work of Jacques Derrida has transformed our understanding of a range of disciplines in the humanities through its questioning of some of the basic tenets of Western metaphysics. This volume is a trans-disciplinary collection dedicated to his work; the assembled contributions – on law, literature, ethics, history, gender, politics and psychoanalysis, among others – constitute an investigation of the role of Derrida's work within the field of humanities, present and future. The volume is distinguished by work on some of his most recent writings, and contains Derrida's own address on "the future of the humanities." In addition to its pedagogic interest, this collection of essays attempts to respond to the question: what might be the relation of Derrida, or "deconstruction," to the future of the humanities. The volume presents the most sustained examples yet of deconstruction in its current phase – as well as its possible future.

Tom Cohen is Professor in the Department of English at the State University of New York, Albany. He is the author of *Anti-Mimesis* (Cambridge, 1994) and *Ideology and Inscription* (Cambridge, 1998). He is also contributing editor of *Material Events: Paul de Man and the Afterlife of Theory* (2000).

JACQUES DERRIDA AND THE HUMANITIES

A Critical Reader

EDITED BY

TOM COHEN

CAMBRIDGE
UNIVERSITY PRESS

PUBLISHED BY THE PRESS SYNDICATE OF THE UNIVERSITY OF CAMBRIDGE
The Pitt Building, Trumpington Street, Cambridge, United Kingdom

CAMBRIDGE UNIVERSITY PRESS
The Edinburgh Building, Cambridge CB2 2RU, UK
40 West 20th Street, New York, NY 10011-4211, USA
477 Williamstown Road, Port Melbourne, VIC 3207, Australia
Ruiz de Alarcón 13, 28014 Madrid, Spain
Dock House, The Waterfront, Cape Town 8001, South Africa

http://www.cambridge.org

First published 2001

Printed in the United Kingdom at the University Press, Cambridge

Typeface Baskerville Monotype 11/12.5 pt.   *System* LATEX 2ε   [TB]

A catalogue record for this book is available from the British Library.

Library of Congress Cataloguing in Publication data
Jacques Derrida and the humanities : a critical reader / edited by Tom Cohen.
p.   cm.
Includes bibliographical references and index.
ISBN 0 521 62370 7 (hardback) ISBN 0 521 62565 3 (paperback)
1. Derrida, Jacques.   2. Humanities – Philosophy.   3. Deconstruction.
I. Cohen, Tom, 1953–
B2430.D484 J33   2001
001.3′092 – dc21   2001025755

ISBN 0 521 62370 7 hardback
ISBN 0 521 62565 3 paperback

For Barbara L. Cohen

Contents

Preface

The present volume may be the first overtly *trans-disciplinary* "reader" devoted to Derrida's work in its current phase. These essays were not only to be "pedagogic" in demonstrating one or more ways to read Derrida's extensions into these fields. They were called together to ask again why or how, "today," Derrida's interventions are to be tracked, and what the consequences of this project stand, perhaps, to be in the institutions of the human sciences or a "Humanities" to come.

Three premises, therefore, underlie the essays gathered here:

(1) That Derrida's work, "today," might be tracked by its interface with a series of different "disciplines," different questions, to make connections for the reader as to how these might work or are underway in scholarship or thinking today: thus, for the first time, a volume in which the somewhat formal questions of Derrida and Law, . . . and Literature, . . . and Aesthetics, . . . and Politics, . . . and Psychoanalysis, . . . and Ethics, . . . and Technology, . . . and Representation, and so on, might be addressed as pretexts for more or less exemplary exploration;

(2) That these essays, virtually or otherwise, would concern themselves less with the polemical contexts of Derrida's past reception – distracting misprisions of "nihilism" or "relativism" or "linguisticism," and so on – than demonstrate by interrogation and performance the "*affirmative* deconstruction" that Derrida has, from the first, insisted was the necessarily transformative premise of his thought;

(3) That these essays might have access to more recent work of Derrida's, or developments which bring into play texts and perspectives (for instance, on hospitality and religion, technicity and the "secret") either unavailable to or unemphasized in earlier treatments of this text.

Collectively, such a trans-disciplinary volume would ask, implicitly, not only the question of the "future of the humanities" in relation to Derrida's work (the title of Derrida's own contribution to the volume) but provide a virtual network or interactive and multi-linked website of cross-referencing essays, a virtual if discontinuous ensemble-effect, perhaps, in which an underlying question would resonate: What is the "state" of the translational project of Derrida, "today," after the narrative and many deaths of deconstruction have been played out, or repeated, or survived? What of the "future" which Derrida's work seems to wager itself on, in the structure (and thematic) of the promise – what can only keep the door open to a coming "event" it cannot effect or guarantee, but which the model of translation, or crossing, would be attendant upon?

Acknowledgements

This volume owes its inception to the late Michael Sprinker, and much of its development and final form to the editorial advice and shaping of Ray Ryan, to whose patience and professionalism the editor is again indebted. I must also extend my professional regard and deep appreciation to Derek Attridge, who lent his time and critical eye to the project from the beginning, and whose input is reflected in the numerous details of the volume itself. Equally decisive, in very different ways, has been the moral and logistical collaboration of Barbara L. Cohen – to whom the volume is dedicated. Throughout the phase of production, review, and organization, Geoff Manaugh has played a critical role in realizing this volume, both in terms of intellectual commentary and technical support. In addition I want to thank Werner Hamacher for discussions and suggestions that helped realize the potential of the project. I would also like to thank Helen Elam and Jason Smith for their generous critical insights.

Biographical chronology

Geoff Manaugh

1930	Born 15 July in El-Biar, French-occupied Algeria; an "indigenous Jew," not a citizen of France.
1935–1941	Attends nursery and primary schools in El-Biar; Article 2 in the *Jewish Statute* (3 October 1940) forbids Jews from teaching and Law.
1942	Expelled from classes as part of a general wave of anti-Semitism. Told by a teacher in class, "French culture is not made for little Jews."
1943–1947	Fails *baccalauréat* in 1947. Publishes some poems in small North African reviews.
1947–1948	Studies philosophy (Bergson, Sartre) at the Lycée Gauthier, Algiers. Passes *baccalauréat* in June 1948. Later that year reads Heidegger and Kierkegaard.
1949–1950	First trip to France. Studies at Lycée Louis-le-Grand. Begins readings of Simone Weil and existentialism. Application to École Normale Supérieure rejected.
1950–1952	Periods of ill health, with cycles of amphetamine/ sleeping pill use. Meets Pierre Bourdieu and Michel Serres, among others; still enrolled at Lycée Louis-le-Grand.
1952–1953	Enrolls at the École Normale Supérieure, where he meets Louis Althusser (also born in Algeria) the first day.
1953–1954	Befriends Michel Foucault, whose lectures he attends. Writes "The Problem of Genesis in the Philosophy of Edmund Husserl" as his higher studies dissertation.
1955	Fails the *agrégation* oral examination (a competitive examination for teaching jobs guaranteed by the State) in philosophy.

1956–1957	Retakes the *agrégation* exam, and passes. Receives "special auditor" status at Harvard University, where he begins reading James Joyce. Marries Marguerite Aucouturier (with whom two children will be raised).
1957–1959	Performs required military service during the Algerian war, serving as a teacher in a children's school outside Algiers.
1959–1960	Receives first teaching post, at a lycée in Le Mans, where he works with Gérard Genette.
1960–1964	Teaching position at the Sorbonne; assistant to Bachelard, Canguilhem, Ricoeur, and Wahl. After declaration of independence for Algeria, Derrida's family moves to Nice. First publications (in *Critique* and *Tel Quel*). Meets Philippe Sollers. Awarded the Jean Cavaillès Prize for his *Introduction* to Husserl's *Origin of Geometry*. Accepts teaching position at the École Normale Supérieure, where he is invited by Althusser and Jean Hyppolite.
1966	Invited by René Girard to participate in a colloquium hosted by Johns Hopkins University, USA, where he meets Paul de Man and Jacques Lacan.
1967	Delivers his paper, "Différance," to the Société française de philosophie. His first three books are published simultaneously.
1968	Participates in various marches during the events of May. First teaching post at the University of Berlin, where he presents *Glas* over the course of a seminar.
1970	Derrida's father, Aimé, dies of cancer at age 74.
1971	Returns to Algeria for the first time in nearly a decade, where he lectures at the University of Algiers. Delivers, in Montreal, "Signature, Event, Context," to the Congrès des sociétés de philosophie de langue française.
1972	Participates in conference on Nietzsche in Cerisy, where other participants include Deleuze, Klossowski, Lacoue-Labarthe, Lyotard, and Nancy. Three more books are published, but a break is made with Sollers and *Tel Quel*.
1975	Begins Fall seminars at Yale, with Paul de Man and J. Hillis Miller.

1979   Helps organize, at the Sorbonne in Paris, the Estates General of Philosophy.

1980   Defends his own *Thèse d'État* at the Sorbonne. Conference at Cerisy ("On the basis of JD's work") organized by Lacoue-Labarthe and Nancy. Honorary Doctorate awarded by Columbia University, New York City.

1981   Visits Prague as part of the Jan Hus Association, which he founds, to teach a "clandestine seminar." Arrested at the airport for allegedly possessing heroin, and jailed. Released upon intervention of the French government.

1982   Appears in Ken McMullen's film, *Ghost Dance*. Begins first steps toward founding, with others, the Collège international de philosophie.

1983   Elected director of the Collège international de philosophie. Joins the main council of the "Foundation against Apartheid." Death of Paul de Man.

1986   Begins collaborations with architect Peter Eisenman, on invitation of Bernard Tschumi, for the Parc de la Villette in Paris.

1987   Begins regular Spring teaching appointment at the University of California, Irvine. Honorary Doctorate awarded by Essex University, UK.

1988   Honorary Doctorate awarded by the University of Palermo, Italy.

1989   Lectures at Cardozo School of Law, New York City, on "Deconstruction and the Possibility of Justice." Honorary Doctorates awarded by Williams College, USA; and the New School for Social Research, New York City.

1991   Derrida's mother, Georgette, dies.

1992   Controversial honorary Doctorate awarded by Cambridge University. Begins Fall seminars at Cardozo School of Law, NYC. Second conference at Cerisy.

1993   Honorary Doctorate awarded by the University of Pécs, Hungary.

1995   Conference in Tuscaloosa, on deconstruction, around the time of the De Man wartime journalism controversy. Honorary Doctorate awarded by Queens College, Ontario, Canada.

1996   Honorary Doctorate awarded by the University of Craiova, Romania.

1997   Third conference at Cerisy. Honorary Doctorate awarded
        by the University of Katowice, Poland.
1998   Honorary Doctorates awarded by the University of Torino,
        Italy, and Western Cape University, South Africa.

The above chronology is based on Geoff Bennington, "Curriculum Vitae," presented in G. Bennington and J. Derrida, *Jacques Derrida* (Chicago: University of Chicago Press, 1991). The reader is pointed to that work for more information concerning the life of Jacques Derrida. I must also thank David Wills for his input to this chronology.

Introduction: Derrida and the future of . . .

Tom Cohen

> Thus we no longer know whether what was always represen-
> ted as . . . "supplement," "sign," "writing," or "trace," "is" not . . .
> "older" than presence and the system of truth, older than "his-
> tory." Or again, whether it is "older" than sense and the senses:
> older than the primordial dator intuition, . . . older than see-
> ing, hearing, and touching . . . not more "ancient" than what is
> "primordial."
>
> *Speech and Phenomena*

> the technical structure of the archiving archive also determines . . .
> its relationship to the future. The archivization produces as much
> as it records the event.
>
> *Archive Fever*

> Of course, if one defines language in such a way that it is reserved
> for what we call man, what is there to say? But if one re-inscribes
> language in a network of possibilities that do not merely encompass
> it but mark it irreducibly from the inside, everything changes. I am
> thinking of the mark in general, of the trace, of iterability, of *différance*.
> These possibilities or necessities, without which there would be no
> language, *are themselves not only human* . . . I am speaking here of very
> "concrete" and very "current" problems: the ethics and the politics
> of the living.
>
> "Eating Well"

I. WAGER

One could speak here of many things: the event horizon, the prosthetic earth, the absolute translation of legacies, the gambling of alternative futures, memory grids that give place to or transform institutions
from within, the hyper-politics of the allomorphic archive, experimental
chronographics – all part of the Derridean wager. Perhaps. What links
them is that they could arise out of a volume of trans-disciplinary essays

which addresses, today, the state of Derrida's project in relation to the "future," if there is a relation as such, of the Humanities, and perhaps the "human."

A break or betrayal, certainly an organizing incision is required at the outset.

While developing over four decades through an astonishing array of styles or strategies, performative experiments, and targeted interrogations, Derrida's project has been entirely consistent with his opening gambit. Here is how Derrida announced this:

> The use of language or the employment of any code which implies a play of forms – with no determined or invariable substratum – also presupposes a retention and protention of differences, a spacing and temporalizing, a play of traces. This play must be a sort of inscription prior to writing, a protowriting without a present original, without an *arche*. From this comes the systematic crossing-out of the *arche* and the transformation of general semiology into a grammatology, the latter performing a critical work upon everything within semiology – right down to its matrical concept of signs – that retains any metaphysical presuppositions incompatible with the theme of *différance*.[1]

How does a reading of the "trace," spacing, the mark, and *différance* transform not only the inherited legacies of the West (for this would amount, only, to an annotation to an archive of knowledge), but actively translate its terms, eviscerate and re-assemble them in difference, interrupt the received programs of perception, interpretation, and experience – and in the process of altering this past or archive, the very functioning of it, hold open the space for the arrival of the unprecedented event, of a virtual or alternative "future" to those programmatically foreseeable (a "future" necessarily *monstrous* since unprogrammed)? That is, whatever Derrida's institutional place or *places* today within the Academic disciplines – and there is no one answer to this, given the play of presence and absence – the stakes of this enterprise never were canonicity, but something perhaps like a translation or recalibration of mnemonic orders to set the stage for, perhaps, other events, decisions, and transformations "to come." Numerous interventions in Derrida's work have targeted specific problems and fields – from law to architecture, literature, ethics, technology, religion, aesthetics, history, politics, and so on – but if one were to try to identify or visualize the "trace," one could not, though nothing could enter the realm of perceptibility, language, thought, or history in its absence. "Older" than history or the senses, it would traverse the site of archival management retaining the possibility of interruption, intervention, much as the mark does all textual agencies on the most micrological of levels, much as "spacing," representable (if at all) by or as mere interval, like a series of slashes, sustains all visibility, all temporalization, all "writing." If Derrida's entire project is a wager nonetheless, it is important to recall the *ante* on the table, which today if anything has only been upped by the impasses which might put the possibility of the "future" in question variably. The upping of the ante – the rendering hyper-political, we might say, of that concerned with the pre-originary effect of thinking the "trace" – has also come from without: say, the University in "ruins," the rule of corporate globalization, "Marxism's" defensive retreat, global warming, and the havoc or eviscerations of terrestrial reserves (species extinction, potable water, fossil fuels, and so on).[2] If the "Humanities" are caught in a double cross-site of University and cultural priorities, they are at once targeted and preserved as a legacy of a humanistic program which archived temporality and value. Out of joint with cultural pragmatisms and consumer culture or the hegemony of techno-science, its monumentalization is as much valued, it seems, as its transformation into active projects of translation would be blocked, returned to a service industry for the maintenance of an ideology of transparency that confirms an arrestation in a rethinking of technicity generally. The broad retreat of contemporary pedagogy in the feudal structure of University rule is too obvious to need addressing, except to note where the *virtual* legacy of the forces, laws, traces, and mnemonic performatives that would be translated – and actively transformed – by alternative relay and reading models threatens the dominant academic sites of today's horizons: at risk of enslavement or reduction to a service capacity, their "future" might depend upon an active translation of linguistic and perceptual premises (hence, a certain model of the "human"). The "Humanities" may appear, at present, pre-inhabited by a *mal d'archive* or "death drive" confirmed by the institutional "pragmatism" which brackets them by fulfilling that drive – subsidiary, all the while, to economic forces that legislate definition and place.

Derrida has his way of pointing to an irreality that can no longer be situated as such in these terms, as in the opening of the third chapter, "Wears and Tears (Tableau of an Ageless World)," in *Specters of Marx*:

The time is out of joint. The world is going badly. It is worn but its wear no longer counts. Old age or youth – one no longer counts in that way. The world has more than one age. We lack the measure of the measure. We no longer realize the war, we no longer take account of it as a single age in the progress of history. Neither maturation, nor crisis, nor even agony. Something else. What is happening is happening to age itself, it strikes a blow at the teleological order of history. What is coming, in which the untimely appears, is happening to time but it does not happen in time. Contretemps. *The time is out of joint.*[3]

To examine "deconstruction" as a wager is, perhaps, not to rehearse again the techniques of reading or the assault on metaphysics that provided the earliest context for the polemics surrounding its reception. It might, instead, direct itself primarily to what Derrida terms affirmative "deconstruction" (of which, differently, there would nonetheless be no other kind).

An incision may be required to resituate these stakes, this *ante* that was on the table before any among us arrived. How is a "future" – if unpreconceived and therefore "monstrous" – held open against the automated closure of installed laws which police and regulate perception, hermeneutic machines that preinscribe decisions, models of reference and action, and so on?[4] If the programming of institutions and regimes of memory management stand to be opened to a radical (and non-human) alterity that welcomes the "event," the received programs we find ourselves in are not only implicitly judged as *faulted*, as forecasting a certain doom, as a *mal d'archive* turned against itself beyond the "histories" of metaphysics or the economies of phallogocentrism that are openly targeted. If there is a *fault* in this state without horizons, that which is "older" than history itself and standing apart from it can critique or recast its program – like the injunction Hamlet receives from the visored ghost ("Do not forget!"), an imparted "knowledge" contradicted by the court or appearances to the point of folly, much as the logics of the "trace" would be contradicted too by the rhetoric of empiricisms, realisms, hermeneuticisms, pragmatisms, materialisms, and so on, for which an assumed transparency of language would be both premise and alibi. It must be possible to hypothesize, as Benjamin does in the *Theses on History*, a rupture, shock, or caesura in which an orchestrated program or past can itself be suspended, disinscribed, and through which other inscriptions can take place, opening new questions and new "responsibilities" that traverse the human and the non-human, animate (or animal) and inanimate, technicity, ethics, and decision. For the "future" cannot arrive without a mark that prepares, or invites, its place – and the site of translation, today, in the fields represented by the "Humanities" or trans-disciplines represented in this volume, offer an occasion to survey that movement, the state of the wager perhaps, its advance or regressions, formalized paralyses or incisions. If we may speak today of *upping the ante* it is as the rendering hyper-political of the pre-originary logic of "trace."[5] What will seem a translation of legacies undertaken by Derridean reading is not from one language into another, such as a new reading technique or set of textual premises. The wager at issue involves how regimes of memory management (hermeneutics) precedent to pre-ception, certainly, program or produce calculable forms of life, decisions, experience, or how the archive is pre-inhabited in this way by an ill, a fault (again), a *mal d'archive* whose formalizations foreclose the "future" in determinant ways.

To approach this site, we may need to recall some of the tools Derrida brings into play. And this is why reading becomes an agency of interven-tion in the opening to redecision not only of mnemotechnic programs and hermeneutic rules, but what Benjamin calls the "sensorium" (by which the world is produced and processed, reference assigned, laws in-teriorized). Reading, that is, which sides with a movement of the "trace" or mark or spacing before any semantic unit or grammar can pretend to legislate sense; reading which, variably, ensconces the text-event in a per-formativity without ground (authorial dictate, generic law, the "proper" more generally); reading as tool and weapon; readings for which, say, the *phoneme* might appear the labyrinthine precedent, and betrayer, of any phenomenology: for only by this disruption of the hermeneutic regime which includes a programming of the senses does an opening to a "fu-ture" or "event" occur that is not, merely, another "tomorrow." Specif-ically, if the Derridean wager offers itself in some ways as transitional, as a bridge or crossing, it might be said to (dis)assemble in the process a grid, a web, a network of disruptive nodes or points in which this is underway but also against which new combinations may be staged or begin to take root. This transitional site is Mosaic to the degree it can ap-pear to exceed one law (or semantic regime) with the prospect of other responsibilities which are no longer only "human" but traverse living and dead, past and future, terrestrial dwelling and ethics. If mnemonic inscriptions program both the senses and interpretive rituals, Derrida's wager may be said, in short, to address what is at issue in disinscribing such a pre-recording – what will be experienced as "loss," no doubt, by certain communities, and hence as a "nihilistic" moment – and re-inscribing otherwise, within a new opening or hospitality to alterity, to a non-human Other. This difference from the perception of "decon-struction" as a nihilist or relativistic practice, even a merely deseman-ticizing one, to that of a project positioning a break with a provenly nihilistic historicism and humanism, in an open wager directed toward a "future" it cannot, itself, expect to arrive on its watch or even rec-ognize, is decisive, and decisive for evaluating what transformations in the disciplines, the Humanities, or the archive itself may or may not be underway.

If reading Derrida entails a labyrinthine movement, then, it is as a performative and at times vertiginous mobility where strategies and logics replicate in explosive variants and viral elaborations. One may choose, as a reader, one among other threads to hold in entering these translational scenes. For if Derrida anticipates and insists on an "other writing" that pre-inhabits and ruptures hermeneutic laws, disinvests master terms, alters the hegemony of conceptual networks from within – if a plethora of strategies and inventions fan out across the field of Western legacies which remark and dislocate received machines of sense – one can pretend to reduce this to two clashing logics: that of the "trace" and that of the received mnemonic program or law.

The "trace" partakes of the logics and movement of the mark and of spacing. If in "human" thought and perception there is language at work, that entails the movement of an irreducible element that can parse, re-arrange, micrologically question or translate – that is, hyperbolically read – how textual events may appear formalized to organize memory, manage knowledge, or legislate (often against themselves) the senses.[6] This factor is sometimes called simply (and somewhat misleadingly) "writing." The mark or trace, occluded from the field of linguistic thought to preserve a fabled transparency of perception or "communication," on which again all rhetorics of realism, historicism, phenomenology, empiricism, pragmatism, mimeticism, and spiritism variably rely, provokes a rereading of the entire field of mnemonic experience or textual legacies as well as all that derives from it: hermeneutic rituals, the programming of so-called perception, the management of political memory, juridical and aesthetic institutions, ethics, the problematic or prospect or definition of temporal inscription. This logic triggers an irreversible scene of translation – a difference or *différance* (at once a temporal and spatial movement) that transports from viewing "human speech acts" as conventions managed by the will to performatives without ground traversed by non-human traces, without a secure horizon of occurrence (without a "now," as opposed to a skein of retentive and protentive traces, gathering, determining, effacing). One can be excused for projecting the figure of a historial bottleneck – as if every problematic, every discipline, must be recalibrated and re-initialized before the play of the "trace."[7] Here would be recast the functioning of the archiving archive out of which experience, decision, and virtual futures would be given space to occur or not. The trace, non-human, dispossesses the economy of a dwelling predicated on a binarized occlusion of the (non-human) Other and opens these networks of mnemonic laws to possible default, to a disassembly that permits a re-assembly maintaining the logics of spacing and trace – that is, a hospitality toward the non-human Other that is structural, open to recalibrations not only of archival politics but the technicity of geothanatological and epistemo-political effects. In this seemingly minimal wager – that of "trace," spacing, or the mark – there would be perhaps nothing more than a gambling of (an) virtual earth(s), assuming that everything which determines human institutions depends on regimes of memory management and the semantic controls that effect it. That is, it involves the possibility or event of dis-inscription and re-inscription.[8]

How would the former be effected? How would the former be proffered, if the pre-recordings precede even our notion of the "past," since they manage the definitions (or produce the narratives) which define anteriority, and how would the latter (re-inscription) be determined and installed so as to make place for the (deferred) possibility of the "event" (which that inscription is)? How does the recording archive produce the event that it (would) records, thus altering the past and rendering the "event" possible? How does this "translation" induced by a thinking of trace – not from one language to another, but within every so-called "language" (of which there never is "one") by an "other language" or writing which does not yet exist but pre-inhabits each – yield an ethics, a politics, a conception of religion haunted by technicity? What shapes or trajectories does an affirmative deconstruction take, as if to say "today"?[9]

2. DIS(AS)SEMBLING MOSAICS

> This concept of responsibility is inseparable from a whole network of connected concepts (property, intentionality, will, conscience, consciousness, self-consciousness.)
>
> "Force of Law"

The trace is unrepresentable unless as a correlative of *spacing* we thought of it metaphorically as a series of slashes or bars (a signature used, interestingly, throughout Hitchcock to dissolve the mimetic pretext of visibility), or in "phonemonological" terms a sort of aural knocking – as at a *séance*, under the table. As in the closing of "Plato's Pharmacy": "The night passes. In the morning, knocks are heard at the door. They seem to be coming from outside, this time . . . Two knocks . . . four . . ."[10] This "knocking" is from an outside which is not one except, perhaps, as an effect whose dispossessing pre-inhabitation is or must be quieted, effaced, or contained (to create an "interior" effect). During the analysis of "Plato's Pharmacy" Derrida stops at the site of *khora* in the *Timaeus*, where he places a bookmark: "Here is a passage beyond all 'Platonic' oppositions, toward the *aporia* of originary inscription . . . The *khora* is big with everything that is disseminated here. We will go into that elsewhere" (160–61). This "elsewhere" will be the non-place of *khora* it/herself, the faux (a)maternal (or "(a)material") prospect of pre-originary inscription, as well as Derrida's later essay of that name, a pre-originary (non)site where programs and inscriptions are installed:

> the being-programme of the programme, its structure of pre-inscription and of typographic prescription forms the explicit theme of the discourse *en abyme* on *khora*. The latter figures the place of inscription of *all that is marked on the world*.[11]

Yet here, too, we are close to imaging within the Derridean weave a site where the disinstallation or re-inscription of world can be, despite its non-place, approached or marked: "a place where everything is marked but which would be 'in itself' unmarked" (109). As for the role Plato has taken in the so-called history of metaphysics: " 'Platonism' is thus certainly one of the effects of the text signed by Plato, for a long time, and for necessary reasons, the dominant effect, but this effect is always turned back against the text" (119–20). "Against the text," like a *mal d'archive* that simultaneously imposes a hermeneutic regime and installs a software whose arc entails eventual self-cancellation.[12] The *mal d'archive*, the "radical evil" of and within the archive, constitutes the archive yet turns it against itself ("There is not one archive fever, one limit or one suffering of memory among others: enlisting the in-finite, archive fever verges on radical evil").[13] What emerges, or can be profiled in this non-site, *khora*, is the backloop of the pre-inscription, the pre-recording which includes, projects, or programs an itinerary – since a "hermeneutic" is also an epistemo-political regime – which will occur according to this law, a history which evades the "event."[14] The logic allows us to conceive, then, of what the event of dis-inscription – for this is the effect of the Derridean readings of Plato alluded to – intervenes in, in optioning another set of horizons:

> *Everything happens as if* the yet-to-come history of the interpretations of *khora* were written or even prescribed in advance, *in advance and reproduced and reflected* in a few pages of the *Timaeus* "on the subject" of *khora* "herself" ("itself"). With its ceaseless re-launchings, its failures, its superimpositions, its overwritings and reprintings, this history wipes itself out in advance since it programs itself, reproduces itself, and reflects itself by anticipation. Is a prescribed, programmed, reproductive, reflexive history still a history? . . . hence what I am saying about

khora gives a commentary, in advance, and describes the law of the whole history of the hermeneutics and institutions which will be constructed *on this subject*, over this subject. (99)

A history whose institutions and hermeneutics in all variations are programmed by the event which that same history stages itself or covers over, turns against ("The archive always works, and *a priori*, against itself"),[15] yet leaves intact as *transperformative* – if such a prescripted itinerary can be called a "history" – is opened anew to disinscription and re-inscription, its pre-recordings rendered again virtual. *Khora* assumes the position of the (non)mother, the undoing of materiality and maternity before what is pre-originary, where the world is assembled by marks which, nonetheless, are to it/herself "neither sensible nor intelligible" (96).

This is the non-site of virtual disinscription and re-inscription of the world, impossible, without relation to phenomenality. *Khora* would be anterior, *ante*, even to archive: "As much as and more than a thing of the past, before such a thing, the archive should *call into question* the coming of the future" (33).[16] The metaphorics of "mother" is exposed as prosthetic, a site of marking and spacing, like the earth, *Geo*, which stands to be re-inscribed at this site which the transperformative draws toward.[17]

The knocking at the *séance* table stands to interrupt, dis-assemble, or micrologically open any mnemonic program or language, like the spacing or trace which attends the spectral setting of an unending translation. This movement of the trace preinhabits the languages and house or legacies of the tradition. I mark these matters since it frames the "deconstructive" project at a slight remove from what I will call the reference wars of the academy whose polemics have at times defined, and cauterized, the intervention at issue – which would be neither that of new techniques of academic reading, as such, nor an aestheticization of the political. If in the knocking of the *séance*, which the logic of the trace or mark signals, the management of anteriority stands to be reconfigured, it is to make an opening of and toward the possibility of the event or the arrival of virtual futures. The model for this is a translation that is without end since it does not move from one to another so-called language. Any given language(s), any monolinguism apprehended as a pretended unity, would appear already spoken by one who (or that) is also not "of" that language, not coincident with it, hence preinhabited by another language experience or language not yet existent – "the ante-premier . . . (or) pre-originary language" ("Monolinguism," 21). This is not introduced by an outside, another language, but recalls Benjamin's inverse trope of *reine*

Sprache,[18] that is, the sheerly (a) material trace-scapes out of which any particular language would be assembled and which would allow a given text to be perpetually resolved into these trace-scapes, in different combinations, by the act of translation as if caught in the transition between two "languages." In the case of the North African Derrida :

> this "inside" of French inscribes within the relationship-to-itself of language, inside its auto-affection so to speak, an absolute outside, the hardly audible or legible reference to that *entirely* other ante-premier language, that degree zero-minus-one of writing which leaves its ghostly mark "in" the so-called monolanguage. This translation translates itself into an internal (Franco-French) translation, playing with the non-identity with itself of all language. No such thing as *one* language exists. (21)

This "structural opening" onto the idea of the future Derrida terms, again, "messianism, that originary promise without a literal content" (23). Translation as hyperbolic *crossing*, or suspended crossing *over* (*Übersetzung*), presents a "structural opening" within the orders of memory, the archive and, independently of all relational defamation, what is called *khora* – the site of pre-inscription. The hospitality of this model to the era of tele-technicity is apparent (and perhaps misleading): the assumption of sheer exteriority without a definition of the "private," the affirmative interface with hypertextual models, the alertness to tropes of "software" that run programs, and so on.

To transpose or translate further or at random, some logics which attend the non-site of *khora* surface not only in the archive or "absolute translation," but in Derrida's analysis of the "apocalyptic tone" ("an apocalypse without apocalypse"), or even literature and "the secret." The political necessity of the latter is stressed, as when the relatively recent or modern "institution" of literature is defined as what allows *everything to be said*: "No democracy without literature; no literature without democracy."[19] Such a *literature* always situated within and against a phantasmal state-control of internalized linguistic censorship marks itself by a logic of "the secret" whose "non-phenomenality is without relation, even negative, to phenomenality" ("Passions," 21). Moreover, if the machinery and presuppositions of reference are retracted and rewired through the non-mystical and contentless formalism of the "secret," the latter's retreat generates the fiction of a relation: "The secret is that one here calls it secret, putting it for once in relation to all the secrets which bear the same name but cannot be reduced to it. The secret would also be homonymy, not so much a hidden resource of homonymy, but the functional possibility of homonymy or of *mimesis*" (21). With the function of the empty "secret" as mere formal assignation rests the alibi of homonymy or *mimesis*, which inversely upholds the machine of representation. The secret doubles over a formal complicity with the state or its aesthetic regime of memory management (since what *mimesis* reproduces is less a real than a coded or commodified anterior trace). This makes "literature" an institution only possible to name as such at its moment of exposure or possible suspension as well. Hence its political double-agency – staking infinite "democracy" but also giving the censor a site of assigned (and controlled, irreal) play, an aestheticization of the *transperformative* that creates another archival reserve (say, in the Academy) to anchor the fictions of reference which literature would simultaneously expose and traverse.[20]

In this case, the blindspot replicates but reverses the misreading of deconstructive style by the rhetoric of political representationalism – that is, since the former resists assignation or *mimesis*, it cannot enter the political debate. The effect cannot be to reproduce the logic of differential translation as a preparatory gesture to a certain crossing – the role of Moses in this process, providing new inscriptions for a "future" he cannot assert or cross over into. It is not accidental that such a Mosaic task recurs attached to Derrida's trajectory, remarked by Blanchot, Derrida, and others.[21] Such a crossing over or out would not be of geopolitical or periodic borders, and is as impossible to assert or describe as the event which, by marking, it makes space for as a repetition (otherwise). One secret of the secret is the utter exteriority of an earth experienced as transformatic surfaces traversed not by mimetic archives which stamp the past and reference as capital or reserve, but a proactive mimesis without model or copy, a weave of alloplastic and allochronic marking networks open to radical alterity. The re-orientation of the political does not involve the positionality of suppressed identity, or tracking "material" conditions reinscribed in a metaphysical archive – a dilemma, within the Academy, that too often links the epistemo-political regimes of neo-conservative archivism (historicism, biographism, domains of transparency and facts) to the mimetic regimentation of "leftist" thought and polemics. An *other* definition of the epistemo-political or of archival politics would be necessitated, as here of another humanity – or Humanities – "beyond the homo-fraternal and phallogocentric schema."[22] Whatever "future" would be provoked or solicited by this incision is made place for through the dismantling evacuation of guardian terms and semantic policing, what can again be rendered virtual – since the archive turns against itself per definition, and may be made to do so doubly – by a retro-proleptic alteration of inscriptions ("archivization produces as much as it records the event" [*Archive*, 17]). These networks collude and collide, perhaps, in a frantic set of rhythms whose translation-effect would be, nonetheless, *irreversible*.

What the spectrality of "trace" stands to re-write, then, is a geotechnity that begins a process of archival transformation rethinking not just dwelling – a dwelling without interiority or reserve (we might add, with fossil fuels, potable water, biodiversity, and so on in mind: indefinite reserves) – which is also to say a de-naturalized "earth," without up or down, without solar origin, without mystical gravity, a zoographicism in which "life" as effect, and the mimetic allomorphism of iterable forms (camouflage, shape-shifting, evolutionary adaption) are rethought across the boundaries once defining "human" and its politically defined imaginary others, a horizon marked by an opening to the absolute and hence non-human Other (as in current work on the "animal").[23] Such a geotechnicity "to come" thought not as the hegemony of techno-science but the latter's redistribution according to archival laws and a mimesis without model or copy remains, without doubt, a limit moment of this wager. Such a rethinking of a dwelling without interiority or an absolute hospitality requires, as a practical step, a trans-architecture.

3. HAUNTED DWELLING, TRANS-ARCHITECTURE

> the affirmation that motivates deconstruction is unconditional, imperative, and immediate
>
>   "Eating Well"

An utterly marginal or occasion piece in this canon may be of use as a hosting mechanism here. In a riff on Bernard Tschumi's architectural writing, Derrida maps a project that tracks, perhaps, the affirmative – if not reconstructive – moment of deconstruction, "a writing of space, a mode of spacing which makes a place for the event" (570).[24] Before any recourse to the clichés surrounding the Derridean effect, the experience of loss and disruption primarily "experienced" by those invested in discursive formations whose transformation would, indeed, be at issue, we might re-emphasize this task of translation itself: in its entirety, in the hospitality it will theorize and attempt to perform toward radical alterity, the Derridean project may (perhaps must) be read as a wager, an intervention, an interruption of a set of programs – metaphysics, phallogocentrism, empiricism, materialism, and so on – and a future it could not name or dictate but only, by this intervention, make possible as an "event." These programs must pass through, or cross, a site of interruption or translation, and why that effect could be referenced (as here) to something as seemingly irreducible, minor, and banal perhaps as "spacing" or the movement of what Derrida will name "trace." Irreducible, prefigural, dependent not on entities but the interval, not on the word or concept but the mark, not on historial agency but that before which "history" must appear as imposed narrative. So if a thinking of the "trace" entails *translation* not from one historical epoch to another but from a certain model of the *oikos* and history – humanist, dependent on posited origins cast within epistemo-critical programs and inscriptions shaped by the era of the Book, among other things – to another, it is not serial, not a matter of substitution, and not a matter of prediction. To interrupt a system that forecloses the possibility of "future" is not necessarily (or at all) "nihilistic." On the contrary, since it cannot propose or dictate the shape of the "event" without falling back into the same trap (or reinforcing it), and since it must lay the groundwork or grid for dis-inscription and the possibility of re-inscription (the ultimate or *hyperpolitics* is, in this sense, mnemonic, a politics of the *archive*), it is not only affirmative but so without a specified object of "faith" to focus upon – as if to say, almost, in the name of an earth not yet arrived though in no way utopian or dialectical.

The affirmative moment would mark itself both as an "experience" beyond the programming of experience ("of" deconstruction, the impossible, trace, and so on), and does not take the form, necessarily, of resuming a program of assurances. It is structural, in excess of the closure of hermeneutic sutures and regimes, with their predictable destinations, and if incomprehensible to the latter, are already implied by the privileged performative of language: the *promise* – the site where the play of retentive traces, or legacies, is projected toward a future reading that cannot arrive in any "present." It is held open to, and mobilized within language by, an effect that is not "human," that is other or Other – yet which, once again, can be referenced to something as irreducible as the mark. The performative of human language is not referred, as in "speech act" theory, to the grounded agency of a speaker, since the performative itself is both given and traversed, constituted and deconstituted, by an abyss of contexts, agencies, lines of force, points, of course letters, but units themselves impossible without marking, spacing, trace – a sort of "materiality without matter." The "translation" spoken

of above occurs, we might say, from the "non-perspective" of the trace –
"older" than history, "older" than the originary, traversing the animate
and inanimate. Yet this scene of crossing that is, at best, in Mosaic fashion
and yet not, prepared, is also a wager without guarantee nor can be. Any
attempt to interrogate the effect of this translation or active reading on
the various discursive disciplines today such as history, or law, or ethics,
or the "institution" of literature – all of which Derrida has performed
interventionist readings within the constituted traditions of – would
draw more or less closer to the site of a wager, and transformation.

Altering the definitional matrices of the *oikos* or dwelling, and hence
hospitality, as if to void each of the metaphorics of interiority, Derrida
speaks of a "transarchitecture" (578). The proffered terms of translation or the new "grid" does "not achieve assembled totality. It crosses
through. To establish a grid" – that is, among other things, the new
language, or terms, or questions that arrive – "is to cross through, to go
through a channel. It is the experience of permeability." "A path must be
traced for another writing" (579) designed (Derrida is still interrogating
Tschumi's work) "to give dissociation its due, but to implement it *per se*
in the space of reassembly" (579). The site of crossing (without *telos*) is, like
reading according to the logics of *trace*, of points (the title of a collection
of Derrida's interviews), a "discontinuous series of instants and *attrac-
tions*": "Each point is a breaking-point: it interrupts, absolutely . . . But
the interrupter maintains together *both* the rupture and the relation to
the other, which is itself structured as both attraction *and* interruption,
interference and difference: a relation without relation" (580). The struc-
turality of trans-architecture, which cannot exile spacing and some form
of terrestrial dwelling, provides the foil of this re(dis)assembly:

> it was necessary to speak of promise and pledge, of promise as affirmation, the
> promise that provides the privileged example of a performative writing. More
> than an example: the very condition of such writing. Without accepting what
> would be retained as presuppositions by theories of performative language and
> speech acts – relayed here by an architectural pragmatics (for example, the value
> of presence, of the *maintenant* as present) – and without being able to discuss it
> here, let us focus on this single trait: the provocation of the event I speak of
> ("I promise," for example), that I describe or trace; the event that I *make* happen
> or *let* happen by marking it. The mark or trait must be emphasized so as to
> remove this performativity from the hegemony of speech and of what is called
> human speech. The performative mark *spaces* is the event of spacing. (580)

Interruption: the trait or mark, somewhere, which then opens the space
for the event, and displaces the self-interpretation and mock-hegemony

of "what is called human speech." Without a mark that persists the event has no place, the "future" no chance, even if that mark cannot name or predict but only provoke or let happen, if (we can add) the mark persists as archive and as interruption:

But this *maintenant* does not only maintain a past and a tradition; it does not ensure a synthesis. It maintains the interruption, in other words, the relation to the other *per se*. To the other in the magnetic field of attraction . . . but first of all to the Other: the one through whom the promised event will happen or will not. For he is called, only called to countersign the pledge [*gage*], the engagement or the wager. This Other never presents itself; he is not present, *maintenant* . . . This Other will be anyone, not yet a subject, ego or conscience and not a man; anyone who comes and answers the promise, who first answers for the promise, the to-come of an event which would maintain spacing, the *maintenant* in dissociation, the relation to the other *per se*. Not the hand being held [*main tenue*] but the hand outstretched [*main tendue*] above the abyss. (580–81)

This bridging hand with connotations of technicity and touch precedent to preception is also the agency of an other writing:

But if it presents neither theory, nor ethics, nor politics, nor narration . . . it gives a place to them all. It writes and signs in advance – *maintenant* a divided line on the edge of a meaning, before any presentation, beyond it – the very other, who engages architecture, its discourse, political scenography, economy and ethics. Pledge but also wager, symbolic order and gamble: these red cubes [Tschumi's grid-figures] are thrown like the dice of architecture. The throw not only programs a strategy *of* events, as I suggested earlier; it anticipates the architecture to come. It runs the risk and gives us a chance. (581)

The reason I have cited this text among many is the logic it presents, under the aegis of trans-architecture, not only for an "affirmative" de-construction (there would be no other), but the wager by which another writing summons a "future" it does not predict or necessarily partici-pate in, without presenting the entire assembly of new arts or disciplines, "gives a place to them all." Another writing of law, of history, of aesthetics, of gender, of literature, of the disciplines or the "Humanities" (or the "human" more generally).

Yet if this "trans-architecture" reflects (perhaps) the entire network of Derridean writings, the vast switchboard and infra-citational movements which cannot cease maintaining interruption simultaneously with a re-assembly that provokes the possibility of the event, it presents itself as a wager. The risk it runs in anticipating this "architecture to come" is being foreclosed, occasioning a more catastrophic event – which, nonetheless, would open a chain for other "futures" that could not be foreclosed.

We can not know, for instance, when or whether the re-inscription of other disciplines or institutions open to (and traversed by) the non-human Other, maintained in and by spacing and the trace, would be "instituted," only that they have a chance and a place where there had been none. "Perhaps."

*

Such might be the wager. Might be, since the certification of "risk" can be deferred: can it occur if re-wired to a web-like elaboration, a master honey-comb of texts and terms through which, and at the expense of which, absolute translation would be provoked – but where any "future," monstrous or disastrous, could not be tracked in those terms? We know, inevitably, it involves regressions in institutional terms, in the cadre of purveyors whose roles may be more viral carriers than agents, and that "translation" need not occur, at all. Moreover, the positioning of a brake before a possible or virtual future is also conservative, that "future" must be solicited, marked, heralded by a recalibration of anteriority (the canonization of alteritous reading models). And what, too, of time? What is its term? What would be its model? Without teleology, conceived as allomorphic, inhabited by backloops and worm-holes, experimental chronographs and elisions for which even the notion of preservation must be barred – that is, what must and can be affirmed would include disappearance, without a trace, what Derrida terms cinders. Or not? One of the enigmas of Derrida's trajectory has always been its viral impact – that is, that where it seems directly assimilated, mimed, written-with, it can at times appear least transformative. And yet the trans-architecture suggested makes or gives a "place" to another, which may not (must not?) be recognizable to or before the hand that the trans-architect extends. Moses would not "cross" the river, a lethe in any event that sheds the recombinant DNA of recognizable legacies in a desert wandering. For the Other to counter-sign – not so much a reader as something, a voice or alterity within an incipient reading – it need (perhaps must) no longer be recognizable, no longer return to the metaphorics of the bridge and the community assigned to its protection. Derrida's work as *transperformative* – as translational and performative wager – seems to require a movement through the inventions and para-words of his work, a curling back or closing off so that that discourse can take up its host or incubate. A community of translators, in effect, both relays or virally communicates and, at moments, closes off. The essays which dis(as)semble and re(as)semble here, the *séances* performed under this table or table of contents, would be performative in the sense, perhaps, of interrogating, recording, exemplifying, holding a place open for further extensions, and enabling that which they cannot predict and which *the* trans-architect *could or would not recognize*. But by then, perhaps, "everything is changed." Or not. "If that's possible, *if there is any* future."[25]

NOTES

1 Jacques Derrida, "Différance," in *Speech and Phenomena*, trans. David B. Allison (Evanston: Northwestern University Press, 1973), 146.

2 The issue of a pause in "deconstruction's" cultural trajectory that raises issues of futurity at today's crossroads reflects its survival of a polemic – neither Habermasian periodizations nor Rortian fantasies of the "private," nor even Gasche's stalwart return to philosophic propriety seems terribly relevant. Beyond the dated polemics, Derrida's work seems at once misleadingly canonized and permanently segregated, marked by media-acceptance and divorced from institutional currency (this would not account, nonetheless, for its vast, often unmarked influence). This moment, which positions the Derridean project at once at its afterlife and unmarked dawn, creates a problem of rhetorical strategy. It will be dealt with, in this volume, by a workman-like, rather than polemicized, review of the state of transformation in specific knowledge-fields.

3 Jacques Derrida, *Specters of Marx*, trans. Peggy Kamuf (New York: Routledge, 1994), 77.

4 "As soon as there are words – and this can be said of the trace in general, and of the chance that it is – direct intuition no longer has any chances." "Passions: 'An Oblique Offering,'" trans. D. Wood in *Derrida: A Critical Reader*, ed. David Wood (Oxford: Blackwell, 1992), 24.

5 The trace is neither living nor dead. It traverses, spectrally and virally, this putative divide, and this non-human, non-biocentric and perhaps non-existent agency opens a thinking that ruptures the humanisms and biocentrisms in which "death" – cast out as other – discretely re-informs the blank territorializations and semantic enclosures of contemporary global culture, opening in Derrida, as well, as rethinking of the "animal." Something like earth too has ceased to be named or marked as natural, maternal, as house with the attendant metaphorics of interiority or dwelling. The radically Other is not referenced, initially, to human subjects as others or the other but to a non-human trace which precedes and networks these: it is this opening, then, which would begin the translation viewed, variably, in a rethinking across the disciplines in light of this logic of "trace," in law, ethics, history, and so on, of the humanities, and of the "human."

6 We recall that for Derrida, "text" is not a figure of what suspends reference and retreats into linguistic play, but rather what marks the confluence of all

historial networks and forces within interpretive spaces and contexts where
their trajectories can be engaged, and performatively clarified or reposi-
tioned: "What I call 'text' implies all the structures called 'real,' 'economic,'
'historical,' socio-institutional, in short: all possible references. Another way
of recalling again that 'there is nothing outside the text.' " ("Afterword:
Toward an Ethic of Discussion," in *Limited Inc.* [Evanston: Northwestern
University Press, 1988], 148.)

7 This scenario Derrida – targeting the metaphysics of presence – seems
to launch after Heidegger's (failed) attempt to overthrow or close "metaphysics," but he does not repeat that fatal rhetoric since, in a way, Derrida
seems to view "metaphysics" simultaneously as the hermeneutic program
producing and produced by a certain (model of) history (linked, with
Heidegger, to "Platonism" [which is not to say Plato]), and as a mere institutionalized effect, rather than a conceptual epoch to be overthrown in a
flawed series of reversals and father–son encounters in which the latecomer
will always have to invent the paternity of the precursor (Plato to Nietzsche
to Heidegger, and so on).

8 And here is why the "trace" is irreducible and suffers what it also effects,
perpetual effacement: if what is called memory programs what is perceiv-
able, if effaced linguistic reference is taken for the real, if inscription predicts
intuition, then the languages of empiricism, or realism, or transparent perception, or pragmatism, and so on, are predicated on compulsory forgetfulness ("The trace has, properly speaking, no place, for effacement belongs to
the very structure of the trace" [*Différance*, 156]). Moreover, each assertion of
referential ground is designed to serve policing roles for one or another variant of the epistemo-aesthetic state – a state like that, perhaps, of Hamlet's
Denmark, in denial of what a certain mnemonic injunction knows to be
true, a state haunted by a crime or fault denied by the courtiers, the laws
pretending to a transparency of "language" or to a facticity of reference
or to ontotheological assertion ("metaphysics"), a state nonetheless ruled
by this denied fault, or king. The Benjamin of *The Theses on History*, to
break the dictates of a "historicism" he allies extraordinarily with fascism,
conjures a rupture within the mnemonic order by invoking non-human,
even *geological* time on the one hand – recalling the paltry thousands of
years of "human" history – and, on the other, a break inhabiting language understood as itself a non-human agency. Derrida invokes across
textual history the movements of the "trace" or mark "older than" history, "older than" the ancient or originary, the ecological or economy of
meanings which hermeneutic conventions guard and police, institute and
tend.

9 The translation of the "Humanities" and the disciplines into a non-humanist
territoriality that would break the bounds of the sciences as such cannot be
mapped, but only put into a performative arena provoked by a series of ne-
gotiations and interventions. One cannot simply say, for instance, that here
psychoanalysis would be reread as a science of memory (among others), law

subjected to a problematic of allo-human "justice," ethics entered into a field of hospitality toward the absolute other, gender remarked from a shifting affirmation of a multitudinous positionality appealing to a site that precedes the power-differentiations of institutional power, aesthetics rewritten from a marginal philosophic category to a problematic where perception itself or phenomenality is programmed, history removed from narrative and teleology, religion positioned over an original technicity, literature made to appeal to a political guardianship of the secret, politics rewritten as the hyperpolitical domain of the "promise" and mnemotechnicity, and so on, since no formula, as formula, translates beyond the viral effect that would, alone, give evidence of an unrecognizable "event." Nonetheless, voided of these insignia, the wager would be – if it is, and if there is true risk here – that the re-planting, or trans-architecting of this geographic alteration sets the stage for other means of decision, other geological accessions than the programs of humanism, historicism, scientism, or the alibis of transparency (empiricism, pragmatism) could yield to in time. For with this break would be, from the beginning, an alteration in the field of temporal marking and intervention, the depolicing of "time."

10 Jacques Derrida, "Plato's Pharmacy," in *Dissemination*, trans. Barbara Johnson (Chicago: University of Chicago Press, 1981), 171.

11 Jacques Derrida, "*Khôra*," in *On the Name*, trans. Thomas Dutoit (Stanford: Stanford University Press, 1993), 106.

12 One cannot escape the ethical implications, Nietzschean in tone, by which Derrida addresses the "future" as something necessarily broken with the programmatic laws of perception and institutional power or reading today – as if these put, in Benjamin's terms, the future and past in jeopardy. If the archival order represents the most political of sites, it is not inert: it is the non-site of inscriptions from which "experience" is shaped, repeated, projected, or generated. But it also turns against itself, constitutively, and not by only programming forms of reading or perception that compel or return us to hierarchized functions or word-concepts that legislate what is "lived," but by turning against itself in the process – much as, say, the text of Plato, in which various "Socrateses" move through variant positions and figures of logics or writing, produces against itself the instituted abstractions of "Platonism," a possibility among others in the text become a blind held against it. If for Derrida the future "can only be for ghosts," it is not only those of the undead or unread (textual) *events* which still rule the earth, seeking the justice of differential reading, but the manner in which a "subject" to come might inhabit an earth not conceived as originary or natural or maternal – rather, as "a 'who' besieged by the problematic of the trace and of differance, of affirmation, of the signature and of the so-called proper name... as destinerring of missive" ("Eating Well," in *Points...: Interviews 1974–1994*, ed. Elizabeth Weber [Stanford: Stanford University Press, 1995], 260). That the juxtaposition of a hyper or radically exteriorized translation of a human subject to come with a transformed notion

of hospitality pre-inhabited, pre-dispossessed and opened to a radical –
hence, non-human – alterity with the "last man" of pre-recorded inscriptions
bears a Nietzschean resonance does not trivialize the break that inhabits this
thought.

13 Jacques Derrida, *Archive Fever: A Freudian Impression*, trans. Eric Prenowitz
(Chicago: University of Chicago Press, 1995), 20. Any alteration in the
archive, including that of the technicity of its postal relays (e-mail), alters
how "life is lived."

14 Within Derrida's encounters with Plato from "Plato's Pharmacy" through
"Envois" in *The Post Card*, "*Khôra*" represents the undoing of a narrative of
progression. Derrida's ongoing production appears, then, irreducible to a
periodizing set of categories, however much that might aid a canonicity the
work both solicits and resists – moving, rather, to contaminate, translate,
performatively inhabit, and disinhabit. The case of Plato is exemplary, however, of the programmaticity of the program, as well as of the false site of its
installation – that is, not as fact or even under "Plato's" signature, but within
a hermeneutical regime co-produced by (and against) this event. Not only
do the inscriptions of this history famously appear marked in the event of
this signature – as if somehow both founded and policed by it – or because
we can pretend that three key texts of Derrida manifest the distinct phases
of production which some critics would highlight ("Plato's Pharmacy" in
Dissemination, "Envois" in *The Post Card*, and the later text, "*Khôra*"). In "Plato's
Pharmacy" it necessarily trades off the image of Plato as "father" of the
West, of metaphysics, of Platonism – a fortuitous monument who persists
within a rhetoric of origination and philosophy which Heidegger's reading
of Nietzsche as, still, a mere inversion of Plato perpetuated (if only to keep
"metaphysics" open long enough for himself to take credit for closing, thus in
turn placing himself in the position ascribed to the displaced Nietzsche, and
so on). But the force of "metaphysics" here turns not quite into a historial fact
but an interpretive effect – as though *there never quite was "metaphysics"* after
all, except as an effect of Plato's text, the storied blind called "Platonism" installed or imposed as a dominant reading, to be sure, but also still just about
to occur (since now the map of historical time appears reversible). Thus
"Plato's Pharmacy" analyzes the pharmacological role of (the deaths of)
Socrates and writing under the fictive if powerful logics of the parricide, the
putting out of Being or father Parmenides (or "Plato"), the theatrical drama
of the overthrow in part. The rhetoric of this presentation keeps the index of
generational replacement, overthrows, dawns, and historical effects in position for the reader, on display repeatedly. (For instance, in the Stranger's
supposed horror at the "parricide" of father Parmenides [241d–42b; "Plato's
Pharmacy," 164–65] – which would make more sense if "Parmenides" had
not, already in the dialogue named after him, deconstructed more or less
literally a young Socrates' hypothesis of the *eidos*.) But Derrida observes that
in Plato the *eidos* and the *typos* or impress (and for that matter, *stoicheia* or
"primal letters") are effects of the same cut: "*typos* can designate with equal

pertinence the graphic unit and the eidetic model" ("Plato's Pharmacy," in *Dissemination*, trans. Barbara Johnson [Chicago: University of Chicago Press, 1981], 159). Derrida refers to this historical installation in the most nuanced and performative way, a way that keeps the course of the subsequent "history" contingent on one of several virtual outcomes or impositions managed by the text's forces: " 'Platonism' is both the general rehearsal of this family scene and the most powerful effort to master it, to prevent anyone's ever hearing of it, to cancel it by drawing the curtains over the dawning of the West" (167). So when the "Envois" section of *The Post Card* detemporalizes any possible genetic narrative by playing on the reversible multi-positionality of the signatorial "p" and "s" of its post-script, with demolitioning inversions of a "father" Plato with an equally (false) paternity of Socrates, as well as of dictation and scribe, forerunner and legatee, *p*rimary and *s*econdary, cause and effect, what might appear to a reader of Derrida's work like a progression from maintaining (barely) a periodizing fiction or paternal metaphorics to the counter-sequentiality of performative chronographs is problematic. For one thing, the premise of a "Derrida" who supplements the Platonic text with deconstructive reversibility could be exposed by returning to writings in the Platonic *oeuvre* that, so to speak, actively read these Derridean moves as if well in advance – such as, for instance, the extraordinary reading scene in the Protagoras, where a (now) elder (dissimulating) Protagoras and young (dissimulating) Socrates between them read Simonides' text citing and reading Pittacus' in an abyssal reading combat of marked power plays of reversible "S"s and "P"s into which "Plato" (and then Derrida) are absorbed, an event destabilizing the platform of Derrida's *post*-script or rendering the inventions of "Envois" another effect, still, of the Platonic text-machine. For a performative reading of how the anagrammatic "Plato" marks a reading of Derrida's "Envois" in advance, thus leaving a counter-signature that disowns the entire imposition of "Platonism," and its history, see my, "P.s.: Plato's scene of reading in the Protagoras," in *Anti-Mimesis from Plato to Hitchcock* (Cambridge: Cambridge University Press, 1994), 45–88. That effect, however, is not to assimilate Derrida's undecidable gesture of post-metaphysical reading to Plato, and hence "metaphysics," still, but as Derrida elsewhere marks, to dissociate Plato's signature from the historical trajectory heavily marked by or as "metaphysics." To render "Platonism" not what Platonic writing institutes as the *eidetic* platform of truth and binarized concepts, but an always possible reading-effect of Plato's work – one instituted, imposed, inscribed in advance as a virtual program that did not bear a Platonic signature any more than it could, in a sense, be verified as having in fact in a sense taken place. "Plato's Pharmacy" marks this switch by an observation in the midst of its phantasmal analyses, that "we are today on the eve of Platonism" (107), thus allowing that this entire heritage were, in fact, delayed, misread, without "overthrow" or even installation, and rather just about to begin (again).

15 *Archive Fever*, 12.

16 It "is not, we repeat, a question of the past . . . It is a question of the future, the question of the future itself, the question of a response, of a promise and of a responsibility for tomorrow" (36).

17 It is, perhaps, in "Circumfession," in Geoff Bennington, *Jacques Derrida* (Chicago: University of Chicago Press, 1993), that the dispositionality of a geo-prosthetic trace appears obliquely marked, echoed and displaced with the mother (Georgette), whose prosthetic demystification – along the lines of the she/it of the *khora* – Bennington devotes a section to in "Derridabase" (207–11). In "Circumfession" the displaced name of Geo echoes through the mother's name ("Uncle Georges, my mother's younger brother who thus bears the same name as his sister, who he often nicknamed Geo" [261]), and, as counterpoint, the "theological" project of G. (the programmatic interlocutor to be evaded, Geoff), emergent nonetheless through a recurrent reference to a "geologic program" (39, 124, 272) – "I catch them out seeing me lying on my back, in the depth of my earth, I mean, they understand everything, like the geologic program" (39) – or the "regular and geological relation between chance and necessity" (294).

18 That is, in Benjamin's "The Task of the Translator," so-called "pure language," by which is meant the networking traces, phonemes, intervals, marks, and so on out into which all language resolves, without "meaning."

19 In "Passions" we read: "Literature is a modern invention, inscribed in conventions and institutions which, to hold on to just this trait, secures in principle its *right to say everything*. Literature thus ties its destiny to a certain non-censure, to the space of democratic freedom (freedom of the press, freedom of speech, etc.). No democracy without literature; no literature without democracy" (23).

20 Werner Hamacher calls Derrida's approach in this regard "the structure of a horizonless performativity." See "Lingua Amissa: The Messianism of Commodity-Language and Derrida's *Specters of Marx*," in *Ghostly Demarcations*, ed. Michael Sprinker (New York: Verso, 1999), 201–202. Such is the predicate of any intervention whatsoever: "Only with this characterization is the ground cleared for the messianic movement, for the Marxist project and a politics of emancipation: it is performing without a performative horizon, the perforation of every horizon, transcendental – and, more exactly, atranscendental – kenosis of all linguistic and non-discursive forms of action."

21 Maurice Blanchot, in "Thanks (Be Given) to Jacques Derrida," develops the figure of Moses as translator of a new law or inscription, asking: "One may wonder what was Moses' 'fault', the fault that will prevent him from reaching the 'promised land'. There are of course a number of privileged answers. But in the desire to reach his destination and rest there is already one hope too many. He may see, but not have" (*The Blanchot Reader*, ed. Michael Holland [Oxford: Blackwell, 1995], 323). Though, within this logic, the problematic of another "Moses" drifts from the agency of a project (like Derrida's) to the position of anyone in the unavowable community who or that partakes of this transition, toward a site that cannot be identified in a "present." Geoff

Bennington explores this metaphorics too in "Mosaic Fragment: if Derrida were an Egyptian . . . ," *Derrida: A Critical Reader*, 97–120.

22 See Jacques Derrida, *The Politics of Friendship*, trans. G. Collins (London: Verso, 1997), 386. Derrida speaks of: "*that* crime in which, allowing for the difference of a repression, the political being of politics, the concept of politics in its most powerful traditions is constituted" (ix).

23 For some preliminary elaborations of an altered problematic of earth, see chapters 6 and 8 of Tom Cohen, *Ideology and Inscription: 'Cultural Studies' after Benjamin, de Man, and Bakhtin* (Cambridge: Cambridge University Press, 1998).

24 This and citations that follow come from Jacques Derrida, "Point de folie – Maintenant l'architecture," trans. K. Linker, from *Architecture Theory since 1968*, ed. K. Michael Hays (Cambridge, MA: MIT Press, 1998), 566–81.

25 *Specters of Marx*, 37.

CHAPTER I

The future of the profession or the university without condition (thanks to the "Humanities," what could take place tomorrow)

Jacques Derrida

This will no doubt be *like* a profession of faith: the profession of faith of a professor who would act *as if* he were nevertheless asking your permission to be unfaithful or a traitor to his habitual practice.

Before I even begin to follow in fact a torturous itinerary, here is the thesis, in direct and broadly simple terms, that I am submitting to you for discussion. It will be distributed among a series of propositions. In truth, it will be less a thesis, or even an hypothesis, than a declarative engagement, an appeal in the form of a profession of faith: faith in the University and, within the University, faith in the Humanities of tomorrow.

The long title proposed for this chapter signifies first that the modern university *should* be without condition. By "modern university," let us understand the one whose European model, after a rich and complex medieval history, has become prevalent, which is to say "classic," over the last two centuries in states of a democratic type. This university claims and ought to be granted in principle, besides what is called academic freedom, an *unconditional* freedom to question and to assert, or even, going still further, the right to say publicly all that is required by research, knowledge, and thought concerning the *truth*. However enigmatic it may be, the reference to truth remains fundamental enough to be found, along with light (*lux*), on the symbolic insignias of more than one university. The university professes the truth, and that is its profession. It declares and promises an unlimited commitment to the truth. No doubt the status of and the changes to the value of truth can be discussed *ad infinitum* (truth as adequation or truth as revelation, truth as the object of theoretico-constative discourses or as poetico-performative events, and so forth). But these are discussed, precisely, *in* the University and in departments that belong to the Humanities. I will leave these enormous questions suspended for the moment. Let us underscore merely by way of anticipation that this immense question of truth and of light, of the

Enlightenment – *Aufklärung, Lumières, Illuminismo* – has always been linked to the question of man, to a concept of that which is proper to man, on which concept were founded both Humanism and the historical idea of the Humanities. Today the renewed and reelaborated declaration of "Human rights" (1948) or as we say in French, "des Droits de l'homme," the rights of man, and the institution of the juridical concept of "Crime against humanity" (1945) form the horizon of *mondialisation* and of the international law that is supposed to keep watch over it. (I am keeping the French word "mondialisation" in preference to "globalization" so as to maintain a reference to the world – *monde, Welt, mundus* – which is neither the globe nor the cosmos.) The concept of man, of what is proper to man, of human rights, of crimes against the humanity of man, organizes as we know such a *mondialisation* or worldwide-ization. This worldwide-ization wishes to be a humanization. If this concept of man seems both indispensable and always problematic, well – and this will be one of the motifs of my thesis, one of my theses in the form of profession of faith – it can be discussed or reelaborated, as such and without conditions, without presuppositions, only within the space of the new Humanities. (I will try to specify what I mean by the "new" Humanities.) But whether these discussions are critical or deconstructive, everything that concerns the question and the history of truth, in its relation to the question of man, of what is proper to man, of human rights, of crimes against humanity, and so forth, all of this must in principle find its space of discussion without condition and without presupposition, its legitimate space of research and reelaboration, *in* the University and, within the University, above all *in* the Humanities. Not so that it may enclose itself there, but on the contrary so as to find the best access to a new public space transformed by new techniques of communication, information, archivization, and knowledge production. (Although I must leave this aside, one of the most serious questions that is posed, and posed here, between the university and the politico-economic outside its public space is the question of the marketplace in publishing and the role it plays in archivization, evaluation, and legitimation of academic research.) The horizon of truth or of what is proper to man is certainly not a very determinable limit. But neither is that of the university and of the Humanities.

This university without conditions does not, in fact, exist, as we know only too well. Nevertheless, in principle and in conformity with its declared vocation, its professed essence, it should remain an ultimate place of critical resistance – and more than critical – to all the powers of dogmatic and unjust appropriation. When I say "more than critical," I have in mind "deconstructive" (so why not just say it directly and without wasting time?). I am referring to the right to deconstruction as an unconditional right to ask critical questions not only to the history of the concept of man, but to the history even of the notion of critique, to the form and the authority of the question, to the interrogative form of thought. For this implies the right to do it performatively, that is, by producing events, for example by writing, and by giving rise to singular *oeuvres* (which up until now has been the purview of neither the classical nor the modern Humanities). With the event of thought constituted by such *oeuvres*, it would be a matter of making something happen to this concept of truth or of humanity, without necessarily betraying it, that is, to the concept that forms the charter and the profession of faith of all universities. This principle of unconditional resistance is a right that the university itself should at the same time reflect, invent, and pose, whether it does so through its law faculties or in the new Humanities capable of working on these questions of right and of law – in other words, and again why not say it without detour – the Humanities capable of taking on the tasks of deconstruction, beginning with the deconstruction of their own history and their own axioms.

Consequence of this thesis: such an unconditional resistance could oppose the university to a great number of powers, for example to state powers (and thus to the power of the nation-state and to its phantasm of indivisible sovereignty, which indicates how the university might be in advance not just cosmopolitan, but universal, extending beyond worldwide citizenship and the nation-state in general), to economic powers (to corporations and to national and international capital), to the powers of the media, ideological, religious, and cultural powers, and so forth – in short, to all the powers that limit democracy to come. The university should thus also be the place in which nothing is beyond question, not even the current and determined figure of democracy, and not even the traditional idea of critique, meaning theoretical critique, and not even the authority of the "question" form, of thinking as "questioning." That is why I spoke without delay and without disguise of deconstruction.

Here then is what I will call the unconditional university or the university without condition: the principial right to say everything, whether it be under the heading of fiction and the experimentation of knowledge, and the right to say it publicly, to publish it. This reference to public space will remain the link that affiliates the new Humanities to the Age of Enlightenment. It distinguishes the university institution from other institutions founded on the right or the duty to say everything, for example religious confession and even psychoanalytic "free association." But it is also what fundamentally links the university, and above all the Humanities, to what is called literature, in the European and modern sense of the term, as the right to say everything publicly, or to keep it secret, if only in the form of fiction. I allude to confession, which is very close to the profession of faith, because I would like to connect my remarks to the analysis of what is happening today, on the worldwide scene, that resembles a universal process of confession, avowal, repentance, expiation, and asked-for forgiveness. One could cite innumerable examples, day after day. But whether we are talking about very ancient crimes or yesterday's crimes, about slavery, the Shoah, apartheid, or even the acts of violence of the Inquisition (concerning which the Pope recently announced that they ought to give rise to an examination of conscience), repentance is always carried out with reference to the very recent juridical concept of "crime against humanity." Because I am preparing to articulate together Profession, the Profession of faith, and Confession, I note in passing and in parentheses (for this would require a long development), that in the fourteenth century it was possible to organize the confession of sins as a function of social and professional categories. The *Sulla Artesana* from 1317 (cited by my colleague Le Goff) prescribes that the penitent in confession be interrogated with reference to his socio-professional status: princes about justice, knights about plunder, merchants, officials, artisans, and laborers about perjury, fraud, lying, theft, and so forth, bourgeois and citizens in general about usury and mortgages, peasants about envy and theft, and so forth.[1]

To repeat, then: if this unconditionality, in principle and *de jure*, makes for the invincible force of the university, it has never been in effect. By reason of this abstract and hyperbolic invincibility, by reason of its very impossibility, this unconditionality exposes as well the weakness or the vulnerability of the university. It exhibits its impotence, the fragility of its defenses against all the powers that command it, besiege it, and attempt to appropriate it. Because it is a stranger to power, because it is heterogeneous to the principle of power, the university is also without any power of its own. That is why I speak of the *university without condition*. I say "the university" because I am distinguishing here, *stricto sensu*, the university from all research institutions that are in the service of economic goals and interests of all sorts, without being granted in principle the independence of the university; I also say "without condition" to let one hear the connotation of "without power" and "without defense." Because it is absolutely independent, the university is also an exposed, tendered citadel, to be taken, often destined to capitulate without condition, to surrender unconditionally. It gives itself up, it sometimes puts itself up for sale, it risks being simply something to occupy, take over, buy; it risks becoming a branch office of conglomerates and corporations. This is today, in the United States and throughout the world, a major political stake: to what extent does the organization of research and teaching have to be supported, that is, directly or indirectly controlled, let us say euphemistically "sponsored," by commercial and industrial interests? By this logic, as we know, the Humanities are often held hostage to departments of pure or applied science in which are concentrated the supposedly profitable investments of capital foreign to the academic world. A question must then be asked and it is not merely economic, juridical, ethical, or political: can the university (and if so, how?) affirm an unconditional independence, can it claim a sort of *sovereignty* without ever risking the worst, namely, by reason of the impossible abstraction of this sovereign independence, being forced to give up and capitulate without condition, to let itself be taken over and bought at any price? What is needed then is not only a principle of resistance, but a force of resistance – and of dissidence. The deconstruction of the concept of unconditional sovereignty is doubtless necessary and underway, for this is the heritage of a barely secularized theology. In the most visible case of the supposed sovereignty of nation-states, but also elsewhere, the value of sovereignty is thorough dissolution. But one must beware that this necessary deconstruction does not compromise, not too much, the university's claim to independence, that is, to a certain very particular form of sovereignty that I will try to specify later. This would be what is at stake in political decisions and strategies. This stake will remain on the horizon of the hypotheses or professions of faith that I submit to your reflection. How to deconstruct the history (and first of all the academic history) of the principle of indivisible sovereignty even as one claims the unconditional right to say everything, or not to say anything, and to pose all the deconstructive questions that are called for on the subject of man, of sovereignty, of the right to say everything, therefore of literature and democracy, of the worldwide-ization underway, of its techno-economic and confessional aspects, and so forth?

I will not claim that, in the torment threatening the university today and within it some disciplines more than others, this force of resistance, this assumed freedom to say everything in the public space has its unique or privileged place in what is called the Humanities – a concept whose definition it will be advisable to refine, deconstruct, and adjust, beyond a tradition that must also be cultivated. However, this principle of unconditionality *presents itself*, originally and above all, in the Humanities. It has an originary and privileged place of *presentation*, of manifestation, of safekeeping in the Humanities. It has there its space of discussion as well as of reelaboration. All this passes as much by way of literature and languages (that is, the sciences called the sciences of man and culture) as by way of the non-discursive arts, by way of law and philosophy, by way of critique, questioning and, beyond critical philosophy and questioning, by way of deconstruction – there where it is a matter of nothing less than re-thinking the concept of man, the figure of humanity in general, and singularly the one presupposed by what we call, in the university, for the last few centuries, the Humanities. From this point of view at least, deconstruction (and I am not at all embarrassed to say so and even to claim) has its privileged place in the university and in the Humanities as the place of irredentist resistance or even, analogically, as a sort of principle of civil disobedience, even of dissidence in the name of a superior law and a justice of thought. Here let us call *thought* that which at times commands, according to a law above all laws, the justice of this resistance or this dissidence. It is also what puts deconstruction to work or inspires it as justice. This right must be without limit, if I may say so, to authorize the deconstruction of all the determined figures that this sovereign unconditionality may have assumed through history. For this, we have to enlarge and reelaborate the concept of the Humanities. To my mind, it is no longer a matter simply of the conservative and humanist concept with which most often the Humanities and their ancient canons are associated – canons which I believe ought to be protected at any price. This new concept of the Humanities, even as it remains faithful to its tradition, should include law, "legal studies," as well as what is called in this country, where this formation originated, "theory" (an original articulation of literary theory, philosophy, linguistics, psychoanalysis, and so forth), but also, of course, in all these places, deconstructive practices. And we will have to distinguish carefully here between, on the one hand, the principle of freedom, autonomy, resistance, disobedience, or dissidence, the principle that is coextensive with the whole field of academic knowledge and, on the other hand, its privileged place of *presentation*, of reelaboration, and of thematic discussion, which in my opinion would more properly belong to the Humanities, but to the transformed Humanities. If I link all of this with insistence not only to the question of literatures, to a certain democratic institution that is called literature or literary fiction, to a certain simulacrum and a certain "as if," but also to the question of the profession and of its future, it is because throughout a history of *travail* (usually translated as "work" or "labor" but I will leave it in French for the moment), which is not only trade or craft, then a history of trade or craft, which is not always profession, then a history of the profession, which is not always that of professor, I would like to connect this problematic of the university without condition to a pledge, a commitment, a promise, an act of faith, a declaration of faith, a profession of faith that in an original way ties faith to knowledge in the university, and above all in that place of the self-presentation of unconditionality that will go by the name Humanities. To link in a certain way faith to knowledge, faith in knowledge, is to articulate movements that could be called performative with constative, descriptive, or theoretical movements. A profession of faith, a commitment, a promise, an assumed responsibility, all that calls not upon discourses of knowledge but upon performative discourses that produce the event they speak of. One will therefore have to ask oneself what "professing" means. What is one doing when, performatively, one professes but also when one exercises a profession and singularly the profession of professor? I will thus rely often and at length on Austin's now classic distinction between performative speech acts and constative speech acts. This distinction will have been a great event in the twentieth century – and it will first have been an academic event. It will have taken place *in* the university and in a certain way, it is the Humanities that made it come about and that explored its resources; it is to and through the Humanities that this happened, and its consequences are incalculable. Even while recognizing the power, the legitimacy, and the necessity of the distinction between constative and performative, I have often had occasion, after a certain point, not to put it back in question but to analyze its presuppositions and to complicate them. I will do so once again today, but this time from another point of view and after having made this pair of concepts count for so much, I will end up designating a place where it fails and must fail. This place will be precisely *what happens*, comes to pass, that at which one arrives or that which happens to us, arrives to us, the event, the place of the taking-place – and which cares as little about the performative – the performative power – as it does about the constative. And this can happen, this can arrive in and by the Humanities.

Now I am going to begin, at once by the end and by the beginning. For I began with the end *as if* it were the beginning.

I

As if the end of work were at the origin of the world. Yes, "as if," I indeed said "as if . . ." At the same time as a reflection on the history of work, that is, *travail*, it is also no doubt a meditation on the "as," the "as such," the "as if" that I will propose to you, and perhaps on a politics of the virtual. Not a virtual politics but a politics *of the* virtual in the cyberspace or cyberworld of worldwide-ization. One of the mutations that affect the place and the nature of university *travail* is today a certain delocalizing virtualization of the space of communication, discussion, publication, archivization. It is not the virtualization that is absolutely novel in its structure, for as soon as there is a trace, there is also some virtualization; this is the "abc" of deconstruction. What is new, quantitatively, is the acceleration of the rhythm, the extent and powers of capitalization of such a virtuality. Hence the necessity to rethink the concepts of the possible and the impossible. This new technical "stage" of virtualization (computerization, digitalization, virtually immediate worldwide-ization of readability, tele-work, and so forth) destabilizes, as we well know, the university habitat. It upsets the university's topology, disturbs everything that organizes the places defining it, namely, the territory of its fields and its disciplinary frontiers as well as its places of discussion, its field of battle, its *Kampfplatz*, its theoretical battlefield – and the communitary structure of its "campus." Where is to be found the communitary *place* and the social bond of a "campus" in the cyberspatial age of the computer, of tele-work, and of the World Wide Web? Where does the exercise of democracy, be it a university democracy, have its *place* in what my colleague Mark Poster calls "CyberDemocracy"?[2] One has the clear sense that, more radically, what has been upset in this way is the topology of the event, the experience of the singular taking-place.

What then are we doing when we say "as if"? Notice that I have not yet said "*it is* as if the end of work were at the origin of the world." I have not said anything whatsoever that was and I have not said it in a principal clause. I left suspended, I abandoned to its interruption a strange subordinate clause ("as if the end of work were at the origin of the world"), as if I wanted to let an example of the "as if" work all by itself, outside any context, to attract your attention. What are we doing when we say "as if"? What does an "if" do? We are acting *as if* we were responding to at least one of several of the possibilities – or to more than one at a time – that I am going to begin to enumerate.

1. *First possibility*: by saying "as if," are we abandoning ourselves to the arbitrary, to dream, to imagination, to utopia, to hypothesis? Everything I am preparing to say will tend to show that the answer cannot be so simple.

2. Or, *second possibility*, with this "as if" are we putting to work certain types of judgment, for example those "reflective judgments" concerning which Kant regularly said that they operated "as if" (*als ob*) an understanding contained or comprehended the unity of the variety of empirical laws or "as if it were a lucky chance favoring our design [*gleich als ob es ein glücklicher unsre Absicht begünstigender Zufall wäre*]."[3] In this latter case, that of the Kantian discourse, the gravity, seriousness, and irreducible necessity of the "as if" points to nothing less than the finality of nature, that is, a finality whose concept, Kant tells us, is among the most unusual and difficult to pin down. For, he says, it is neither a *concept of nature* nor a *concept of freedom*. Therefore, although Kant does not say as much in this context and for good reason, this "as if" would itself be something like an agent of deconstructive ferment since it in some way exceeds and comes close to disqualifying the two orders that are so often distinguished and opposed, the order of nature and the order of freedom. The opposition that is thereby disconcerted by a certain "as if" is the very one that organizes all our fundamental concepts and all the oppositions in which they are determined and in which they determine, precisely, what is proper to man, the humanity of man (*phusis/techné, phusis/nomos*, nature *versus* humanity, and within this humanity, which is also that of the Humanities, one finds sociality, law, history, politics, community, and so forth, all set within the same oppositions). Kant also explains to us, in effect, that the "as if" plays a decisive role in the coherent organization of our experience. Now, Kant is also someone who attempted, in an extremely complex fashion, to both justify and limit the role of the Humanities in teaching, culture, or the critique of taste.[4] This was recalled and analyzed in a magisterial fashion by two of my friends and colleagues to whom I owe a lot: Sam Weber in an inaugural book in many ways, and one

that is very dear to me, *Institution and Interpretation*,[5] followed recently by a remarkable article on "The Future of the Humanities,"[6] and Peggy Kamuf who treats this same text of Kant's in her admirable book on *The Division of Literature, or the University in Deconstruction*.[7] Sam Weber and Peggy Kamuf say decisive things, and I refer you to them, concerning what is happening between deconstruction, the history of the university, and the Humanities. What I am trying to explore here would be another avenue on the same site, another path through the same landscape. And if my trajectory appears different here, I will doubtless cross their tracks at more than one intersection. For example, in the reference to Kant. There is nothing surprising in the fact that the *Third Critique* comes back with such insistence in the United States in all the discourses on the institutions and the disciplines tied to the Humanities, on the problems of professionalization that are posed there. Kant also has a whole set of propositions on this subject, notably on work, craft, and the arts, both the liberal arts and the salaried, mercenary arts, but also on the conflict of the faculties – something I discussed many years ago in *Economimesis* and *Mochlos*.[8] This recurrent appeal to Kant may be especially remarked, in fact, in the United States where, for reasons that should be analyzed, the term *Humanities* has known a particular history and still appears at the twentieth century's end in the figure of a problem, with a semantic energy, a conflictual presence, and resonance that it has doubtless never had or that it lost in Europe and no doubt everywhere else in the world where American culture is not prevalent. There are certainly interwoven reasons for this, in particular that of the effects of the worldwide-ization underway that always passes by way of the United States, its political, techno-economic, and techno-scientific power, in a more unavoidable and visible fashion.

3. Finally, *third possibility*, does not a certain "as if" mark, in thousands of ways, the structure and the mode of being of all objects belonging to the academic field called the Humanities, whether they be the Humanities of yesterday or today or tomorrow? I will not hasten for the moment to reduce these "objects" to fictions, simulacra, or works of art, while acting as if we already had at our disposal reliable concepts of fiction, of art, or of the work. But if one were to follow common sense, couldn't one say that the modality of the "as if" appears appropriate to what are called *oeuvres*, singularly *oeuvres d'art*, the fine arts (painting, sculpture, cinema, music, poetry, literature, and so forth), but also, to complex degrees and according to complex stratifications, to all the discursive idealities, to all

the symbolic or cultural productions that define, in the general field of the university, the disciplines said to be in the Humanities – and even the juridical disciplines and the production of laws, and even a certain structure of scientific objects in general?

I have already quoted two of Kant's "as if"s. There is at least one more. I would not subscribe to it without reservation. With it, Kant seems to me to place too much confidence in a certain opposition of *nature* and *art*, at the very moment when the "as if" makes it tremble, just as we saw happen a moment ago to the opposition of *nature* and *freedom*. But I recall this remark *for two reasons*: on the one hand, so as to suggest that what is perhaps at issue here is changing the sense, the status, the stake of the Kantian "as" and "as if," which would be a subtle displacement but one whose consequences seem to me limitless; on the other hand, I am preparing to cite an "as if" that describes an essential modality of experience of works of art, in other words, of that which, to a large extent, defines the field of the classical Humanities insofar as it concerns us here today. Kant says that "in a product of beautiful art, we must become conscious that it is art and not nature; but yet the purposiveness in its form must seem to be as free from all constraint of arbitrary rules as if it were a product of mere nature."[9]

In a provisional way and so as to introduce from a distance my remarks, my hypotheses, or my profession of faith, I wanted to draw your attention to this troubling thing we do when we say "as if" and to the connection this troubling thing, which looks like a simulacrum, might have with the questions I am preparing to address, the conjoined questions of profession and confession, of the university with or without condition – of the humanity of man and of the Humanities, of work [*travail*] and of literature.

For what I would like to attempt with you is this apparently impossible thing: to link this "as if" to the thinking of an event, that is, to the thinking of this thing that *perhaps* happens, that is supposed to *take place*, that is supposed to find its place – and that *would* happen here for example to what is called *le travail* (work). It is generally believed that, in order to happen, to take place, an event must interrupt the order of the "as if," and therefore that its "place" must be real, effective, concrete enough to belie the whole logic of the "as if." What happens, then, when the place itself becomes virtual, freed from its territorial (and thus national) rootedness and when it becomes subject to the modality of an "as if"? I will speak of an event that, without necessarily coming about tomorrow, would remain perhaps – and I underscore *perhaps* – to come: to come *through* the university, to come about and to come *through* it, *thanks* to it, *in* what is called the university, assuming that it has ever been possible to identify an *inside* of the university, that is, a *proper essence of the sovereign university*, and within it, something that one could also identify, properly, under the name of "Humanities." I am thus referring to a university that would be what it always should have been or always should have represented, that is, from its inception and in principle: sovereignly autonomous, unconditionally free in its institution, sovereign in its speech, in its writing, in its thinking. In a thinking, a writing, a speech that would be not only the archives or the productions of *knowledge* but also performative works, which are far from being neutral utopias. And why, we will wonder, would the principle of this unconditional freedom, its active and militant respect, its effective enactment, its *mise en oeuvre*, be confided above all to the new "Humanities" rather than to any other disciplinary field?

By putting forward these questions, which still resemble virtual desires taken for realities, or at best barely serious promises, I seem to be professing some faith. It is as if I were engaging in a profession of faith. Some would say perhaps that I am dreaming out loud while already engaging in a profession of faith. Assuming that one knows what a profession of faith is, one may then wonder who is responsible for such a profession of faith. Who signs it? Who professes it? I do not dare ask who is its professor but perhaps we should analyze a certain inheritance, in any case a certain proximity between the future of the academic profession, that of the profession of professor, the principle of authority that derives from it, and the profession of faith.

What does *to profess* mean in sum? And what stakes are still hidden in this question as concerns *travail*, work, career, trade, craft (whether professional, professorial, or not), for the university of tomorrow and, within it, for the Humanities?

This word "profess" of Latin origin (*profiteor, fessus sum, eri; pro et fateor*, which means to speak, from which comes also fable and thus a certain "as if"), means, in French as in English, *to declare openly, to declare publicly*. In English, says the *OED*, it has only a religious sense before 1300. "To make one's profession" means then "to take the vows of some religious order." The declaration of the one who professes is a *performative* declaration in some way. It pledges like an act of sworn faith, an oath, a testimony, a manifestation, an attestation, or a promise, a commitment. To profess is to make a pledge while committing one's responsibility. "To make profession of" is to declare out loud what one is, what one believes, what one wants to be, while asking another to take one's word and believe this declaration. I insist on this performative value of the declaration that professes while promising. One must underscore that constative utterances and discourses of pure knowledge, in the university or elsewhere, do not belong, as such, to the order of the profession in the strict sense. They belong perhaps to the craft, career, the "métier" (competence, knowledge, know-how), but not to the profession understood in a rigorous sense. The discourse of profession is always, in one way or another, a free profession of faith; in its pledge of responsibility, it exceeds pure techno-scientific knowledge. To profess is to pledge oneself while declaring oneself, while *giving oneself out to be*, while promising this or that. *Grammaticum se professus*, Cicero tells us in the *Tusculanes* (2, 12), is to give oneself out to be a grammarian, a master of grammar. It is neither necessarily to be this or that nor even to be a competent expert; it is to promise to be, to pledge oneself to be that on one's word. *Philosophiam profiter* is to profess philosophy: not simply to be a philosopher, to practice or teach philosophy in some pertinent fashion, but to pledge oneself, with a public promise, to devote oneself publicly, to give oneself over to philosophy, to bear witness, or even to fight for it. And what matters here is this promise, this pledge of responsibility, which is reducible to neither theory nor practice. To profess consists always in a performative speech act, even if the knowledge, the object, the content of what one professes, of what one teaches or practices remains on the order of the theoretical or the constative. Because the act of professing is a performative speech act and because the event that it is or produces depends only on this linguistic promise, its proximity to the fable, to fabulation, and to fiction, to the "as if," will always be formidable.

What relation is there between professing and working? In the university? In the Humanities?

II

From my first sentence, as soon as I began to speak, I named *le travail*, work, by saying "*As if* the end of work were at the beginning of the world."

What is work, that is, *le travail* (I believe we will have to keep this word in French here)? When and where does *un travail* take place, its place? For lack of time in particular, I cannot enter into a rigorous semantic analysis. Let us recall at least *two features* that concern the university. *Le travail* is not merely action or practice. One can act without working and it is not certain that a *praxis*, in particular a theoretical practice, constitutes, *stricto sensu*, *un travail*. Above all, whoever works is not necessarily

granted the name or status of worker, *travailleur*. The agent or the subject who works, the operator, is not always called a *travailleur* (*laborator*)
and the sense seems to be modified when one goes from the verb to
the noun: the *travail* of whoever *travaille* in general is not always the labor of a "travailleur." Thus, in the university, among all those who, in
one way or another, are supposed to be working there (teachers, staff or
administrators, researchers, students), some, notably students, as such,
will not ordinarily be called "travailleurs" as long as a salary (*merces*) does
not regularly compensate, like a commodity in a market, the activity of
a craft, trade, or profession. A fellowship or scholarship will not suffice
for this. The student may very well work a lot, he will be held to be a
travailleur, a worker, on condition of being on the market and only if in
addition he performs some task, for example, here in the US, that of the
teaching assistant. Inasmuch as he studies, purely and simply, and even
if he studies a lot, the student is not held to be a *travailleur*. Even if (and
I will insist on this in a moment) every craft, trade, or career is not a
profession, the worker is someone whose work is recognized as a craft,
trade, or profession on a market. All of these social semantics are rooted,
as you know, in a long socio-ideological history that goes back at least
to the Christian Middle Ages. One may thus work a lot without being a
worker recognized as such in the society.

Another distinction will count for us more and more, which is why I
pay it considerable attention right away: one can work a lot, and even
work a lot *as a worker*, a *travailleur*, without the effect or the result of the
work (the *opus* of the operation) being recognized as a "work," this time
in the sense not of the productive activity but of the product, *l'oeuvre*, that
which *remains* after and beyond the time of the operation. It would often
be difficult to identify and objectify the product of very hard work carried
out by the most indispensable and devoted workers, the least well treated
workers in society, the most invisible ones as well (those who dispose of
the trash of our cities, for example, or those who control air traffic, more
generally those who guarantee the mediations or transmissions of which
there remain only virtual traces – and this field is enormous and growing
steadily). There are thus workers whose work, and even whose productive
work, does not give rise to substantial or real products, only to virtual
specters. But when work gives rise to real or realizable products, one must
then introduce another essential distinction within the immense variety
of products and structures of products, within all the forms of materiality,
of reproducible ideality, of use and exchange values, and so forth. Certain
products of this working activity are held to be objectivizable use or

exchange values without deserving, it is believed, the title of *oeuvres* (I can say this word only in French). To other works, it is believed that the name of *oeuvres* can be attributed. Their appropriation, their relation with liberal or salaried work, with the signature or the authority of the author, and with the market are of a great structural and historical complexity that I will not analyze here. The first example of *oeuvres* that come to mind are *oeuvres d'art* (visual, musical or discursive, a painting, a concerto, a poem, a novel), but since we are interrogating the enigma of the concept of *oeuvre*, we would have to extend this field as soon as we tried to discern the type of work proper to the university and especially in the Humanities. In the Humanities, one no doubt treats in particular *oeuvres* (*oeuvres d'art*, either works of discursive art or not, literary or not, canonical or not). But in principle the treatment of works, in the academic tradition, depends on *a knowledge that itself does not consist* in *oeuvres*. To profess or to be a professor, in this tradition that is, precisely, undergoing mutation, was no doubt to produce and to teach a knowledge even while professing, that is, even while promising to take a responsibility that is not exhausted in the act of knowing or teaching. But, in the classical-modern tradition that we are interrogating, to know how to profess, or to profess a knowledge, or even how to produce a knowledge is not to produce *oeuvres*. A professor, as such, does not sign an *oeuvre*. His or her authority as professor is not that of the author of an *oeuvre*, a work. It is perhaps this that has been changing over the last few decades, encountering the frequently indignant resistance and protestations of those who believe they can discern, in writing and in the language, between criticism and creation, reading and writing, the professor and the author, and so forth. The deconstruction underway is no doubt not unrelated to this mutation. It is even its essential phenomenon, a more complex signal than its detractors admit and which we must take into account. In principle, if we refer to the canonical state of certain conceptual distinctions, and if we rely on the massive and largely accepted distinction between performatives and constatives, we may deduce from it the following propositions:

1. All work, all *travail* (work in general or the work of the worker) is not necessarily performative, that is, it does not produce an event; it does not make this event, it is not by itself, in itself, the event, it does not consist in the event it speaks of, even if it is productive, even if it leaves a product behind, whether or not this product is an *oeuvre*.

2. Every performative doubtless produces something, it makes an event come about, but what it *makes* in this way and *makes come about in this way* is not necessarily an *oeuvre*; it must always be authorized by a set of

conventions or conventional fictions, of "as if"s on which an institutional community is founded and to which it agrees.

3. Now, as traditionally defined, the university would be a place identical to itself (a non-substitutable locality, rooted in the ground, limiting the substitutability of places in cyberspace), a place, a single place, that gives rise only to the production and teaching of a *knowledge* [*savoir*], that is, of knowledges [*connaissances*] whose form of utterance is not, in principle, performative but theoretical and constative, even if the *objects* of this knowledge are sometimes of a philosophical, ethical, political, normative, prescriptive, or axiological nature; and even if, in a still more troubling fashion, the structure of these objects of knowledge is a structure of fiction obeying the strange modality of the "as if" (poem, novel, *oeuvre d'art* in general, but also everything that, in the structure of a performative utterance – for example of the juridical or constitutional type – does not belong to the realist and constative description of what is, but produces the event on the basis of the qualified "as if" of a supposed established convention). In a classical university, in conformity with its accepted definition, one practices the study, the *knowledge* of the normative, prescriptive, performative, and fictional possibilities that I have just enumerated and that are more often the object of the Humanities. But this study, this knowledge, this teaching, this *doctrine* ought to belong to the theoretical and constative order. The act of *professing* a doctrine may be a performative act, but the *doctrine* is not. This is a limitation concerning which I will say that *one must* indeed, at the same time, conserve it *and* change it, in a non-dialectical mode:

1. One must reaffirm it because a certain neutral theoreticism is the chance for the critical and more-than-critical (deconstructive) unconditionality that we are talking about and that, in principle, we all uphold, we all declare to uphold, in the university.

2. One must change while reaffirming this limitation because it must be admitted, and professed, that this unconditional theoreticism will itself always suppose a performative profession of faith, a belief, a decision, a public pledge, an ethico-political responsibility, and so forth. Here is found the principle of the unconditional resistance of the university. One may say that, from the point of view of this classical auto-definition of the university, there is no place in it, no essential, intrinsic, proper place either for non-theoretical work, for discourses of a performative type, or, *a fortiori*, for those singular performative acts engendering *today*, in certain places in the Humanities today, what are called *oeuvres*. The classical auto-definition and auto-limitation that I have just evoked characterized the

academic space reserved formerly for the Humanities, even where the
contents, objects, and themes of these produced or taught forms of knowledge
were of a philosophical, moral, political, historical, linguistic, aesthetic,
anthropological nature, that is, belonged to fields where evaluations,
normativity, and prescriptive experience are admitted and sometimes
constitutive. In the classical tradition, the Humanities define a field of
knowledge, sometimes of knowledge production, but without engendering signed works or *oeuvres*, whether these are works of art or not. I will
once again invoke Kant in order to define these classical limits assigned
to the traditional Humanities by those who demonstrate their necessity.
Kant sees there first of all a "propaedeutic" to the Fine Arts rather than
a practice of the arts. *Propaedeutic* is his word. The *Third Critique* specifies
that this pedagogic preparation, this simple introduction to the arts will
come at that point in the order of knowledge (the knowledge of what
is and not of what *ought to be*) where it must not involve any "prescriptions" (*Vorschriften*). The Humanities (*Humaniora*) must prepare without
prescribing: they would propose merely forms of knowledge that, moreover, remain preliminary (*Vorkenntnisse*). And without bothering, in this
text, with considerations of the long and sedimented history of the word
"Humanities," Kant discerns there solely the study that favors the legal
communication and sociability among men, that which gives the taste
of the common sense of humanity (*allgemeinen Menschensinn*). There is,
then, a theoreticism here, but also a Kantian humanism that privileges
the constative discourse and the form "knowledge." The Humanities
are and must be sciences. Elsewhere, in "Mochlos," I tried to lay out my
reservations on this subject even as I saluted the logic one finds at work in
The Conflict of the Faculties. This theoreticism limits or forbids the possibility for a professor to produce *oeuvres* or even prescriptive or performative
utterances in general; but it is also what permits Kant to withdraw the
faculty of philosophy from any outside power, notably from State power
and guarantees it an unconditional freedom to say what is true and to
conclude as to the subject of truth, provided that it does so *in the inside*
of the university. This final limitation (to say *publicly* all that one believes
to be true and what one believes one must say, but only *inside* the university), has never been, I believe, either tenable or respectable, in fact
or by law. But the transformation underway of public cyberspace, which
is public on a worldwide scale, beyond state-national frontiers, seems to
render it more archaic than ever. And yet I believe (this is *like* a profession of faith that I address to you and submit to your judgment) that the
idea of this space of the academic type, which has to be protected by

a kind of absolute immunity, as if its interior were inviolable, is an idea we must reaffirm, declare, and profess endlessly – even if the protection of this academic immunity (in the sense in which we speak of biological, diplomatic, or parliamentary immunity) is never pure, can always develop dangerous processes of auto-immunity, and must not prevent us from addressing ourselves to the university's outside, without any utopic neutrality. This freedom or immunity of the University and above all of its Humanities, is something we must lay claim to while committing ourselves to it with all our might – not only in a verbal and declarative fashion, but in work, in act, and in what we make happen with events.

Against the horizon of these preliminary reminders and these classic definitions, one may see certain questions taking shape. They have at least *two forms*, for the moment, but we might see them change and become more specific as we go along.

1. First, if this is indeed the way things are, if in the classical and modern academic tradition (up through the nineteenth-century model) normative and prescriptive performativity, and *a fortiori* the production of *oeuvres*, must remain foreign to the field of university work, even in the Humanities, foreign to their teaching, that is, in the strict sense of the word, to their theory, to their theorems as discipline or doctrine (*Lehre*), then what does it mean "to profess"? What is the difference between a trade or craft and a profession? And then between any profession and the profession of the professor? What is the difference between the different types of authority granted to craft or trade, to profession, and to the profession of the professor?

2. Second, has something happened to this classical-modern university and to these Humanities? Is there something happening to it or promising to happen to it that upsets these definitions, either because this mutation transforms the essence of the university, and in it the future of the Humanities, or because it consists in revealing, through the seismic activities underway, that this essence has never conformed to these definitions however obvious and indisputable they are? And here once again the question "what does it mean 'to profess' for a professor?" would be the fault line of this seismic activity underway or still to come. What happens not only when one takes into account the performative value of "profession" but when one accepts that a professor produces "*oeuvres*" and not just knowledge or pre-knowledge? To make our way toward the definition of this type of particular performative action that is the act of professing, and then the act of profession of a professor, and

then finally of a professor of Humanities, we must pursue further our
analysis of the distinctions between *acting, doing, producing, working, work in
general, and the work of the worker*. If I had the time, I could recall once again
and discuss some conceptual distinctions Kant makes between art and
nature, *tekhné* and *physis*, as well as between *Tun* (*facere*) on the one hand
and, on the other, acting (*Handeln*), realizing (*wirken*) in general (*agere*), or
between the product (*Produkt*) as *oeuvre* (*Werk, opus*) on the one hand, and
effect (*Wirkung, effectus*) on the other hand.[10] In the same passage, Kant
distinguishes between art and science, art and craft (*Handwerke*), liberal
art (*freie Kunst*) and mercenary art (*Lohnkunst*). Let us return for a moment
to my equivocal expression: *the end of work*. It may designate the suspension, the death, the term of the activity called work. It can also designate
the object, the aim, the product, or the *oeuvre* of the work. All action, all
activity, as we were saying, is not work. Work is no more reducible to the
activity of the act than it is to the productivity of the production, even if,
out of confusion, these three concepts are often linked. We know better
than ever today that a gain in production can correspond to a dimin-
ishing of work. The virtualization of work has always, and today more
than ever, been able to complicate infinitely this disproportion between
production and work. There are also activities and even productive activities that do not constitute work. The experience of what we call work,
travail, signifies also the passivity of a certain affect; it is sometimes the
suffering and even the torture of a punishment. *Travail*, is that not *tri-
palium*, an instrument of torture? If I underscore this doloristic figure of
punishment and expiation, it is not only in order to recognize the biblical legacy ("in the sweat of thy face shalt thou eat bread"). It is Kant,
once again, who sees in this expiatory dimension of work a universal
trait that transcends biblical traditions.[11] If I underscore this expiatory
interpretation of work, it is also so as to *articulate* or in any case interrogate
together two phenomena that I am tempted today to gather into the same
question: why is it that, on the one hand, we are witnessing throughout
the world a proliferation of scenes of repentance and expiation (there is
today a theatrical worldwide-ization of the confession, of which we could
cite many examples) and, on the other hand, a proliferation of all sorts
of discourses on the end of work?

   Work supposes, engages, and situates a living body. It assigns it a
stable and identifiable place even there where the work is said to be
"non-manual," "intellectual," or "virtual." Work thus supposes a zone
of passivity, a passion, as much as it does a productive activity. Moreover,

we must also distinguish between social work in general, craft or trade, and profession. Not all work is organized according to the unity of a craft or a statutory and recognized competence. As for "crafts" or "trades," even precisely where they are gathered under these names by legitimate institutions or by corporations, not all of them are called, not all of them can easily be called, in our languages, professions, at least when these languages remember their Latin. Even if this were not impossible, one would not easily speak of the profession of the seasonal farm worker, the priest, or the boxer since their know-how, their competence, and their activity suppose neither the permanence nor the social responsibility granted by the, in principle, secular society to someone who exercises a profession by freely committing himself to accomplish a duty. One would more easily and above all speak of the profession of physician, lawyer, professor, as if profession, linked more to the liberal and non-mercenary arts, implied a pledge of responsibility freely declared, very nearly under oath – in a word *professed*. In the lexicon of "professing," I will emphasize less the authority, the supposed competence, and the guarantee of the profession or of the professor than, once again, the pledge to be honored, the declaration of responsibility. For lack of time, I must leave aside this long history of the "profession," of "professionalization" that leads to the current seismic activity. Let us retain, all the same, one essential trait. The idea of profession supposes that beyond and in addition to knowledge, know-how, and competence, a testimonial commitment, a freedom, a re-sponsibility under oath, a sworn faith obligates the subject to render ac-counts to some tribunal yet to be defined. Finally, all those who exercise a profession are not professors. We will thus have to take account of these sometimes hazy distinctions: between work, activity, production, trade or craft, profession, professor, the professor who dispenses a knowledge or professes a doctrine, and the professor who can also, as such, sign *oeuvres* – and who is perhaps already doing so or will do so tomorrow.

III

As if, I said at the outset, the end of work were at the origin of the world. I am indeed saying "as if": *as if* the world began there where work ends, as if the *mondialisation du monde* (which is what I call in French the *worldwide-ization of the world*, in short, what you call, in this country, globalization) had as both its horizon and its origin the disappearance of what we call *le travail*, this old word, painfully laden with so much meaning and history: *work, labor, travail,* and so forth, which always has the sense of real, effective, and not virtual work.

By beginning or by pretending to begin with an "as if," I am neither entering into the fiction of a possible future nor into the resurrection of an historical or mythical past, still less of a revealed origin. The rhetoric of this "as if" belongs neither to the science fiction of a utopia to come (a world without work, "at the end without end," *in fine sine fine* of an eternal sabbatical rest, a Sabbath without evening, as in St. Augustine's *City of God*) nor to the poetics of a nostalgia turned toward a golden age or an earthly paradise, toward that moment in Genesis when, before there is sin, the sweat of laboring brows would not yet have begun to flow, either in man's toil and plowing or in woman's labor of childbirth. In these two interpretations of the "as if," science fiction or memory of the immemorial, it would be *as if* in fact the beginnings of the world originarily excluded work; there would *not yet* or *no longer* be work. It would be *as if,* between the concept of world and the concept of *travail,* there were no originary harmony, thus no given accord or possible synchrony. Original sin would have introduced work into the world and the end of work would announce the terminal phase of an expiation. The logical skeleton of this proposition in "as if" is that the world and work cannot coexist. One would have to choose the world or work, whereas according to common sense, it is difficult to imagine a world without work or some work that is not *of the world* or *in the world.* The Paulinian conversion of the Greek concept of *cosmos* introduces into the Christian world, among many other associated meanings, the assignation to expiatory work. I recalled a moment ago that the concept of *travail,* work, is laden with meanings, history, and equivocations, and that it is difficult to think it beyond good and evil. Although it is always associated simultaneously with dignity, life, production, history, the good, freedom, it connotes no less often evil, suffering, pain, sin, punishment, servitude. But the concept of world is no less obscure, in its European, Greek, Jewish, Christian, Islamic history, between science, philosophy, and faith, whether the world is wrongly identified with the earth, with the humans on earth, here below or with the heavenly world above, or with the cosmos, or with the universe, and so forth. Successful or not, Heidegger's project, beginning with *Sein und Zeit,* will have sought to remove the concept of world and of being-in-the-world from these Greek or Christian presuppositions. It is difficult to put any faith in the word "world" without careful prior analyses, and especially when one wants to think it with or without work, a work whose concept branches out into the notions of activity, of the doing or *making* of technics, on the one hand, with passivity, affect, suffering, punishment, and passion, on the other hand. Whence the difficulty of understanding the "as if" with which I began: "as if the end of work were at the origin of the world." Once again, I am thinking this phrase in French, and I insist on that since the French of "globalization," *mondialisation*, marks a reference to this notion of world charged with a great deal of semantic history, notably a Christian history: the world, as we were saying a moment ago, is neither the universe, nor the earth, nor the terrestrial globe, nor the *cosmos*.

No, in my mind, this "as if" should not signal either toward the utopia or the improbable future of a science fiction or toward the dream of an immemorial or mythological past *in illo tempore*. This "as if" takes account, in the present, of two commonplaces, and it puts them to the test: on the one hand, there is a lot of talk about the end of work and, on the other hand, there is just as much talk about a "globalization," a worldwide-ization of the world, a becoming-world of the world. And these are always associated with each other. I borrow the expression "end of work," as you have doubtless already guessed, from the title of a recent but already well-known book by Jeremy Rifkin, *The End of Work: The Decline of the Global Labor Force and the Dawn of the Post-Market Era*.[12] As you also know, this book gathers up a fairly widespread sort of *doxa* concerning the effects of what Rifkin calls the "Third Industrial Revolution." This revolution has the potential, in his opinion, to be "a powerful force for good and evil," and the "new information and telecommunication technologies have the potential to both liberate and destabilize civilization" (xviii). I don't know if it is true that, as Rifkin claims, we are entering "a new phase in world history": "fewer and fewer workers will be needed to produce the goods and services for the global population." "*The End of Work*," he adds naming thus his own book, "examines the technological innovations and market-directed forces that are moving us to the edge of a near workerless world" (xvi).

What would be the consequences of this from the point of view of the university? To know whether these propositions are literally "true," one would have to agree about the meaning of each of these words (end, history, world, work, production, goods, etc.). I have neither the means nor the time and therefore no intention to discuss directly either this book or this serious and immense problematic, notably the concepts of world and work that are mobilized here. Whether or not one adopts the premises and the conclusions of a discourse like Rifkin's, one must recognize at least (this is the minimal consensus from which I will set out) that something serious is indeed happening or is about to happen to what we call "work," "tele-work," virtual work, and to what we call "world" – and therefore to the being-in-the-world of what is still called man. We must also admit that this depends for a large part on a techno-scientific mutation that, in the cyberworld, in the world of the Internet, of e-mail, and of cellular telephones, affects tele-work, the virtualization of work and, at the same time as the communication of knowledge, at the same time as any putting-into-common and any "community," the experience of place, of taking place, of the event, and of the *oeuvre*: of that which happens, comes about, or as I would prefer to say, that which *arrives*.

I am not going to enter into this problematic of the so-called "end of work," which was not altogether absent from certain texts of Marx or Lenin. As for the latter, he associated the progressive reduction of the workday with the process that would bring about the complete disappearance of the State.[13] Rifkin sees in the third technological revolution underway an absolute mutation. The first two revolutions, that of steam, coal, steel, and textile (in the nineteenth century) and then that of electricity, petroleum, and the automobile (in the twentieth century), did not radically affect the history of work. This is because they both freed up a sector where the machine had not penetrated and where human labor, non-machine and non-substitutable by the machine, was still available. After these two technical revolutions comes ours, therefore, the third one, that of cyberspace, micro-computing, and robotics. Here, it seems that there exists no fourth zone where the unemployed can be put to work. A saturation by machines heralds the end of the worker, thus a certain end of work. End of *Der Arbeiter* and his age, as Jünger might have said. Rifkin's book treats teachers and more generally what he calls the "sector of knowledge" as a special case within the mutation underway. In the past, when new technologies replaced workers in some sector or another, new spaces appeared to absorb the laborers who lost their jobs. But today, when agriculture, industry, and services lay off millions because of technological progress, the only category of workers spared would be that of "knowledge," an "elite of entrepreneurs, scientists, technicians, computer programmers, professional educators, and consultants" (xvii). But this remains a narrow sector, unable to absorb the mass of the unemployed. Such would be the dangerous singularity of our age. Rifkin does not speak of unemployed teachers or aspiring professors, in particular in the Humanities.

I will not treat the objections one could make to these kinds of discourse, in their generality, neither as concerns the so-called "end of work" nor with regard to the so-called "worldwide-ization." In both cases, which are moreover closely linked, if I had to treat them head-on, I would try to distinguish, in a preliminary fashion, between the massive and hardly contestable phenomena that are registered with these words, on the one hand, and, on the other, the use people make of these words without concept. In fact, no one will deny that something is indeed happening to work in this century, to the reality and to the concept of work – active or actual work. What is happening there is indeed an effect of techno-science, with the worldwide-izing virtualization and delocalization of tele-work. What is happening indeed accentuates a certain tendency toward the asymptotic reduction of work-time, as work in real time and localized in the same place as the body of the worker. All of this affects work in the classic forms we have inherited, in the new experience of borders, of the nation-state, of virtual communication, of the speed and spread of information. This evolution goes in the direction of a certain worldwide-ization; it is undeniable and fairly well known. But these phenomenal indices remain partial, heterogeneous, unequal in their development; they call for close analysis and no doubt new concepts. Moreover, between these obvious indices and the doxic use – others might say the ideological inflation – the rhetorical and often hazy complacency with which everyone gives in to the words "end of work" and "globalization," there is a gap. I do not wish to bridge this gap in a facile way and I believe one must sternly criticize those who forget it is there. For they attempt thereby to induce forgetfulness of zones in the world, populations, nations, groups, classes, individuals who, massively, are the excluded victims of the movement called "the end of work" and "globalization" or "worldwide-ization." These victims suffer either because they lack the work they would need or else because they work too much for the salary they receive in exchange on a worldwide market that is so violently inegalitarian. This capitalistic situation (there where capital plays an essential role between the actual and the virtual) is more tragic in absolute figures than it has ever been in the history of humanity. Humanity has perhaps never been further from the worldwide-izing or worldwide-ized homogeneity of "work" and "without work" that is often alleged. A large part of humanity is "without work" just where it would like to have more work, and another has too much work just where it would like to have less, or even to be done with a job that is so poorly paid on the market. This history began a long time ago. It is interwoven

with the real and semantic history of "craft," "trade," and "profession."
Rifkin is acutely conscious of the tragedy that could also ensue from this
"end of work" that does not have the sabbatical or dominical sense it has
in the Augustinian *City of God*. But in his moral and political conclusions,
when he wants to define the responsibilities to be assumed in the face of
"the technological storm clouds on the horizon," in the face of "a new age
of global markets and automated production," he comes back to – and
I believe this is neither fortuitous nor acceptable without examination –
the Christian language of "fraternity," of "qualities not easily reducible
to or replaceable by machines," of "renewed meaning and purpose in
life," of "renewal of community life," of "rebirth of the human spirit";
he even envisions new forms of charity, for example "providing shadow
wages for volunteering time, imposing a value-added tax on the products
and services of the high-tech era to be used exclusively to guarantee a
social wage for the poor in return for performing community service"
and so forth (291–93).

   If I had had the time to retrace it with you, I would no doubt still have
insisted, on the time of work, while taking frequent inspiration from the
research of my colleague Jacques Le Goff. In the chapter "Temps et
travail" in his *Un autre Moyen Age*, he shows how, in the fourteenth century, there already coexisted demands for prolonging and demands for
reducing the duration of work (69–71). We have here the premises for
workers' rights and a right to work in the form in which they will later
be inscribed in human rights. The figure of the humanist is a response to
the question of work. In the theology of work that dominates the period
and that is no doubt not dead today, the humanist is someone who begins
to secularize the time of work and the monastic time schedule. Time,
which is no longer just a gift of God, can be calculated and sold. In the
iconography of the fourteenth century, the clock sometimes represents
the attribute of the humanist[14] – the same clock that I am obliged to
watch and that keeps a strict watch over the lay worker that I am here.
I would have liked to speak to you for hours about the *hour*, about that
purely fictional countable unit, about this "as if" that regulates, orders,
and makes time (*fiction* is what *figures* but also what *makes*), the time of
work outside and within the university, where everything, courses, seminars, lectures, is counted by hourly segments. The "academic quarter
hour" is itself regulated by the hour. Deconstruction is also the question of the hour, a crisis of the unit called "hour." It would also have
been necessary to follow the trace of that tripartite classification that,
since the ninth to eleventh centuries, has divided society into the three

orders of clerks, warriors, and workers (*oratores, bellatores, laboratores*); and then the hierarchy of crafts (noble or servile, licit or illicit, *negotia illicita, opera servilia*, forbidden on Sunday) (89). Le Goff shows how the unity of the world of work, as distinct from the world of prayer and the world of war, if it ever existed, "did not last very long" (102). After the "contempt for the crafts . . . a new frontier of contempt is laid down which passes through the middle of new classes, and even the middle of the professions" (ibid.). Although he does not distinguish, it seems to me, between "craft" and "profession" (as I believe one must do), Le Goff also describes the process that gives birth in the twelfth century to a "theology of work" and to the transformation of the tripartite schema (*oratores, bellatores, laboratores*) into "more complex" schemas, which is explained by the differentiation of economic and social structures and by a more extensive division of work (165). In the twelfth and thirteenth centuries the "scholarly craft" appears as the hierarchy of *scolares* and *magistri* that will be the prelude to universities. Abelard had to choose between *litterae* and *arma*. He sacrificed "*pompa militari gloriae*" for "*studium litterarum.*" I would be tempted to situate the profession of the professor, in the strict sense, at this highly symbolic moment of the pledge by which, for example, Abelard assumed the responsibility to respond to the injunction or the appeal: "*tu eris magister in aeternum*" (179), even if, as Le Goff emphasizes, he continued to describe his career in military terms, dialectics remaining an arsenal and the *disputationes* battles. It is often the figure and the name of *philosopher* (181), of the professor *as* philosopher, that becomes necessary in a new situation. The university is thought and is represented from the privileged place of the philosophical: within and outside the Humanities. There is nothing surprising in Kant's granting such a privilege to the Faculty of Philosophy in his architecture of the university. If for deconstruction, to a certain extent at least, philosophy is at once a privileged reference, resource, *and* target, this may be explained no doubt in part by this dominant tradition. In the twelfth and thirteenth centuries, scholarly life becomes a craft or trade (*negotia scholaria*). One then speaks of *pecunia* and *laus* to define what compensates the work and research of new students and scholars. Salary and glory articulate between them economic functioning and professional conscience.

What I wish to suggest with these meager historical indications is that one of the tasks to come of the Humanities would be, *ad infinitum*, to know and to think their own history, at least in the directions that we have just seen open up (the act of professing, the theology and the history of work, of knowledge and of the faith in knowledge, the question of man, of the world, of fiction, of the performative and the "as if," of literature and of *oeuvre*, etc., and then all the concepts that we have just articulated with them). This deconstructive task of the Humanities to come will not let itself be contained within the traditional limits of the departments that today belong, by their very status, to the Humanities. These Humanities to come will cross disciplinary borders without, all the same, dissolving the specificity of each discipline into what is called, often in a very confused way, interdisciplinarity or into what is lumped with another good-for-everything concept, "cultural studies." But I can very well imagine that departments of genetics, natural science, medicine, and even mathematics will take seriously, in their work itself, the questions that I have just evoked. This is especially true – to make one last reference to the Kant of *The Conflict of the Faculties* – besides medicine, of law schools and departments of theology or religion.

I must now hasten my conclusion. I will do so in a dry and telegraphic manner with seven theses, seven propositions, or seven professions of faith. They remain altogether programmatic. Six of them will have only a formalizing value of serving as reminders, of reassembling or recapitulating. The seventh, which will not be sabbatical, will attempt a step beyond the six others toward a dimension of the *event* and of the *taking-place* that I have yet to speak of. Between the first six theses – or professions of faith – and the last, we will get our foothold in preparation for a leap that would carry us beyond the power of the performative "as if," beyond even the distinction between constative and performative on which we have up until now pretended to rely.

The Humanities of tomorrow, in all their departments, will have to study their history, the history of the concepts that, by constructing them, instituted the disciplines and were coextensive with them. There are many signs that this work has already begun, of course. Like all acts of institution, those that we must analyze will have had a performative force and will have put to work a certain "as if." I just said that one must "study" or "analyze." Is it necessary to make clear that such "studies," such "analyses," for the reasons already indicated, would not be purely "theoretical" and neutral? They would lead toward practical and performative transformations and would not forbid the production of singular *oeuvres*. To these fields I will give therefore six, and then seven thematic and programmatic titles, without excluding, obviously, cross-fertilizations and reciprocal interpellations.

1. These new Humanities would treat the history of man, the idea, the figure, and the notion of "what is proper to man" (and a non-finite

series of oppositions by which man is determined, in particular the traditional opposition of the life form called human and of the life form called animal). I will dare to claim, without being able to demonstrate it here, that none of these traditional concepts of "what is proper to man" and thus of what is opposed to it can resist a consistent scientific and deconstructive analysis.

The most urgent guiding thread here would be the problematization (which does not mean the disqualification) of these powerful juridical performatives that have given shape to the modern history of this humanity of man. I am thinking, for example, of the rich history of at least two of these juridical performatives: *on the one hand*, the Declarations of the Rights of Man – *and of the woman* (for the question of sexual differences is not secondary or accidental here and we know that these Declarations of the Rights of Man were being constantly transformed and enriched from 1789 to 1948 and beyond: the figure of man, a promising animal, an animal capable of promising, as Nietzsche said, remains still to come) and, *on the other hand*, the concept of "crime against humanity," which since the end of the Second World War has modified the geopolitical field of international law and will continue to do so more and more, commanding in particular the scene of worldwide confession and of the relation to the historical past in general. The new Humanities will thus treat these performative productions of law or right (rights of man, human rights, the concept of crime against humanity) there where they always imply the promise and, with the promise, the conventionality of the "as if."

2. These new Humanities would treat, in the same style, the history of democracy and the idea of sovereignty, which is also to say, of course, the conditions or rather the unconditionality on which the university and within it the Humanities are supposed (once again the "as if") to live. The deconstruction of this concept of sovereignty would touch not only on international law, the limits of the nation-state, and of its supposed sovereignty, but also on the use made of them in juridico-political discourses concerning the relations between what is called man and woman. This concept of sovereignty has been recently at the center of very poorly thought-out and poorly conducted debates, in my country, on the subject of man–woman "parity" in access to political offices.

3. These new Humanities would treat, in the same style, the history of "professing," of the "profession," and of the professoriat, a history articulated with that of the premises or presuppositions (notably Abrahamic, biblical, and above all Christian) of work and of the worldwide-ized

confession, at the very point where it goes beyond the sovereignty of the head of state, of the nation-state, or even of the "people" in a democracy. An immense problem: how to dissociate democracy from citizenship, from the nation-state, and from the theological idea of sovereignty, even the sovereignty of the people? How to dissociate sovereignty and unconditionality, the power of sovereignty, the powerlessness of unconditionality? Here again, whether it is a question of profession or confession, it is the performative structure of the "as if" that would be at the center of the work.

4. These new Humanities would treat, in the same style, the history of literature. Not only what is commonly called History of literatures or literature themselves, with the great question of its canons (traditional and indisputable objects of the classical Humanities), but the history of the concept of literature, of the modern institution named literature, of its links with fiction and the performative force of the "as if," of its concept of *oeuvre*, author, signature, national language, of its link with the right to say or not to say everything that founds both democracy and the idea of the unconditional sovereignty claimed by the university and within it by what is called, inside and outside departments, the Humanities.

5. These new Humanities would treat, in the same style, the history of profession, the profession of faith, professionalization, and the professoriat. The guiding thread could be, today, what is happening when the profession of faith, the profession of faith of the professor, gives rise not only to the competent exercise of some knowledge in which one has faith, not only to that classical alliance of the constative and the performative, but to singular *oeuvres*, to other strategies of the "as if" that are events and that affect the very limits of the academic field or of the Humanities. We are indeed witnessing the end of a certain figure of the professor and of his or her supposed authority, but I believe, as should now be obvious, in a certain necessity of the professoriat.

6. These new Humanities, finally, would thus treat, in the same style, but in the course of a formidable reflexive reversal, both critical and deconstructive, the history of the "as if" and especially the history of this precious distinction between performative acts and constative acts that seems to have been indispensable for us up until now. It will surely be necessary (things have already begun) to study the history and the limits of such a decisive distinction, and to which I have made reference today as if I believed in it without reservation up until now, as if I held it to be absolutely reliable. This deconstructive work would concern not only the original and brilliant *oeuvre* of Austin but also his rich and

fascinating inheritance, over the last half-century, in particular in the Humanities.

7. To the seventh point, which is not the seventh day, I arrive finally now. Or rather: I *let perhaps* arrive at the end, now, the very thing that, by *arriving*, as an *arrivant* or arriving one [*en arrivant*], by taking place or having place, revolutionizes, overturns, and puts to rout the very authority that is attached, in the university, in the Humanities:

1. to knowledge (or at least to its model of constative language),
2. to the profession or to the profession of faith (or at least to its model of performative language),
3. to the *mise en oeuvre*, the putting to work, at least to the performative putting to work of the "as if."

That which happens, takes place, comes about in general, that which is called event, what is it? Can one ask with regard to it: "What is it?" It must not only surprise the constative and propositional mode of the language of knowledge (S is P), but also no longer even let itself be commanded by the performative speech act of a subject. As long as I can produce and determine an event by a performative act guaranteed, like any performative, by conventions, legitimate fictions, and a certain "as if," then to be sure I will not say that nothing happens or comes about, but what takes place, arrives, happens, or happens *to me* remains still controllable and programmable within a horizon of anticipation or precomprehension, within a horizon period. It is of the order of the masterable possible, it is the unfolding of what is already possible. It is of the order of power, of the "I can," or "I may." No surprise, thus no event in the strong sense. Which is as much as to say that, to this extent at least, it does not happen, it does not come about, or as I would say in French: *cela n'arrive pas*, it does not arrive. For if there is any, if there is such a thing, the pure singular eventness of *what* arrives or of *who* arrives and arrives *to me* (which is what I call the *arrivant*), it would suppose an *irruption* that punctures the horizon, *interrupting* any performative organization, any convention, or any context that can be dominated by a conventionality. Which is to say that this event takes place only to the extent where it does not allow itself to be domesticated by any "as if," or at least by any "as if" that can already be read, decoded, or articulated *as such*. So that this small word, the *as* of the "as if" as well as the *as* of the "as such" – whose authority founds and justifies every ontology as well as every phenomenology, every philosophy as science or knowledge – this small word, *as*, is then everywhere the name of the very issue, not to say the target of deconstruction. It is too often said that the performative produces the event of which it speaks. One must also realize that, inversely, where there is a performative, an event worthy of the name cannot arrive. If what arrives belongs to the horizon of the possible, or even of a possible performative, of its power of the "I can," "I may," it does not arrive, it does not happen, in the full sense of the word. As I have often tried to demonstrate, only the impossible can arrive. By frequently pointing out about deconstruction that it is impossible or the impossible, and that it was not a method, a doctrine, a speculative meta-philosophy, but *what arrives, what comes about*, I was relying on the same thought. The examples with which I have attempted to accede to this thought (invention, the gift, forgiveness, hospitality, justice, friendship, and so forth) all confirmed this thinking of the impossible possible, of the possible *as* impossible, of an impossible-possible that can no longer be determined by the metaphysical interpretation of possibility or virtuality. I will not say that this thought of the impossible possible, this other thinking of the possible is a thinking of necessity but rather, as I have also tried to demonstrate elsewhere, a thinking of the "perhaps," of that dangerous modality of the "perhaps" that Nietzsche speaks of and that philosophy has always tried to subjugate. There is no future and no relation to the coming of the event without experience of the "perhaps." What takes place does not have to announce itself as possible or necessary; if it did, its irruption as event would in advance be neutralized. The event belongs to a *perhaps* that is in keeping not with the possible but with the impossible. And its force is therefore irreducible to the force or the power of a performative, even if it gives to the performative, to what is called the force of the performative, its chance and its effectiveness. The force of the event is always stronger than the force of a performative. In the face of what arrives to me, happens to me and even in what I decide (which, as I tried to show in *Politics of Friendship*, must involve a certain passivity, my decision being always the decision of the other), in the face of the other who arrives and arrives to me, all performative force is overrun, exceeded, exposed.

This force in keeping with an experience of the "perhaps" keeps an affinity or a complicity with the "if" of the "as if." And thus with a certain grammar of the conditional: what *if* this arrived? This, that is altogether other, *could well* arrive, this *would* happen. To think *perhaps* is to think "if," "what if?" But you see quite clearly that this "if," this "what if," this "as if" is no longer reducible to all the "as if"s that we have been talking about up until now.[15] And if it is declined according to the verbal mode of the conditional, this is also to announce the unconditional, the eventual, or the possible event of the impossible unconditional, the altogether other – which we should from now on (and this is something else I have not yet said or done today) dissociate from the theological idea of sovereignty. Basically, this would perhaps be my hypothesis (it is extremely difficult, and almost impossible, impossible to prove): it would be necessary to dissociate a certain unconditional independence of thought, of deconstruction, of justice, of the Humanities, of the University, and so forth from any phantasm of sovereign mastery.

Well, it is once again in the Humanities that one would have to make arrive, make happen, the thinking of this other mode of the "if," this more than difficult, im-possible thing, the exceeding of the performative and of the opposition constative/performative. By thinking, *in* the Humanities, this limit of mastery and of performative conventionality, this limit of performative authority, what is one doing? One is acceding to that place where the always necessary context of the performative operation (a context that is, like every convention, an institutional context) can no longer be saturated, delimited, fully determined. The brilliant invention of the constative/performative distinction would basically still have sought, in the university, to reassure the university as to the sovereign mastery of its interior, as to its proper power, a power of its own. One thus touches on the very limit, *between the inside and the outside*, notably the border of the university itself, and within it, of the Humanities. One thinks *in* the Humanities the irreducibility of their outside and of their future. One thinks *in* the Humanities that one cannot and must not let oneself be enclosed within the inside of the Humanities. But for this thinking to be strong and consistent requires the Humanities. To think this is not an academic, speculative, or theoretical operation; it is not a neutral utopia. No more than saying it is a simple enunciation. It is on this always divisible limit, it is at this limit that what arrives arrives. It is this limit that is affected by the arriving and that changes. This limit of the impossible, the "perhaps," and the "if," this is the place where the university is exposed to reality, to the forces from without (be they cultural, ideological, political, economic, or other). It is there that the university is in the world that it is attempting to think. On this border, it must therefore negotiate and organize its resistance. And take its responsibilities. Not in order to enclose itself and reconstitute the abstract phantasm of sovereignty whose theological or humanist heritage it will perhaps have begun to deconstruct, if at least it has begun to do so. But in order to resist effectively, by allying itself with extra-academic forces, in order to organize an inventive resistance, through its *oeuvres*, its works, to all attempts at reappropriation (political, juridical, economic, and so forth), to all the other figures of sovereignty.

I do not have time to justify any further my profession of faith. I do not know if what I am saying here is intelligible, if it makes sense. I especially do not know what status, genre, or legitimacy the discourse has that I have just addressed to you. Is it academic? Is it a discourse of knowledge in the Humanities or on the subject of the Humanities? Is it knowledge only? Only a performative profession of faith? Does it belong to the inside of the university? Is it philosophy, or literature, or theater? Is it a work, *une oeuvre*, or a course, or a kind of seminar? I have numerous hypotheses on this subject, but finally it will be up to you now, it will also be up to others to decide this. The signatories are also the addressees. We don't know them, neither you nor I. For if this impossible that I'm talking about were to arrive perhaps one day, I leave you to imagine the consequences. Take your time but be quick about it because you do not know what awaits you.

NOTES

1 Jacques Le Goff, *Un autre Moyen Age* (Paris: Gallimard, 1999), 172.

2 Mark Poster, unpublished manuscript, "CyberDemocracy: Internet and the Public Sphere."

3 *Kritik der Urtheilskraft*, Einleitung, IV and V, in *Kantswerke, Akademische Ausgabe*, V, 181 (XXVII) and 184 (XXXIV).

4 Ibid., § 60.

5 Samuel Weber, *Institution and Interpretation* (Minneapolis: University of Minnesota Press, 1987), 143.

6 Samuel Weber, "The Future of the Humanities," in C.S. de Beer, ed., *Unisa as Distinctive University for our Time* (Pretoria: Interdisciplinary Discussion Forum, University of South Africa, 1998).

7 Peggy Kamuf, *The Division of Literature, or the University in Deconstruction* (Chicago: University of Chicago Press, 1997), 15.

8 Jacques Derrida, "Economimesis," in Sylviane Agacinski *et al.*, *Mimésis (des articulations)* (Paris: Aubier Flammarion, 1975), trans. Richard Klein, in *Diacritics* 11, 2 (1981); "Mochlos ou le conflit des facultés," in *Philosophie* 2 (1984), "Mochlos; or, The Conflict of the Faculties," trans. Richard Rand and Amy Wygant, in Richard Rand, ed., *Logomachia: The Conflict of the Faculties* (Lincoln: University of Nebraska Press, 1992).

9 "An einem Producte der schönen Kunst muss man sich bewusst werden, dass es Kunst sei und nicht Natur; aber doch muss die Zweckmässigkeit in der Form desselben von allem Zwange willkürlicher Regeln so frei scheinen, als ob es ein Product der Blossen Natur sei" (*Third Critique*, § 45, 306 [179]).

10 *Third Critique*, § 43; cf. also Jacques Derrida, "Economimesis," 59.

11 See Kant, *Religion Within the Limits of Reason Alone*, trans. Theodore M. Greene and Hoyt H. Hudson (New York: Harper Torchbooks, 1960), unnumbered note, 67–68.

12 Jeremy Rifkin, *The End of Work: The Decline of the Global Labor Force and the Dawn of the Post-Market Era* (New York: G. P. Putnam's Sons, 1995).

13 V.I. Lenin, *L'Etat et la Révolution* (Paris: éditions sociales), 175.

14 Le Goff, *Un autre Moyen Age*, 78.

15 This "as if" is no longer simply philosophical. It is thus, for all these reasons, not that of *The Philosophy of the As If* (*Die Philosophie des Als ob*) by Vaihinger. Nor is it the one to which Freud alludes, when he makes reference to Vaihinger's work, at the end of the third chapter of *The Future of an Illusion*.

CHAPTER 2

Derrida and literature

J. Hillis Miller

For I have to remind you, somewhat bluntly and simply, that my most constant interest, coming even before my philosophical interest I should say, if this is possible, has been directed towards literature, towards that writing which is called literature.

What is literature?

– Jacques Derrida, "The Time of a Thesis, Punctuations"

Literature is everywhere in Jacques Derrida's writing. It is there from one end to the other of his work, even in essays or books that superficially do not seem to involve "literature." If Derek Attridge had not already invented or borrowed the phrase "Acts of Literature" as the title for his fine anthology of Derrida's writings about literature[1] I might have called this chapter "Derrida's Acts of Literature." The phrase "acts of literature" is a double genitive, subjective and objective at once. It names acts performed by literature, and at the same time acts that create or comment on literature. In what sense can literature, or writing about literature, or writing literature, or reading literature be an "act"? That is one of my main questions here.

Derrida, along with all the other things he is (as this volume testifies), is one of the great literary critics of the twentieth century. By saying he is a "literary critic" I mean not just that he has contributed to literary theory from a philosophical perspective but that he has written, or presented in seminars, detailed, persuasive, and brilliantly original readings of literary works by a long list of what are usually considered "major authors" along with some "minor" ones: Mallarmé, Shakespeare, Poe, Melville, Joyce, Celan, Baudelaire, Ponge, Genet, Blanchot (the *récits*, not the criticism), Kafka, Proust, and less known authors like Jos Joliet. What Derrida has written about Mallarmé's "Mimique," Baudelaire's "La fausse monnaie," Joyce's *Ulysses*, Celan's poetry, or Kafka's "Before the Law," looks like literary criticism to me. I think we must take Derrida at his word when he says that literature has been his "most constant interest," and also believe him when, in another place, he asserts that "deconstruction . . . is a coming-to-terms with literature."[2]

The quickest way to get at Derrida's definition of literature, strangely enough, is by way of his speech act theory. Derrida's speech act theory, as readers of "Signature Event Context" and "Limited Inc a b c . . . " will know, centers on a critique of J. L. Austin and a polemical rebuttal of John Searle's attack on Derrida by way of what the latter calls "iterability." Iterability is the lever Derrida uses to reverse the hierarchy by which Austin (and Searle) expel literature from the domain of "felicitous" speech acts. Austin calls literature, along with speaking in soliloquy and acting on the stage, "parasitical" on normal speech acts. Literature is "non-serious," "infelicitous," "etiolated" (in the sense that white asparagus is kept from turning green by being covered and kept from sunlight). "I must not be writing a poem," says Austin – if I want to utter a felicitous speech act, that is.

For Derrida, however, since iterability is an intrinsic feature of any language or any mark taken as a sign, it cannot be excluded from the analysis of any speech act or sign whatsoever. Iterability is a feature of language or the mark in general, even of utterances that seem to be controlled by being spoken once and once only by an "I" present to itself and others in the correct circumstances, e.g. "I pronounce you man and wife," said by the minister in a correctly performed church wedding that marries this particular couple once and for all (unless they divorce by way of another speech act). Even such utterances are always already internally divided or multiplied (both at once) by their "structure of repeatability." The marriage ceremony would not work as a way of doing things with words if it were not repeatable. The "normal" and "serious" speech act cannot be used to set aside and devalue in advance "non-serious" ones.

Literature is for Derrida the possibility for any utterance, writing, or mark to be iterated in innumerable contexts and to function in the absence of identifiable speaker, context, reference, or hearer. This does not mean that the referential function of language is suspended or annulled in literature. The referential function of language cannot be suspended or annulled. It does mean, however, that a reader, for example, will, most probably, search in vain for a "real life" referent for the "Kate Croy" to whom the first paragraphs of Henry James's *The Wings of the Dove* refer. I say "most probably" because you never know for sure. Nevertheless, the narrator of that novel, as opposed to its author, speaks as if Kate Croy had had a real, verifiable existence outside language or "literature":

"She waited, Kate Croy, for her father to come in, but he kept her un-
conscionably...." Nothing, it appears, distinguishes this sentence from
language that would have been used in a biography of a real Kate Croy,
just as nothing would distinguish a fictitious telephone book from a real
one, until you tried to dial the numbers in the fictitious one, that is.

What, then, is literature? There is no such thing, for Derrida, if one
means an infallible test for determining that you have a genuine piece of
literature in hand. Literature is not some essence hidden inside a given
text. Any piece of language, oral or written, can be "taken as literature,"
not in the sense that we can make it function any way we like, but in
the sense that the possibility of being taken as literature is intrinsic to it,
just as the serious is built on the non-serious, not the other way around.
Literature depends on the possibility of detaching language from its firm
embeddedness in a social or biographical context and allowing it to play
freely as fiction.

Much work in literary study as a university-based institutionalized
endeavor has always been an attempt to treat what could be taken as
literary works as though they were historical, social, or autobiographical
documents, that is, as though they were not literature. This includes these
days important aspects, though not all aspects, of so-called cultural studies, the latest version of the way to teach and write about literature that
has been dominant throughout all its modern institutionalization since
the late nineteenth century. The institution of literary study, including,
of course, most journalistic reviewing, is, paradoxically, a vigorous and
multifaceted attempt to suppress, efface, cover over, ignore, and forget
the properly literary in literature, that is, what is improper about literary language or about any language when it is taken as literature. By
"improper" I mean possibly detached from what we ordinarily assume is
its proper referential or performative use, its "serious," "non-etiolated"
use. Here is Derrida's way of expressing this. The passage is taken from
the interview of Derrida by Derek Attridge that opens the latter's admirable anthology of Derrida's writings on literature. The passage must
be read carefully in order to distinguish what Derrida says from what
so-called deconstruction is often vulgarly said to assert, that is, that everything human is "all language" or "all wanton subjectivity":

Literature has no pure originality in this regard. A philosophical, or journalistic,
or scientific discourse, can be read in a "nontranscendent" fashion. "Transcend"
here means going beyond interest for the signifier, the form, the language (note
that I do not say "text") in the direction of the meaning or referent (this is Sartre's
rather simple but convenient definition of prose). One can do a nontranscendent

reading of any text whatever. Moreover, there is no text which is literary *in itself*. Literarity is not a natural essence, an intrinsic property of the text. It is the correlative of an intentional relation to the text, an intentional relation which integrates in itself, as a component or an intentional layer, the more or less implicit consciousness of rules which are conventional or institutional – social, in any case. Of course, this does not mean that literarity is merely projective or subjective – in the sense of the empirical subjectivity or caprice of each reader. The literary character of the text is inscribed on the side of the intentional object, in its noematic structure, one could say, and not only on the subjective side of the noetic act. There are "in" the text features which call for the literary reading and recall the convention, institution, or history of literature. ("An Interview with Jacques Derrida," *AL*, 44)

The odd terminology here ("transcendent," "noematic," "noetic") is borrowed from "phenomenology," more particularly from Edmund Husserl. Several of Derrida's earliest books are devoted to Husserl. He pays homage to Husserl's continued influence on his thinking in the much later "Time of a Thesis," cited hereafter as TT. Rodolphe Gasché is to this degree right to say that Derrida belongs within the phenomenological tradition, but immediately after the passage quoted above Derrida firmly establishes his distance from Husserl. It is just literature or "literarity" that puts phenomenology "in crisis." This means that the Husserlian terminology as Derrida uses it is twisted to new uses that in the end put Husserlial certainties, for example the primacy of consciousness, radically in question: "I believe this phenomenological-type language to be necessary, even if at a certain point it must yield to what, in the situation of writing or reading, and in particular literary writing or reading, puts phenomenology in crisis as well as the very concept of institution or convention (but this would take us too far)" (*AL*, 44–45).

Derrida uses Husserl's language to make several rapid moves. "There is no text which is literary *in itself*," he says. "Literarity is not a natural essence." So much for the idea that literature can be identified and segregated, kept separate, for example in courses that teach "literary works" in "literature departments." Why is this? The answer, first, is that any piece of language whatsoever can be read either as literature or as not literature. This, as I have said, works both ways, both to say that a telephone book can be read as literature and that *Madame Bovary* can be read as sociological or biographical evidence, side by side with memoirs, letters, and newspaper stories. What is the difference between the two ways of reading? The difference, in Derrida's quaint phenomenological terminology, one of the few places Derrida overtly uses Sartre, is between

a transcendent and a non-transcendent reading. A "transcendent" reading goes beyond the text in the direction of what it means or refers to, as
we use a telephone book to ring up a friend. This is what Sartre says we
use prose for. A non-transcendent reading remains with the form and
language, the signs themselves, perhaps even their materiality as marks
on the page, though Derrida does not say that here. (Elsewhere, for example in the book on Celan, he does talk in his own way, with Celan's
help, about the materiality of inscription.) Such a reading suspends or
brackets the "transcendent" reading that any discourse also calls for.

The passage cited from Derrida, however, says more than this. It
might be thought from what he has said that making a transcendent or
non-transcendent reading is a matter of subjective choice. "It's a free
country," as the somewhat ironic United States slang phrase has it. This
would seem to match what is often described as Derrida's irresponsible
"relativism" or "nihilism." Such characterizations are dead wrong, as
Derrida's paragraph scrupulously explains. "Of course," says Derrida,
"this does not mean that literarity is merely projective or subjective – in
the sense of the empirical subjectivity or caprice of each reader." Why
not? Derrida gives two related but by no means identical answers to
this question. The first depends on the Husserlian distinction between
noematic and noetic. The prefix, *noe-* is from the Greek *noesis*, "intelligence, understanding," from *noein*, "to perceive," from *nous*, "the mind."
Noetic means "apprehended by the intellect alone," while *noematic* refers
to features in what is to be known that makes them knowable, subject
to *noesis*. "Intentional" is a Husserlian term that describes the way the
mind reaches out toward things to know them. "Consciousness is always
consciousness of some object or other, never a self-enclosed emptiness":
this is a basic phenomenological credo. Literarity, the possibility of being
taken as literature, is not in the mind but in the text. One can see the
fine line Derrida is walking here and see also how much is at stake in
getting it right. "The literary character of the text is inscribed on the
side of the intentional object, in its noematic structure, one could say,
and not only on the subjective side of the noetic act." The "not only"
here is the tightrope walking. It means, if I understand it, that the act of
making a given piece of discourse literature does involve the mind, as it
has internalized conventions and rules, as well as knowable, "noematic,"
features of the discourse itself.

Derrida, however, says still more than this. Taking a piece of language
as literature also involves that complex set of conventions, rules,
institutions, and historical features that are both within text and within

the mind of the one who performs the act (a speech act) of taking a given text as literature. This means that the mind of the person who says or implies, "I declare this is literature," is not a private subjectivity, "but a subjectivity which is non-empirical and linked to an intersubjective and transcendental community . . . The essence of literature, if we hold to this word essence, is produced as a set of objective rules in an original history of the 'acts' of inscription and reading" (*AL*, 44, 45). When we take something as literature we do not act as private and sequestered egos. The cultural community to which we belong, with all its rules and institutions, acts through us, or we act in its name and with its authority. Key words here are "produced" and "acts." The essence of literature, if it can be said to have an essence, is not something that descends from on high, from some supernal realm. It is "produced" by occasions of writing and reading that are historically embedded "acts." The history is "original" both in the sense that it is special to our tradition and not legitimately universalizable to "world literature" at every time and place and in the sense that it is originary or originating. It comes into existence or is "produced" by specific historical acts of inscription and reading.

More broadly speaking, just what, for Derrida, are the rules, conventions, and institutions that define the "literary character of the text"? Derrida gives a specific and somewhat surprising answer to that question. Literature as an institution in the West, says Derrida, is linked to democracy and to freedom of speech, the freedom, in principle, though never of course quite in fact, to say or write anything, or to perform any symbolic act. This means that literature, as an institution in the West, has a quite short history. It arose with Western-style democracies, in the late seventeenth century, and would disappear if they disappeared. Literature could disappear, and "civilization" would not necessarily disappear at the same time, assuming you think Singapore, say, which hardly has free speech, is an example of civilization. Here is the way Derrida himself expresses this:

Literature is a modern invention, inscribed in conventions and institutions which, to hold on to just this trait, secure in principle its *right to say everything*. Literature thus ties its destiny to a certain noncensure, to the space of democratic freedom (freedom of the press, freedom of speech, etc.). No democracy without literature; no literature without democracy . . . The possibility of literature, the legitimization that a society gives it, the allaying of suspicion or terror with regard to it, all that goes together – politically – with the unlimited right to ask any question, to suspect all dogmatism, to analyze every presupposition, even those of the ethics or the politics of responsibility. (*Passions*, 28)

A key word here is "invention." Literature is not an "essence" but an "invention," something particular writers in particular societies at particular historical moments have made up on the basis of possibilities inherent in language, just as (though not quite "just as") the steam engine was invented on the basis of possibilities inherent in water. I shall later explain further why this word "invention" is so important and just what Derrida finds or invents in that word. The passages just quoted give the lie to claims that Derrida, or "deconstruction" in general, are ahistorical, ignore history, or do not follow Fredric Jameson's injunction "always historicize." Here is an exigent historicizing if there ever was one. It is a historicizing of literature that would make big problems with current (and much older) attempts to universalize the Western concept of literature and study things called "Chinese literature" or "Indian literature" or "Native American literature." It would also remind us that calling Homer's *Odyssey* or Sophocles' *Oedipus the King* or Virgil's *Aeneid* or Dante's *Divine Comedy* literature in our modern sense of that word is anachronistic.

Derrida draws the most extreme and disquieting consequences from his association of literature with democracy and free speech. Literature, guaranteed by the principle of free speech, affords the possibility to disclaim responsibility. I can always say, and get away with saying, "any resemblance to real persons is purely coincidental," or with saying "that is not me speaking my own opinions but an imaginary character or narrator." Here is the way Derrida puts this extreme irresponsibility of literature:

But this authorization to say everything paradoxically makes the author an author who is not responsible to anyone, not even to himself, for whatever the persons or the characters of his works, thus of what he is supposed to have written himself, say and do, for example. And these "voices" speak, allow or make to come – even in literatures without persons and without characters. This authorization to say everything (which goes together with democracy, as the apparent hyper-responsibility of a "subject") acknowledges a right to absolute nonresponse, just where there can be no question of responding, of being able to or having to respond. This non-response is more original and more secret than the modalities of power and duty because it is fundamentally heterogeneous to them. We find there a hyperbolic condition of democracy which seems to contradict a certain determined and historically limited concept of such a democracy, a concept which links it to the concept of a subject that is calculable, accountable, imputable, and responsible, a subject having-to-respond [*devant-répondre*], having-to-tell [*devant-dire*] the truth, having to testify according to the sworn word ("the whole truth, nothing but the truth"), before the law [*devant la loi*], having to reveal the secret, with the exception of certain situations that are determinable and regulated by law (confession, the professional secrets of the doctor, the psychoanalyst, or the lawyer, secrets of national defense or state secrets in general, manufacturing secrets, etc.). This contradiction also indicates the task (task of thought, also theoretico-practical task) for any democracy to come. (*Passions*, 28–29)

This passage says a mouthful, as they say. It associates literature with a certain radical irresponsibility. This follows from the definition of literature as the right to say anything. That in turn follows from iterability's radical potentiality as Derrida defines it as a feature of all utterances both constative and performative, both truth-saying and act-doing. Literature is an exploitation of the possibility that any utterance may be "non-serious." It is always possible to say, "That is not me speaking but an imagined persona or character in a literary work." I am not an axe-murderer. I have just written a novel in which I imagine an axe-murderer and tell the story of his life (Dostoevsky's *Crime and Punishment*). Indeed the assumption that the narrator of a novel, for example, must not be identified with the author, however tempting and plausible that identification may be, is the most commonplace of assumptions in literary criticism these days. It follows from this that there is a radical fissure, or contradiction, or heterogeneity in democracy. On the one hand democracy is based on the notion of the accountable individual who can be held responsible for what he or she has said or done, including what he or she has written, be hailed before the law and compelled to tell the truth, the whole truth, and nothing but the truth (unless it is self-incriminating), that is, be compelled responsibly to respond, or else be held in contempt of court. On the other hand the freedom to say everything in literature means the right not to respond, a right to absolute non-response, to keep secret. Derrida associates this hyperbolic right to non-response with the democracy to come (*a venir*, but with a pun on *avenir*, the future), and, as I shall show, with the secret, if there is such a thing, one of the most enigmatic areas of Derrida's recent thought. Literature keeps a secret that does not have to be revealed, or rather that cannot by any means, from gentle interrogation all the way up to torture, be revealed. Literature, like Bartleby in Melville's "Bartleby the Scrivener," does not respond. It says "I should prefer not to," when we say, "Answer me! Stand and unfold!"

The most puzzling sentence in this passage is the one that says, "these 'voices' [in literature] speak, allow or make to come – even in literature without persons and without characters." That Derrida is asserting that the speech of characters or narrators in literature only makes obvious the disconnection of what is written in even non-narrative works from its author is clear enough, but what does he mean by "speak, allow or make to come"? Allow or make to come *what?* The phrase is followed by a dash. What is the difference between "allow" and "make" here? Either allowing or making would be speech acts, though of different sorts. Literature allows something to happen or makes something happen. That happening is a coming, though of just what Derrida does not say, in his oddly incomplete locution. Nor is the original French any less enigmatic: " Et ces 'voix' parlent, laissent ou font venir –" (*Passions*, 66). I shall return to this enigma. That is a promise.

I seem to have reached a somewhat dismaying endpoint or even impasse in my progressive identification of just what Derrida means by "literature" or "the literary" or "literarity." It is dismaying because it seems to confirm just what Derrida's critics or critics of so-called deconstruction hold against him (or it): it is irresponsible, nihilistic, radically relativistic. Here is Derrida apparently saying that literature is an excuse for saying or writing any damn thing that comes into your mind, even the most scandalous or subversive or negative, and then saying when challenged, "I refuse to respond. I am not responsible or responsive. It is my duty not to respond. I must keep literature's secret. That is not me speaking or writing. I am just giving an example of how it is possible to speak or write in that way, and I defy you to prove otherwise." Is there any way to go beyond this hyperbolic endpoint or end of the line as it disappears into the infinity of a radical detachment from the social responsibility we expect from serious writers either of literature or of literary criticism and theory?

Here we encounter the most difficult and strangest aspect of Derrida's ideas about literature. It is also perhaps the least expected because it does not fit the prejudices we may have developed from reading vulgar accounts of so-called "deconstruction." This aspect of Derrida's literatures is one place in his work where he is unfaithfully faithful to his Husserlian heritage. Just because "literature," that is, some utterance or text taken as literature because all sorts of rules and conventions lead us to do so, can be detached from its empirical context and allowed to play freely as fiction (any resemblance to real persons, living or dead, is purely coincidental . . .), such a text creates or reveals, responds to, the ideal existence of what it names. In "The Time of a Thesis" Derrida asserts not only that his first interest was literature but that around 1957 (that is forty years ago before the year when I am writing this) he registered, as they say in France, a thesis on "The Ideality of the Literary Object" (TT, 36). What does that mean? That thesis as such was never written, so we can never know what it might have said. In another sense, everything Derrida has written about literature since then, including all his acts of practical criticism, are, we can guess, parts of the endless elaboration of that unfinished project. He relates this project to Husserl, to a "bending" of Husserl. This gives a clue as to what that thesis might have contained: "It was then for me a matter of bending, more or less violently, the techniques of transcendental phenomenology to the needs of elaborating a new theory of literature, of that very peculiar type of ideal object that is the literary object, a bound ideality Husserl would have said, bound to so-called 'natural' language, a non-mathematical or non-mathematizable object, and yet one that differs from the objects of plastic or musical art, that is to say from all of the examples privileged by Husserl in his analyses of ideal objectivity" (TT, 37). The passage just quoted tells the reader several important things. To call a literary work an "object" borrows Husserlian terminology that names not "object" in the ordinary sense of a material object like a stone or a jug but anything that is the "object" of an intentional act of consciousness, anything that consciousness "intends" or attends to. As opposed to mathematizable objects that are, so it seems, free of any cultural or historical determination, as number, algebra, and graphing seem to be free, the literary object is bound to so-called natural language, limited by its forms. Henry James's *The Golden Bowl* is bound to the English language at a certain stage of its historical development, just as Baudelaire's "La fausse monnaie" is bound to the French language. To translate either is to some degree to traduce it, to denature it. Nevertheless, like a triangle or a square, a literary work is an "ideal object." What in the world does this mean? A triangle is an ideal object because its existence does not depend in the least on any particular triangles, for example ones I inscribe with a ruler on a piece of paper. Even if every single inscribed triangle of every sort, including accidental ones formed, for example, by twigs falling from a tree, were to disappear the ideal triangle would still exist. Derrida's somewhat outrageous project was to transfer that presumption to the literary object and to claim that it too is ideal. This would mean that though the reader can have access to the "world" opened up by *The Golden Bowl* only by reading *The Golden Bowl* and in no other way, nevertheless that realm would remain in existence as an ideal object even if every single copy of *The Golden Bowl* were destroyed. It is in this sense that Derrida speaks of "the ideality of the literary object." It is an implacable obligation to that ideality of the literary object that gives the writer the duty of non-response or non-responsibility, that is, a refusal in the name of, on the authority of, a greater responsibility, as when Derrida says, "This language and these thoughts, which are also new responsibilities, arouse in me a respect which, whatever the cost, I neither can nor will compromise."

What Derrida says in *Passions* about the link of literature to the secret and in "Psyché: l'invention de l'autre" about invention as allowing and making to come – will help us to understand better this strange counter-intuitive concept of literature. Attending to these will also return me to my claim that Derrida's idea of literature is closely intertwined with his theory of performative utterances. "Psyché: Invention of the Other" centers on a reading of Francis Ponge's little eight-line poem, "Fable." It is the exuberant concentrated general assertions of the concluding pages that interest me most here, but these, it should be remembered, grow out of the Ponge reading and are enabled by them. Derrida could not have said what he says about the invention of the other without the help of that reading. In these final pages he distinguishes between two forms of invention, the invention that returns to the same and the invention that responds to a call from the wholly other. The first kind, "paradoxically," "invents nothing," since it is an extrapolation from what already exists and has been institutionalized: "Invention amounts [*revient*] to the same, and it is always possible, as soon as it can receive a status and thereby be legitimatized by an institution that it then becomes in its turn" (*AL*, 339). That is the ordinary sense of "invention." The other invention, the one that interests Derrida, "peut, selon un croisement de chance et de nécessité, produire le nouveau d'un événement" (Psyché, 58) [can, through a merging of chance and necessity, produce the new of an event] (*AL*, 340). Here is one sequence in Derrida's writing where a return to the original French is necessary, since every sentence in these concluding pages plays on the resources of double meaning and nuance in the French language. Invention is here taken in the double sense that is justified by its etymology from *inventio*. "Invention" means both make up and find already there. This distinction between two forms of invention turns on that double meaning, and Derrida plays throughout these pages on associated French words, *avenir*, "future," *venir*, "come," *revenir*, "return, come back to," *aventure*, "adventure," *événement*, "event," and so on. The impossible invention (in both senses at once and in neither) of the wholly other invokes a new notion of speech acts, since the standard one is too tied to the ideas of rules and institutions that are firmly in place and that are not changed by a given performative utterance. This invention is "beyond the speech act" (*AL*, 318). The literary object, we now know, is ideal in the sense of having been there all along. It is more discovered than invented by the words of the work, though even that gives the writer too much autonomy. The literary object is accessible only through the words of the work, but it was always already there. On the one hand there is the invention of the possible, an extrapolation from what we already have. This is "invention du même par laquelle l'autre revient au même" (Psyché, 59) [invention of the same by which the other turns back into the same]. On the other hand "l'autre n'est pas le possible. Il faudrait donc dire que la seule invention possible serait l'invention de l'impossible. Mais une invention de l'impossible est impossible, dirait l'autre. Certes, mais c'est la seule possible: une invention doit s'annoncer comme invention de ce qui ne paraissait pas possible, sans quoi elle ne fait qu'expliciter un programme de possibles, dans l'économie du même" (59) [The other is not the possible. One must say that the only possible invention would be of the impossible. But an invention of the impossible is impossible, the other would say. Certainly, but it is the only possibility: an invention must announce itself as invention of that which would not appear possible, without which it does no more than make explicit a program of possibles, within the economy of the same]. A moment later Derrida speaks of this invention of the other as another invention that does not discover the other through a performative utterance but that uses words to "allow" the other "to come," and by no means "makes" it come. This gives the explanation of the puzzling phrase encountered earlier, "allow or make to come." We also know now what unspoken phrase lies beyond that dash. It is the words "le tout autre," the wholly other. Invention in the second more radical and authentic sense, impossible invention, "donner lieu a l'autre, laisser venir l'autre," gives a place to the other, lets the other come. This is done by that activity of opening, destabilizing language that Derrida's own linguistic practices exemplify. Only such language can leave places or spaces, *lieux*, as it might be said, within which the other intervenes, or does not intervene. You can never know beforehand what will happen or whether anything at all will happen. A speech act performing this other kind of invention is never an infallible magic. As Derrida says, I must "destabiliser les structures de forclusion pour laisser passage a l'autre" [destabilize the structures of foreclosure in order to allow passage to the other] as Ponge's language in the first line of "Fable" employs ordinary syntax and diction to destabilize them: "Par le mot par commence donc ce texte" [With the word *with* commences then this text]. Nevertheless, I do not make the other come. The call and the coming comes from the other direction, from the other, the "tout autre," the wholly other: "il ne peut être inventé que par l'autre, depuis la venue de l'autre qui dit 'viens' et auquel la réponse d'un autre 'viens' paraît être la seule invention désirable et digne d'intérêt" (60) [It cannot be invented except by way of the other, by way of the coming of the other who says "come" and to which the response of another "come" appears to be the sole invention that is desirable and worthy of interest]. The other comes or does not come, as it happens, through "the chance of an encounter," "even if the inventiveness of the greatest genius is needed to prepare to welcome it" (*AL*, 342). I can only let it come, though that letting is itself a speech act of a peculiar kind, requiring the greatest genius with words.

Nor is it a we or a community of researchers in the usual sense, working according to rules, that is the agent or the result of invention: "what is promised here is not, is no longer or not yet, the identifiable 'we' of a community of human subjects, with all those familiar features we wrap up in the names *society*, *contract*, *institution*, and so forth" (*AL*, 342). Nevertheless this impossible invention is "the only invention in the world, the only invention of the world" (*AL*, 342). It is the invention of the world because it is truly inaugural, initiatory, even legislative. Like a declaration of independence it lays down new rules that imply a new "we," a new community, even a new political order. The other invents me, and through what I do invents others, a community. My work then is somehow to use language "laisser venir l'aventure ou l'événement du tout autre" (Psyché, 61) [to give a place to the other, let the other come]. This other, it is important to note, is not singular but plural: "L'autre appelle à venir et cela n'arrive qu'à plusieurs voix" (61) [The call of the other is a call to come, and that happens only in multiple voices]. Derrida exemplifies that by having his essay end in a dialogue of give and take between two voices letting the other come or within which the other has come, in multiple voices. The multiplicity of voices is crucial here. It forbids or forecloses the temptation to think of the other, the wholly other, as some Platonic "One." In speaking just at the end in a rapid exchange of different voices, each other to the other, and in the exuberant doubleness or duplicity of its wordplay, the essay does what it talks about. It makes an opening or place for the others to come.

So far so good, but it is still not clear just why this justifies the apparent irresponsibility of the non-response Derrida associates with literature and with literature's right to say everything and not take responsibility for it. We can see how what is said in that way comes from the wholly other that is neither made nor found but allowed to come in a literary work. This would mean that I can say, "This is not me speaking but the wholly other speaking through me. Don't hold me responsible for it." I might say in passing that, as Derrida recognizes, it is doubtful if this would cut much mustard when used as an excuse if I were hailed before the law for advocating the overthrow of the government or for writing something judged obscene or for burning my country's flag. The principle of accountability is much more successfully and forcefully institutionalized than the contradictory freedom not to respond that follows from democratic freedom of expression. That is what Derrida means by saying freedom of speech is a principle but never a complete actuality even in a "free country." Certainly that freedom is being severely curtailed in the United States again of late, for example in attempts to regulate the Internet. Nevertheless, why would this hypothetical judge, however much he respected free speech, not also be justified in demanding that the author respond in the name of that ideal work that is the source of his work and that its words incarnate, however inadequately and incompletely, just as a triangle inscribed on paper embodies the ideal triangle that would go on existing even if all material embodiments were destroyed? The author ought to be able to testify in the name of the ideality of the literary work and tell us more about it, for example about those aspects he left out accidentally or on purpose but should in principle know. "Come on now, tell the truth. I'll jail you for contempt if you don't answer. Are those your own opinions or are they opinions you deplore and are just representing so we can deplore them too?" This would invite or command the author to make a comparison, so to speak, between the ideal triangle and the one crudely inscribed on paper.

It is just here, however, that Derrida's concept of the secret as a fundamental feature of literary works intervenes to make response to such a demand not only undesirable in the name of a higher responsibility to keep silent but also in principle impossible, just as it invalidates any pseudo-Husserlian paradigm of comparing the ideality of the literary object with its embodiment in this particular copy of, say, *The Wings of the Dove* I hold in my hands at this moment. Such a comparison is impossible because the only access anyone, including the author, has to that ideality is through the words of the work, through the original manuscript or through one or another of its printed copies that have allowed the ideality to come. Literature's association with the secret means a certain superficiality or lack of depth in literary works. We (including the author) can know only what they say. What is not said cannot by any means be known, even by the author. The reading of Baudelaire's "La fausse monnaie" depends crucially on knowing whether the speaker's friend was telling the truth or lying when he said the alms he gave the beggar was counterfeit money. This, as Derrida insists in *Given Time*, we cannot ever know. It remains an impenetrable secret. The reader of *The Wings of the Dove* would immensely like to know just what was in that letter the dying Milly Theale wrote to Densher and that his fiancée Kate Croy throws, unread by either of them, in the fire. This the reader can never know. It is a perpetual secret, taken by Milly with her into her grave. This event indicates graphically (in both senses) the connection of the secret with death and therefore suggests some deep connection of literature with death. A work of literature is always in one way or another or in many ways at once an act of survival, of living on after someone's or something's death. Death is a displaced name or figure for the wholly other, but only one name, no more adequate or "literal" than any other. Derrida works this out in detail in his series of readings of Blanchot's "récits," *La folie du jour* (*The Madness of the Day*) and *Arrêt de mort* (*Death Sentence*), collected in *Parages*. The secrets literature holds are as superficial as the words imprinted on the surface of the pages and as unfathomably deep as death. Speaking of Baudelaire's characters in "La fausse monnaie" Derrida says: "Ces personnages de fiction n'ayant aucune consistance, aucune épaisseur au-delà de leur phénomène littéraire, l'inviolabilité absolute du secret qu'ils portent tient d'abord à la superficialité essentielle de leur phénoménalité, au *trop-évident* de ce qu'ils donnent à voir" (*Donner le temps*, 194). Of a true secret, if there is such a thing, one cannot even say that it exists, since one knows in principle nothing at all about it. This is why Derrida consistently, in talking about the secret, says, "the secret, if there is such a thing." Here is Derrida's most concentrated and most eloquent expression of the connection he sees between the secret and acts of literature as he has defined them in their association with democracy, freedom of expression, and the right to non-response:

There is in literature, in the *exemplary* secret of literature, a chance of saying everything without touching on the secret. When all hypotheses are permitted, groundless and ad infinitum, about the meaning of a text, or the final intentions of an author, whose person is no more represented than nonrepresented by a character or by a narrator, by a poetic or fictional sentence, which detaches itself from its presumed source and thus remains *locked away* [*au secret*], when there is no longer even any sense in making decisions about some secret behind the surface of a textual manifestation (and it is this situation which I would call text or trace), when it is the call [*appel*] of this secret, however, which points back to the other or to something else, and holds us to the other, then the secret impassions us. Even if there is none, even if it does not exist, hidden behind anything whatever. Even if the secret is no secret, even if there has never been a secret, a single secret. Not one. (*Passions*, 29–30)

The reader will see how Derrida's thought about the secret is tied to his sense of the exemplary status of literature as the privilege of saying anything and not being held responsible for it as the personal statement of an author. All hypotheses about the meaning of a text are permitted not because the reader can make it mean anything he or she likes but because there is in principle no access to the secret originary ground that might verify any one of them. The reader cannot make decisions about some secret hidden beneath the surface of a text because, if that secret is really secret (if there is such a thing as a secret, which remains a secret), it is in principle absolutely impossible to uncover this secret. There is absolutely no way to read Milly's letter to Densher or to know whether that coin in "La fausse monnaie" was counterfeit or not. Literature is the place especially to look for the secret because it is by convention detached in special ways from its "transcendence" or referential gesture and because the literary work is an exemplary case of what Derrida means by "text or trace," though all texts have these features. It is the inaccessibility of the secret, the wholly other at the origin of the work, that constitutes the call that is transmitted by the work and that Derrida here calls being "impassioned" by the secret, following the title of the essay, which is "Passions," and playing on a double implication in the word: passion in the etymological sense of something suffered, as one speaks of Christ's passion on the cross, and in the not quite contrary sense of aroused desire. We are impassioned by the call of the secret to find out the secret, though this is a passion destined to remain unsatisfied. The secret in a literary work impassions us in both senses. As he put this in another place: "The inaccessible incites from its place of hiding."

This is, more or less, *mutatis mutandis*, what Derrida thinks literature is, or rather what it does, since literature is, for him, not an essence but an act. It is an act, as I have shown, of an exceedingly peculiar kind, since it does not make but allows to come.

The one remaining question, for me here, is how these assumptions, latent or overt, as they gradually become more explicit as his work progresses, have determined or inflected his actual procedures of practical criticism. These are the "close readings" that I began by saying earn

Derrida the right to be considered one of the great literary critics of the twentieth century and, I hope, of the new one too, since we have by no means heard the last from him. Here I am then, nearly at the end of my time or space or allotted number of words, still before the door, *ante portam*, of what I promised to do, that is account for the way Derrida actually does literary criticism, performs acts of literature in that particular sense. To do so in detail would be an interminable job, since each such essay is to some degree unique, idiomatic. Each employs its own special strategies of reading appropriate to what is idiomatic about the work in question. That is one reason it is difficult, if not impossible, to learn from Derrida's work how to do literary criticism, unless what you learn is that you are always alone before the work, on your own in reading it, forced to invent your own way to allow it to come through in your writing. If the wholly other does not come except in multiple voices, each work is a unique and irreplaceable opening that allows the others to come or rather to come in their not coming. Of each work might be said what the doorkeeper in Kafka's parable says to the man from the country at the moment of his death: "this gate was made only for you. I am now going to shut it" (*AL*, 210). Nevertheless, some indications can be briefly made.

Henry James's imagination was so fecund and so inexhaustible that he had to limit the données of his novels to just a few characters in a limited situation in order to hope to finish even a novel of many hundreds of pages. Still, notoriously, James had to huddle his conclusions and settle for "misplaced middles." In a similar way Derrida can see so much in so little that he most often deals with short works or with delimited citations from works. Moreover he deals with them from the perspective of a single question, theme, or problematic. An example would be the problematic of the gift in the reading of Baudelaire's prose poem "La fausse monnaie" in *Donner le temps* (cited hereafter as *DT*). What Derrida says of that problematic could be said of all his literary criticism: "nous partons toujours de textes dans l'élaboration de cette problématique, de textes au sens courant et traditionnel des lettres écrites, voire de la littérature, ou de textes au sens de traces différantielles suivant un concept que nous avons élaboré ailleurs" (*DT*, 130). Literature, the reader can see, is an exemplary case of a general feature of all texts, that is, that they are "traces différantielles." Derrida's procedures of practical criticism are derived not so much from American "close reading" of the "new critical" kind as from the French tradition of "explication de texte," which is not quite the same thing. The latter is a pedagogical device that calls for close attention to grammatical, rhetorical, and syntactical features of a given text, as well as to biographical and historical contexts. It has a different underlying ideology from the American New Criticism. Its goal is to perpetuate the French language and to teach clear writing as well as good reading by close acquaintance with model texts from tradition. Derrida was trained in *explication de texte*. It leaves its traces on his work in the sober pedagogical tone proceeding from careful citation and minute attention to linguistic detail. Nevertheless, Derrida's readings are a hyperbolic, extravagant, even outrageous explosion of that method. It is as though he had said, "You want *explication de texte*, unfolding of what is latent in semantic and syntactical details? I'll show you what really happens if you do that conscientiously." What happens is, for example, eighty-six pages devoted to the word "yes" in Joyce's *Ulysses*.

Derrida's literary criticism often bears the marks of its original preparation for oral delivery at some conference or in those seminars he has been giving yearly in Paris and in the United States for decades. In the midst of "The Law of Genre," for example, he says there would be an immense amount more to say about the "interpretative alternatives," the "particularly rich combinatory of possibilities," of the two sentences he had begun by uttering and then iterating with a difference. He will abstain, he says, "in order not to exceed my time limit and out of respect for the law of genre and of the audience" (*AL*, 127). In spite of this respect, he has more than once exceeded his time limit, for example in the oral delivery of *Limited Inc.* in English at Yale or in the presentation of *Ulysses Gramophone* at the Joyce conference at Frankfurt. An admirably inexhaustible fecundity of invention or creativity characterizes Derrida's acts of literature. His essays are exuberant, exorbitant, excessive, iterative, hyperbolic, too long to fit their prescribed limits, and still leave much unsaid or only hinted. What, if anything, justifies this hyperbolic excess, these linguistic hijinks and jokes? This feature of Derrida's writing has often been held against him. He cannot be serious if he makes so many jokes and so outrageously plays on words. The answer to such objections must be that he does it out of respect for the texts he reads, since they demand from him not just a reading in the sense of a passive description of meaning, but a carrying over into the work of criticism of the work's performative force. Derrida feels an obligation to try to make his essays speech acts allowing that "wholly other" to come if it happens to come. "I am careful to say 'let it come,'" says Derrida, "because if the other is precisely what is not invented, the initiative or deconstructive inventiveness can consist only in opening, uncloseting, destablising foreclusionary structures so as to allow for the passage toward the other. But one does

not make the other come, one lets it come by preparing for its coming"
(*AL*, 341–42). If Ponge does this "by bending these rules [of the conventional performative utterance] with respect for the rules themselves
in order to allow the other to come or to announce its coming in the
opening of this dehiscence" (*AL*, 340), Derrida in his turn justifies the
linguistic exuberance of *Limited Inc.* (cited hereafter as *LI*), and by implication of his work in general, including his literary criticism, by saying,
"I multiply statements, discursive gestures, forms of writing, the structure of which reinforces my demonstration in something like a practical
manner, that is, by providing instances of 'speech acts' which by themselves render impracticable and theoretically insufficient the conceptual
oppositions upon which speech act theory in general . . . relies" (*LI*, 114).
The dilations of Derrida's essays result in part from a sense of the richness of "play" hidden in apparently straightforward, idiomatic sentences
or in brief texts like Ponge's "Fable," partly from the extreme difficulty
of getting said what Derrida wants to say or doing with words what he
wants to do. It is not all that easy to grasp what he means by *différance* or
just what he is saying about literature and the law in "Before the Law,"
especially since the intuition (though that is not quite the right word) of
a certain unsayable or something unavailable to cognition is, I claim,
the motivation of all his work. "The inaccessible incites from its place of
hiding." It incites speech or writing in an interminable, never successful,
never satisfactory, never complete, attempt to "get it right," or "do it
right," as Derrida tries first this way and then that and then another formulation, each extending a given essay further and further and allowing
it to conclude only arbitrarily, without ever really coming to an end in
the sense of reaching an endpoint or telos. Paul de Man's essays, to give
a counter-example, characteristically work from received opinion about
a given work through a close reading to an often scandalous concluding
formulation that could only have been earned by the reading (e.g.: "From
this it can be seen that the impossibility of reading should not be taken
too lightly."[3]) Derrida's essays work in a reverse way. They often begin
with a concentrated enigmatic statement or speech act that the rest of
the essay unfolds through the close reading of some text. "The Law of
Genre," for example, begins with two strange sentences: "Genres are
not to be mixed. I will not mix genres" (*AL*, 223). One of Derrida's most
important essays on rhetoric (in the sense of figures of speech), "White
Mythology," begins with two exceedingly enigmatic sentences, full of
puns, wordplay, hidden allusions. The rest of the essay, in a manner of
speaking, "explains" this beginning: "De la philosophie, la rhétorique.

D'un volume, à peu près, plus ou moins – faire ici une fleur, l'extraire, la monter, la laisser, plutôt, monter, se faire jour – se détournant comme d'elle-même, révolutée, telle fleur grave – apprenant à cultiver, selon le calcul d'un lapidaire, la patience . . . [From philosophy, rhetoric. That is, here, to make from a volume, approximately, more or less, a flower, to extract a flower, to mount it, or rather to have it mount itself, bring itself to light – and turning away, as if from itself, come round again, such a flower engraves – learning to cultivate, by means of a lapidary's reckoning, patience . . .].[4] The unfolding, however, in principle might be endless. This happens not only according to the law that out of the right kind of concentration on the little comes an inexhaustible much that might take a lifetime and more to explicate, in the etymological sense of "unfold," but also according to the law that says the little part is greater than the whole and contains it, circumscribes it. Derrida has formulated this law more than once, for example in *Given Time*: "Encadré, enchèssé, bordé, le plus petit devient, métonymiquement, plus grand que le plus grand – qui le borde et le cadre" (*DT*, 123). A figure for this is the little patch of yellow wall in Vermeer's "View of Delft" that so fascinates Proust's Bergotte at the moment of his death and that is, as Derrida observed in his seminar on this episode, bigger than the whole in the sense of including it, just as this one episode contains the whole novel in miniature, as the minuscule part of a fractal repeats the pattern of the whole. Proust's "récit de la mort de Bergotte," says Derrida, is an "art inoué de la composition en abyme, c'est à dire de l'inscription dans la partie d'un tout plus petit que ses parties ou du détail plus grand que le tout comme ce petit pan de mur jaune dans lequel va mourir en s'abêmant Bergotte, inclusion du tout dans la partie qui signe le deuil et jusqu'au deuil de soi" (unpublished seminar of Dec. 7, 1994) [Proust's "récit de la mort de Bergotte," says Derrida, "is an unheard of art of composition 'en abyme,' that is to say of the inscription in the part of a whole smaller than its parts or of a detail larger than the whole like this little patch of yellow wall in which Bergotte is going to die as if he were falling into an abyss, inclusion of the whole in the part which subscribes oneself to mourning and even to mourning for oneself "]. Derrida builds a whole essay on an apparently limited feature of the author's writing or on a single word or phrase that is then interrogated at length or on a peripheral work, like the small text by Mallarmé, "Mimique," or Ponge's brief poem, "Fable," or a small piece of Kafka's *The Trial*. Derrida's presupposition is that in literary criticism it is better to concentrate microscopically on a part than to make big generalizations about the whole based on a telescopic view of the whole. Often the part that expands in this way, turning the part to whole relation inside out, is a single word, sometimes a common word like "yes," sometimes an odd word like "subjectile" (in an essay on Artaud). The complexity Derrida finds in the little part is sometimes a depth in the word itself, sometimes an inexhaustible web of sideways connections that connect the word to uses in other authors or elsewhere in Derrida's own work. Derrida's two essays of literary criticism on "law," "Before the Law" and "The Law of Genre," are inextricably connected to his other writings about law, for example the book entitled *Force de loi*.

One might think Derrida has chosen texts that fit his presuppositions about literature, but in many cases the literary critical essays are occasional. He was invited to a conference on Celan or Joyce and, if he accepted, had to produce something on their work, or he was invited to a conference on genre and had to produce something that would fit that (the essay on Blanchot's *Madness of the Day*, "The Law of Genre"), or, for many years, he was appointed to give seminars at the École Normale Supérieure on prescribed philosophical texts or topics and had to fit whatever he said in those seminars about literature to those prescriptions. The essay on Kafka's "Before the Law" was originally part of a course at the École on Kant's *Critique of Practical Reason*.

Derrida, it is true, often juxtaposes a work of literature with a philosophical, anthropological, psychoanalytical, or otherwise "non-literary" work or topic (Baudelaire with Mauss, Genet with Hegel, Kafka with Kant, Poe with Lacan, and so on). Or the literary criticism arises as part of a prolonged interrogation of a large topic or problematic (the gift for the Baudelaire essay; reading, ethics, and the law for the Kafka essay; the problematic of signature for the book on Ponge; bearing witness for the Celan book; the problematic of that strange performative utterance that is "saying yes" for the book on Joyce, and so on). This must not, however, be misunderstood. The part once more overflows and encompasses the whole. The literary work is read for its own sake, and, as Derrida clearly asserts, as something that takes precedence over the abstract or "philosophical" expressions. It takes precedence because it gives unique and irreplaceable access to the truth about the given topic.

As "Psyché: l'invention de l'autre" shows, however, the unorthodox speech act structure Derrida finds there as a defining characteristic of literature is not just characteristic of "literature" in the usual sense of canonized works. The exemplary status of literature, for Derrida, the reason why he remains fascinated by it, returns to it, discusses it so brilliantly and indefatigably, as in the essays on Celan, Joyce, Ponge, Blanchot, Shelley, Shakespeare, and so on, is that literature in an exemplary way brings into the open, exposes, that structure of response to the wholly other, the secret, the "tout autre," that is, for Derrida, the basis of the new ethics, the new politics, the democracy to come, he would put in place of the one Austin wants to preserve at all costs. Such a linguistic structure also appears in philosophy, politics, psychoanalysis, and so on, for example in the Declaration of Independence that created by the fiat of a speech act the United States of America.[5] Literature is the place to study iterability, not just in what happens thematically in a given work, but in the way it works. All Derrida's acts of literary criticism are for the sake of showing this, as in what he says about Joyce's "oui-dire," saying yes, in *Ulysses*, or about bearing witness in Celan's poetry, or about the fabulous in Ponge, or about *l'arrêt de mort*, the arrest of death, in Blanchot, and so on. All Derrida's essays on literature in one way or another focus on the special way these works are performative in the anasemic sense he specifies in "Psyché" – using the rules against the rules to inaugurate something wholly new in response to a call from the "others": "l'autre appel à venir et cela n'arrive qu'à plusieurs voix."

Each of Derrida's essays centers on an attempt to formulate through an obedience to the actual words of the work in question the special, the idiomatic way the other is invoked or allowed to come in its not coming in this particular work. In the essay on Mallarmé, "La double séance (*The Double Session*)," this is the way the temporal to and fro of dissemination around what Mallarmé calls the hymen executes endless verbal dances over the perpetually absent origin: "between desire and fulfilment, perpetration and remembrance: here anticipating, there re-calling, in the future, in the past, *under the false appearance of a present*" (quoted from Mallarmé's "Mimique," Derrida's "text" in the essay, *AL*, 130). In the Celan book, *Schibboleth*, the focus is on the here and now of dating in poetry that makes each poem commemorate or perform a unique act of bearing witness that is an idiomatic password but that nevertheless is repeated in anniversaries of that date and that invokes our assent in a new bearing witness each time the poem is read. *Ulysses Gramophone*, one of Derrida's most wonderfully exuberant, outrageously inventive, prolonged, and even comic essays, mingling chance and necessity, centers on the saying *yes* that is the performative act *par excellence* letting or allowing the other to come, or not to come, as it happens to happen. In "Before the Law" the absent origin, the wholly other, is given its Kafkan name of "the law," *das Gesetz*. It is in this essay that Derrida says, "the inaccessible incites from its place of hiding" (*AL*, 191). The essay provides, with Kafka's help, a cascade of formulations of the consequences of this inciting: "Reading a text might indeed reveal that it is untouchable, literally intangible, *precisely because it is readable*, and for the same reason unreadable to the extent to which the presence within it of a clear and graspable sense remains as hidden as its origin"; "What *must not* and cannot be approached is the origin of *différance*: it must not be presented or represented and above all not penetrated . . . The secret is nothing – and this is the secret that has to be kept well, nothing either present or presentable, but this nothing must be well kept . . . It is both obscene and unpresentable"; "Here, we know neither *who* nor *what* is the law, *das Gesetz*. This, perhaps, is where literature begins . . . Here one does not know the law, one has no cognitive rapport with it; it is neither a subject nor an object *before* which one could take a position" (*AL*, 197, 205, 207).

I give now a final example of this demonstration of the way all Derrida's essays of literary criticism are in consonance or resonance, echo one another at a distance, or are at least metonymical, each its own special door to the wholly other: in the preface to *Parages*, which brings together Derrida's set of essays on Blanchot's "récits," Derrida says these strange fictions by Blanchot "have remained inaccessible to me," and though the essays he has written about them do not testify to an access gained at last, nevertheless, "in their very dissimulation, in the distancing of the inaccessible *as such*, because they give onto it in the act of giving it names, they have presented themselves to me afresh" (*AL*, 222). Here once more is the assertion that reading and literary criticism are instigated by the "inaccessible." Whether or not I am justified in what I say about Derrida, in my bearing witness to what I have found there, can only be told through a detailed reading of these essays. Whether Derrida is justified or not can be told only by going back to read the literary works, to Derrida's reading of which his essays bear witness in their turn. Such responsible, responsive reading, incited by the inaccessible in its place of hiding, a reading leading from gate to gate, sideways, and in a receding series of gates within, is the life (and perpetually deferred dying) of literary study.

Translations Supplied by Author (J. Hillis Miller)

NOTES

1 See Jacques Derrida, *Acts of Literature*, ed. Derek Attridge (London and New York: Routledge, 1992), cited hereafter as *AL*.
2 "Deconstruction in America," cited in ibid., 1.
3 Paul de Man, *Allegories of Reading* (New Haven: Yale University Press, 1979), 245.

4 Jacques Derrida, "La mythologie blanche: la métaphore dans le texte philosophique," *Marges: De la philosophie* (Paris: Minuit, 1972), 249 [trans. Alan Bass, "White Mythology: Metaphor in the Text of Philosophy," in *Margins of Philosophy* (Chicago: University of Chicago Press, 1982), 209].

5 See "Declarations of Independence," etc., in *AL*.

FURTHER READING

Clark, Timothy. *Derrida, Heidegger, Blanchot: Sources of Derrida's Notion and Practice of Literature*. Cambridge: Cambridge University Press, 1992.

Derrida, Jacques. *Acts of Literature*. Ed. Derek Attridge. New York: Routledge, 1992.

Hartman, Geoffrey. *Saving the Text: Literature/Derrida/Philosophy*. Baltimore: Johns Hopkins University Press, 1981.

Kerrigan, William and Joseph H. Smith, eds. *Taking Chances: Derrida, Psychoanalysis, and Literature*. Baltimore: Johns Hopkins University Press, 1984.

Leitch, Vincent B. *Deconstructive Criticism: An Advanced Introduction*. New York: Columbia University Press, 1983.

Muller, John P. and William J. Richardson, eds. *The Purloined Poe: Lacan, Derrida, and Psychoanalytic Reading*. Baltimore: Johns Hopkins University Press, 1988.

Royle, Nicholas. *After Derrida*. Manchester: Manchester University Press, 1995.

Sub-stance, 7. Fall 1973. "Literature . . . and Philosophy? The Dissemination of Derrida."

Taylor, Mark, ed. *Deconstruction in Context: Literature and Philosophy*. Chicago: University of Chicago Press, 1986.

CHAPTER 3

Derrida and gender: the other sexual difference

Peggy Kamuf

> What will the index be? On which words will it rely? Only on
> names? And on which syntax, visible or invisible? Briefly, by which
> signs will you recognize his speaking or remaining silent about what
> you nonchalantly call sexual difference? What is it you are thinking
> beneath those words or through them?
>
> – Derrida, "*Geschlecht*: Sexual Difference,
> Ontological Difference"

The expectation for this chapter is that it talk about gender in the company of Derrida's thought. The point would be to see how such a companion or accompaniment might influence the direction taken by talk
when it turns to the subject of gender. Naturally, one should try to meet
this expectation as far as possible. To do so, of course, one will need
to write in some particular language, preferably a language in which
talk about gender can be understood, in which the word "gender" is in
common use. Even if the choice of language for this chapter were not
already limited by other conditions, this expectation to talk about gender would limit the choice to English. One can write "gender" only in
English.

Such a limitation is only reasonable. It does, however, complicate
the task we are expected to accomplish here. Because Derrida does not
write in English, he does not write in the language to which the word
"gender" belongs. It is thus highly probable that he has never written that
word as such or even intended the ordinary meaning it has in English
through the use of the related French word "genre." In French, words,
more specifically nouns, have a *genre*, masculine or feminine, there are
genres in a specialized literary historical sense, and there is *genre* in general
(genus, kind, manner, fashion), but *genre* is not gender if one means by
that a sexual classification. The French noun *sexe* seems to be the closest
translation to what Anglophones have generally intended by the word
gender, especially in recent times. "Genre" and "gender" form a pair of

what translators commonly call "faux amis" or "false friends," the kind that betray each other and part company.[1]

At the very least, this means that one cannot begin responding to the expectation for this essay by indexing all the occurrences of "gender" in Derrida's very considerable *oeuvre*. On the contrary, we must assume that there is none and that Derrida has literally had nothing to say about gender, at least nothing to say about it by that name. It also means, therefore, that if we expect to speak on the subject in Derrida's company, without leaving our companion in the lurch like a false friend, then we can only do so at the conjunction of more than one kind of difference: gender or sexual difference, but also language difference, which makes for the differences between "gender" and "genre," "gender" and "sexe," "sex" and "genre," and so forth. The complication seems inevitable, and with it comes the risk that a discussion of language difference and the consequent problems of translation have to lead one off the subject of gender difference. After all, what does the one have to do with the other?

As we shall see, Derrida would most probably say that they have everything to do with each other. That assertion is likely to sound surprising and not only in an English-speaking context. Before we attend more closely to this surprising notion, and before we thereby risk losing track of the theme of gender, against all expectation for this chapter, let us try to hear how that theme is playing in English alone.

Consider, for example, the distinction often made in English between sex and gender. What is the difference invoked by this subsisting distinction in our language? To begin to outline an answer, we can turn to one of the most frequently cited authorities on the question. Judith Butler, perhaps more than anyone else currently writing in English, has raised our general awareness of the problems inherent in the supposition that sex can be reliably distinguished from gender and vice versa. In a book devoted essentially to contesting that supposition, Butler writes: "Originally intended to dispute the biology-is-destiny formulation, the distinction between sex and gender serves the argument that whatever biological intractability sex appears to have, gender is culturally constructed . . . Taken to its logical limit, the sex/gender distinction suggests a radical discontinuity between sexed bodies and culturally constructed genders."[2] When she goes on to point out, however, that this distinction must itself in fact be discursively produced, Butler is able to make appear a continuity in the place of the supposed "radical discontinuity" between the two terms: the seemingly prediscursive, "natural" domain of sex, since it is produced by and as discourse, is above all cultural, which means that the prediscursive is first of all discursive. With that, Butler is able to show how the distinction collapses: "perhaps this construct called 'sex' is as culturally constructed as gender; indeed, perhaps it was always already gender, with the consequence that the distinction between sex and gender turns out to be no distinction at all" (Butler, 7). The distinction turns out to be no distinction. Within a certain *discourse*, we may now quite correctly use sex to mean gender and gender to mean sex.

Yet, in speaking of "discourse," "discursive production," and so forth, Butler is clearly not making an argument about the *language* in which she can write both "sex" and "gender" and maintain a distinction between them. Indeed, the clarity of this argument depends altogether on being able still to distinguish them without risk of confusion. In other words, the collapse of the *discourse* of sex/gender depends on the *language* of "sex" and "gender" upholding the distinction *against* collapse. It is impossible to say, therefore, which of these movements – the collapse or the maintenance of the distinction – is more essential, more necessary to the understanding afforded by her argument. And consequently, one cannot say for certain that some notion of gender (or sex, there being no difference finally) is dependent on a discourse rather than on a language. Nor can one affirm with any certainty that an argument such as this one has moved beyond the discourse of sex and gender rather than merely reinscribing the very terms of the opposition it sought to displace.

That reinscription, without any significant displacement, may be in fact the overall effect (if not the intent) of Butler's argument here seems to be confirmed in the passage with which it concludes and which proposes other differentiating terms in place of the collapsed distinction. Butler writes:

> It would make no sense, then, to define gender as the cultural interpretation of sex, if sex itself is a gendered category. Gender *ought not to be conceived merely* as the cultural inscription of meaning on a pregiven sex (a juridical conception); gender *must also designate* the very apparatus of production whereby the sexes themselves are established. (7, emphases added)

We have added emphases in order to bring out one apparent connection made between what is still being called "sex" and "gender" despite the demonstrated uselessness of that distinction. The connection seems to be a mere addition: gender is not only this but also this. However, with this dual definition of gender, Butler is adding a discursive operation, which is called an operation of production, to another operation, which is here called inscription ("the cultural inscription of meaning"). While this addition follows as a consequence of the collapse of a discursive distinction (between sex and gender), it also *makes* a distinction between what is being called inscription and what is being called production. These terms would be related otherwise than by simple addition or repetition: they are, it is implied, in a clear relation of difference, which must therefore be marked by two different terms. "Gender ought not to be conceived merely as the cultural *inscription* of meaning on a pregiven sex (a juridical conception); gender must also designate the very apparatus of *production* whereby the sexes themselves are established" (emphases added). If we follow the logical relations implied by this choice of differentiating terms, it would seem that gender as production produces the sexes, whereas gender as inscription receives them pregiven from this other productive apparatus. This means that the conception of gender as "cultural inscription" on the received sexes is being thought as secondary and dependent on the operation that is here being called production. Thus at one level what is formulated as a simple addition (not merely this gender but also this gender) is at another level (but within the same syntax) formulated as an order of priority that makes gender as inscription a phenomenon secondary to and dependent on gender as production.

The move we have just retraced in Butler's analysis raises a number of questions. For example: why is inscription the term chosen to distinguish the secondary, derived (sense of) gender from the other, the first, the "apparatus of production" as it is called? And then, likewise, why is production the term chosen to distinguish the more powerful, more originary (sense of) gender? These terms, one must suppose, have certainly not been chosen at random. This choice, then, raises further questions: what is one doing when one displaces the binary distinction of the sexes and the genders (male/female or masculine/feminine or man/woman, which are implicated with every other binary known to man or to woman) into this other distinction between production and inscription? What trait or traits allow(s) one to make a distinction between these terms that is more reliable than the collapsed distinction between sex and gender? And in making such a distinction is one doing something that is more like a production or more like an inscription?

To address this last question, one would have to take into account what we have already noted: the fact that Butler's analysis cannot dispense with *inscribing* a terminological or lexical difference between "sex" and "gender" even as it works to produce a collapse of that difference. Because, therefore, the argument we are reading requires both the collapse and the maintenance of its distinctions, because it must describe the collapse of terms in a language that clearly holds them apart, because, in other words, it can seem to *produce* something like an idea or concept of *no* difference between its terms only by *reinscribing* the difference between them, the new distinction would have to be no less collapsible than the one it has displaced. The assertion of the priority of production over inscription must be inscribed to be produced.

As we said, in order to notice this effect, one must pay attention to the specific language in which it is being produced or inscribed. (Which does not mean that, if it goes unnoticed, the effect is any less effective or even productive, that is, *reproductive* of its own terms, a fact that finds confirmation perhaps in the frequency with which this argument is referred to or otherwise repeated. Judith Butler is, as we said, unquestionably one of the most cited authorities on the question we are examining.) The argument, however, seems quite deliberately designed not to call attention to its own language in this way. This distraction from what one could call the scene of inscription in a particular language is the very doubtful ground on which Butler seeks to establish the priority of what she calls, following Foucault, "the apparatus of production" over inscription. And in fact, the priority asserted in the above passage will never again be put in question in the analyses that follow in the rest of this book.

That this ground is indeed doubtful may be gauged by recalling the principal argument of Derrida's *Of Grammatology*. Moreover, his analyses there allow one to suggest provisional answers to at least some of the questions in the swarm of those we have just asked about Butler's move from the collapsed sex/gender distinction to the clear priority of production over inscription. What her terminological choice repeats or reproduces is the tendency Derrida identified and analyzed to figure inscription as a secondary operation, a writing, which is itself produced by something else, some other, more originary operation. Because this gesture has been so regularly and persistently repeated, Derrida was able to isolate it as an identifying trait of what he called, in *Of Grammatology* and elsewhere, the metaphysics of presence. This phrase, which has come to function as something like deconstruction's watchword (meaning what one is *on watch for*, if not against), economically designates the mode of thinking from a self-present and undifferentiated origin. What Derrida shows is that, however else such an origin may have been represented throughout the Western tradition, it has been most constantly characterized as *prior to* writing. There is thus the metaphysical tradition of a certain writing about how writing (or inscription) is always a secondary operation. Butler's choice of the term "inscription," which she wants to make secondary to "production," seems therefore still to belong, at least in part, to this tradition.

But just as clearly Butler's gesture is more complex if only because, in another sense, it also resembles or imitates Derrida's. More specifically, her marking of the collapse of the sex/gender distinction repeats a recognizable procedure of deconstruction that Derrida worked out, and, once again, very thoroughly in *Of Grammatology*: the hierarchized terms of a binary opposition are reversed, the secondary or derived term is generalized as *différance*, which will have "produced" the opposition in the first place (although Derrida would never describe *différance* as "producing" differences or oppositions and still less as an "apparatus of production"). Likewise, in Butler's analysis, the distinction of sex from gender is said to be "produced" by the discursive condition identified with the second term; gender is thereby generalized as something like *différance*. Nevertheless, the generalization that Butler performs also leaves intact and undeconstructed the trait of secondary inscription. Thus, despite a certain recognizable outline of the deconstructive procedure, of which Butler makes such good use, a distance is also inscribed from the kind of thinking one associates foremost with Derrida.

We are suggesting that this distance can best be measured as the one traversed – or not – between sexual/gender difference and language difference. When gender as discursive production is said somehow to precede gender as inscription, then this "productive" *différance* is explicitly encoded as *not* originally a kind of writing. The point is not whether this dismissal of writing holds up or even whether Butler wants it to hold up; the point is rather that the argument rests finally on a mode of *exclusion* of inscription and therefore of what it itself is doing when it writes "sex" and "gender" in a particular language. For that is indeed what can be said to differentiate inscription from production as they appear to be used here: production is chosen to be the more general or powerful term because it seems not to be tied to any language and therefore to any language in particular, a language of inscription, this one, for example, in which however often we describe the collapse of the binary couple of either sex or gender, we are, uniquely perhaps, able to inscribe it again in those same terms, as I have just done.[3] Uniquely, in your or my idiom of English, another pair is reiterated.

It is in the engagement with this necessary inscription that Derrida's thinking of "gender" (although inscribed by other names) plots some paths across the distance between sexual difference and language difference, between generality/genderality and its marking, which can only take place in a particular language. If, then, we began this chapter by pointing out that, in all probability, Derrida has never written the word gender, it was in order to call attention right away to the inscription of *something other*, perhaps an other (than) sexual difference on the body of his language. Instead of a general reproduction of gender, by that name and therefore only in one particular language, there would be the inscription in a different language of another "generalization." But if gender is indeed being generalized *in other names* by that writing, then this leaves open the possibility that anything or everything Derrida has written can be taken to refer its reader somewhere or somehow to (a) sexual difference.[4] That probability is even a certainty if one takes as seriously as one should *dissemination* as Derrida has described it and which he understands to be at work in every text as its possibility, that is, the possibility of its coming to find a reader.[5] This term can still be heard in its so-called sexual (that is, genital) sense: a dis-semination, where the prefix has a privative value. It would be a non-semination, a non-generative non-reproduction of the seed and the semen, which is the masculine essence. But the word has not just a privative sense, because it also says *dissemination*, the scattering of the semantic or semiotic value of signs. Between these levels, between the body of signs and the genitally sexed body, the act of semination is itself dis-seminated, meaning it does not reproduce itself, no "itself" can reproduce itself. This important term for Derrida has therefore also to be heard as a calculated, strategic displacement of the term reproduction, above all sexual reproduction, and *a fortiori* of the term Butler privileges: production, as in "apparatus of production." As a descriptive name for the transferential movement of meaning, dissemination explicitly detaches that process from the transmission of a father's seed, which would be reproduced only in sons. Indeed, as Derrida has used it, it makes detachment from the original "seed" of meaning, or from the kernel of an original intention to mean, the condition of the transfer. If it retains a mark of gendered, genital sexual difference, that is also so as to scatter the mark in a generalization without gender, a generalization of gender's mark. As we have just described its double operation, "dissemination" emulates several other strategically deployed terms in Derrida's texts where once again a genitally sexual sense gets remarked.[6] Such a deliberate sexualization of the general language of philosophical or analytic discourse is a strategic move as well against or at least in tension with the kind of neutralization of sexual difference that has traditionally characterized it. We will have more to say about this tradition and its affinities for a neutralized sexuality.

To admit such a generalization, a sexualization of *différance*, is also to admit as an ongoing possibility that sexual difference will not always be marked or inscribed by its most common or general name in a given language. This is yet another reason it would be strictly impossible to recognize the limits of a theme of gender or sexual difference running through Derrida's text. The possibility of thematizing this difference, and all the difference it makes, is throughout put in question there, explicitly in innumerable places and implicitly at every stroke with which the text imprints itself. The problem, therefore, for our essay, which is still attempting to meet the expectation to talk about gender in Derrida's company, is that we are left with no clearly or certainly pertinent way to proceed. There is no one thread to follow; instead there are the innumerable threads of "sexuality's" thematic name disseminated through every other term. One has only to choose.

For the sake of simplicity, however, let us choose to follow the thematic name of "sex" a little further into Derrida's text. Perhaps, in this way, we can be led to glimpse a place or a space of its dissemination. We can begin with the title of an essay, since a title is one such thematic marker. If we are looking for our clearly marked theme, then the title, "*Geschlecht*: Sexual Difference, Ontological Difference," cannot be a bad place to start since it names or cites sexual difference twice, in two different languages.

The essay is a reading of Heidegger and what he had to say about sexual difference. But the question one must immediately entertain is whether indeed he had anything at all to say about it. For Heidegger apparently referred only minimally, if at all, to sex, sexual difference, or gender. In this way, at least, Heidegger's thought seems worlds away from, for example, Butler's preoccupations. But what if it could be shown that the gesture with which the one silences sexual difference is essentially the same as the gesture with which the other speaks apparently of little else? What happens when the difference collapses between naming and not naming "sexuality" by whatever name it is given in a language? Is there then even still a word, one word, with which to name, rather than silence sexual difference? And if not, does that mean sexual difference will have been disseminated somehow beyond the binary mark of gender, the $+/-$ marking of the two and only two? We will take up these questions again in conclusion, after first having followed closely this reading of Heidegger's silencing of sex.

This silence is remarkable if only for the fact that his contemporaries are Freud and psychoanalysis, for whom sexual difference is presumed to be speaking everywhere. In that contrasting light, the silence calls attention to itself; indeed Derrida suggests it may even sound rather "haughty, arrogant, or provoking in a century when sexuality, commonplace of all chatty talk, has also become the currency of philosophic and scientific 'knowledge,' the inevitable *Kampfplatz* of ethics and politics."[7] Derrida's note of sarcasm here, which mocks "the commonplace of all chatty talk [*lieu commun de tous les bavardages*]," seems to be reserved for one feature of this scene of our century of psychoanalysis: the name of "sexuality."

This is made clear when the essay continues by questioning Heidegger's silence, in the sense of questioning whether he *did* indeed maintain silence on "sexuality." In order to assert this with certainty, one would have to be able to index everything Heidegger ever wrote. And yet, were one to propose drawing up such an index, one would first have to decide how to answer certain questions, which Derrida lists as follows:

What will the index be? On which words will it rely? Only on names? And on which syntax, visible or invisible? Briefly, by which signs will you recognize his speaking or remaining silent about what you nonchalantly call sexual difference? What is it you are thinking beneath those words or through them? . . . What measure would seem to suffice to allow that silence to appear as such, marked and marking? Undoubtedly this: Heidegger apparently said nothing about sexuality by name in those places where the best educated and endowed "modernity" would have fully expected it given its panoply of "everything-is-sexual-and-everything-is-political-and-reciprocally." (396; 381)

If, on the other hand, rather than asking such questions, one were just to follow the common nouns already found in any index, then one would try to track down every mention of "sexuality" in Heidegger. But, of course, one would have to look for it in another language, German, where it more or less translates into the word "Geschlechtlichkeit." Only more or less, however. This difference of language is naturally not insignificant since it is also a difference in the possibilities for the dispersion of some sexual sense or the sense of the sexual that occur in German as in no other language. These possibilities are held in reserve by *Geschlecht*, of which sex, in the sense of one sex or the other, is only one possible translation: "genre, family, stock, race, lineage, generation" are others.[8] In other words, what in English we call sex or sexuality is inscribed in German with a word that also serves to gather up a family group, a generated line of descent. Essentially Derrida's essay titled "*Geschlecht*" is going to be concerned with following the double movement that scatters or disseminates "sexuality" through this term that *marks out* belonging to one *Geschlecht* and not another, that is, one family, stock, kind, gender, sex, etc.[9] He's interested in tracing the movement of a dissemination that gets gathered up under the mark of *Geschlecht*. *Geschlecht* derives from the verb *schlagen*, to strike a blow ("one of the most prevalent senses of *schlagen* is to mint or stamp a coin").[10] This also clearly suggests that with *Geschlecht*, unlike the term "gender," there is as much reason to speak of its *inscription* as of its production.

Despite these initial and unavoidable complications, Derrida proceeds as if one could rely on an index to check Heidegger's references to sexuality. He is thereby taken to a page on which Heidegger invokes the term *Geschlecht*, in the plural *Geschlechter*. It occurs in a passage where he is explicitly negating that *Dasein* can be said to have a sex or to be one of either of the two sexes. Because *Dasein* must be thought of as neutral, then, as Heidegger writes: "That neutrality means also that *Dasein* is neither of the two sexes [*keines von beiden Geschlechtern ist*]" (400; 386). First let us recall that *Dasein* is the name chosen, in Heidegger's great work *Being and Time*, for the kind of being concerned with its own existence (*Dasein*, being-there, existence) in the world with others. One reason this name is chosen is its neutrality. The existence called *Dasein* is, for example, that of neither a male nor female being, neither man nor woman. Yet, as Derrida remarks, this neutralization does not mean to say that *Dasein* is asexual, without sexual existence; it is a neutralization only of the sexual duality, of *sex-duality*, if you will, rather than *sexuality*. It is the binarity of sexual difference and not sexuality as such that for Heidegger must be neutralized. Moreover, suggests Derrida, this might at least partially explain why, when he is led to specify the neutrality of *Dasein*, Heidegger thinks first of sexual neutrality: the neuter is neither one of two (*ne-uter*) and the binary division of "man" that most quickly comes to mind is the sexual division (401; 386).

One should thus understand Heidegger's negation of *Dasein*'s belonging to either of two sexes as above all not a negation of a more general sexuality, more general than the classification by *Geschlecht*: a pre-dual, non-binary sexuality. On the contrary, this negation would be necessary to open the thinking of *Dasein* to a sexuality freed from its determinations by metaphysical binarity. It would be a more general "sexuality" before or beyond the logical division by two; a sexuality not yet or no longer *according to binary reason*. And thus in some sense more powerful than reasoned sexuality. Heidegger makes this clear as the passage Derrida is quoting continues: "But such asexuality is not the indifference of an empty nullity, the feeble negativity of an indifferent ontic nothing. In its neutrality, *Dasein* is not just anyone no matter who, but the originary positivity and power of the essence" (402; 387).

As this language clearly indicates, the neutralization of sexual difference is a movement that adopts the path of a negation ("neither of the
two sexes") in order to bring out the positivity and the power, or one
could say the potency, of *Dasein*'s non-dual sexuality. The problem, however, is how to neutralize *Dasein*'s belonging to one of two sexes without
neutering its sexual power. This is a problem for Heidegger in his language, the language of *Dasein*, which means both the language to which
the term *Dasein* belongs (German) but also the language as spoken (or
rather written) here by *Dasein*. *Dasein* seems to be proper to some one
language, someone's language. Indeed, the fact that Heidegger's English
translators most often leave this term in German suggests that it has the
force of a quasi-proper name. *Dasein* is not a proper name in the common sense, of course. On the contrary, it is a very common name for
existence in a certain language. Nevertheless, this effect of properness
must be related to what Heidegger wants us to understand about *Dasein*,
that it is, as he puts it, "in each case mine."

With this figure of *Dasein*'s properness or "mineness," there is another
face put on the problem of articulating its neutrality without negating the
force of its existence and its sexuality. To ask the question of the meaning
of Being or to analyze existence from the place of *Dasein* that is in each
case mine is to turn inside out, as it were, the space of neutral objectivity,
to reinscribe objectivity within its "subject," who is therefore not a subject
inquiring as to or into objects but a mode of being that relates to itself
by questioning its own, each time my own, existence. Heidegger's bold
deconstruction of the space of the metaphysical subject requires that he
negate the neutrality of *Dasein* in the sense of the neutrality supposed to
detach the inquirer from the inquiry. *Dasein*, which is each time mine,
is defined, we could say, as that which is above all not neutral toward
its own Being, its own *being there* or *da sein*. As Heidegger puts it in the
opening of his treatise:

We are ourselves the entities to be analysed. The Being of any such entity is *in
each case mine*. These entities, in their Being, comport themselves towards their
Being. As entities with such Being, they are delivered over to their own Being.
Being is that which is an issue for every such entity. [*Das Sein ist es, darum es diesem
Seienden je selbst geht.*][11]

We have just identified two modes of *Dasein*'s neutrality or non-
neutrality. On the one hand, *Dasein* is neutral, for example, with regard
to belonging to either of the two sexes. On the other, *Dasein* is in each
case mine because it is not neutral as regards its Being, which, as we just

read, is said to be "an issue for every such entity." These two modes, however, are also thought by Heidegger to be in a certain relation of subordination. The neutralization of Dasein's belonging to one of two sexes *follows from* its non-neutrality as regards its own Being in the world with others. With this ordering, Heidegger means to recall the priority of ontological difference, the difference of Being, over every other difference; before *Dasein* can be said to be, for example, of one sex or the other, it is, or we might say in a more Heideggerian tone, it must be or even it *bes* the Being that it is. Since, therefore, Heidegger wants to speak principally of the ontological difference of *Dasein* he will naturally have little to say about sexual difference, which is a secondary phenomenon.

What one may remark, however, along with Derrida, is that this subordination reproduces one of the oldest gestures of the philosophical discourse Heidegger is attempting to deconstruct. This discourse, as dictated by "the most traditional philosophemes," is one that derives, deduces, or distances sexuality "from every originary structure" and it is repeated, in Derrida's phrase, "with the force of a new rigor" when Heidegger neutralizes the mark of sexual difference in order to proceed with the analysis of *Dasein* (410; 397). With this rigorous repetition, in other words, Heidegger stiffens up the reasons for maintaining the ban on speaking of *Dasein* as essentially *Geschlechtlich*, belonging to one of two sexes or, as we say, having a sex. The strongest or most rigorous reason Heidegger provides is to recover the power of "sexuality." Derrida thus aligns this aspect of Heidegger's thought with what he himself has shown to be constantly at work whenever a philosophical discourse subordinates the difference made by sex-duality to a more general difference. One has reason to suspect that this structure of thinking, which defines the limits of the pertinence of sex-duality, also reproduces within those limits the enforced subordination of one sex to the other. This latter effect of Heidegger's ontological discourse is among those that Derrida's essay is engaged in undoing.

He does so principally, as we will see, by calling attention to gestures taking place in a space of inscription. These gestures describe a "kind of strange and very necessary displacement" (402; 388) and the space of their inscription would be in fact a "transformation or deformation of space."[12] Like non-neutral *Dasein* that is in each case mine, this transforming, deforming displacement does not align with the space of an interiority, an enclosable space bounded by some fundamental distinction of inside from outside. The displacement occurs wherever some such distinction is made since it can only be made at the limit of *Dasein*, where the self-relating mineness of *Dasein* in itself, in its "interiority," is put in relation to some not-self, some exteriority. The transformed space of *Dasein*, then, is inscribed, strangely but necessarily, as a relation to some other, some other *Dasein*, but also perhaps some other *than Dasein*.

This space of *Dasein*, then, would be that of deconstructing relations to some other than itself. We can always ask to know if these relations are sexual, that is, if *Dasein* is having sexual relations. But to whom would we address such a question? From whom would we expect an answer to it? Is that not a question *Dasein* can only answer for itself? For who can presume to say that *Dasein* has this or that sex, in other words, that *Dasein* is having sex, or what sex is for a *Dasein* that is in each case mine? If it is always mine, then it is only for me to say. But, on the other hand, if it is only for me to say, then to whom or to what do I say it, which I must if in fact there is a relation to some other that is, as we say, sexual?

Such questions begin to sound unbearably indiscreet. Since we have been led to invoke our sense of discretion, let us go back to the way in which Derrida is reading Heidegger's apparent silence on the sexuality of *Dasein*. The silence is perhaps to be heard as discretion, a "transitive and significant silence (he has silenced sex) which belongs . . . to the path of a word or a speech he seems to interrupt" (397; 382). Silence is aligned here with interruption of speech, the active non-saying of something, the secreting of discretion. What is interesting and important to note, however, is that Derrida's reading does not follow the trace of some secret, which it would work to reveal, but the trace only of the secreting, of the *active* non-saying, which is to be traced as the displacement of a non-said through a discourse. The protocol of reading here is therefore not first of all a hermeneutic, but a remarking of written gestures whereby some sexual body discreetly covers itself. Thus, the questions guiding the reading do not amount to the necessarily indiscreet one: what is the secret that is being hidden? Rather Derrida asks: "What are the places of this interruption? Where is the silence working on that discourse? And what are the form and determinable contours of that non-said?" (397; 382). These questions, in other words, do not ask the discreetly covered body to bare itself; rather they propose that one follow the determinable contours of a form that has given body to a textual corpus.

These determinable contours, however, belong to no naturally given body that we think we know. Instead, the outlines of a textual body are difficult to trace and cannot be modeled as an object in space or a substantial body. That it does not represent an object does not mean, however, that it corresponds to nothing real. These are the real gestures of a strangely different corpus that is neither body nor object but a *relation* between at least two. It is the relation realized in the act of reading, which is prerequisite to encountering the gestures of a text. As we have already remarked, Derrida's reading of Heidegger follows the traces of such gestures. More precisely, it *re-marks* these gestures in the course of its reading, the reading it is doing or performing. We will take a few examples of these re-marks.

The next occurrence of *Geschlecht* that Derrida isolates is found in a passage that once again neutralizes sexual difference. This time Heidegger adds quotation marks around the word *Geschlechtlichkeit*, but he also adds an *a fortiori* that, as Derrida remarks, "raises the tone somewhat." This tonal remark concerns the *a fortiori* reason one must hold *Dasein* to be sexually neutral. The term Heidegger in fact uses here is not the logical Latin term, but a German adverbial phrase that invokes, albeit from some distance, the law: *erst recht*, literally "first by law" but usually translated as "with all the more reason," "all the more so." What is properly, rightly, or by law first is the stronger reason, the more forceful reason, that which has the all the more reason, or as one says in French "plus forte raison."[13] Heidegger is speaking of a *Selbstheit*, selfhood, or, to use a more technical term, ipseity of *Dasein* that is neutral with regard to any being-me or being-you, any egoism or altruism, an ipseity "not as yet determined as human being, me or you, conscious or unconscious subject" (404; 390). With regard to all of these divisions, the being-a-self of *Dasein* is neutral, asserts Heidegger, "and with all the more reason [*erst recht*] with regard to 'sexuality' ['*Geschlechtlichkeit*']."

About this insistence on the *a fortiori* or stronger reason, Derrida remarks quite simply: if the reason is so strongly obvious, then why insist on it? Why does it not go without saying? He then points out in strictest logic that the

movement of this *a fortiori* is logically irreproachable on only one condition: It would be necessary that the said "sexuality" (in quotation marks) be the assured predicate of whatever is made possible by or beginning with ipseity, here, for instance, the structures of "me" and "you," yet that it not belong, as "sexuality," to the structure of ipseity, an ipseity not as yet determined as human being, me or you, conscious or unconscious subject, man or woman. Yet, if Heidegger insists and underlines ("with all the more reason"), it is because a suspicion has not yet been banished: What if "sexuality" already marked the most originary *Selbstheit*? If it were an ontological structure of ipseity? If the *Da* of *Dasein* were already "sexual"? What if sexual difference were already marked in the opening up to the question of the sense of Being and to the ontological difference? And what if neutralization, which does not happen all by itself, were a violent operation? (ibid.)

If indeed there is violence here, it subsists in the traces of the invoked law or order of reasons, in the structure of derivation from a first ipseity presupposed as without sexual difference in itself. Invoking the greater, stronger, or more powerful reason as that which necessitates this neutralization, one has perhaps covered over a weaker reason, a reason that is rather a nagging suspicion or even a fear, which has not yet been banished and perhaps can never be banished: perhaps "sexuality" already marks the most originary being-self and is an ontological structure of ipseity. For if the only logically correct or faultless order of reasons here means that "sexuality" *must* be the predicate of everything made possible by the being-a-self of *Dasein*, but does not, itself or as itself, belong to what it makes possible, then a strange displacement of the ordered derivation or predication has been effected. "Sexuality" would have to be said to *participate without belonging* to everything made possible beginning with ipseity, and thus ipseity itself would have to be inscribed already within a strange sexuality without "sexuality" or "*Geschlechtlichkeit.*"[14]

The problem is quite clear. The ipseity or self-relation that Heidegger wants to mark out as that of a *Dasein* not indifferent to its own being would be, as Derrida phrases it, a "minimal relation to itself as relation to Being, the relation that the being which we are, as questioning, maintains with self and with its own proper essence . . . Neutrality, therefore, is first of all the neutralization of everything but the naked trait of this relation to self" (399; 384). But if it is said to be first of all or above all (*erst recht*) *sexual* neutrality, then this implies that some *other* sexual non-neutrality, some *other* sexual difference has first of all to be neutralized, reduced, or withdrawn *so that* one may isolate the "naked trait" of self relation. For *Dasein* properly to name such a naked self-relation, this other sexual difference must be withdrawn and, by withdrawing, *give* one the possibility of thinking something like a self, the being-a-self of sexually neutral *Dasein*. *Dasein* itself and as a self would be something like a gift of the other sexual difference, the one that withdraws just as every other sexual couple or coupling does, behind some folded tissue: curtain, veil, venetian blind, *rideau, jalousie*, and so forth.[15] The problem, then, is this gift, whereby *Dasein* is given (a) sex, and at the same time – and this is what we call birth – given all that is made possible by being a self. If the self relation is thus given, then it cannot be thought of as *first of all* a self relation, but necessarily as a relation to something else than the self it is given. One cannot think the self beginning with itself.

The question remains why this impossibility should be thought to create a problem. In other words, why does the necessity of the non-self-relation seem to make for a problem rather than a gift? This question can only be pursued by the more specific one: for whom does it make problems? We are suggesting that Derrida is isolating the problems it makes for Heidegger, quite singularly, but at the same time he is opening up the possibility for thinking non-self-relation in terms *also* of gift and not just of problem. We will later propose at least one consequence of this for the notion of sexual reproduction as that which gives life.

Like the problem of *Dasein*'s sexual neutrality with which we began, the problem we've just alluded to is also one for Heidegger's language, the language in which he would inscribe "Geschlechtlichkeit" so as to neutralize it, erase it, or withdraw it. This is where the tissue of his text must fold back over its own inscription. As Derrida points out, the appearance of the quotation marks on "Geschlechtlichkeit" should not be overlooked (Heidegger writes: "with all the more reason with regard to 'sexuality' ['*Geschlechtlichkeit*']"). And as he often does when analyzing this punctuation, he cites in passing the distinction made in speech act theory between use and mention. According to that distinction, as Derrida writes, "the current sense of the word 'sexuality' is 'mentioned' rather than 'used'" (405; 390). There is, however, some reservation regarding this distinction, signaled here by Derrida's own use of quotation marks on the terms "mentioned" and "used." Is not Heidegger's mention of "*Geschlechtlichkeit*" also a kind of use, and does not this neutralizing "mention" of sexuality also have the allure of a not-indifferent and perhaps even violent "use," the operation of quotation, a citation to appear, *erst recht*, before the law? In that guise, "sexuality" would be, Derrida suggests, "cited to appear in court, warned if not accused" (405; 390). The bracketing of "sexuality," its furtive appearance under citation could suggest some scene of guilt, a fault that the court of ordered reasons *must* contain at the risk of contaminating the original structure of ipseity and of *Dasein*. Derrida suggests that this is perhaps what is at stake here for Heidegger: "For in the end, if it is true that sexuality must be neutralized *a fortiori*, *erst recht*, why insist? Where is the risk of misunderstanding? Unless the matter is not at all obvious, and there is still *a risk of mixing up once more* the question of sexual difference with that of Being and ontological difference" (404; 390; emphases added). Or, put in somewhat different terms: "Above all, one must protect the analytic of *Dasein* from the risks of anthropology, of psychoanalysis, even of biology." That is, *Geschlechtlichkeit* is a thematizable, representable object for these sciences, but not for the fundamental ontology that Heidegger wants to adumbrate and that he wants to protect from contamination by these other disciplines. One way he does so is to avoid thematizing sexuality in that name. *Geschlechtlichkeit*, therefore, will be set aside or rather withdrawn behind the curtain set hanging between the quotation marks placed around the word.

At this point, then, Heidegger's text exposes an order of forced reasons. This exposition follows a strictly logical path, but in so doing it also exposes (itself to) a certain risk. And this risk is determined *erst recht* as the risk of mixing or contamination. But an exposition, in addition to the senses of philosophical or logical argument and of exposure to risk or to contamination, also remarks a spatial movement, an ex-position, a transformation or deformation of positioned, oppositional space. There is thus a fold in the order of reasons that exposes itself here, in other words, makes itself visible or phenomenalizes itself. The phenomenon of this exposition, however, occurs as the ex-posing of a *text*, rather than an object in conventionally lighted oppositional space. How does Heidegger's text expose itself in all these senses at once? And how does this irreducible semantic plurality come to displace and reinscribe the figure of a contaminating sexual duality?

If Heidegger's "all the more reason" is a blow struck in the name of a certain non-contamination of *Dasein*'s ontological difference by sexual difference, then this *coup de force* or forced neutralization, by raising the tone, also calls attention to what "does not happen all by itself" but must be forced to happen, *performed as perforce*. Above the surface of the text's argument, a gesture juts out (provided at least that someone remarks it) to put sexuality in its place, but the same gesture cannot prevent the appearance of the strange displacement whereby sexuality, by not belonging to ipseity, nevertheless belongs to everything it makes possible. Only a *coup de force* here can decide that this non-belonging of "sexuality" does not indicate a more general structure of sexual difference rather than a more restricted one, a contaminated structure of ontologico-sexual difference rather than one that determines sexual difference to be logically dependent on the being-a-self of *Dasein*, which would only thereupon receive the predicate of sexual. This latter order of implication or derivation, whereby a contaminating sexual difference is contained, would be what has to be preserved by the strategy of neutralization.

And yet, it is the movement of neutralization itself that brings out or allows to appear in this strange, non-phenomenal light a sexual difference that contaminates all others. Or rather, since this language of contamination signals already the decision by the court of forced reason, let us resume the language of gift we introduced above. As we were saying, there would be a sexual difference, an *other* sexual difference, that *gives* all others or that *gives* itself in the guise of all other differences.

This general space of the other sexual difference would thus also be the possibility of transformation or deformation of a certain engendering power of "sexuality." One touches here, in other words, on the limit of the determination of sexuality as it has always been understood: reproduction, engenderment, genital sexuality. As that which "gives life" to this deformed space, that is, puts it in motion, sexual difference has now also to be heard in another sense, before or beyond this limit that defines the most general sense of "life" as sexually engendered life, this life here. "Sexual difference" would then also have to be heard without this general sense, without a generalizable sense of the "life" it gives. This other sexual difference invokes an unheard-of sense, its tones muffled as it were within parentheses: (sexual) differe/ance.

The textual gesture we have just retraced is not that of some body but of a covering or silencing of the body, its withdrawal from discursive space. For all that, the sexed or sexual body is not simply absent. Rather it is withdrawn but into the folds of a text. Because it is folded in this way, a text does not lay itself out flatly or in a straight line. But also because it is folded, a text somewhere exposes the manner in which it still harbors the force of whatever sent it into waves for a start (call it the sextual drive). That is why, when he comes to formalize this structure, Derrida briefly sketches the outline of a form that is not stable but rather a movement that is being somehow driven. This movement in discursive space can be traced through the displacement of a *pair* of terms, always a pair or at least a duality. The paired duality functions something like the negative and positive terminals of a battery that charge and discharge the *dynamis* driving the movement. Here, then, is the brief sketch Derrida draws of this drive or transmission system:

> By a kind of strange and very necessary displacement, it is sexual division itself that leads to [*porte à*] negativity; so neutralization is at once the effect of this negativity and the effacement to which thought must subject it to allow an original positivity to become manifest. Far from constituting a positivity that the asexual neutrality of *Dasein* would annul, sexual binarity itself would be responsible, or rather would belong to a determination that is itself responsible, for this negativation. To radicalize or formalize too quickly the sense of this movement . . . we could propose the following schema: it is sexual difference itself as binarity, it is the discriminative belonging to one or another sex, that destines or determines (to) a negativity that must then be accounted for. (402–403; 388)

This is a formalization of what Heidegger does when he negates sexual binarity in order to retrieve an original positivity of sexuality. The formalized schema will be taken a little further, but first let us remark the initial strangeness in this movement. Sexual division or sexuality "leads to" negativity: that is, it carries toward, it puts in motion (*porte à*) but it also carries that motion in itself against itself since the movement is toward a negation of itself as binarity. A fold is created here when sexual difference carries within "itself" its own limited determination as binarity. Binarity with its negative and positive poles, in other words, is at once the determination to be negated and that which determines, makes necessary, or destines to the negation. This effect of an implicated fold within the movement, which, moreover, folds or doubles around binarity, is marked at the articulation of negative and positive terms: neutralization. That "neutralization," we read, "is at once the effect of this negativity and the effacement to which thought *must* subject it to allow an original positivity to become manifest" (emphases added). In other words, the neutralization must submit to the double neces- sity to inscribe a negativity and efface it, to inscribe it by effacing it. And since the neutralization is itself but the movement through this in- scription and effacement of negativity, it carries toward and away from "itself," toward and away from this strange ipseity marked already by sexual division. Sexual difference is "itself" divided, it divides its own location.

It is this power system driven by positive and negative poles that Derrida remarks when he takes the formalization a step further. What he traces is the implied or enfolded negative term corresponding to the positive pole of power in Heidegger's language ("In its neutrality, *Dasein* is not just anyone no matter who, but the originary positivity and power [*Mächtigkeit*] of the essence"). The enfolded, withdrawn structure is drawn out by means of Derrida's translation of Heidegger's term into its implied opposite: powerlessness, or, depending on how one wants to hear it, impotence.

Going still further, one could even link sexual difference thus determined (one out of two), negativity, and a certain "impotence" [*impuissance*]. When returning to the originality of *Dasein*, of this *Dasein* said to be sexually neutral, "originary positivity" and "power" [*puissance*] can be recovered. In other words, despite appearances, the asexuality and neutrality that must first of all be withdrawn from the binary sexual mark, in the analytic of *Dasein*, are in fact on the same side, on the side of *this* sexual difference – the binary – to which one might have thought them simply opposed. (403; 388; translation modified)

If we follow Derrida's example and remark the use of quotation marks, then we see the terms "impotence" and "power" being both used and mentioned here. There is mention or citation (but also translation) of Heidegger's term "Mächtigkeit," in the phrase "Mächtigkeit des Wesens," the power (potency) of the essence, of originary positivity. "Impotence" ("impuissance," with the always possible sense of "impossibility") is the word Derrida unfolds out of the implied system of Heidegger's discourse. The term, therefore, is not a quotation or "mention" of what actually appears as the discourse is written. But neither is it simply being used in some context, a context that would serve to determine whether or not we hear the term in its strictly sexual sense (genital impotence) or any one of its many other possible uses: powerlessness of whatever sort, impossibility in general. (But what would that be: "impossibility in general"? We'll leave this question suspended for the moment.) The quotation marks on "impuissance" signal a suspension of all these senses and all possible contexts of the term's use. But the quotation marks, because they cite only an implied term in Heidegger's discourse, also point very precisely to the contours of an active silencing, the withdrawal of the sexual mark. Derrida remarks that Heidegger "will never directly associate the predicate 'sexual' with the word 'power,' the first remaining all too easily associated with the whole system of sexual difference that may, without much risk of error, be said to be inseparable from every anthropology and every metaphysics" (403; 389). But also no doubt Heidegger avoids this association because the sexual mark invariably reiterates the link between positive and negative poles, potency and impotence. Despite that, however, insofar as non-dual sexuality is recovered as a positivity, the power one strives to withdraw from the binary poles of negative and positive is also, still, once again getting its charge from that binary system. That is why one can say that the "asexuality and neutrality that must first of all be withdrawn from the binary sexual mark . . . are in fact on the same side, on the side of *this* sexual difference – the binary – to which one might have thought them simply opposed." The binary opposition is therefore both withdrawn and redrawn. This back and forth describes the movement of its displacement through a system, its repeated inscription and effacement.

In addition to placing quotation marks around the interpolated term "impuissance," Derrida traces another typographical gesture in the same passage. There is also a use of italics that marks out "*this* sexual difference" for special emphasis. I would suggest that the deictic "this" receives its emphasis by force of dissemination. I would also therefore be tempted to read this device as something like a *coup de force* that is both analogous to and a displacement of Heidegger's "with all the more reason." Specifically, it re-marks difference or division at the site of the deixis, which is the index of a gesture, the possibility of any reference to *this here* and of any relation of this "this" to itself. It thus situates the dividing limit at which every ipseity, every "this, here, now," is posed and exposed, displaced into another "this," into another's here and now. In other words, *"this* sexual difference" carries toward an immediate multiplicity of senses, illimitable by any two; but it also continues to signal *this* singular sexual difference here, in all its impossible binarity. This "this" uncannily appropriates and expropriates the ipseity of every "myself" when it divides its mark, on the page, and splits its location, deforming the former space of binary opposition. The italicized deictic "this" imprints, inscribes, or strikes sexual difference (*"this* sexual difference") with the force of its dissemination.

Would not such a *coup de force* have to reinscribe the whole machinery of "puissance," power, potency, or *Mächtigkeit?* Perhaps, but only on the condition of remaining strangely powerless in itself, only on the condition that it be suspended in advance – disseminated – from the other to which or to whom it is consigned as a sign to be read, or not, in *this* text *here. "This* sexual difference," which is to say, at once, the other (and the other's) sexual difference. Sexual difference divides – itself. It thus divides its proper meaning and this division inscribes (itself as) a text. The general name of humanity's gender deconstructs.

Nothing is perhaps less certain of success than the project to recapture the originary power of "sexuality" by neutralizing sex-duality. Whether in Heidegger's discourse or, very differently, in a discourse like Judith Butler's, that gesture has to remain implicated without neutrality in *this* sexual difference, which thereby also reinscribes its binary trait. No power of sexuality that does not also, at the same time, get transmitted as an im-power, an impotency. Heidegger's discourse perhaps sought to dissimulate or discreetly silence this inscription of "impower" by, in one of those gestures Derrida re-marks, "never directly associat[ing] the predicate 'sexual' with the word 'power'." He would thereby have wanted to avoid falling back into a strictly binary sexual domain, but perhaps he was also secretly re-connecting sexuality to an absolute power, a power without implication in im-power. Butler's discourse would seem to make this connection without dissimulation, in the open: it is overtly a discourse of sexual politics, rather than always only potentially or in secret. That is, sexuality is connected by its discursive arguments to a system it calls the "apparatus of production." But we have also seen that, as the condition of its identifying a source of production that is not yet an inscription, such a discourse attempts to hide in plain sight its own articulations, there where it must draw on the binary trait and reinscribe it. Such an attempt, if it could ever succeed, would dissimulate the text *as* text, that is, as both more and less than the vehicle of a discourse's conceptual generalizations. It would thereby also spell the end of whatever can still come to be inscribed of the other sexual difference, beyond, before, or within the binary, and thus the end of any transformation of the relations held in place by sex-duality.

If such an inscription is still possible, however, then oddly enough it can announce itself in the figure of impossibility, of that im-power Derrida unfolds at the point at which his reading, we might say, poses another signature on Heidegger's text. When we earlier suspended the question: What is impossibility in general?, it was this scene of a signature that we were anticipating. For would not impossibility *in general* have to include the impossibility of that very generalization? If so, then it is always somewhere being restricted in the general sense, specified as the impossibility of this or that, of this one or that one. It is this necessary limitation of impossibility that allies it with the restricting effects of signature on generalizing discourse, *a fortiori* discourse on gender. Such effects are remarked everywhere in the gender-less texts signed "Jacques Derrida."[16]

Somewhere closer to the beginning of this chapter, we asked: "What if it could be shown that the gesture with which the one silences sexual difference is essentially the same as the gesture with which the other speaks apparently of little else?" Perhaps what happens in that eventuality is that terms like "gender," "Geschlecht," "sexe," and so forth will indeed have come to be neutralized but in another fashion. They would have been neutralized for use as reliable markers of the *general* theme of sexuality inscribing discourse in a language.

– By "neutralized for use," do you mean that these terms have been put out of commission, rendered useless, and therefore discourse has to drop them? Or, on the contrary, do you mean they have been shorn of whatever would make them useless, such as the necessity to translate between languages, and turned into conceptual tools with which a discourse can construct itself?

– Whichever. In either case and in all cases, the theme plays only when some non-concept, some impossible concept, something like a proper name, picks it up as an instrument of quasi-musical inscription. And begins to write in more than one voice, more than one language.

NOTES

1 Although this incommensurability is well known to translators between the two languages, it has not to my knowledge been the object of much if any reflection by those who regularly write about the relation between "sex" and language. The title of a collective work directed by Luce Irigaray, for example, *Sexes et genres à travers les langues* (Paris: Grasset, 1990), would seem to promise just such an engagement with this difference between English and at least the other languages represented in the collection (French and Italian). But any reader with this expectation who reads through the collection, beginning with Irigaray's own long introduction, is very soon disappointed. It is partly this oversight, which is certainly not limited to Irigaray and her epigones, that the present article seeks to interrogate.

2 Judith Butler, *Gender Trouble: Feminism and the Subversion of Identity* (New York: Routledge, 1990), 6.

3 Butler often effects this reinscription more or less explicitly through a kind of translation. The need to translate another language, however, rarely if ever prompts any remark as to the referential constraints of the target language, English. For instance, an essay on Simone de Beauvoir begins by citing the famous line from *The Second Sex*: "One is not born, but rather becomes, a woman." Butler then proceeds to offer a paraphrase that ignores whatever implications follow from the fact of de Beauvoir's own language: "Simone de Beauvoir's formulation distinguishes sex from gender and suggests that gender is an aspect of identity gradually acquired" ("Sex and Gender in Simone de Beauvoir's *Second Sex*," *Yale French Studies* 72: 35). De Beauvoir, of course, any more than anyone else writing in French, says literally nothing about gender and consequently about its possible distinction. For a similar commentary on the same Beauvoirian formulation, see *Gender Trouble*, 111–12.

4 This condition has certainly not been missed by Derrida's readers and has prompted enormous commentary, both favorable and unfavorable. To take only a recent index, several book titles in the last few years mark the conjunction of either Derrida's name or deconstruction with an interest in sexual difference: for example, Diane Elam, *Feminism and Deconstruction* (New York: Routledge, 1994); Nancy J. Holland, ed., *Feminist Interpretations of Jacques Derrida* (University Park, PA: Pennsylvania State University Press, 1997); Penelope Deutscher, *Yielding Gender: Feminism, Deconstruction, and the History of Philosophy* (London and New York: Routledge, 1997).

5 On this important term, see David Wills's impeccable glossary in this volume.

6 Of these, "hymen" and "invagination" commonly carry a reference to the female body. Derrida was led to comment on the choice of these terms in an interview that deals largely with sexual difference: see Jacques Derrida and

Christie V. McDonald, "Choreographies" in Peggy Kamuf, ed., *A Derrida Reader: Between the Blinds* (New York: Columbia University Press, 1991), 453.

7 Jacques Derrida, "*Geschlecht*, différence sexuelle, différence ontologique," in *Psyché, Inventions de l'autre* (Paris: Galilée, 1987), 396 [trans. Ruben Berezdivin, "'Geschlecht': Sexual Difference, Ontological Difference," in Kamuf, ed., *A Derrida Reader*, 381]. Further references to both the original and the translation will be given in that order in the text.

8 As given in French in Derrida's essay, these possible translations of *Geschlecht* are listed as "sexe, genre, famille, souche, race, lignée, génération." Although "genre" is in turn translated (or not) as "genre" in the English version, one could argue that this is an instance where Derrida is using the term to mean something very close to gender.

9 In fact, the principal part of the reading of the dispersion, and even decomposition, of the term *Geschlecht* through Heidegger's text will be consigned to another essay, which is a companion to this one: "Heidegger's Hand (*Geschlecht* II)" [trans. John P. Leavey, Jr., in John Sallis, ed., *Deconstruction and Philosophy: The Texts of Jacques Derrida* (Chicago: University of Chicago Press, 1987)]. There is also a third *Geschlecht* essay: "Heidegger's Ear: Philopolemology (*Geschlecht* IV)" in Jacques Derrida, *The Politics of Friendship*, trans. George Collins (London: Verso Press, 1997). On the missing number in this sequence – *Geschlecht* III – see "Heidegger's Hand."

10 David Krell, *Intimations of Mortality: Time, Truth, and Finitude in Heidegger's Thinking of Mortality*, as cited in Jacques Derrida, "Heidegger's Hand (*Geschlecht* II)." As for the standard meanings of *Geschlecht*, Krell writes: "First, it translates the Latin word *genus*, being equivalent to *Gattung*: *das Geschlecht* is a group of people who share a common ancestry . . . Of course, if the ancestry is traced back far enough we may speak of *das menschliche Geschlecht*, 'human kind.' Second, *das Geschlecht* may mean one generation of men and women . . . Third, there are male and female *Geschlechter*" (ibid.).

11 Martin Heidegger, *Being and Time*, trans. John Macquarrie and Edward Robinson (New York: Harper and Row, 1962), 67.

12 Derrida and McDonald, "Choreographies," in Kamuf, ed., *A Derrida Reader*, 453.

13 Derrida has often interrogated idiomatic French expressions formed with "raison." In *Given Time*, the expressions "donner raison à l'autre" (to concede that the other is right) and "avoir raison de l'autre" (to prevail over the other) receive thorough attention as key to what is at stake in the opening of a gift "*destined* not to have reason, to be wrong, as if one had to choose between reason and gift (or forgiveness). The gift would be that which does not obey the principle of reason: It is, it ought to be, it owes itself to be without reason, without wherefore, and without foundation," *Given Time: I. Counterfeit Money*, trans. Peggy Kamuf (Chicago: University of Chicago Press, 1992), 156. For another deployment of the idioms of "raison," in an essay on Heidegger, see "Comment donner raison," trans. by John P. Leavey, Jr. as "How

to Concede, with Reasons," in Derrida, *Points... interviews (1974–1994)*, Elisabeth Weber, ed. (Stanford: Stanford University Press, 1995).

14 The necessity of this syntax of "without" has been shown by Derrida at several junctures, notably in his readings of Blanchot. We refer in particular to "The Law of *Genre*," an essay on the notion of *genre*, the false friend of "gender," where the necessity is retraced in its most generic terms: "I would speak of a sort of participation without belonging – a taking part in without being part of, without having membership in a set. The trait that marks membership inevitably divides, the boundary of the set comes to form, by invagination, an internal pocket larger than the whole; and the outcome of this division and of this unbounding remains as singular as it is limitless," trans. Avital Ronell, *Glyph* 7: 206. The invagination described here would be another term with which to name the strange movement of displacement that reinscribes all oppositions within an itself that is itself without closure. On the choice of this term, see above, note 10.

15 This topos of natural discretion or modesty that must cover sexual coupling was most forcefully put in place perhaps by Rousseau, who argued as well, of course, that the responsibility for this modesty has always been assigned to the female of the species. Whenever "sexual difference" is being thought solely on the basis of this discreetly hidden genital act, then it remains also to some extent a Rousseauvian difference.

16 This includes all texts Derrida has signed or will sign. See, however, especially the discussion of Hegel's signature on the conceptual machinery of the dialectic, in *Glas*, trans. John. P. Leavey, Jr. and Richard Rand (Lincoln: University of Nebraska Press, 1986).

FURTHER READING

Butler, Judith. *Gender Trouble: Feminism and the Subversion of Identity*. New York and London: Routledge, 1990.

Cornell, Drucilla. *Beyond Accommodation: Ethical Feminism, Deconstruction, and the Law*. New York: Routledge, 1991.

Derrida, Jacques. "Choreographies: An Interview with Jacques Derrida." Trans. Christie V. McDonald. *Diacritics* 12, 2 (1982).

"Geschlecht: Sexual Difference, Ontological Difference." Trans. Ruben Berezdivin. In *A Derrida Reader: Between the Blinds*. Ed. Peggy Kamuf. New York: Columbia University Press, 1991.

Given Time, I: Counterfeit Money. Trans. Peggy Kamuf. Chicago: University of Chicago Press, 1992.

"Heidegger's Hand (Geschlecht II)." Trans. John P. Leavey, Jr. In *Deconstruction and Philosophy: The Texts of Jacques Derrida*. Ed. John Sallis. Chicago: University of Chicago Press, 1987.

"The Law of Genre." Trans. Avital Ronell. *Glyph* 7.

Spurs: Nietzsche's Styles. Trans. Barbara Harlow. Chicago: University of Chicago Press, 1978.

Deutscher, Penelope. *Yielding Gender: Feminism, Deconstruction, and the History of Philosophy*. London and New York: Routledge, 1997.

Elam, Diane. *Feminism and Deconstruction*. New York and London: Routledge, 1994.

Grosz, Elizabeth. "Ontology and Equivocation: Derrida's Politics of Sexual Difference." In Nancy J. Holland, ed., *Feminist Interpretations of Jacques Derrida*. University Park, PA: Penn State Press, 1997.

Johnson, Barbara. "Gender Theory and the Yale School." In Johnson, *A World of Difference*. Baltimore: Johns Hopkins University Press, 1987.

Holland, Nancy J. "The Treble Clef/t: Jacques Derrida and the Female Voice." *Philosophy and Culture*, vol. II. Ed. Venant Cauchy. Montreal: Beffroi, 1987.

Kamuf, Peggy. "Deconstruction and Feminism: A Repetition." In Nancy J. Holland, ed., *Feminist Interpretations of Jacques Derrida*. University Park, PA: Penn State Press, 1997.

Kofman, Sarah. "a cloche." In Hugh J. Silverman, ed., *Derrida and Deconstruction*. New York: Routledge, 1989.

Meese, Elizabeth. *(Ex)tensions: Re-figuring Feminist Criticism*. Urbana: University of Illinois Press, 1990.

Rapaport, Herman. *Heidegger and Derrida: Reflections on Time and Language*. Lincoln: University of Nebraska Press, 1989.

Spivak, Gayatri Chakravorty. "Displacement and the Discourse of Woman." In Mark Krupnick, ed., *Displacement: Derrida and After*. Bloomington: Indiana University Press, 1983.

Vinken, Barbara. "Republic, Rhetoric, and Sexual Difference." In Anselm Haverkamp, ed., *Deconstruction is/in America*. New York: New York University Press, 1995.

CHAPTER 4

Derrida and aesthetics: Lemming (reframing the abyss)

David Wills

A discussion of Derrida's treatment of the aesthetic as developed in *The Truth in Painting*,[1] referring specifically to Kant's Third Critique, is not the place for the manner of facile narrative abandon that comes with a personal reminiscence. Such a story would, I suppose, need to be kept outside of and apart from the subject here. Even though, remaining completely cut off from any other purpose, it might, in Kant's terms, display the beauty he calls that of a "mere formal finality." It is, however, hard to imagine a narrative that would be "estimated on the ground of . . . a finality apart from an end,"[2] some story that would come to be in being excised, at one fell swoop, with no blood or trace of its rupture, like his impossibly neatly cut tulip (*Critique*, 80n; cf. *TIP*, 82–95). Thus I won't recount how my father, the one with the wooden leg, at the time when he, his wife, and four young children had been thrown out of their religious sect, kept very much outside of and apart from it, though only relatively so – all that is too complicated to explain in the space allotted here[3] – I won't recount how he, wanting to keep us in the house and apart from and outside of movie theaters (this was before television in the place I grew up in) at a time when, on account of our religious banishment, the family's social contacts were very much reduced, being reconciled to the fact that a suitable use for the image could be found if only it were contained within certain parameters, for a while took to renting creationist nature films that, come certain hallowed evenings, he would screen for us. The only one I remember from this distance was about lemming (like "sheep," in English the same signifier can go for singular and plural). This is not the place for that sort of story, for when Kant wrote his Third Critique he didn't appear to rely on anything like films he had seen of lemming. Yet at least some of his references were drawn from comparable documentary representations of the exotic placed alongside the familiar iconic commonplaces of the European experience. Thus he mentions in the same breath a church and a New Zealander's tattoo, or

Savary's impression of the pyramids and the tourist's perplexity vis-à-vis St. Peter's basilica.[4] The latter reference is a focus of Derrida's reading of Kant in "Parergon" in *The Truth in Painting*, and, as he notes:

> Kant never went to have a closer look, neither to Rome nor to Egypt. And we must also reckon with the distance of a narrative, a written narrative in the case of Savary's *Letters*. But does not the distance required for the experience of the sublime open up perception to the space of narrative? (*TIP*, 142)

How much space, the question becomes, separates something like Savary's *Letters* from the narrative represented by a series of reminiscences, or even a single one? How might such a space be circumscribed and what would distinguish it from an abyss? We don't have to make any imaginative leaps to get there; just follow the simple storyline of a logical progression. Derrida, in referring to Savary, is discussing the sublime and again lighting upon Kant's examples, as he had done so tellingly in respect of the Third Moment of the Analytic of the Beautiful. There, we recall (being careful not to reminisce), Kant listed types of ornamentation – *parerga* – such as "frames of pictures or the drapery on statues, or the colonnades of palaces" as examples of "adjuncts" that augment the delight of taste by means of form. His list opened a taxonomic can of worms that Derrida saw as gnawing away at the whole architectonic structure of the Critiques (*Critique*, 68; cf. *TIP*, 53–78). Kant returned to the example of a frame two sections later but not in its own right, rather as the support for decorations he was to cite as an example of free or self-subsisting beauty: "So designs *à la grecque*, foliage for framework or on wallpapers, &c., have no intrinsic meaning; they represent nothing – no Object under a definite concept – and are free beauties." Those designs are contrasted with the aforementioned Maori tattoos, which, for being found on a human being, become dependent or "appendant" forms of beauty (*Critique*, 72–73). The foliage on the frame cannot, for Kant, be compared with the tattoo on a New Zealander's body. This is a strange contrast that Derrida does not follow up on, although by means of other contrasts (parrot, humming-bird, bird of paradise, crustaceans vs. man, woman, child, horse) he is able to conclude that Kant's "anthropologistic recourse . . . weighs massively, by its content, on this supposedly pure deduction of aesthetic judgement" (*TIP*, 108). Lemming, therefore – this insistence on frames, creatures, and Maori tattoos having brought me back to my film of them – might pose something of a problem for Kant's distinction between free and dependent beauties. Perhaps they are not beautiful at all, certainly not like birds of paradise, though in the film I found them rather cute. Would I choose one for a pet over a crawfish? Probably. Unlike the horse, they do not appear to have any anthropological utility, although a plague of them might plough clear through a landscape. Nonetheless it is in terms of their end, perhaps even of their finality apart from an end, that they come to mind in this impertinent narrative reminiscence, in my father's film of them viewed in a protected living-room in a land where even the tattooed chins existed mostly in picture-books, with respect to which this Norwegian rodent was exoticism itself, poles apart, utterly exorbitant. These lemming, having imposed themselves here where they have no place, will be dispatched to the other end of oblivion, for in the end and of their end and finality the only image I retain is of a horde of them implacably scurrying towards the cliff, countless thousands driven by the eschatological mandate of the sea, never pausing an instant to contemplate the awful sublimity of it all but disappearing into the abyss like this _____

In Kant's *Critique of Judgement* the judgment that gives rise to aesthetics serves to connect "the realm of the natural concept, as the sensible, and the realm of the concept of freedom, as the supersensible," those two realms developed in each of the preceding Critiques and between which there nevertheless exists a "great gulf," an abyss. Judgment will be the "middle term between understanding and reason," rendering possible a transition between them (*Critique*, 14–15). This aporetic contrast between what is on the one hand separated by an abyss and on the other joined by a process of transition is the motor for Derrida's reading of the Third Critique as an (unavowed) problematic of the frame, something that, from a certain point of view, would have appeared to be unavoidable once Kant had set out to divide architectonically the entire human conceptual field. Thus for all the latter's attention to the delimitation of the object of understanding, for all his distinctions between the limit and the boundary,[5] when it comes to matters that must eventually bear upon the work of art, frames will attract little more attention than a passing reference as an example of ornamentation, a *parergon* or *hors d'oeuvre*, supposedly outside the work, a work whose status as an object will thus have been unproblematically presupposed.[6] And as if to underscore the conceptual naiveté of that unproblematical presupposition, exposing it in spite of himself as a symptom that belies the logic of his argument, Kant will mention the decidedly "external" frame in the same breath as references to clothing on a statue and colonnades of palaces. How clothing can be external to a statue, or a column external to the building it holds up, in the same way that a frame is presumed to be external to a painting, is the quandary that escapes Kant and endlessly intrigues Derrida.

Derrida, in contrast, gives the frame the explicit status of the focus or "center" of his discussion of the work of art, as explained in the preface entitled "Passe-partout":

This partition of the edge is perhaps what is inscribed and occurs everywhere [*se passe partout*] in this book; and the protocol-frame is endlessly multiplied in it . . . that's the whole story, to recognize and contain, like the surrounds of the work of art, or at most its outskirts: frame, title, signature, museum, archive, reproduction, discourse, market, in short: everywhere where one legislates on the *right to painting* by marking the limit, with a slash marking an opposition [*d'un trait d'opposition*] which one would like to be indivisible. (*TIP*, 7, 11)

But he also gives the frame graphic status, by means of the diacritical mark his text has recourse to in order to separate the somewhat fragmentary sections of the four chapters of "Parergon," the first essay in *The Truth in Painting*. That mark, a half-crochet, a ∟, is a not-too-distant relative of our quotation mark, used in the first printed books of the fifteenth century to distinguish between text and commentary. It was the mark of a "lemma": "When F. Reiner printed the Bible with the Postills of Nicholas of Lyra at Venice in 1482–3, he introduced a single half crochet ∟ before a passage in the text, and another after the corresponding *lemma* in the accompanying commentary."[7] Derrida's half-crochets illustrate the complex set of relations that obtain among the marks constituting a piece of writing, among different texts and formats, especially as determined by any attempt to fix external limits to such marks. The word "lemma," which in the fifteenth century referred to the proposition drawn from a classical source or holy writ that was quoted, and served as a heading for the commentary that followed it, now means both an assumed, and therefore accessory proposition on the basis of which an argument will proceed, and a similar proposition given as a title. It is thus something fundamental to the argument which occupies an accessory or marginal position, albeit with the prominence of a title or headword; something like a frame that forms the basis of a conceptual or aesthetic structure while appearing to remain more or less exterior to it. "Lemmata" (Fr. *Lemmes*) is Derrida's title for the first (of four) part(s) of "Parergon" and he points thereby to the relation between that essay, as introductory seminar or general heading, and the discussions of philosophical treatments of the aesthetic – Kant, Hegel, and Heidegger – that he will subsequently develop (at least in two out of those three cases) in his book. But more particularly he points to his following chapter in which he analyzes the absence, from Kant's treatise on the aesthetic, of any treatment of the seemingly very necessary question of framing, as if its completely unproblematic status allowed it to function as the unstated lemma that framed Kant's whole text. For, according to Derrida, philosophical discourses on art in general – and, one might add, discourses on the aesthetic in general – presume to go straight through the frame on their way to what is supposed to be the center of the work. The case where this is examined most closely – the question surrounding the identity of two shoes in a painting by van Gogh – is the subject of the final part ("Restitutions") of *The Truth in Painting.*

However, what is finally most noteworthy about the "lemmata" that one might logically presume to lie enclosed within the half-crochets that regularly punctuate Derrida's book is the fact that they consist of nothing more than blank space. In his text, one half-crochet appears at the end of an empty line, then, following some blank lines, a mirror image of the same mark appears at the beginning of a new line. His half-crochets point less to a lemma than to the abyss of difference produced by a lemma, to a process of negotiation of abyssal textual spaces that we might nickname by means of the neologistic gerund *lemming*. For Derrida's commentary is in fact an analysis of an absence, the absence of any rigorous philosophical discourse on the frame in Kant. The headwords by Kant on the frame that one might, according to Derrida's logic, expect to serve as the basis for a discussion of the Third Critique, cannot be found in the Enlightenment philosopher's writings.

One could even advance the hypothesis that, by means of Derrida's diacritical caprices, the half-crochets or symbolic frames that one might ordinarily expect to enclose the written text and allow for separations to be made between each fragment are in fact turned inside out, rendered abyssal, such that the reader is called upon to view this text the

way she might imagine a series of paintings with frames that "face" outwards, whose corners have had their means of support dislocated from
them; paintings exposed in all their vulnerability to what lies outside
them, flimsily or impossibly held together by the four imaginary apices
of the open half-crochets; as if the frame had been divided in four and
its corners flipped inwards to meet at the "center." For it is just such a
deconstruction of the frame, its chiastic dispersal or "reconstitution" as
an x or $+$ that occupies and erases the center of the work, that Derrida will propose, especially in his piece on Adami's paintings ("+R").
Either that, or its "replacement" by a lacing effect, a "frame" gone all
soft and pliable and made to function by being sewn in through the
front and out through the back of the canvas, like the laces of the shoes
in van Gogh, such as Derrida will ask us to imagine by the end of his
book. That deconstructive faultline is visible in the open corner of every
one of the half-crochets appearing throughout "Parergon," in the imper-
fect joint that reduces these typographical extravagances from being the
solid supports of a self-enclosed artistic object to the simple (though never
single) lines, brushstrokes, *traits*, traces or marks whose essential dehiscence and disseminative drift he has been drawing attention to since he
began writing.

What I am trying to emphasize in the final analysis is the very graphic
effect of the archaic diacritical marks appearing in Derrida's text. It is
these half-crochets, and the spaces they mark out, that constitute perhaps
the most explicit example of the figural in Derrida's writing. I say "in
Derrida's writing," in contrast to the paintings by others – Cranach,
Fantuzzi, Robert, Caron, Goya, Adami, Titus-Carmel, van Gogh – that,
as one might expect, illustrate or exemplify what *The Truth in Painting*
"says." Those aesthetic objects are not "in" his text in the same way
that these diacritical marks are. The drawings, paintings, and sculptures
that are reproduced side by side with what he writes do not inscribe its
radical heterogeneity – even if, in the case of Adami's works, they are
the very exemplar of it[8] – in the same way that these foreign, discarded,
archaic marks of punctuation do. But the idea of radical heterogeneity is
the first principle of Derrida's relation to the art object, just as, as I shall
shortly explain, it is his first principle *tout court*. He sees a painting not just
surrounded but "invaded" by discourse and writing; and, conversely,
a writing, any writing, constituted by the two senses of the graphic,
the semantico-syntactic, and the figuro-pictorial. The minimal trace of
this – yet its effects are incommensurable – is the space in and around
letters and words, the very visuality that necessarily gives those linguistic

elements some sort of aesthetic sense simultaneous with their coming to meaning. The graphicality of language is the condition of possibility, for example, of poetry, epitomized by Mallarmé's *Un coup de dés*, a constant Derridean reference. In order to account for such a spatio-linguistic function Derrida's analyses of writing often concentrate on the syntactic as a troubling as well as a reinforcement of the semantic, the means by which the self-extensions of language as the graphic other of the scriptural come into play as both a cohesive and disruptive force.

Nowhere is this more obvious than in that pivotal work in Derrida's corpus that is the 1974 text, *Glas*.[9] Not that *Glas* was the first time he formalized, as it were pictorially, the work of a double writing, for various earlier pieces such as "Tympan" (in *Margins*) or the reading of Mallarmé in "The Double Session" (*Dissemination*) similarly foregrounded the play of textual configurations. But in *Glas* the spatio-syntactic relation between two columns of writing, the fact of their juxtaposition, apposition or opposition, gives rise to troubling and provocative semantic networks, primarily between Hegel and Genet. Furthermore, by means of a series of judas (read "JD") holes, one is privy, as in a primal scene, to a visual deployment of autobiographical or signatory effects. And nowhere is Derrida's writing more graphic, in every sense of the word, for one of the main figures that *Glas* explicitly draws out for the reader, by means of those two columns, is that of a double erection, of the tumescences and detumescences of what he terms a play of *bande/contrebande*.[10] *The Truth in Painting*, published in French four years after *Glas*, is to some extent written in the shadow of those columns, such that Derrida's "outing" – thanks to Genet – of Hegel's absolute knowledge, at least implicitly performed in the earlier text, is shown to have its parallel in the spatial and conceptual inversion that gives rise to the subsequent analysis of Kant's incongruous parergonal columns. *Glas* sets the scene at the beginning of "Lemmata" when Derrida quotes himself from the 1974 text and asks us to "imagine the damage caused by a theft which robbed you only of your frames, or rather of their joints, and of any possibility of reframing your valuables or art-objects" (*TIP*, 18).

The effects of a language as spacing, and the grammatico-figural effects of such a spacing, come into focus again in the last essay of *The Truth in Painting*. In "Restitutions," Derrida's "defense" of Heidegger against Schapiro comes down, to some extent at least, to the role played by a comma. Derrida is analyzing Heidegger's sentence "Van Gogh's painting is the disclosure of what the product, the pair of peasant's shoes, is in truth," and the ambiguity between the painting as product, and the shoes as object within the painting, that arises from Heidegger's appositional gloss. The discussion – Derrida's essay takes the form of a polylogue of a number of voices[11] – goes like this:

– Your refinement around the syntax of "the product, the pair of shoes" seemed incredible to me. So everything would be played out in the suspense of this apposition, on the point of a comma between "the product" and "the pair," this pause setting down the pair a little to one side of the product, of a slightly longer interval between the two words.
– what is the size [*pointure*] of a comma?
– It isn't a matter of a temporal interval between two, of which one is "pair," but of this syntactic fact that "the pair" is in apposition, doubling the product, with a doubling that is nonetheless narrowing, stricter, straighter (the product, *here for example*, the pair). So the space of *this* painting is assigned by the *pointure* of the comma which *itself*, as comma, like a shoe, never says anything. (*TIP*, 326)

It would be tempting to stop on this comma and go no further than this extract from "Restitutions" in order to develop all I have to say regarding Derrida's figural graphism, his painterly writing. One could start with the proliferation of italics, unfinished sentences, and interrupted dialogue; move on to the punning on "*pointure*" – what is the point of a comma? what is the *periodicity* of a comma? what is the sharpness of a comma? – that has the reader see writing as a series of trompe-l'oeil effects. All that would have to be dealt with before one came to analyze what the text says in relation to Heidegger's essay, and his use of punctuation, before one came to the stability or instability of the figural forms that constitute the shoes in van Gogh's painting.[12] As a result, one might try to distract attention from the choice between peasant clodhoppers (for Heidegger) or city-dweller brogues (for Schapiro) that is the controversy motivating the whole discussion. Instead, following Heidegger's step into ambiguous syntax, these shoes might suddenly be transformed, by the apposition and comparison of, on the one hand (or foot), a mentioned, then a used comma, and, on the other, a shoe – "as comma, like a shoe" – into something resembling the slippers with exorbitant curled-up toes worn by a mythological dancer in the court of an ancient satrap (as evocatively orientalist as a Maori tattoo). For the comma, "framed" or contextualized thus by Derrida's commentary, becomes the mark of that pause or interval by means of which space doubles as writing, or conversely the means by which language devolves upon the arabesque, those chiastic functions of what we call the graphic being for him the whole aesthetic gambit.

From this point of view the matter of the aesthetic necessarily returns to a question of the framing of space, and it cannot but be related to the space, or spacing that constitutes every mark as "iterable." This is the principle of radical recontextualization that Derrida develops in *Limited Inc.*[13] Once one accepts that sense "moves" in order to function, and Derrida insists that there must be such a break with the intactness of a self-presence in order for there to be any meaning whatsoever – a play of sense rather than some impossibly ideal immediate and permanent transparency of meaning – then limiting the extent of that "movement" or spacing becomes an insoluble problem or question. From this point of view language and meaning take place as a form of rupture; they occur over an abyss. Structurally, they represent the same sort of impossible but necessary bridge that Kant unwittingly identified in configuring his Critiques. This means that language and meaning are forever in the business of contextualization, which also means they are forever in the business of framing, framing an abyss; in the business of *lemming*. That framing or bridging is what permits something to make sense rather than operate as the freefloating drift of signification; but the very same, and necessary law of the abyss that opens the play of meaning, makes ascribing limits to it ultimately impossible. At the outside – an "outside" that cannot be defined or delimited – there is in fact that sort of freefloating drift that the law of context seeks to prevent. In Derrida's terms, no context is saturable (*Limited Inc.*, 12). The frame of linguistic meaning is, therefore, as unstable as that of a work of art, or rather, the unsettling effects – wordplay, the borders of nonsense – that are supposed to be peripheral, even exterior to the real business of meaning, are in fact structurally intertwined, laced throughout the most basic functions of language. If, as Derrida says, logically extending language's structural instability, every linguistic unit is capable of being taken out of its context and reinserted in a different one, then every word is subject to the rearrangement of elements that goes by the name of the *anagram*. The idea of the anagram returns us to the aesthetic or graphic in language, the painterly if you wish, for it has letters dancing before our eyes, words taking on new shape and form.

Derrida seems to be aware of this in the approach(es) he takes in his analysis of Kant. Following the latter's paradoxical logic of a beauty that is derived from the disinterest of pleasure, he declares himself enjoined on the one hand to obey Kant's argument on its own terms, to follow it (*"je la suis"*). But on the other hand he will necessarily stray from that argument, turning it to his own purposes, changing its apparent order, drawing it away from itself or "seducing" it (*"je la séduis"* (*TIP*, 43) (indeed, "duction" in general will be a focus of the third essay in *The Truth in Painting*, that on work by Gérard Titus-Carmel):

How to treat this book [*The Critique of Judgement*]. Is it a book. What would make a book of it. What is it to read this book. How to take it. Have I the right to say that it is beautiful. And first of all the right to ask myself that

⌐
∟   for example the question of order. A spa-
tial, so-called plastic, art does not necessarily prescribe an order of reading. I can move around in front of it, start from the top or the bottom, sometimes walk around it.

. . .

   But a book. And a book of philosophy. If it is a book of metaphysics in the Kantian sense, hence a book of pure philosophy, one can in principle enter it from any point: it is a sort of architecture . . . one ought to be able to begin anywhere and follow any order. (*TIP*, 49–50)

In the context that Derrida's discussion has by this point established, that of frames, of the shape of a discourse, of a text like *Glas*, of insertions and interruptions that disturb the tranquil integrity of a work, and more specifically here the question of order, the possibility of intervening to change the order, one may, in turn, read his "seduction" of Kant's critique in more than one way. Since what necessarily occurs, on his account, is a type of corruption of the syntagmatic integrity of the Kantian argument, one is tempted to read in the verb *je séduis* its own improbable anagram, namely the neologism *je désuis*. That might mean "I de-follow" or "I un-follow," or "I subject Kant's logic to a throw of the dice (*un coup de dés*)"; or again, "I insert into it the disruptive effects of a fragment of my own signature (*un coup de D*)." The signature, after all, represents the whole gambit of the frame; in a painting it is normally juxtaposed to, and draws the eye towards the frame. It acts as an opening in or an incursion upon the pure pictorial integrity of a work of art that threatens to rewrite the lines of force of the visual field; it is the anagrammaticalizing force par excellence, acting as a "drive" [*pulsion*] produced within the "whole field of historical, economic [and] political inscription" (61) that begins with the wall on which the work of art is hung, and that the frame, naively conceived, purports to keep separate from it.
   The anagrammatical possibility also weighs upon the principle of mimetic representation whose theoretical assurance would preserve the

integrity of the work just as surely as the frame seeks to do in physical terms. The presumption that the content of the work derives from the world outside in a form of one-to-one correspondence means that the frame is just a frame, an insubstantial structure that fades into insignificance to allow an automatic commerce to take place between the inside and outside of the work. If what is within the frame really reflects what is outside it then there really is no frame, or so the argument of analogical mimesis would go. In *The Truth in Painting* the matter of mimesis is given only passing mention, for it is the focus of an earlier essay on Kant's *Critique*, "Economimesis," that analyzes the management and domestication of signification by means of mimetic representation. And indeed, in that essay Derrida again disrupts, or should we say *derails* the logical order of Kant's discourse on taste (*le goût*) by pointing to what it presumes yet circumvents, namely the most literal sense of taste that passes via the olfactory, and by extension everything relating to *le dégoût* ("disgust"). It will be through the idea of what taste cannot stomach (*le vomi*) that a more violently authentic articulation between inside and outside will come to be understood.

Thus the deconstruction of *analogical* mimesis involves, implicitly if nothing else, a detour through the *anagrammatical* possibility (there could be no more graphic form of anagrammatical return and confusion than vomit), for the presumed transparency of mimetic representation comes thereby to be rearranged or reconfigured according to a logic of spacing and of inscription.

* * *

Keeping the inside in and the outside out, the frame is inevitably double: "according to the logic of the supplement, the parergon is divided in two. At the limit between work and absence of work, it divides in two" (*TIP*, 64). But the division of space that materializes in a particular form in the frame is, of course, only the outside effect of an iterability that infects the pictorial field as much as the scriptural, of an originary heterogeneity that is revealed in the simplest trace, line or brushstroke, in everything that is drawn; in the condition of possibility of drawing that Derrida refers to as the *trait*:

it is never common, nor even one, with and without itself. Its divisibility founds texts, traces and remains . . . A trait never appears, never itself, because it marks the difference between the forms or the contents of the appearing. A trait never appears, never itself, never for a first time. It begins by retrac(t)ing [*se retirer*].

I follow here the logical succession of what I long ago called, before getting around to the turn of painting, the *broaching* [entame] of the origin: that which opens, with a trace, without initiating anything. (*TIP*, 11)

If one were to posit anything like an architectonics of Derridean philo-sophical discourse, one would have to argue that whether it is a matter of aesthetics, politics or ethics, access to it is consistently articulated across this threshold concept of the trait as a function of iterability. In these terms the 1971 essay, "Signature event context," appears dissemina-tively seminal, that is to say inscribing its law of heterogeneity in chiastic intersections across a wide variety of texts.[14] One finds it traversing *The Truth in Painting* by means of the references made in the preface to ques-tions of speech act theory, to Cézanne's "promise" to tell the "truth in painting," to the possibility of a pictorial performative, a painting act. In fact that preface was presumably written about the time (1977) Derrida was following up on the English translation of "Signature event con-text" and becoming involved in the debate with Searle, work now pub-lished together in *Limited Inc*. It is perhaps significant, therefore, that what Derrida goes on to develop as the "emblem" for the *topos* of the trait, in his preface to *The Truth in Painting*, is, as the title of that preface makes explicit, the passe-partout. Not a masterkey so much as the variable and multiple template or mat, the mobile frame within a frame that doubles the surface of the work in a play of planes and perspectives. Starting, as he says, long ago, and leading to the seemingly very different con-cerns of his more recent work, Derrida has consistently drawn on the logic of iterability to address, always from a different perspective and in a different format, the structural and conceptual aporias that that logic gives rise to. As he states in the interview appended to the English reprint of the Searle debate, subtitled "Toward an Ethic of Discussion," "iterability is at once that which tends to attain plenitude and that which bars access to it . . . iterability retains a value of generality that covers the totality of what one can call experience or the relation to something in general" (*Limited Inc.*, 129). As a result, "questions of right, of morality and of politics" come to be "inscribed in an exchange of arguments that is ostensibly so limited, even academic and 'micrological,' concerning the structure of speech acts, of intentionality, of citation, of metaphor, of writing and of the signature, of philosophy and of literature" (ibid., 112). Given this generalizing impulse to iterability, called in other con-texts "undecidability," given that it applies as much to "right, morality and politics" as to the "integrity" of a work of art, are we to interpret as a chance anagrammatical effect, or a logical necessity, the fact that we can read an "e-t-h-i-c-s," albeit in a form that would have to be seduced out of its own framework, within the lexical bounds of an aest-h-e-t-i-c-s? What would it mean to relate, in such an intimate if contorted, should we say "perverse," way, two domains of thinking that are usually held to be poles apart (except of course when they come into contact)? What I am saying here is on one level this: the aesthetical or aestheticizing gesture often pretends to be able to bracket out of consideration matters of, say politics or ethics; it claims often to be apolitical or anethical, art for art's sake alone. But critical evaluation of such a gesture will generally find it to be less apolitical or anethical than representative of an ethics of bad faith or of a conservative politics. A double paradox is in operation: politics and ethics follow aesthetics in the latter's retreat from politics and ethics; and the discourse of politics and ethics, rejecting aesthetics for its abstraction from political and ethical questions, nevertheless seeks to reclaim it as a legitimate domain for those very questions, to redeem aesthetics by relinking it to the political and ethical. This therefore brings us back to a problematic of framing, one that is not well served by a classical conception of the frame as unanalyzed separation between two interiorities, or between an interiority and an exteriority. I suggest that the relation between aesthetics and ethics is in fact more like the sort of abyssal involution that allows one to find an anagram of one functioning within the other.

As we have seen, and as Derrida does not let us forget, the abyss (and bridging the abyss) was very much Kant's initial problem in the Third Critique. The introduction to Kant's essay may be said to be framed by the abyss, at its beginning and at its end. First, between sensible and supersensible "there is a great gulf fixed, so that it is not possible to pass from the former to the latter" but "the latter is *meant* to influence the former... There must, therefore, be a ground of the *unity* of the supersensible that lies at the basis of nature" (*Critique*, 14). And again later: "the realm of the concept of nature ... and that of the concept of freedom ... are completely cut off from all reciprocal influence ... by [a] broad gulf... It is not possible to throw a bridge from one realm to the other. – Yet ... [the faculty of judgment] provides us with the mediating concept between concepts of nature and concepts of freedom" (37–38). Kant's concept of the gulf is thus that of an abyss that fails to deal with its own abyssality, that will consequently be drawn down into it by the mobile and transformative frame, or the contortions of its own argument. Or, if you wish, the dividing or framing line between nature and freedom is subdivided, self-dividing to make room for judgment. This is no simple ground of unity or bridge but an aporetic or undecidable abyssal enfolding that involves a rewriting of relations of difference. In Derrida's analysis, Kant's Third Critique cannot simply bridge the abyss or provide a middle ground between reason and understanding; the sort of passe-partout it seeks to provide for the two philosophical constructions between which it is situated finds itself *mis en abîme*; drawn back into the abyss it is designed to reduce once the frame that it is attempts to deal with matters parergonal. This means that judgment cannot be the external framework for nature on one side and freedom on the other without also functioning as something internally necessary to each. Now only the most general structural comparison can be drawn between nature and freedom as systematically developed in Kant's Critiques, and the aesthetic and ethical questions that are given explicit treatment in one of Derrida's texts or another. But, I would argue, it is according to the same logic of abyssally enfolded difference analyzed via Kant that the iterability that Derrida identifies through the spacing functions of language and, within the domains of aesthetics and the plastic arts, in the heterogeneous self-divisions of the frame and the signature is again brought explicitly to the surface as the aporia of undecidability that orients important discussions of the political and ethical.

Space will allow me to enter into only one detail of those discussions, one which, however, relates most closely to the emphasis I have already given to Derrida's deconstruction of the frame. I refer to the question of order and what I have previously called the *anagrammatical* effect of iterability, by means of which every utterance, in being repeated, is resituated, recontextualized, and rearranged. That structural potential for rearrangement, not knowing in advance how it will next appear, is what makes for the "undecidable," what we might take as the ethical form of the aesthetic "iterable" were it not that Derrida's logic shows such a distinction to be reductive. In terms of the frame, iterability can be understood as a type of torsion that inverts the foursquare surround to the work and reinscribes it as chiastic lines of force internally traversing and exceeding its supposed self-enclosed content. It allows for the radically heterogeneous reconfiguration of elements staged by the centrifugal effect of the signature, the proper name melting into brushstrokes as it hovers on the edge of the canvas. Iterability "begins" as the minimal *différance* that permits signification to function at all, breaching undifferentiated sameness to permit articulation, but which, laced throughout each level of articulation or the successive configurations of context, exceeds any given context's "desire" for saturability. What I wish to underline here is that the anagrammaticalizing torsion of iterability inverts a logic that might appear to ensue from its destabilizing effects. Whereas one might be tempted to read in it, and in undecidability, the abdication of the responsible use of language – "if meaning cannot be confined to the context it wishes to be confined to, then one might as well say anything; if undecidability can never be reduced, then nothing can be said *decisively*" – in fact, as Derrida has made explicit on any number of occasions, the opposite (or a type of opposite) is true. For example, in "Afterword: Toward an Ethic of Discussion," Gerald Graff to some extent represents those caricatures of deconstruction that have been borrowed by any number of Derrida's detractors, from abusively reductivist journalistic characterizations to the serious tones of a philosopher like John Searle. As Derrida's replies to Graff's questions make clear, far from preventing decision, undecidability allows for it:

[the] undecidable opens the field of decision or of decidability. It calls for decision in the order of ethical-political responsibility. It is even its necessary condition. A decision can only come into being in a space that exceeds the calculable program that would destroy all responsibility by transforming it into a programmable effect of determinate causes. There can be no moral or political responsibility without this trial and this passage by way of the undecidable. (*Limited Inc.*, 116)

Once the concept of decision is understood to reside within the space of possibility opened by iterability – no decision without the opening towards decidability that constitutes undecidability, just as there is no meaning without the opening towards an uncontrollable drift of meaning – then the well-posed and firmly constructed frame that decision is supposed to place around the event of decidability, cutting it off, bringing it to a close (in French a judicial decision is an *arrêt*, a decree that stops discussion), becomes subject to the conceptual torsion or anagrammatical reversal that I am outlining here.[15]

In a later essay, "Force of Law," Derrida will similarly advance the iterable or undecidable as the condition of possibility of justice, of a justice that exceeds the mechanical application of law:

I think that there is no justice without this experience, however impossible it may be, of aporia. Justice is an experience of the impossible . . . Every time that something comes to pass or turns out well, every time that we placidly apply a good rule to a particular case . . . we can be sure that law (*droit*) may find itself accounted for, but certainly not justice . . . Law is the element of calculation, and it is just that there be law, but justice is incalculable, it requires us to calculate with the incalculable; and aporetic experiences are the experiences, as improbable as they are necessary, of justice.[16]

and in concluding with three examples of aporias, he repeatedly underlines the affirmative force of undecidability in terms similar to those just cited:

The undecidable, a theme often associated with deconstruction . . . is not merely the oscillation of the tension between two decisions; it is the experience of that which, though heterogeneous, foreign to the order of the calculable and the rule, is still obliged . . . to give itself up to the impossible decision, while taking account of law and rules. A decision that didn't go through the ordeal of the undecidable would not be a free decision, it would only be the programmable application or unfolding of a calculable process. It might be legal, it would not be just. ("Force of Law," 24)

The passage through the aporia of the iterable or undecidable[17] is thus marked by the surprise of a sort of conceptual anagram, reversing the terms (but in such a way as to permanently displace them) of what might appear as a logical insistence. It is therefore no surprise to find an experience of the ethical abyss in Derrida's work that parallels yet rewrites his analysis of the parergonal abyss in Kant's aesthetics.

The judicial and ethical aporia or experience of the impossibility that, Derrida argues, is the condition of possibility of justice is examined in more than one recent essay in terms of the extreme situation represented by the story of Abraham's sacrifice of his son Isaac.[18] There, responding to or answering a call from one competing necessity, God, means turning one's back on an equally pressing priority, that of kinship. In Derrida's reading this is less a religious quandary than the staging of the dilemma of every human relation and indeed every relation to another: in being responsible towards one individual, one other being, one automatically and necessarily neglects all the other others. Nor is it the same dilemma as that between the individual and common good, for Derrida is talking about the infinity of every possible other individual relation. Building on the work of Emmanuel Levinas, Derrida has expressed this aporia by means of the formulation "*tout autre est tout autre*," which can mean "every other is every other" (every one is equally "worthy") as well as "every other is wholly other" (it is only in recognizing another in his/her utter difference that one can begin to relate to him/her).

In many ways there could not, therefore, be a more graphic representation of the abyss than in terms of this gulf of utter difference that separates one being from another, yet that abyss is held to be the basis of every possible relation. It is only by keeping utter otherness in play that, for example, relations can be developed on the basis of forms of mutual human respect rather than succumb to loyalties based primarily on kinship, race, sex, or indeed class, profession, and so on, any of the common ties that can be shown to have caused enmities and conflicts, even genocides, throughout history. In a sort of converse configuration of the problematic of the frame in aesthetics, where the painting traditionally sought to exist as a pure interiority containing a meaning that could nevertheless be at the same time separated from yet accessed by the exteriority that surrounded it, the relation between beings can only be articulated through this abyss of utter exteriority or otherness. Now of course it would be reductive to assimilate a being to a painting, to claim that the relation between two beings is anything like that between a painting and the wall that surrounds it, or even like that between the painting and a spectator observing it, although, as I shall discuss in conclusion, something of a structural comparison does hold. What is clear, however, is that the gulf of utter otherness between beings is abyssal in the same way that Derrida shows a frame to be.

That is so in the first place simply because, as I have already explained, however impossible this might seem, the abyss necessarily remains the space of a relation and a form of negotiation; otherwise there is no relation. Wherever there is the abyss there is framing of the abyss, there is *lemming*. Conversely, unless the two elements of the relation are, in the final analysis, wholly other one with respect to the other, there is no relation (of difference) either, just undifferentiated sameness. The abyss is thus the space of an aporetic difference; everything hinges on how it is framed. But, in the second place, this deconstruction of the space of difference – like that of the frame supposed to separate inside from out – does not create abyssal effects as it were within the space "between" the elements of the relation without also bearing upon the integrity of those very elements. The utter otherness of the relation between beings thus calls into question, rearranges, and anagrammaticalizes the very being and status of those beings. That this is so becomes clear when Derrida analyzes the relation between human and animal in his recent essay, "L'animal que donc je suis" ["The Animal That Therefore I Am"]. He begins by stating the uneasiness he feels faced with a cat looking at him naked and goes on to raise a series of questions concerning the presumed distinctions made by the philosophical tradition (Aristotle, Descartes, Kant, Heidegger, Levinas, and Lacan are his principal examples) between man and animal based on knowledge of nakedness (and thus good and evil), rationality, language, priority, and so on. And, in the sort of conceptually anagrammatical move that I have been drawing attention to, he plays on the French homonym "*je suis*" that means both "I am" and "I follow" to reverse and displace the hierarchical relation that has consistently relegated the animal to second place and, with a rapidly accelerating pace beginning about two centuries ago, led to a treatment of animals raised for human consumption that would, to say the least, be incomprehensibly shocking to preceding generations. And the scandal of that relation begins with the enormous presumption of an opposition between a single species (man) and every other one of the millions of other living species reduced to a single denomination (the animal). Thus the animal that, in Descartes, and his successors' terms, I, as thinking human, am therefore not – *je pense donc je (ne) suis (pas un animal)* – becomes for Derrida both the animal that he recognizes himself to be and that which, in an anagrammatical reordering of the philosophical tradition, he recognizes himself as following or coming after. *L' animal que donc je suis* here means "the animal that therefore I am (following)."

From this point of view the animal – for example the cat that is not shy about following one into the bathroom – exists in the abyss of a particularly differential otherness. Different from the sameness of another human yet also different from the incommensurable other of an inanimate object, its gaze serves to undermine the ontological security of the human animal that so confidently distinguishes itself from it. The cat appears as something like a passe-partout occupying, and framing, a median space between human animality and the inanimate.[19] It is therefore perhaps no accident that, as Derrida notes, the animal figures in his own writings "gain in insistence and visibility, become active, swarm, mobilize and get motivated, move and become moved more and more as my texts become more explicitly autobiographical [he will later say 'zootobiographical']."[20] As if the conceptual recognition, not to say exploitation, of an animal other necessarily called into question the scriptural assurance or detachment of the third person, called for the first person of an autobiographical writing. Or conversely, as if in giving oneself over to the framing, iterabilizing, or exiling of self and of ontology that is constituted by an autobiography, one necessarily awakened in oneself a consciousness of one's fellow animals. For if, as the lesson of iterability also teaches us, every writing is testamentary, then the particular staging of one's own obituary that is an autobiography might well be expected to bring one face to face with one's animal and mortal nakedness.

Among the creatures from his work that Derrida lists in "The Animal
That Therefore I Am" are Kant's horse, birds, and crustaceans, as well
as the fish of "+R" (the second essay of *The Truth in Painting*), which,
with its *ichtus* cut and pasted as *ich*, and anagrammaticalized as *chi*, could
well read as the most fertile nexus of relations among framing, animals,
and autobiography of any of his writings. The drawing, by an Adami
inspired by and quoting from *Glas*, of a fish hooked and emerging from the
water, is analyzed by Derrida as the figuration of a play or competition
of his signatures, signatures that Adami also draws on the surface of
the work. It brings to mind the law of the countersignature that, for
Derrida, constitutes the work of art in institutional terms.[21] The work is
countersigned, of course, when a museum pays for it and hangs it in its
gallery; but it is also countersigned by being recognized or endorsed by
a viewer (who may or may not depend on the institution of the museum
in signing on to that recognition). The countersignature is thus a type of
supplementary frame – there is never ever a single frame, such is the law
of the passe-partout – that is placed like an institutional blessing upon
the work by the spectator and that takes place in the abyss of difference
separating the viewer from it. Not a recognition of or response to the same
wholly other that is involved in the relation of one human with another;
nor of the different wholly other that is the recognition of or response to
another animal; but nevertheless an articulation of otherness by means
of an iterative framing of the abyss of difference, for, repeating Derrida,
"iterability retains a value of generality that covers the totality of what
one can call experience or the relation to something in general" (*Limited
Inc.*, 129). Furthermore, it is an articulation that is not without ontological
risk, however negligible that might seem. Countersigning means writing
one's name as it were on the work, even if by proxy, performing some
sort of autobiographical, and thus testamentary or obituary function. In
doing the work the favor of according it institutional status, endorsing
it, the spectator also cedes something of himself or herself to it, steps
somewhat or somehow into the frame of it, enters into a relation with it,
falls into the abyss. Yet we have seen that every frame reframes both of the
"entities" it separates and joins. Thus, we should also look for a converse
of that sort of partial signing of one's name within the ambit of the work of
art, a converse to the way in which the spectator in effect bleeds into the
work, something from within the frame that extends outside it to connect
across the abyss of distinction that is also the space of its relation with the
viewer. Derrida proposes a figure for that in "Restitutions," in the laces
that weave in and out of the van Gogh shoes and, he supposes, in and out

of the canvas itself; configuring thereby a particularly innovative form of framing. Tellingly, that lacing "begins," on the canvas itself, by encircling the space of van Gogh's signature, reinforcing the corporeal provenance of the work of art. For the mark of the proper name represents the imprint of a singular body and reestablishes the structure of the aesthetic as an articulation that implies, to some extent at least, a relation between the body of the artist and the body of the spectator.

Thus in seeking to identify some means by which, in a form of "response" to the countersignature bestowed upon the work by its spectator, or in a reciprocal reframing of ontological relations, the work extends outside itself, we might propose something like a tattoo, an inscription on the body of the viewer, a work of art engraved upon the visage. The tattoo already encountered in Kant is not exactly drawn from that perspective, yet it does, in spite of itself, raise questions about the frame. It is an example of a dependent beauty, banished outside the framework of free beauties by the fact of its attachment to the human: "A figure might be beautiful with all manner of flourishes and light but regular lines, as is done by the New Zealanders with their tattooing, were we dealing with anything but the figure of a human being" (*Critique*, 73). A design *à la grecque* qualifies, as does a design of foliage on a frame, but not the tattoo on the frame of a Maori body. I shall not repeat here the obvious questions about such categories that, as I have already developed, are the basis of Derrida's analysis in *The Truth in Painting*. For me, however, it is precisely such a tattoo effect that, in a disseminative de-/recontextualization of the object of contemplation, gets imprinted upon the spectator in every experience of the aesthetic. From the beginning, still at the end. Hence, an abyss apart from the cultural practices of native New Zealanders, existing nevertheless in a complex set of relations with them, I sit in my father's living room with the light from moving images flickering its changing momentary imprint upon my face, content, I imagine, to cast a detached aesthetic gaze upon the wonders of nature unfolding before my eyes, now parrots, hummingbirds, birds of paradise, now lemming, entrancing and drawing me inexorably closer and closer to the edge, of everything, of every given frame, in lockstep inscrutable animal logic that obviously understands more than I ever could, about life and death for instance, about life–death that, as Derrida suggests,[22] everything has yet to be learned and relearned, teeming and advancing to the very edge that seems not to be perceived as an edge, just the commencement of another falling, a different case of the frame, a turn in the disseminative warp, the space of lemming, noun and gerund, animal otherness and reframed function of being and becoming abyssal, they fall and splash out of sight, out of the frame of aesthetic contemplation and ethical comprehension, into the quandary of an unfathomable martyrdom, holocaust or hecatomb, our names for it cannot sound the utter conceptual and ethical otherness of it, yet this much is clear, it is only over that edge and in that abyss, in the adventure to come where the frame gets unhinged and the relations redrawn, only from that perspective and in the necessary and impossible thinking of such an abyss, in short via such lemming, that aesthetics and ethics can even begin.

NOTES

1 Jacques Derrida, *The Truth in Painting*, trans. Geoff Bennington and Ian McLeod (Chicago and London: University of Chicago Press, 1987). Hereafter referenced in the text as *TIP*.

2 Immanuel Kant, *The Critique of Judgement*, trans. James Creed Meredith (Oxford: Clarendon Press, 1973), 69. Hereafter referenced in the text as *Critique*.

3 See my *Prosthesis* (Stanford: Stanford University Press, 1995), 106–13.

4 §16 (Analytic of the Beautiful, Third Moment): "Much might be added to a building that would immediately please the eye, were it not intended for a church. A figure might be beautified with all manner of flourishes and light but regular lines, as is done by the New Zealanders with their tattooing, were we dealing with anything but the figure of a human being." §26 (Analytic of the Sublime): "This explains Savary's observations in his account of Egypt, that in order to get the full emotional effect of the size of the Pyramids we must avoid coming too near . . . The same explanation may also sufficiently account for the bewilderment, or sort of perplexity, which, as is said, seizes the visitor on first entering St. Peter's in Rome" (*Critique*, 73, 99–100).

5 See, for example, Immanuel Kant, *Prolegomena to Any Future Metaphysics*, trans. and ed. Gary Hatfield (Cambridge: Cambridge University Press, 1997), in particular 104–11.

6 The extent to which the Third Critique concerns the work of art is, of course, open to question, given the "superiority which natural beauty has over that of art" (*Critique*, 158). As Gilles Deleuze remarks: "he who leaves a museum to turn toward the beauties of nature deserves [Kant's] respect," Gilles Deleuze, *Kant's Critical Philosophy: The Doctrine of the Faculties*, trans. Hugh Tomlinson and Barbara Habberjam (London: Athlone Press, 1984), 56. The work of art necessarily "presupposes an end" (173) that will relegate it to the category of dependent beauties like the tattoo, in spite of the status of free beauty given to the foliage on a frame.

7 M. B. Parkes, *Pause and Effect: An Introduction to the History of Punctuation in the West* (London: Scolar Press, 1992), 53.

8 Among Adami's drawings are a series of *Studies for a Drawing after* Glas that include complicated framing effects within the drawings, quotations from *Glas*, and even imitation (or forgery) of Derrida's handwriting and signature.

9 Here and elsewhere I refer to the dates of the original French publications.

10 Cf. Fr. *bander*, to have an erection.

11 We are told in the "lemmatic" note opening the essay that there are "n + 1 – female – voices" (256), the undecidability of the number, and the gender of the voices rendering the differences, both graphic and spatial, among them, abysmally multiple.

12 The unsympathetic interpretation would be that Heidegger falls into the same trap as Schapiro in allowing for the slippage by means of which an object can simply be taken out of a painting and attributed to its rightful owner. The sympathetic interpretation would be that Heidegger recognizes a permeability of the frame and, as it were, weaves his discursive logic in and out of the work of art.

13 "By virtue of its essential iterability, a written syntagma [earlier: "the traits that can be recognized in the classical, narrowly defined concept of writing, are generalizable"] can always be detached from the chain in which it is inserted or given without causing it to lose all possibility of functioning," Jacques Derrida, *Limited Inc.* (Evanston: Northwestern University Press, 1988), 9.

14 "The X (the chiasmus) (which can always, hastily, be thought of as the thematic drawing of dissemination)," "Hors livre," in *Dissemination*, quoted in *TIP*, 166.

15 One might read the deconstructive enterprise in general, in its most "classic" sense of an inversion and displacement of hierarchies such as that between speech and writing, in terms of the same idea of conceptual anagrammatical torsion. Any number of commonplace ideas about deconstruction, relying on and repeating the logocentric gestures Derrida attempts to displace, can be seen to have things quite back-to-front. See, for a recent example, Derrida's assertion that *différance*, far from encouraging delay and suspense, underscores urgency (Jacques Derrida and Bernard Stiegler, *Echographies, de la télévision* [Paris: Galilée-INA, 1996], 18); or this close historical case: during the Clinton impeachment hearings, Monica Lewinsky was praised for speaking straightforwardly and not giving in to the "deconstructions" of language that Clinton supposedly indulged in. The unspoken logic was as follows: Clinton can be called a deconstructionist, because he uses language loosely; since he doesn't believe language means what it says, he can distort it. Deconstructionists can tell lies because they hold language to be iterable, meaning to be undecidable. Let us reverse, or anagrammaticalize that logic: it is only because language is iterable, which means that lies are structurally indistinguishable from truth, only "because of deconstruction," therefore, that honesty can be a virtue. If the words a liar uttered immediately identified themselves as untrue, truth and untruth, and hence honesty and dishonesty, would be transparently apparent facts of language. There

would be no virtue in them, nothing to be gained from encouraging one rather than the other.

16 Jacques Derrida, "Force of Law: the 'Mystical Foundation of Authority'," in Drucilla Cornell, Michel Rosenfeld and David Gray Carlson, eds., *Deconstruction and the Possibility of Justice* (New York: Routledge, 1992), 16.

17 As Derrida explains, it is never simply a matter of a passage through the aporia to a "post-aporetic" space, for we are dealing with structural effects: "The ordeal of the undecidable that I just said must be gone through by any decision worthy of the name is never past or passed." Thus the undecidable is less a moment and more an uncanny doubling or haunting: "The undecidable remains caught, lodged, at least as a ghost – but an essential ghost – in every decision, in every event of decision" (24).

18 See, for example, his *The Gift of Death*, trans. David Wills (Chicago: University of Chicago Press, 1995), and "La Littérature au secret," in *Donner la mort* (Paris: Galilée, 1999), as well as "L'animal que donc je suis," in Marie-Louise Mallet, ed., *L'Animal autobiographique* (Paris: Galilée, 1998), translation forthcoming in *Critical Inquiry* Winter 2001.

19 It should not be presumed that within differential structures of otherness there is a simple opposition to be made between animate and inanimate, any more than between human and animal. One might, following Derrida on supplementation, articulation, and grafting, argue in terms of an originary *prosthetization* of the animate, as I have attempted to do in *Prosthesis*.

20 "L'animal que donc je suis," 285, my translation.

21 See "The Spatial Arts: An Interview with Jacques Derrida," in Peter Brunette and David Wills, *Deconstruction and the Visual Arts: Art, Media, Architecture* (New York: Cambridge University Press, 1994), 16–19.

22 See for example the discussion in the "Introduction" to his *Specters of Marx*, trans. Peggy Kamuf (New York: Routledge, 1994), xviii–xix; and in "L'animal que donc je suis," 280–82.

FURTHER READING

Beardsworth, Richard. *Derrida and the Political*. New York: Routledge, 1996.

Brunette, Peter and Wills, David. *Screen/Play: Derrida and Film Theory*. Princeton: Princeton University Press, 1989.

Brunette, Peter, and Wills, David, eds. *Deconstruction and the Visual Arts: Art, Media, Architecture*. New York: Cambridge University Press, 1994.

Derrida, Jacques. "L'animal que donc je suis." In Marie-Louise Mallet ed., *L'animal autobiographique: autour du travail de Jacques Derrida*. Paris: Galilée, 1999.

"Economimesis." Trans. Richard Klein. *Diacritics* 11: 2 (1981).

"Force of Law: The 'Mystical Foundation of Authority'." Trans. Mary Quaintance. In Drucilla Cornell, Michel Rosenfeld, and David Gray Carlson eds., *Deconstruction and the Possibility of Justice*. New York: Routledge, 1992.

"Forcener le subjectile." In Paule Thévenin and Jacques Derrida, *Antonin Artaud: Dessins et portraits*. Paris: Gallimard, 1986.

The Gift of Death. Trans. David Wills. Chicago: University of Chicago Press, 1995.

Glas. Trans. John P. Leavey Jr. and Richard Rand. Lincoln: University of Nebraska Press, 1986.

Limited Inc. Ed. Gerald Graff. Evanston: Northwestern University Press, 1988.

Memoirs of the Blind. Trans. Pascale-Anne Brault and Michael Naas. Chicago: University of Chicago Press, 1995.

The Truth in Painting. Trans. Geoff Bennington and Ian McLeod. Chicago: University of Chicago Press, 1987.

Derrida, Jacques and Stiegler, Bernard. *Échographies, de la télévision*. Paris: Galilée/Institut national de l'audiovisuel, 1996.

Kant, Immanuel. *The Critique of Judgement*. Trans. James Creed Meredith. Oxford: Clarendon Press, 1973.

Melville, Stephen, and Readings, Bill, eds. *Vision and Textuality*. Durham: Duke University Press, 1995.

Plissart, Marie-Françoise and Derrida, Jacques. *Right of Inspection*. Trans. David Wills. New York: Monacelli Press, 1998.

Rapaport, Herman. *Is There Truth in Art?* Ithaca: Cornell University Press, 1997.

CHAPTER 5

Derrida and representation: mimesis, presentation, and representation

Marian Hobson

The Poet is a powerful magician, creating visions taken for real (the implications of the figure of Prospero in Shakespeare's *The Tempest*, or Alcandre in Corneille's *L'Illusion comique*); the Poet is a dangerous liar in society or a hanger-on weaving confidence tricks in the family (Tannegui Lefèvre, 1697; the figure of Trissotin in Molière's *Les Femmes Savantes*). And the products of his fancy may be wondrous sights, or on the contrary misleading, even dangerous, illusions. These accounts of the work of poets from the classical European tradition of the sixteenth and seventeenth centuries are not localized there but operate in a long tradition running back to Plato or beyond, and forward to the actual danger run by the author of *Satanic Verses*. They are one sort of answer to the question of the relation between art and truth, which is really two questions, at least. One: does art proffer objects which can be measured against truth? Does it, for instance, make sense to say of a painting or a poem that it is "true"? And second: what is the status of the imaginary object that is the product of art? When we see the figure of Hamlet on the stage, surely we are not seeing Ralph Fiennes, but somehow a ghostly superimposition of the prince onto the body of the actor?

It is at least partly in these terms that Derrida raises the question of the relation between truth and literature in "The Double Session" published in 1970 and then in the volume *Dissemination*, 1972. He does so explicitly in relation to the history of that relation. We shall see that even the position of the article in the volume points to a history, for it acts as a hinge, between work on Plato ("Plato's Pharmacy") and an article, "Dissemination," built round what might be called "ultra-modernity," round a novel by the French novelist Philippe Sollers. Mallarmé, the middle article's subject, acts as an articulation between Plato and modernity. The discussion of mimesis, of writing and literature as "mimemes," copies, points back to the considerations of form, of representation, and of ideology of the first article, but in fact forward as well to work on the

132

phantasm in *Glas* (1974) and to its expansion in *Specters of Marx* (1993), to which there can only be this brief allusion here (see Hobson, 1998). Instead, the present chapter will elaborate the question of "representation," and sketch the links Derrida provides to its role in history and in criticism. It will start from two passages in "The Double Session." These function rather differently. A footnote, treating of mimesis in Plato, makes of it a kind of contradiction, one might say a logical trap, which is said to generate a good part of the history of literary criticism; the more extended passage, in the text, elaborates this, relating it to seventeenth- and eighteenth-century aesthetics, and to work of Heidegger's. The present chapter will follow the question of representation and truth through to "Restitutions" in *The Truth in Painting* (1978), where the way it is discussed has changed very markedly. From a "machine," the claws of which close round a problem, we have moved to a complexly layered dialogue in an indeterminate number of voices, which strands out from the question of truth in painting: what kind of truth is there behind a painted object, to what does it refer, if it does refer? – leading the reader to a more diffuse and more difficult set of problems: what are the relations between the objects which may be painted and what critics say about them? Finally, the chapter will show briefly how the justification for grouping ideas, for staging them in a history at all, is discussed in relation to "representation" ("Sending").

But, at this preliminary stage in these considerations, there has to be sounded a note which is methodological and cautionary. Though the remarks above have remained with the vocabulary in the works of Derrida to be discussed (mimesis, truth, representation) they have treated the three texts or excerpts from texts thematically. This is to treat them as if they were parts of the philosophical domain of aesthetics. In a sense, they are that – highly illuminating commentaries on the texts they take as base (Plato, Mallarmé, Heidegger). But even at this preliminary stage, there must be caution: we have to incorporate questions of how the thread is woven in to Derrida's work, and not merely of what it is, what thread or threads. Even though the question is explicit, to sketch the pattern above, with however many precautions, is to fit Derrida's work into preset or traditional channels, when precisely much of his thought is deliberately resistant to such a tack. However tempting, it is inaccurate to speak as if he had worked in or on a domain, here in our concerns, "aesthetics." The end of this chapter, on Derrida's article "Sending," will look at some reasons for this, in considering some of his remarks on the history of the word "representation."

The problem of thematicism, of grouping ideas – or metaphors – into sets of items which can be associated by some common property, or by some title is one of the major problems in approaching Derrida. His vocabulary is very mobile, and if attention is not paid to his manner of writing, a reductionism is practiced which misses a good deal in the work. Here in the present article, this difficulty can perhaps be turned: he has taught philosophy all his life, for a long time the preparation for the formidable examination, the "agrégation." The traditional, preexisting questions, which form the staples of this as of every exam in any educational institution have then been present to his mind. Even though they do not constitute the evident shape of his writings, he does, we shall see, strand these questions into his thinking. The relation of the painting to the painter, the status of the painted object, are twisted together with less familiar ones: how we connect what we see in a picture not just with the picture's "reference," how we speak of that connection, how we make that connection just by speaking. And how there are elements in the picture which undo that connection, which force a movement on.

I MIMESIS (*DISSEMINATION*, 201–20)[1]

"The Double Session," the middle article in *Dissemination* [1972], starts with an epigraph – a textual effect, a typographical maneuver which points forward to *Glas* – an excerpt from Plato's *Philebus*, 38e–39e, followed by a quotation from Mallarmé's "Book." Into this Platonic excerpt is inserted Mallarmé's "Mimique," a passage of prose. The implication of the epigraphs is that something happens between the Platonic *mimesis* and Mallarmé's "Mimique."

At the beginning, Derrida explicitly places his article between literature and truth (and in a side-swipe at Sartre, denies that it will confine itself to the question "what is literature"[2]). This relation of "between"[3] is quickly defined by its outlines, its frame, as a *history* "of a certain play between literature and truth" (208), a history organized not by mimesis but by a "certain interpretation of *mimesis*" (209). So it becomes clear, right at the beginning of this chapter, that this history is being designated as part of a specific conceptuality – dependent, we are told, on the idea of sense and on the presence of the truth of sense. Derrida is fully exploiting here the ambiguity of the word "sense" in French: sense, yes, but also direction. Now history, events unfolding through stages in time, must surely have direction. But do they have sense? What might be the relation of this process through temporal stages and sense? I will return to the question at the very end. For the present, it is hinted at this point in the article that literature is but a moment of something wider: "A history of literature if one accepts the idea that literature was born of it and died of it" (183 cf. 187).

The wider history indicated here is very wide indeed: from Plato to avant-garde writing; but as the restriction which is twice put forward by a conditional clause suggests, it is also quite local, for it points to the history of literature that forms the perspective of the group publishing the journal in which Derrida's article appeared, *Tel Quel*. It is its editor, Philippe Sollers, whose novel *Nombres* is the text from which the last article in *Dissemination* takes its departure. "The Double Session," like the *Tel Quel* group in its work on Mallarmé, gives the poet a key role in the development of modern writing. They all recast the light in which it was common to place him at that time: as a Platonist-Hegelian, whose capital letters designate entities – "the Book," "the Idea" – from among a cast of idealized, slightly effete Platonic abstractions. They present on the contrary a Mallarmé at the cutting edge of modernity, one whose work involves a reshaping of the relation between idealism and materialism. Derrida, quoting J. Hyppolite (philosopher, and one of his teachers) speaks of "a materialism of the idea" (235). Now Julia Kristeva, in her book *The Revolution in Poetic Language* published in 1974, but building on work undertaken earlier, will make a bold attempt to get Mallarmé to run in the Marxist marathon; it is a break-out from the then usual communist party critiques of avant-garde writers for being hopelessly divorced from the social changes in whose midst they were living.[4] She will put him forward not as an avant-garde poet inhabiting remote towers, but as a turning point, the opener-up of modern literature, an explorer of language, a worker whose praxis is linguistic and revolutionary. Derrida will in his preface "Outwork" hint at a courteous, tacit disagreement with Kristeva over the possibility of using the poles "materialist"/"idealist" of ideology or of literature, or of attaining so quickly a "real" causality, "historical, economic, political, sexual etc." (43). Kristeva aligns "poetic," "material," and "materialist", which she opposes to representation (so that neither language nor literature are representational). Language used in literary ways has a real subversive effect, she argues, which can be related to political and social agitation.

Derrida on the other hand does not operate such a polar model, but one which is slightly skewed. As he often reminds us, to take the opposite pole of an argument is still to remain within its sphere of operation – for instance, to call something "unjust" accepts the frame supplied by the relevant concept of the just. So he does not reverse the authority and relevance of truth's rule over mimesis – for truth is the law of mimesis – but displaces it. Representation is not rejected in favor of the directly concrete (Kristeva, on the contrary, in search of a materialist aesthetics, is interested in the poem as sound effect). Instead, through a replicating of mimesis, the distinction between the imitated and the imitation is broken down. In Mallarmé's "Mimique", the mime "installs a pure medium of fiction"; there is not representation, remembering the past or anticipating the future, but copy without prior model. This is a difficult conception, but needs to be grasped to understand Derrida's position at this point.

In what Derrida shows to be a fictional quotation, Mallarmé writes: "the scene illustrates but the idea, not any actual action" (175). (Derrida here, as elsewhere, in *Specters of Marx* for instance, argues that the distinction between the effective or real and the phantasmatic is not a stable one.) The common-sense relation between a model and its copy, which is one of cause and priority, is disturbed. The Mallarméan mime, Derrida argues, delivers activity which is reduplication without origin. The present of his pantomime is strung between the future of desire and its accomplishing, or an act and its memory: it is a "false appearance."

This makes of truth not an external authority which the work of art is to mold itself to, but a function in a wider movement. Moreover, Mallarmé's quotation may be fiction too; the quotation, in spite of its quotation marks, may be invented, and it may be the Mime, Derrida suggests, who imitates nothing which preexists his mime, whose whole mime is a "gestual writing" (199). Mallarmé's writing does not reflect its own writing (it is not then what was called in French critical theory of the 1950s a "mise en abyme"). For though it refers to writing, that writing is not its own: it does not write directly about itself writing. Mallarmé's passage ends in fact with the surprise that silence exists between the sheets already written and the glance reading them. This end then does not mirror, but winds back to its beginning: the silence in a musical afternoon, with fluttering thoughts which the poet is challenged to translate. This shape is not that of insertion and is not that of a system closed on to itself, though it does refer to itself (202); see section II below where I show how it is greatly developed in "Restitutions."

To capture the relation of literature and truth in "The Double Session", as we shall see, a "logical machine" is set up which snaps shut round a strange contradiction in the aesthetic tradition's approach. In the value of mimesis as explored in classical aesthetics are revealed two opposed attitudes to imitation, ones which together take the form of a double bind: art is inferior to nature if it imitates nature at less than the level of perfect replication; but if it attains that level, or even if it should improve on its model, it is still not equal to it, for it is subsequent, and thus not superior but perhaps dangerous (it can be taken for it).

The first sketch of the history of the play between literature and truth is confined to Plato and to a very long footnote. Platonic *mimesis* is summarily traced out and the machinery of what is called its "network," its "logic," its schema (211–13) reconstructed. Taking two of the key passages in the Platonic corpus dealing with mimesis and with the ontological status of the mimetic image (around *Republic* 398a and *Sophist* 241b), three points are made. The first implies that Plato has a double attitude to mimesis – Homer is expelled from the city for practicing it; Parmenides criticized for ignoring it, for leaving us with no method of speaking of false words or false opinion without contradiction. We need to be able to make them out as "images [idols] or likenesses [icons] or imitations [mimemes] or appearances [phantasms] or ... the arts which have to do with them" (*Sophist* 241e). The second point in the footnote relates mimesis to "diaresis," the method used to catch the Sophist, that of division of every question into two branches (as if for a rat running a maze). The Sophist is driven between two forms of mimesis, *eikastic* and *phantastic* (235d, *Dissemination*, 212). Eikastic mimesis uses as paradigm the proportions of the original, whereas the phantastic corrects what is painted in perspectival fashion, according to the distance and angle it is seen from (235e; 236a). "So artists abandon the truth and give their figures not the actual proportions but those which seem to be beautiful." It appears but is not like, it can be called an appearance or "phantasm" (236b).

It is the third point in Derrida's footnote which constructs what I called the trap that mimesis forms. Inverted commas which are suspensive but not quotational appear, around the "sort of logical machine," the mechanism of the trap. And around terms that link here with the history of literature already mentioned. For "prior" to the philosophical "decision," a kind of mimesis which was not ashamed or hugger mugger was possible. The implication of these terms specialized by the quotation marks is that a separation or "decision" between "good" and "bad" mimetism is worked through to the point where a complex is carved up into opposed poles. These words in their punctuational guards indicate that in these articles of *Dissemination*, a history of reason (among other histories) is being sketched, and that in these Platonic texts, the *Phaedrus*, the *Sophist*, the *Republic*, a reassignment of values occurs, following which, mimesis will be ontologically inferior, less real. Derrida summarizes this thus: Plato is suggesting that there is a good mimesis and a bad mimesis, but the good mimesis, though good, cannot cease to be imitation, and thus somehow less existent than the real.

Pre-Platonic values in art have been regressed to by modernity, Derrida suggests. After Plato, and before modernity, mimesis as a "logical machine" produces a double valuation of what does the imitating, and a double set of consequences derivable from the relation to being which it is given. At this point the note becomes schematic. The two values given to the "imitant" by Plato and the tradition which follows him each have three consequences, but both branches of the fork snap shut round the ontological inadequacy of the imitant. The copy is "flakey," it doesn't have full existence, as if "existence" were a color which it could have more or less tincture of. On one side, it is, however resembling, nothing; on the other, it is something, but never, however perfect, as existing as its model. Derrida here has exhibited a pattern of arguing and of thinking which is deeply embedded in our tradition, perhaps unavoidable, but nonetheless problematic.

This "schema" explicates with great acuity the aesthetics of the seventeenth and eighteenth centuries – and Derrida develops this further in the main flow of the article, by giving examples. The schema or "logical machine" is sharp: it will, Derrida is quite right, generate "all the clichés of criticism to come" (186 end of note; Hobson, 1982). The footnote shows how in classical writing on art, art can be superior to nature, and yet always have a shadowy existence which makes it less than nature; the note is a powerful threading together and articulation of aesthetic truisms. The trap is that whether the copy is attributed being or not, that being is always less than its source.

Now in the body of Derrida's text, two forms of relation of art to truth are put forward: the revealing of what is hidden in forgetfulness, given the Greek word for truth, *aletheia*, or the measured equality of proportion to a model, given the Latin word, *adæquatio* (219). These are the two forms of relation to truth explored by Heidegger in "Plato's doctrine of truth" (1931–32) and mentioned briefly in *The Origin of the Work of Art* (1935–36), in which he traces truth-as-adequation back to the root "wid" of the words *eidos* and *idea*, a root which refers to a visual stratum in the words. These imply a correct, true relation between knowledge and what is known. *Aletheia*, which was undivided into what appears and its appearance, is replaced by *adæquatio*, where what appears and its appearance can be measured against each other (Derrida argues of both that they are ruled by the "process of truth"). Derrida explicitly, though politely, resists the chronological sequence that Heidegger had seen in them – suggesting instead that reference, as a part of a "truth process," be displaced, not canceled, by the "operation of a certain syntax." It is, says Derrida, the undecidable trait of an effort of writing which effects this operation – and by "undecidable" refers to famous work by the mathematician Kurt Gödel, where sentences which were true but not provable within any given version of formalized arithmetic were exhibited, and where it is impossible to decide between two determinate statements which are apparently contradictory alternatives.

This "undecidable" can be pondered as a thematic thread but must also be understood in the relation in which it is proffered, as "the operation of a certain syntax." In doing that, one sees more clearly what is meant both by "deconstruction" and by the methodological warning given above. For later in his article Derrida will make of Mallarmé, rightly, an artist with syntax, capable of activating radically different meanings within the same phrase. But he will himself do this at several points, among them in a phrase written in the long footnote. Of the copy, Derrida writes that it is "inferior to the model in its essence at the moment when it can replace it," and thus be "primé" – "dominated by" or, on the contrary, "given an advantage." The possibility of this opposed pair of meanings is created by the passive of a verb "primer" whose meaning, or one of them, is "advantage" created by dissymmetry in the set-up of an oppositional game (royal tennis, the *jeu de paume*). Derrida has written a sentence which swings between two opposed readings. It is as if "deconstruction" is itself evolving, and the locus of that evolution is work on mimesis. For thematics only registers the contradiction; whereas syntax also lets it operate. Of it can be said what Derrida in the "passe-partout," preface to *The Truth in Painting*, says of a phrase by Cézanne, "I owe you the truth in painting and I will tell it to you": its force derives from the capacity to play with the determinations of the context without making itself indeterminate.

II PRESENTATION ("RESTITUTIONS OF THE TRUTH IN POINTING," *THE TRUTH IN PAINTING*, 257–382)[5]

It was in a footnote that Derrida situated his work on mimesis as part of a history of the relation between literature and truth; it focused on tensions in the Platonic texts round the nature of appearance. (These, the art historian Ernst Gombrich has suggested, may relate to a crucial turning in Greek artistic practice: the systematic encouragement to look at art works in terms of appearance [Gombrich, 1960; Klein, 1970].) In this Platonic setting out of the tracks on which aesthetic problems run right down to the eighteenth century, the copy, however perfect, is less than the model; it has less existence, it is ontologically weaker than the original. Derrida, in setting out so clearly the paradoxical shape of the arguments associated with mimesis, and siting them in a historical cursus, is also perhaps moving out of this pattern of deconstruction. What is a relation of strain and contradiction becomes less fraught, as the title "Restitutions of the truth in pointing" of the article on painting in *The Truth in Painting* already suggests. Here, different approaches, different perspectives on painting, are stranded into a discussion which is in the form of what is called a "polylogue." That is, a multivoiced conversation, where the different speakers are not identifiable separately except typographically, and where, we are told, one of the voices is feminine. These different perspectives are those of different relations to the truth of works of art, but the approaches are also those of different aesthetics to which names – Kant and Heidegger – can be attached. We will see in this following section that the principle line of inquiry is no longer the two-pronged relation of copy to model (less perfect or more perfect, but always less real). Instead, it is one which builds in reflection on itself: how are works of art, and commentary on that art, connected?

A panoply of models for truth is laid out right at the beginning of the introduction to the whole volume, "passe-partout." The quotation which gives the book its title is taken, we have seen, from a letter by Cézanne; truth is in painting, and is owed. "I owe you the truth in painting and I will tell it to you" (2). Derrida very quickly draws out of the promise at least four senses: truth restituted or unveiled – *aletheia*; truth as relation to a model – *adæquatio*; truth presented or represented through painting, that is, truth in the domain of painting; what is true about painting.

Aletheia and *adæquatio* were, as we have seen, types of structure given to truth by Heidegger. They had appeared already in "The Double Session." But there are in "Restitutions" other structures which have been further developed in *Glas* (1974): fetish but also "ghost." One of the Greek terms for "appearance" was "phantasma," a word also applied to "ghost," as well as sharing its root "phan" with words like "fancy" and "fantasy." "Ghosts" flitter through the third article of *The Truth in Painting*, "Restitutions of the truth in pointing" (at both beginning and end, 257, 373), for ghosts,[6] apparitions, like the Platonic appearance of art, are neither present nor absent, neither existing, nor dead – "then what we call a likeness, though not really existing, really does exist" (*Sophist*, 240b). Unlike the footnote of "The Double Session," where the appearance raises the question of the relation of painting-copy to its source, here it asks the question of what we are seeing, and how we make out what we are seeing. Derrida speaks of "spectral analysis" (377). The starting point is a couple of references by Heidegger in *The Origin of the Work of Art* to a painting of shoes by van Gogh, and the reply to those references by the American art historian Meyer Schapiro. The painted shoes play complex roles in Heidegger's *The Origin of the Work of Art*, and in the Schapiro text which both answers it and criticizes it. Heidegger is attributing the shoes to an old peasant woman, Schapiro restoring them to van Gogh. Here, as a preliminary remark, Derrida points out that both Heidegger and Schapiro omit the possibility of fetishism which the shoes raise. They omit the question of whether the picture that they are probably talking about could not be a picture of two shoes from the same foot ("probably" for Schapiro has reminded the reader that there is a whole series, and that Heidegger does not identify the painting clearly, though he responds to a query by letter). There are two points to be made here round the question of fetishism. First, the fetish is one model of truth: to speak of "fetish" is to set up something as the "real thing", subject to some kind of ban or taboo, for which the fetish is a substitute and equivalent. Both Schapiro and Heidegger then are neglecting the possibility that van Gogh's picture itself raises the question of whether as a picture it refers to something out there, a pair of shoes belonging to someone, or whether rather to objects freighted with phantasmatic investments. But, second point, if the shoes are for the same foot, then the complex left–right complementarity of the human body may be left aside in van Gogh's painting. There may be two shoes of the same side, each other's "perfect double." Derrida develops different possibilities of what this might mean, different ways of thinking the relation between "real" shoes and painted ones. The painted shoes, even if of the same foot, may bear "physiognomical" traces (370) to make them part of a pair, and traceable back to real ones; or there may be no pair sensible in the painting, the shoes can't be put together either to each other or to other absent ones (375). The painted shoes in this second possibility cannot be *compared*, measured up to a truth external to the picture, to which they might be adequate. By neglecting the possibility of fetishism, both Schapiro and Heidegger may be writing in the wake of Kant, and of his "transcendental aesthetic" (375) where space–time is the form of pure *a priori* intuition concerned, and lays down, however minimally, norms, frames, and measures associated with an oriented human body.

Derrida, I shall argue, has displaced the question Heidegger poses. Heidegger's aim was to work back to an earlier point in the tradition, where it was accepted that the work of art presents truth. He sought to indicate to us the consciousness or the predatory assumption of disponibility which orient our present modern response. But this Heideggerian aim may be invested with other, uninvestigated freights, as Schapiro suspects. Instead, in Derrida's case, it is as if his text works round the question of speaking about art, rather than about the question of truth in art. The latter is however the question to which Heidegger constantly returns. He nowhere builds into his response an awareness of the verbal nature of his work; on the contrary, as we shall see, he puts forward in the figure of a peasant woman a model for unaware discourse.[7] And one can indeed wonder whether discourse can be made aware without the formal device of reflexivity, of "mise en abyme": whether it can be done without a self-consciousness which diffracts and distances the relation to what is being spoken about?

Schapiro is giving van Gogh's shoes back to the painter, a restitution away from the Heideggerian pathos, as Schapiro takes it, of peasantry, and the modest lack of claims which the philosopher has woven round them. Derrida, in looking very minutely at the articulation of the argument, will not allow at least one of the voices to disagree. But the Heideggerian position is given a great deal more space, and its freight more latitude. Heidegger is turning away from the classical opposition of subject/object, away from the sense of an autonomous subject dealing with clearly defined already given objects; rather, he investigates the way things are given to us. Hence, models of truth like *adæquatio* are queried, for the measure of an impression to its model implies that the model-object is already given. Heidegger is laying suspicion on the attitude he called "aesthetic." In *The Origin of the Work of Art*, Heidegger is disrupting another pair of opposites, "form" and "matter" which as he says are central to all theories of art and aesthetics. This pair are presented with a kind of recoil at "a conceptual machinery that nothing is capable of withstanding" (27) that they, once they are linked with the distinction object/subject, have put at our disposal. For they have led, it is implied, to "purpose" as the account of the relation between form and matter. We, as autonomous subjects, induce a form onto matter, to make of it our instrument, to cause it to follow our purposes, to make of it a purposive object.

Heidegger offers a scale of concepts (*Ding, Zeug, Werk*) which refines the distinction between "form" and "matter" and complicates any answer to the question: what sort of thing is a work of art, what is the "thingness" of the work? "Serviceability," instead of "purpose," is a testimony to preparation, something like the van Gogh shoes, between the thing and the work of art. As Derrida points out, one of the references to a van Gogh painting occurs in a paragraph which is denying that an art work's truth can be adequation to an already existing object, which is "rendered"; so *contra* Schapiro, Heidegger is unlikely to be referring to the painted objects as if they were a real pair of shoes.

His suspicion of the distinction between "form" and "matter" which is at the basis of much aesthetic theory leads to an examination of the work of art (*Werk*) in relation to the "thing" (*Ding*) and to the "product" or "stuff" (*Zeug*). They are "at home" not as a purpose, but in being "serviceable," something like the shoes, a testimony to a preparation, something between the thing and the work of art. The reader's understanding of how the suspicion of "form" and "matter" functions strengthens with the context Heidegger gives it. For he soon attributes the shoes to a peasant woman: they are a "pictorial presentation" of something everyone knows, they are "serviceable," and if we seek out the service, then they are what they are on the feet of the peasant woman, and they are the more genuine, the less they have been thought about, or even looked at, or felt. Heidegger argues that while we only see in general a pair of shoes, we won't understand this "stuff"; and after a re-creation in words of the world of the peasant woman, a world of "wordless joy" and "uncomplaining anxiety as to the certainty of bread" (34), he allows that perhaps we only see this from the picture. In other words, it is the painting's lack of words that helps us understand the silent unself-consciousness of the woman. The "serviceability" of the shoes is ratcheted down away from purpose and use, and rooted in "reliability" by virtue of which the woman is "admitted" to the "silent call of the earth" and is certain of her world. In another negative route which Heidegger lays out for the reader (he or she has already been an observer, whereas the peasant woman is a bearer of the shoes), the "productness" of the shoes is not available through a description or report or explanation of a set of shoes really lying in front of us, but only by bringing ourselves (in mind) in front of the painting by van Gogh. Van Gogh's work reveals what "stuff," what "*Zeug*," the pair of peasant shoes is. Unlike aesthetic theories, it is not ruled by beauty nor by the representation of what is at hand, mimesis; instead, it is a happening of truth (38).[8]

What is meant by this happening? The word-picture of the peasant woman, whose response is in wordless affect or bodily movement
("shaking," "trembling"), privileges tacit knowledge – she knows without observation and reflection. Heidegger likewise denies that what he is
getting at is an explanation of *Zeug* through the picture; on the contrary,
the picture allows this "stuff" to be found. It is a "revelation" of the being
of the shoes. This is how the picture can be said to bring about truth. In
this section of the *Origin*, it is as if there were a refusal of speech about
the work of art; instead the work itself has spoken (35), truth "happens"
in the work.

Now, in spite of its form as a commentary which follows Heidegger
intermittently if very closely, it seems as if the article in which Derrida
discusses this section is quite different. As we shall see, the different voices,
the self-reference through development of his own specialized vocabulary however cautious, however multifaceted, do raise the question of
speaking about a work of art. Yet this question itself "happens" rather
than is pointed out – the Derridean text is not one of facile contradiction,
but respectful and, as no doubt intended, encourages the reading of the
Heideggerian text.

It is then as if "Restitutions of truth in pointing" sets out to be a
conscious work, but conscious in a novel way. It develops a "spectral
analysis" not by leaning on the distinction between painted and real,
but by raising the question of how a work of art coheres, or on the
contrary, separates off bits of itself, disseminates. But this question is not
put forward (318) by remaining with the strokes of paint, nor with the
painted shoes (adequate reference, Schapiro's truth) nor by moving out
of them into an unveiled present (*aletheia*, Heidegger's). Instead, Derrida
takes Heidegger's description of the gaping boot to point to the way
he moves out of the traits of the painted shoe (the space of the inside
shoe is imaginary, in a way different from the space of the shoe itself,
not directly created by the paint but indicated beyond). It is the reason
for this movement beyond in Heidegger's passage on the picture which
is elusive: the question of what it is to be in the picture, to stay with
the picture. It may be (second suggestion) that the pictorial structure,
the paint strokes, encourage the movement of the eye outside, or rather
inside, the pictorial space; or it may be (first suggestion) that the mere
use of speech, not paint, causes the going beyond the painting, bringing
in what is not purely visible.

Heidegger's rhetoric is strangely unconscious; it is not considering this
question of inside and outside. This is even clearer in the next section

(not commented on by Derrida in this article) where he evokes a Greek temple which opens a world round itself; and then a "speechwork" which is no copy but transforming, which does not speak of battle, but each actual word fights the battle, and places before the decision as to what is holy and what unholy, what great and what small, what courageous and what cowardly (41–43). So these works do not represent; they are not copies of anything – they present. In the work, the happening of truth is at work. This is in spite of spare, despairing words a couple of pages earlier: "world-withdrawal, and world-decay can never be undone." Now Derrida builds into his commentary the question of language in a way that Heidegger does not, however much his work speaks of language. It is as if Derrida were suggesting a possibility of truth in painting which is not representation, but not presentation either. We do not have a mere copy, but nor is there pure parousia, presence or event. Instead, a faceted truth concerned with how we place the inside or outside of the picture, with our speaking of it.

In Heidegger's paragraph, the truth of the "serviceable" appears at the moment of the mention of the shoes being unlaced and sprawling open, as Derrida points out (345–46). Derrida imports his own particular lexis at this point: "unstrictured" ("déstricturé") to link with "detachment," to suggest how at this very moment when Heidegger is emphasizing how little we can work out about the shoes (not where the shoes are standing, only in an indeterminate space, no clue to their use), there is a turn to highly charged language, to an understanding of what *Zeug* is. It is a maneuver by Heidegger to call for reconnection, for adherence.

The adherence Heidegger has turned to is not personalized or subjective: it is given a further charge Derrida points out, one of a "loser takes all" structure. The very fact that the shoes are of little value gives them more value. Their "preoriginary reliability" (352) is an adherence to all that "earth" means in these texts. This is expressed in a kind of baptism, one that supposes the "fiability" of language but also produces it. But in Derrida's text, winding in and out of this exposition-justification of the tone of pathos in the passages round the peasant woman and the van Gogh picture, is another voice. The reattaching (which straddles "adherence" and the purpose of the laces in the open shoes) has as its condition the fiability, but this other voice makes of it an umbilical cord. We through Heidegger have got beyond the polar couples matter/form, subject/object, utility/production to a preoriginary contract. At the same time, suggests this other voice, we have regressed to the mother of all traps, "the mirror play of the world" (355).

Are these laces then a "mise en abyme," a mirroring of the problem of connection and disconnection? In its movement back and forth, Derrida's text can move to what Kant had called "free [wandering] beauty," to what precisely does not have a concept, not even a figure, to tie it. In Kant's adherent beauty, consonant with human purposes, negativity works with sense. Whereas in a pure judgment of taste there is no concept of what the object ought to be (Kant, *Critique of Judgement*, §16). Derrida's difficult summary ("without" and "sense" are homophones in French) "sans thème" makes of the object something which is and is not linguistic. Wandering beauty has a form which is as if there were a purpose when there is none; it has been interrupted, cut off. Adherent beauty gives the example of what it is that is missing in wandering beauty.

Should we then assemble the laces as a figure of the continuity/ discontinuity of the text? Cause them to "adhere?"

Something quite different in fact seems to be going on in "Restitutions of the truth in pointing." A voice in the polylogue invites us to leave this old language. Another? the same? voice refuses van Gogh's painting of shoes as a *mise en abyme* of itself. The question is a standard one of pictorial illusion: does the picture invite you to remember that it is a picture, not real shoes, while you are looking at it? Is the van Gogh an allegory of this kind of aesthetic detachment, of Kantian disinterest? (341). The voice refuses the representation of representation, the *mise en abyme*. What may be the same voice comments that "I" takes words like "mark," "border," "margin" to avoid saying "says," "show," "represent," "paint," "so many words that this system works to deconstruct" (342), and the examples are all words which Derrida has made a good deal of use of. Instead, the question of detachment is developed in the French word's bureaucratic sense of representation, *secondment*. It becomes part of the question not of Kantian "disinterest" but of how a painted work holds itself both together and apart; and perhaps how it may be spoken of without being lent a spurious unity.

To see this more clearly, we should turn to the first chapter in the volume. It works round a term, *parergon*, appearing only once in Kant's *Critique of Judgement*, and in fact only added to the second edition (1793). The *parergon*, Derrida suggests, closes up the artistic work, making it available on the market, liberating its plus value. It is made necessary by an internal lack of determinacy in the work, a lack of certainty about where and whether it needs to come to an end (71) (as photographs of details of paintings may bring home to us nowadays). The frame cooperates with the work bringing it together at the same time as it strains and cracks under the pressure of what it helps to produce (75). *Parergon* then does not point to an outside transcending the picture, but to a push-and-pull relation between interior and exterior. In what is framed there is something lacking, something inviting outside pressure. This description of an art work is far from notions of richness, plenitude, fullness, such as critics tend to attribute to art, as Derrida had shown to refute it in his work on Mallarmé; but also far from allowing the work internal necessity, allowing it to make a kind of world around it, as Heidegger does.

In the article "Restitutions," the first reading of van Gogh's shoes suggests the possibility of a kind of reflexivity: the "stuff," "product," is half way between a thing and a "work." One of Derrida's voices had twice picked up the possibility of a *picture* of a pair of shoes representing the shoes' half-way status between thing and product. The first time, the painting is made lacking in the way the parergon is: "It exhibits – in shoes – its lack of itself, one could almost say its own lack" (298) (of the parergon: 56). Van Gogh's shoes at the point Heidegger refers to them seem to be between "stuff" and "artwork." For, Derrida says, the three things, thing, stuff and (art) work are not simply related, as Schapiro believes; although "stuff" is between the other two, the direction of Heidegger's argument is to make the art work and the thing closer. The picture will have the presentation made in it "in presence and self-sufficient" (299). In describing this Derrida is already pushing close to van Gogh's picture: "like a lace . . . each mode of being of the thing, passes inside then outside the other. From right to left." And bringing further the question of what brings the points together "It makes the thing sure of its gathering . . . The shoe picture is a product (of art) which is like a thing, presenting (and not representing, we shall come to this) a product (shoes) etc." (299).

The second time explicates the different logical structure Derrida attributes to "stricture". Whereas detachment leads to opposition, which is not difference, the stricture defers but does not join up, so that it can take account of the shoes' being neither detached nor attached (340). Instead of linking the painted shoes back to a real man (van Gogh, as Schapiro is anxious to do) as his real shoes, Derrida introduces the term "in *restance*"(313) which is used in another important article, "Limited Inc a b c . . . " (1977). There it is defined as the "minimal possibility" for a sign's reuse. Derrida in his sentence's word play on "se passer" (313) (to pass between, to do without) seems just for a moment to make of the painted object, the shoes, the same kind of non-present remainder, to give it the minimal idealization he gives to the sign. "Stricture" and "destricture" seem then to bring together and to pull apart, the painted object, that is, what we speak of when we speak of the picture.

Heidegger, however, no more nor less naive than Schapiro, attributes the shoes to someone – to a peasant. Is this to contradict his own discourse round *adæquatio* when he asks whether, when we say that art corresponds to truth, we mean that van Gogh's painting takes off a copy from the real and transfers this into a product of artistic production? Heidegger's apparent movement from *adæquatio* to *aletheia*, from truth measured off in a copy to a truth which reveals, from representation to presentation, however much force it may have, still regresses to what are in fact ideological preinvestments, in Heidegger's case, to 1930s values of simplicity and groundedness. It is at this point in Derrida's discussion that we realize that the bootlaces are not a "mise en abyme of the whole picture." The laces sneaking in and out of the painted eyelets pull together the argument by figuring it (321). We move between the painted and the "real" shoes, in and out of the frame.

Derrida in "Restitutions" has developed a way of talking about a painting which doesn't box us into a recursive series "talking about talking about...."; it winds between the van Gogh, and the layers of talking about the van Gogh: Heidegger's, Schapiro's and his own. The possibility of the "sense/without of the pure cut" of the Kantian "wandering beauty" is there to perturb the smooth integration of the painted object into discourse. It detaches itself, as a painted object, from its background, at the same time as it is part of that background, linked into it.

III REPRESENTATION ("ENVOI," IN *PSYCHÉ*, 109-44)[9]

Throughout Derrida's work there is a meditation on what sort of conceptual unity we can obtain, at how high a price. In *Of Grammatology* there is a mulling over of the role of the word as unit on which we rely as some kind of last element for analysis (20). In "Sending: on representation," Derrida reflects on the word "representation" which has a long history not just in an aesthetic sense but as the translation of the German *Vorstellung*, or *Darstellung*, a key term in epistemology. Can one find a semantic kernel, which is common to each use of the word? Derrida doubles back round this question, to an article by Heidegger, "The Age of the World Picture," in which he develops the history of representation sketched out in a couple of sentences in *The Origin of the Work of Art* (30). Modernity is marked by the development of the object, in front of and at the disposal of a subject who is the measure of all things. And Derrida explicates the relation between "presentation" and "representation" in this history: in representation the presentation comes back as a double, a copy, and the idea as a picture of the thing which is at our disposal.

In this Heideggerian history, Derrida points out, the Cartesian epoch of representation relies on a strand in Greek thought which is not one of representation, but which prepares the conception of the world as "picture" (through the root "wid" of *eidos* and *idea*, which implies a visual stratum, as we have seen above). Heidegger orders his history according to epochs, which are each unified by a destiny of being as a "sending."[10] Greek, medieval, and modern periods are separated by their different relation to being. It is these relations which allow the epochs to detach themselves. The Greek period knows no separation into object and subject; it is speech which gathers together and safeguards man's imperiled being even as he is still exposed to chaos (129). The medieval period relates to being as to a created being. The modern period makes of being an object which is over against man, at his disposal. It is the period of representation. Derrida then moves on, in the guise of questions, to one that has been hinted at earlier: in asking what is representation, in collecting the different usages, the question is whether there is a common semantic kernel, which would imply that the term "representation" can be stood in for, represented by other words and phrases.

In the Heideggerian history, the "sending" through epochs comes out in representation. But that representation is the forgetting of, the standing in for, something earlier, which it represents, which was threatened and had to be reassembled and safeguarded. The pattern given to representation is itself representation. Derrida hints that this pattern itself implies that the sending, the history of being was always threatened in its unity, that it is not primordially one but is multiple.

Heidegger had himself suggested that the epoch of representation, of accounting and counting, was drawing to a close. In "The Double Session," as in the third article in *Dissemination*, modernity had doubled back to a pre-mimetic point. Here, in "Sending: on representation," representation and what it had substituted are indissoluble. One can see now the relation between this conclusion, for such it is, and the way "Restitutions" is written: "We should perhaps work things out so as to tell ourselves this story differently, from relays to relays of relays, in a destiny

which is never sure of gathering itself, identifying itself, or making itself
determinate" (*Psyché*, 142).

NOTES

1 Jacques Derrida, *Dissemination*, trans. B. Johnson (London: The Athlone
  Press, 1981).
2 There are several other such remarks in the volume. Sartre's *What is literature*
  was published in *Situations*, II, 1948.
3 The word "between," "entre," plays an important role in the article: in
  French it is a near homonym of the word "antre," cave, and the word-play
  is used to suggest a hinging between semantics and syntax.
4 It is ultimately, also, an attempt to get the position of the intellectual rethought
  by the left wing, to reverse the disparagement of work done through thinking that Sartre, for instance, had gone along with. Kristeva's contains a very
  interesting critique of the Marxist division of superstructure and infrastructure as representations of society, and a suggestion that "representation" be
  replaced by "praxis."
5 Jacques Derrida, *The Truth in Painting*, trans. G. Bennington and I. McLeod
  (Chicago and London: The University of Chicago Press, 1987).
6 "Phantasm," like "fetish," in *Glas* points to models of truth. "Fetish" has as
  its counter-value the particular "truth" for which it has been substituted.
  But it works as an implicit reminder of what it is substituted for, provoking a
  double bind of denial and recognition. "Phantasm" is a way of dominating
  a difficulty by working it into a structure of clear binary opposition, by
  determining difference as opposition (*Glas*, 209–210a).
7 In the second section of "The Origin of the Work of Art," trans. A.
  Hofstadter, in *Poetry, Language, Thought* (New York: Harper and Row, 1971),
  15–88, the object of art spoken of is a Greek temple. Heidegger has chosen
  an example which "copies nothing" and which doesn't speak.
8 Heidegger's concern is for the narrowly aesthetic attitude imposed by
  the loss of context due as much to modern museology as to the passing
  of time.
9 An incomplete translation: "Sending: on representation," trans. P. Caws and
  M.A. Caws, in *Social Research* 49: 2(Summer 1982), 294–326.
10 Heidegger is moving between the words *schicken*, to send, *Geschichte*, history
  (there is a relation between the two words), and *Geschick*, fate.

FURTHER READING

Derrida, Jacques. *Dissemination*. Trans. B. Johnson. London: The Athlone Press,
  1981.
  Glas. Trans. J.P. Leavey and R. Rand. Lincoln: University of Nebraska Press,
  1986.

"Limited Inc a b c . . .", *Limited Inc.* Ed. G. Graff. Evanston: Northwestern University Press, 1988.

Of Grammatology, trans. G.C. Spivak. Baltimore: Johns Hopkins University Press, 1974.

"Sending: on representation." Trans. P. Caws and M.A. Caws, in *Social Research* 49: 2 [an incomplete translation of "Envoi," *Psyché: inventions de l'autre.* Paris: Galilée, 1987].

Specters of Marx. Trans. Peggy Kamuf. New York: Routledge, 1994.

The Truth in Painting. Trans. G. Bennington and I. McLeod. Chicago and London: The University of Chicago Press, 1987.

Gombrich, E.H. *Art and Illusion: A Study in the Psychology of Pictorial Representation.* London: Phaidon, 1960.

Heidegger, Martin. "Plato's Doctrine of Truth" (1931–2), in *Gesamtausgabe*, vol. IX.

The Origin of the Work of Art. Trans. A. Hofstadter. In *Poetry, Language, Thought*, 15–88. New York: Harper and Row, Publishers, 1971.

"The Age of the World Picture." Trans. W. Lovitt. In *The Question Concerning Technology and Other Essays.* New York: Harper and Row (Harper Torchbooks), 1977.

Hobson, Marian. *Jacques Derrida: Opening Lines.* London: Routledge, 1998.

The Object of Art: The Theory of Illusion in Eighteenth-century France. Cambridge: Cambridge University Press, 1982.

Kant, Immanuel. *Critique of Judgement.* Trans. and introduction by J.H. Bernard. New York and London: Hafner Publishing Company, 1966.

Klein, R. *La Forme et l'intelligible.* Paris: Gallimard, 1970.

Kristeva, Julia. *The Revolution in Poetic Language.* Trans. M. Walker, introd. L.S. Roudiez. New York: Columbia University Press, 1984.

Sartre, Jean-Paul. "What is literature," *Situations* II. Trans. B. Frechtman, introd. D. Caute. London: Methuen, 1978.

CHAPTER 6

Derrida and philosophy: acts of engagement

Christopher Fynsk

On the horizon of this chapter, a question: What does it mean to "accompany" Derrida? If the task of a companion volume is to offer guidance or paths for an eventual accompaniment, or if it is even to *be* a form of accompaniment, then those who participate in such an effort must surely pause along the way to ask about the nature and conditions of such an undertaking. What acts (of reading, of writing, or of speech) constitute "accompaniment," presuming that this is even possible? In general: What is it to accompany, in thought, and *who* accompanies? More specifically, who accompanies *Derrida*? If it were a matter of simple "expertise," then little problem would exist; the task for the guide would be clearly indicated, and the nature of "following" would be evident. But any "expert," even any casual reader of Derrida will know that accompaniment cannot be so unproblematic a notion. Indeed, any reader who has attended to Derrida's meditations on friendship and the ethical relation (in the sense of the term he takes from Levinas) will know that joining Derrida on the the path of his thinking means something very different from "following." They will hardly be surprised, for example, at the way Derrida recoils, in a recent volume, at the thought of a *traveling* companion.[1]

So where does this leave those who would "accompany" Derrida? Are they destined, like all those students and commentators who have taken the risk of writing in (or *to*) his name, to abandonment? Are they not always already abandoned by the one they would join? Let us be clear here. There can be few teachers active today who are as generous as Jacques Derrida, few who are as solicitous, as mindful of those who have come to him. He knows, he teaches the relations between thought, memory, and thanks in innumerable acts of remembrance and respect. But he also knows the forgetting and the solitude – an experience of the desert, he calls it – that is the condition of approach to the other or to the strange: the other within (one who does not accompany) and the other without. How do we join that solitude, or gain a distance that is still accompaniment? Or is our task to part company when we glimpse that lesson, when "expertise" becomes engagement? Should a "companion" volume serve, ultimately, to mark the point of separation?

Or is it the case that true accompaniment *begins* at the point of separation, and, further, that no reader would be drawn to that point had accompaniment not already begun – had they not already met Derrida at a crossing of paths, and had they not heeded an invitation? For the step from "expertise," however accomplished, to "engagement" is an impossible one if it has not already been made. Strictly speaking, there is no path from the order of the concept ("theory") to the form of performative response that Derrida names "thought." How many times has Derrida had to write that terms like *différance* or "trace" are not philosophemes or conceptual *topoi*, that the exigencies to which they answer (and which they help draw forth) escape the order of conceptual exposition? No doubt, a reader will never grasp the transformative force of a term like *différance* without grasping the theoretical field within which it intervenes (a field that ranges from transcendental phenomenology to structural linguistics). But the reader must also have grasped the thinking engagement that *prompted* Derrida to advance such a term if that force is ever to strike them. To engage the thought, they must have already been engaged by it – a relation must have opened, they must have assumed its engagements, in some way, as their own. Let this accompaniment be as technically sophisticated as it will – it can only become "accompaniment" by moving toward a relation that has already opened, and always for the sake of a new affirmation of that relation, a repetition of the "yes" that the reader has elected to share.

But how are we to think such engagement? The paths, in fact, are many, and it would be perfectly possible to move directly to Derrida's own thematization of it. We could turn, for example, to Derrida's discussion of the "Yes" in "Nombre de oui,"[2] or to the "*viens*" ("come") in his formidable, but also infinitely generous essay on Blanchot entitled "Pas."[3] We could turn to the readings of Levinas, readings that, like the analysis of Blanchot, engage in their own way with the affirmative movement that invited them. Then there are the readings of Benjamin, Marx, and de Man, each of which thematizes an originary engagement from which it proceeds. I will in fact attempt to approach portions of the latter essays, but I propose to do so along a more indirect path, and by response to another invitation, another demonstrative performance of Derrida's fundamental engagements. I refer here to Derrida's efforts on behalf of the institution of philosophy in France, and to the invitation that appears in one of the founding initiatives by which Derrida has attempted to secure the institutional conditions for philosophical practice and for a *thought* of philosophy's own engagements. This path will provide me the opportunity of underscoring the *performative* character of the acts of engagement to which I have referred in my title, of demonstrating the "fundamental" reach of Derrida's engagement with the thought of the performative itself.[4]

I propose, therefore, to turn initially to Derrida's extensive writings on the institution of philosophy,[5] and specifically to two essays that issued from his efforts to help create and set underway the Collège International de Philosophie – two founding documents for an institution that has helped shape philosophical work in France over the last decade. These essays, "Titres" and "Envois," stand independently, though the first, an exposition of the historical and philosophical exigencies to which the Collège would respond, is in many ways preparatory for the statement – the invitation, let us say – Derrida advances in the second. By reading them together, we can appreciate the performative force and the scope of Derrida's propositions in "Envois," or "Sendoffs," as it is translated in English.[6]

"Titres" proceeds from a gesture that is characteristic of many of Derrida's initiatives: an enumeration of the historical signs that call for the initiative in question. In this case, the signs pointing to the necessity of founding something like a Collège International de Philosophie (the conditions that "entitle" it to exist) belong to what Derrida labels "a re-awakening of the philosophical," a new demand for philosophy of national and international proportions that cannot be met within the governing institutional frameworks. This demand for philosophy is in fact inseparable, in Derrida's eyes, from an *expiration* of the traditional entitlements of philosophy and the institutional structures founded in its name (at least from the time of the creation of the University of Berlin and in the wake of Kant's definition of the juridical authority of "the tribunal of reason"). "The end of philosophy" and the spreading impact of the discourses engaged in *thinking* that end are thus among the motifs that constitute what Derrida understands as a set of multiple (perhaps *irreducibly* multiple) demands for a new philosophical undertaking. "The end of philosophy" counts among those motifs because this closure appears not just under the pressure of philosophical critique, but also by way of philosophy's *exposure* to events that are beyond the purview of traditional philosophy and require new forms of philosophical engagement. Events such as:

1. A new *global* configuration of ethical and juridical issues that have emerged with the modern phenomena of nuclear terror, totalitarianism, genocide and torture, urbanization and ecological catastrophe, and world health issues such as the AIDS pandemic – global issues for which the founding concepts of morality and law (already shaken by critiques emanating from philosophy and psychoanalysis) have proven profoundly inadequate.[7]
2. Techno-scientific developments that challenge traditional concepts of life and death (as in medical technology) or space and time (as in developments in the media and communication – transformations that alter the very meaning and constitution of "public space").
3. A resurgence of religious movements and associated political forces throughout the world that place new forms of pressure on the values of "reason" or on notions such as "democracy."
4. "Cultural" displacements – transformations in the arts and their material bases, or transformations in "forms of life." Derrida cites in this regard the fundamental challenges presented by feminist thought.

The list can (and should) be extended. "Titres" and "Sendoffs," already powerfully suggestive of the global transformations that require new forms of philosophical response, also anticipate Derrida's meditations on topics such as racism, the global economy, democracy, and law (a topic visible throughout the later essays collected in *Du droit à la philosophie*). But my aim here is not to survey Derrida's inventory of the signs that constitute a new demand for philosophy, or to seek to complete the list (even if the exercise would be instructive). Indeed, any effort to map or to represent "adequately" the new situation of philosophy would only reproduce the theoretical drive to objectify and master a field, whereas Derrida's first point, once again, is that the field of transformations that solicit a new philosophical undertaking *exceed the purview* of the theoretical or philosophical gaze as it is traditionally instituted. It is not a matter of an overwhelming range of phenomena, an unmanageable empirical abundance; it is a matter, rather, of transformations that exceed philosophy's "phenomenalizing" or objectifying potential. Accordingly, Derrida hypothesizes that the synthesis of the many signs to which he has referred – signs that *solicit* philosophy without being quite *for* philosophy – cannot be accomplished by any established discourse. Their interpretation, he says,

Traverses and exceeds, though perhaps without disqualifying them, all of the discourses and all of the thematics that pretend to govern [this interpretation], for example philosophy (under all its forms, in particular philosophy of language, philosophy of history, hermeneutics, philosophy of religion), the human sciences (for example, sociology, in all its forms, even the sociology of knowledge; history, even the history of the sciences and techniques; political science or political economy, psychoanalysis, etc.) or the "natural" sciences, supposing that the latter distinction still stands up to analysis. In other words, the charter of such a college must not exclude this possibility, that the thought that would prove to be able to measure up to this unity of the epoch, if there is an "epoch," a unity, and a measure, is perhaps no longer scientific or philosophical, in the currently determinable sense of these terms. And in truth it is this indetermination and this very opening that we designate, in this context, with the word "thought."[8]

"The horizon, the task, and the destination" of a new Collège International de Philosophie, Derrida asserts, is outlined by the demand for such a "thought."

I will return shortly to Derrida's "schematic" for a possible elaboration of this thought. But before turning to "Sendoffs," I would like to underscore two important and related points made by him in the light of his diagnostics of the new philosophical exigencies. The first is that the challenge to philosophy's hegemonic position as arbiter of rational inquiry – a challenge to the entire "univertical" ordering of knowledge in the space of the *universitas* – obliges philosophy (or the "thought" that would succeed it) to entertain an open set of *transversal* relations with emergent forms of knowledge and their technical elaborations. Throughout *Du droit à la philosophie*, and particularly in "Sendoffs" and "Titres," we find a call for *translation* and *transference* – multiple passages (of thought) across institutional boundaries and into entirely new problematics and institutional (or extra-institutional) spaces. The collapse of philosophy's traditional "over-arching" position exposes it, as I have asserted, to the necessity of rethinking its relation to the multiple orders of knowledge and practice. It must think its *implication* in these multiple orders even as it thinks their role in it (the "philosophy" in medicine, law, or linguistics, for example, and, reciprocally, the linguistics, law, or medicine in philosophy), and it must find new forms of engagement with the transformations in which it is implicated. The latter imperative – and this brings me to my second point – entails a fundamental recasting of the theory/practice relation, a new thought of theory, praxis, and what Derrida chooses to continue to call *poiesis*. The need for such a recasting is occasioned first of all, and as we have already noted, by technological developments throughout the sciences and arts. To think these forms of knowledge/practice and their solicitation of philosophy, new forms of *competence* are required of thought; philosophy must rethink technical and artistic performance, and it must rethink its own capacity to engage such performance. It must rethink the *"savoir faire"* of the multiple forms of knowledge/practice and think its possible participation in those forms (not just its implication, but its capacity for performative engagement).

These imperatives lead Derrida to devote a section of "Titres" to what he terms "performativity." Moving from a discussion of the need for a new thought of the knowledge/practice relation to the topic of the performative dimension of language, Derrida asserts that the new Collège should take the risk and the wholly original step of placing the question and even the requirement of "performativity" at the heart of its concerns. No institution of research and teaching, he says, has accorded full legitimacy (the right to full exercise and recognition) to the performative character of language. To be sure, Derrida is well aware that there has always been a place in the university for discussion of the rhetorical effects of language, or its "force"; but his argument is that no institution has recognized *de droit* the place of the *event* in the discourses it sanctions – namely the possibility that those discourses could alter the contract that authorizes them. No institution has sanctioned (and above all, sought) an alteration of the symbolic order it represents – an act of speech, in other words, that would constitute an intervention in the symbolic. Derrida's words are measured on this topic. "Titres" is, after all, an official document, and Derrida is not one to celebrate naively the transgressive powers of symbolic acts (he knows too acutely the ruses of representation and "entitlement"). But when he suggests that the first step in engaging a thought of the performative might involve research into its "institutional aspect," he is doing more than proposing a novel topic of study – a topic that he has himself developed at some length in his reading of Benjamin (in "Force of Law," to which I will return, and in texts such as "Declarations of Independence"). He is also implicitly inviting the Collège to consider the "exorbitant" foundation of its own instituting acts and the transformations to which its founding charter are subject. Though "Titres" touches only briefly on this question, it seems clear that Derrida believes that the initial step of considering the "institutional aspect" of the performative should be taken in relation to the institution of philosophy itself, and ultimately because the deconstructive analysis of philosophy's founding acts helps point to a way of thinking *what calls for philosophy* in the transversal movements that Derrida proposes to the Collège, i.e., in philosophy's engagements with other modes of knowledge/practice.

What does an analysis of philosophy's instituting performative reveal? Derrida sketches an answer in the preface to *Du droit à la philosophie*, and in explicit reference to the initiatives outlined in "Titres." Having observed that any "pragmatic" determination of what may be defined as "philosophy" requires a concept of the essence of the philosophical, and, reciprocally, that any determination of that essence of an "originarist" sort (as in Heidegger) must presuppose a performative "act of language" that marks philosophy's inscription in a given language and an institutional and social function,[9] Derrida goes on to observe that philosophy's founding contract is unstable – by law. Citing the opening declarations of "Titres" (a set of questions more than a set of declarations, in fact: "Why philosophy?," "Why philosophy today?," etc.), Derrida goes on to write:

The whole chapter that opens in this manner will mark the aporia of a community that proposes to found itself on a contract without prior example, a dissymetrical contract inscribing in itself non-knowledge and the possibility given at every instant of breaking the contract, of deforming or displacing not only its particular terms, but its constitutional axiomatic or its essential foundations, even up to the idea of the contract or the institution. No doubt, an auto-foundation or auto-institution always proceeds in this manner, as in the origination of states. But the fiction of a constative knowledge and an irreversibility are always there and are structurally indispensable. Here, on the contrary, it is through fidelity to a quasi-contract that is absolute and without history, to a pre-contractual engagement that the institutional contract might be put back into question in its very presupposition, and even in its essence as a contract. It is always in the name of a more imperative responsibility that one suspends or subordinates responsibility to a constituted seat of authority (for example, the State; but also a given figure of philosophical reason).[10]

The philosophical engagement is always subject to suspension by reason of a more fundamental engagement, an always prior responsibility of thought (a responsibility that is *to* philosophy, Derrida suggests, but to an always more responsible philosophy, more faithful to the "promise" of philosophy). *Before* any instituting act, therefore, but also inseparable from it, is what he names, in *Specters of Marx*, an "originary performativity."[11] In *Du droit à la philosophie*, and in reference to philosophy's engagements in relation to the other, he names it a "yes."[12] As we consider Derrida's own performative in "Sendoffs," we will approach this "yes" and Derrida's implicit suggestion that a thought of this engagement will provide the path for understanding what calls for philosophy in the new conjuncture to which the Collège seeks to respond.

In speaking of a performative in "Sendoffs," I am referring to the quite forceful and demonstrative gesture Derrida makes in advancing a proposition for setting the Collège on a path toward the thought he identifies in "Titres" as "the horizon, the task, the destination [*destination*]," of this new institution.[13] This *coup d'envoi* for the Collège is a proposal for a program of research devoted to the thought of "destination" itself. What does he advance with this term (which I have translated, somewhat neutrally, with its cognate)? It is, first of all, not a thesis, nor a topic, nor a category, in any of the traditional philosophical senses of these terms. As a strategic intervention for engaging the limits of the philosophical itself, it has a more "schematic" character; it condenses and formalizes possibilities for thinking philosophy's engagement of the transversal passages to which philosophy is called. Derrida evokes, in this respect, its "performing" and "performative" value[14] as a strategic lever for intervening in the current conjuncture, a conjuncture marked by a singular turn in the problematic he identified in "Titres" as "the end of philosophy." On the one hand, he says, the turn (and return) to philosophy on the part of the social and natural sciences takes the form of a meditation on ends or finality (which, along with the question of "transmission," in all its breadth, forms the basic lines of Derrida's guiding schema[15]). This turn meets in philosophy itself a fundamental transformation of the problematic of ends and transmission in the form of a new thought of "dispensation," "sending" ("*l'envoi*"), and the gift – a thought that no longer belongs to philosophy proper (construed as onto-theology) and has the force to recast both the history of philosophy as a thought of Being and all the fundamental questions of philosophy and science: the hoary questions of truth, meaning, reference, objectivity, and history (among others).

As many will recognize, an explicit and unembarrassed appeal is made here to Heidegger's thought of the "gift" and "sending" of Being, and to everything that follows from Heidegger's gesture of thinking essence in general from the relation he thinks with the phrase "*es gibt.*" To be sure, these "destinal" relations, preceding and opening the possibility of any relations of predication and communication (all subject/object or "intersubjective" relations) have been subjected to their own "recasting" in Derrida's thought of the trace and *différance*, and Derrida is quite clear in reiterating that his translation of Heidegger is profoundly transformative.[16] Nevertheless, it is worth emphasizing that Derrida does not shy from taking over the Heideggerian legacy in all its *fundamental* reach.

Of course, the term "fundamental" must also be subject to a "destinal" reworking (it must be thought precisely from "engagement," from "sending off," from a contracting of relation that is also a setting underway). But Derrida underscores powerfully that the new Collège must not fail to assume it in response to the demand for such reflection emanating from all the sites to which philosophy is called:

> Even if we had not been convinced of it in advance, our consultations have provided us with an eloquent proof: the demand for this type of research is very marked today, and it is capable of mobilizing great forces and taking original forms. For reasons and along directions that remain to be analyzed, this "fundamentalist" thought has given in to a sort of intimidation before the sciences, all the sciences, but especially the human and social sciences. It can and should find a new legitimacy and cease being ashamed of itself, as has sometimes been the case over the past two decades. This can be done without regressions and without a return to the hegemonic structures.[17]

Derrida thus returns to the "fundamental" exigencies to which he answered in entertaining the thought of a "grammatology" in the volume by that name – exigencies that have been largely lost to view in the translation of this thought in the various "critical" discourses (and even the institutions of deconstruction) in the English-speaking world, but that are perhaps beginning to re-emerge by virtue of the alarming turn in the fortunes of philosophy and humanistic research, at least in the English-speaking academies. For many, it has become painfully obvious that a new thought of the humanities is now required – an *affirmative* thought of their potential implication (and need) in disciplines throughout the fields of knowledge. Indeed, it is the latter exigency that has prompted me to turn to this particular Derridean performance, this demonstrative gesture addressed to the Collège and to all of those concerned by its mission.

So, what would a thought of "destination" offer to a Collège de Philosophie in this conjuncture defined by "the end of philosophy" and by philosophy's exposition to a set of transformations that do not surrender to the synthesizing hold of the concept? Beyond the challenges to the founding concepts of philosophy and science already enumerated, it offers, Derrida hints, a thought of the conjuncture itself: a thought of the "con-" and "dis-" junctions that mark philosophy's relation with itself and with other orders of discourse and practice, but also a thought of the *time* of these expositions, a thought of their event. The thought of destination is also, and perhaps first of all, a thought of another historicity.[18] "Sendoffs," limited by its pragmatic occasion, does not elaborate on the latter motif.[19] But it obviously anticipates the elaborations to come in texts such as *Specters of Marx*, a volume in which Derrida captures the resistance of the time ("our" time, any time) to epochal summation by way of a meditation on the famous phrase from *Hamlet*: "the time is out of joint." As Derrida might well have said in "Sendoffs," had he sought a less affirmative and engaging tone, the time is out of joint for philosophy (are not the many appearances of Polonius another historical sign of its end?). But Derrida finds in this very disjunctive condition the source of a promise – a messianic and emancipatory promise:

> But with the other, is not this disjuncture, this dis-adjustment of the "it's going badly" necessary for the good, or at least the just, to be announced? Is not disjuncture the very possibility of the other? How to distinguish between two disadjustments, between the disjuncture of the unjust and the one that opens up the infinite asymmetry of the relation to the other, that is to say, the place for justice? Not for calculable and distributive justice . . . Not for calculable equality . . . but for justice as the incalculability of the gift and singularity of the an-economic exposition to *autrui*. "The relation to *autrui* – that is to say, justice," writes Levinas.[20]

As we might anticipate, the step from a thought of destination, as Derrida describes it in "Sendoffs," to a thought of justice, as it is evoked here, is a short one. In *Specters*, it is made via an interrogative appeal to Heidegger's translation of *dike* in "The Anaximander Fragment" as *Fug*, or "jointure." "The Anaximander Fragment," Heidegger tells us, offers a thought of justice founded not on an economy of vengeance or retribution, but rather on an enjoined or "destined" order or "jointure" in Being, an order whose an-economic gift is attended by an irreducible dis-order (*Un-fug*). Derrida's critical move vis-à-vis Heidegger is to draw out the necessity of this "dis-" and to unsettle, in this manner, Heidegger's characteristic emphasis on a gathering measure in Being. For Derrida, the thought of a necessary dis-jointure in every destined order offers the link to a possible thought of an experience of history that is the condition for the notion of justice he pursues throughout his latest works.

This is not the place to second Derrida's engagement (re-engagement) with Heidegger's meditation in "The Anaximander Fragment" by working through the compelling motives for his critical reading. But I would like to linger just a little longer at this juncture where a thought of destination opens upon a thought of justice. For this juncture is marked, and thought, by Heidegger with a notion that Derrida does not pursue, but that points back powerfully to the motif of "performativity" that is at the heart of Derrida's proposals for the new Collège and may therefore help us grasp the link (or create a new one) between his understanding of the performative event and his understanding of the interruptive relation that leads him to speak increasingly of a "messianic" experience of justice. I refer here to Heidegger's thought of "usage" – *der Brauch*. *Der Brauch* is in fact the term with which Heidegger translates the "*kata to kreon*" with which the Anaximander fragment opens. "*Entlang dem Brauch*," Heidegger offers for this phrase: order and disorder are enjoined *according to usage*. What is this usage? At the level at which it is evoked here (the "ontological" level, we might say – indeed, Heidegger suggests that we are dealing in this instance with the oldest and most original thought of Being in its difference from beings), it names the interruptive relation between Being and the "there" of its truth. More precisely, and no less technically, it names for Heidegger the interruptive appropriation of the human essence to language, in *Ereignis*, that gives all relation. It is "*the relation*" as Heidegger says in his essay, "The Way to Language"[21]: the contraction of relation that lies at the origin of the "setting underway" of language itself, and thus at the origin of any gift of language, including its gift of itself or its gift of Being. With his thought of the relation of usage, Heidegger obliges us to think the *es gibt* that Derrida has given us to think so powerfully in recent years, from an "*es brauchet.*" At the heart of every gift, there is usage.

Heidegger approaches the thought of usage most frequently and most overtly from an implicit rethinking of his early thought of the "essential praxis" of the human Dasein. I would suggest, in fact, that "usage" is the term with which he rethinks the relation between *physis* and *techné* that so preoccupied him throughout the thirties. And I would add that he is rethinking both praxis and *poiesis* from the "pragmatics" of usage to which he refers in his Parmenides lectures when he undertakes his analysis of praxis as *Handlung*. In effect, he justifies his translation of *to kreon* as "*der Brauch*" (he justifies this translating *Sprachgebrauch*) by thinking the term from its linguistic proximity to the Greek *keir* (the hand). Thus he thinks all forms of *praxis* and *poiesis* in relation to a "*Handlung*" that is an "aletheic" comportment of delivering something to its essence, or according to it what is properly its own (to paraphrase Derrida's own reference to this notion in *Specters*[22]). But Heidegger insists in all his discussions of "*Handwerk*" and "*Handlung*" that human usage must be thought from a prior "use" of the human in *Ereignis* for the destining of Being. Let me try to be precise here, because I mean to mark a dimension of Heidegger's reflection on "*Handlung*" that Derrida himself, in his superb discussion of the hand, does not address.[23] Heidegger makes it quite explicit that all *Handlung*, as a "delivering" comportment of usage, takes its possibility from a grant (a destining, let us say), that opens within language. All *Handlung*, as Derrida notes precisely, is thought by Heidegger *from* the essence of language and from the manner in which language gives relation in giving itself. So we must think human "usage" from the *es gibt* of language and Being. But the gift of language presupposes, in Heidegger's analysis, a prior dis-position of the human essence, a prior appropriation to language that is the ground of the subsequent (taking this, as well as "prior," in a logical sense) "yes" to language by which human kind accedes to the grant of language, its *Zusage*. (This is the "yes" that Derrida has made resound so powerfully – a yes that redoubles the originary exposure to which I am referring.) Once again, the human essence is "used," Heidegger says, for the appropriative movement by which language is first set underway in its essence, its *Wesen*. Heidegger's description of this latter usage (he calls it the *"er-eignend-brauchende Be-wegung"*[24]) is swift, even elliptical. Nevertheless, it is clear that with the notion of usage, Heidegger is thinking the finitude of language itself – the limit (the relation) that is traced in its setting underway. At this limit is a "human essence" that, as mortal, *offers* relation in its very powerlessness with regard to truth, a *"nicht vermögen"* that is the ground of the comportment of *Gelassenheit*.[25] Capable of death, as Heidegger said in *Being and Time*, mortals know an in-capacity in relation to truth. The task for mortals, as Heidegger suggests throughout his later work, is to recover relation to this delivering usage, this (non)ground of human destination – to assume in a free usage ("a free use of the proper," as Hölderlin said) its originary abandonment or exposure in this *er-eignend-brauchende Be-wegung*. This "free usage," Heidegger tells us, would be first of all a *Sprachgebrauch* that remarks the double character of the human implication in language, the way humankind is lent to language and lends itself to language (unreservedly – there is no economy here) in an originary assent to a relation always already contracted.

To restate this schematically once again: a relation to the human essence lies at the origin of language's gift, in Heidegger's account; the comportment of *Gelassenheit* proceeds from this originary exposure. But Heidegger adds that language could not give itself ("speak," as he puts it) without a kind of active assent, a listening that is defining for language and already a kind of speaking. Humankind must accede to language's address, in advance, for language to come to the word. Before any speech, there must be a kind of "yes," a "yes" that remarks and assumes the originary exposure that is the distinguishing trait of the human essence. A "free *Sprachgebrauch*" would assume and countersign the "yes" to language that already redoubles the originary exposure of the human essence that is at the limits of language.

Might this notion of a "free *Sprachgebrauch*" describe Derrida's acts of engagement? An easy answer is at hand (has there been a "freer" philosophical usage than Derrida's in the latter part of the twentieth century?). And we are certainly not far from Derrida's own account of the structure of engagement; with this rapid sketch of the multifold structure of the human engagement with language as it is understood by Heidegger, I have held closely (as I suggested along the way) to Derrida's own "fictive," "quasi-analytic" account of the "yes" in "Nombre de oui," a schematic unfolding of both the originary performative that is the condition of every performative and the repetition (always "free," always forgetfully reassuming) that is necessary to it.[26] But before entertaining, in conclusion, the pertinence of this account for Derrida's own philosophical "pragmatics," I want to suggest that the "use-value" of this appeal to Heidegger's notion of usage lies in the way it points to the necessity of thinking the indissociably "existential" and "ontological" dimensions of the thought of the performative event to which Derrida points in "Sendoffs." Neither "existential" nor "ontological" are quite adequate here by reason of terminological inertia,[27] but they will perhaps serve to point provisionally to a dimension of experience to which Derrida appeals in *Specters of Marx* in evoking the messianic relation he attempts to think under the name of "justice."[28] By thinking the performative event from a notion of usage, it might well be possible to recover something of the bodily and historical dimensions of the "speech act" that have evaded most appeals to this concept. Moreover, the notion of usage (involving, as it does, the human relation to language) helps underscore the point that the "mystical foundation of authority," as Derrida thinks it, lies in a relational structure that *announces* itself or *is announced* in every performative act.[29] For, every performative (at least in the strong sense of this term that Derrida tries to think) proceeds from an originary engagement that is an engagement with language itself – an opening to language that is an opening *of* language. The performative, as Derrida understands it, is always a linguistic "sendoff," and it is always accompanied by an affirmative engagement. Here, in this linguistic event, we have the "silent companion" of every performative act.[30] Here, in the strictest sense, is what *calls* for philosophy, for a translation of philosophy, in the events of discourse and practice to which philosophy is now exposed in the current conjuncture. In every instance of a performative usage, in every performative event (and it is precisely the *eventful* character of the performative to which philosophy is now exposed), philosophy finds itself potentially addressed with a question of destination and with the dimensions of this question I have tried to elaborate: the question of the conjuncture, and with it the question of justice. For, in every case, there is an engagement with the other, an interrupting exposition.

But again, will this general account of engagement and address capture Derrida's own acts of commitment, and thereby the conditions for accompanying him? It may well do so in a "quasi-analytic" manner, but it is no doubt essential to respect Derrida's insistence on the singularly ascetic character of the engagement he seeks to affirm in his writing.[31] This asceticism, and the distance from Heidegger (among others) that it entails is forcefully articulated in *Specters* when Derrida draws out the disjuncture implicit in all jointure, and argues that the "exposition" to which I have pointed in Heideggerian terms (the relation to an "impossible" implied by Heidegger's notion of a human powerlessness) must be understood far more radically than Heidegger ever allowed. It must be understood in and from an abyssal structure of experience that involves a constant ex- or dis-appropriation. The "yes" to justice or to democracy, proceeding from an immemorial exposure, and projecting or enjoining upon its messianic promise as an opening always *possibly* to come, unfolds in an ever more arid or empty space, a "desert in the desert," as Derrida says, "a desert pointing toward the other, an abyssal and *chaotic* desert, if 'chaos' describes first of all the immensity, the unmeasure, the disproportion in the saying of an open mouth, in the waiting – or in the call – of what we are naming here, without knowledge, the messianic: the coming of the other, the absolute and unanticipatible singularity of the coming *as justice.*"[32] It is from such an experience and such a *call* that Derrida reads Marx in *Specters*. Its structure is *universal*, Derrida argues,[33] but its singular repetition as an *inherited* injunction[34] bears a distinct signature. It resonates in *Specters* with the force, the "weak messianic power"[35] that is proper to the "originary performative" – but only inasmuch as it is assumed by Derrida in a new engaging act, a new "messianic" claim.

Derrida "accompanies" Marx, we could say. Might this be a model for the "accompaniment" sought here (in this volume) in relation to Derrida himself? A model, at least, for the repeating engagement required by any accompaniment in writing or thought? If it can, if *perhaps* we can accompany Derrida from the basis of an engagement like the one Derrida undertakes in relation to Marx (and the modality of this "perhaps" marks the fact that such accompaniment, *when it is given*, can never be a *certain* acquisition, and can only unfold in a form of supposition), then it remains essential to underscore that such accompaniment cannot be undertaken without the risk of new engagements, new responsibilities. There is the responsibility of discrimination, first of all ("accompaniment," like inheritance, requires choice, as Derrida emphasizes in relation to the multiple "words" of Marx). We must be willing to *read* Derrida, not just apply his "concepts," cite him as an authority among others, or take his text as an object of scholarship. Then there is the indissociable responsibility of renewed commitment to an other that dis-appropriates every contracted bond. Few, undoubtedly (at least today), will assume the term "messianic" for this engagement, while others will applaud at the way Derrida has raised the stakes with this *gage*. But the yes, however it is thought, must be unreserved in its opening to alterity, and it is clear that one cannot predict the paths onto which it may open. We see, therefore, that to join Derrida in thought is to advance toward the possibility and responsibility of a freeing accompaniment – a "sendoff." It is to advance with him to a point of departure.

NOTES

1 See Catherine Malabou and Jacques Derrida, *La contre-allée* (Paris: Louis Vuitton, 1998), 13.
2 In *Psyché: Inventions de l'autre* (Paris: Galilée, 1987), 639–50.
3 In *Parages* (Paris: Galilée, 1986), 19–116.
4 I hope to meet, in this way, my promise to Tom Cohen and Derek Attridge, who invited me to address the topic of the performative from the perspective of phenomenology. The latter is an immense task whose first condition of fulfillment, I believe, is a demonstration of the performative force of Derrida's engagement with the performative. Here again, many paths are available, starting with the most obvious one: Derrida's engagements with speech act theory. Had I followed so many others along this well-beaten path, I would have attempted to consider Derrida's playful performances in his articles on Searle and link them to the early essay on mimesis ("The Double Session" – is Derrida, writing, not like the mime of Mallarmé's "Mimique"?) and to the later essay on invention ("Inventions de l'autre") where the same "mimetic" power of language, its capacity to fold on itself, is engaged through a poem by Ponge whose first line is "Par le mot 'par' . . . ," a poem in which Derrida finds a deconstruction of the performative/constative distinction and a more originary notion of the performative. One path among so many. But I believe that a stronger imperative carries us today to the "originary" performative I have sketched above. I am convinced that a failure to grasp this dimension of Derrida's writing is at the heart of the failure to realize an "accompaniment"

that is more than a formalist commentary. The failure to grasp Derrida's engagements lies at the heart of the failure to realize the political and ethical role of deconstruction.

5 These writings are collected in *Du droit à la philosophie* (Paris: Galilée, 1990) and range from the earliest essays written for GREPH (the "Groupe de recherches sur l'enseignement de la philosophie") – an initiative to which I devoted an essay some years ago: "A Decelebration of Philosophy," in *Diacritics* 8, 2 (Summer 1978): 80–90 – to the more recent work on behalf of the Collège International de Philosophie.

6 "Sendoffs," trans. Thomas Pepper, with D. Esch and T. Keenan, in *Yale French Studies* 77: *Reading the Archive: On Texts and Institutions*, ed. E.S. Burt and Janie Vanpée: 7–43.

7 Derrida does not evoke the contemporary concept of "globalization" (a concept he would undoubtedly want to question) in this essay of 1982, but his enumeration of issues clearly indicates his attention to this new challenge to the articulation of philosophy's *topoi*.

8 *Du droit à la philosophie*, 560.

9 *Du droit à la philosophie*, 20. Derrida is working here through the imperatives of a thought of "finite transcendence." While the act of thought is not *reducible* to the determinations of its socio-political or linguistic context, it cannot be abstracted from its finite, always historical, inscription.

10 Ibid., 35.

11 *Specters of Marx*, trans. Peggy Kamuf (New York: Routledge, 1994), 31.

12 "The thought of this 'yes' *before* philosophy, *before* even the question, *before* research and critique, does not signify any renunciation of philosophy, or of what might follow it or follow from it. This thought *can*, and one might even think that precisely it *must* engage itself there. It can do so inasmuch as, under the form of obligation or debt, it finds itself already *engaged*, already inscribed in the space that is opened and closed by this *gage* – given to the other, received from the other. But it traces a kind of strange limit between all these determinations of the philosophical and a deconstructive thought that is engaged *by* philosophy without belonging to it, faithful to an affirmation whose responsibility places it *before* philosophy, but also *in advance* of it" (*Du droit à la philosophie*, 28).

13 Ibid., 561.

14 Ibid., 587.

15 Derrida gives the following, summary description of the reach of this motif: "Let's not unfold this problematic in its most easily identifiable dimensions yet (destination and destiny, all the problems of the end and thus of limits or of confines, ethical or political aim, teleology – natural or not – the destination of life, of man, of history, the problem of eschatology (utopian, religious, revolutionary, etc.), that of the constitution and the structure of the sender/receiver system, and thus of the dispatch or sendoff and the message (in all its forms and in all its substances – linguistic or not, semiotic or not), emission, the mission, the missile, transmission in all its forms,

telecommunication and all its techniques, economic distribution and all its conditions (producing, giving, receiving, exchanging), the dispensation of knowledge and what we now call the *"finalisation"* of research or of techno-science, etc.)" ("Sendoffs," 14).

16 *Du droit à la philosophie*, 29.

17 Ibid., 592.

18 *Specters*, 74–75.

19 A regrettable limitation, perhaps, since it clearly points to a farther-reaching thought of the event than the one subsequently offered by Alain Badiou (whose understanding of the question of language remains far short of what would be required by a consequent thought of "performativity" in the sense sought by Derrida). See Badiou's *Manifeste pour la philosophie* (Paris: Éditions du Seuil, 1989).

20 *Specters*, 22–23.

21 This phrase does not appear in the English translation, "On the Way to Language." See Martin Heidegger, "Unterwegs zur Sprache," *Gesamtausgabe*, vol. XII (Frankfurt am Main: Klostermann, 1985), 229.

22 *Specters*, 26.

23 Derrida consistently leaves untouched the problematic of usage at the "on-tological" level, and nothing in his argument will help us determine whether he is avoiding the topic, unaware of it (which seems unlikely), or simply un-interested. It seems quite possible to me that he declines engagement with it in Heidegger's text because it would oblige him to take up the issue of Heidegger's references to a "human essence" that is appropriated to lan-guage in *Ereignis*. Derrida's resistance to any appeal to the philosopheme of *"l'homme"* (however "deconstructed") could well explain a reluctance to work with the term. At the same time, however, it is possible to find traces in his text of a thought of "usage" like the one I am attempting to explore. In "Force of Law," for example, Derrida evokes a "heteronomy" in the "mad" act of decision (one that answers to the urgency of every *just* decision): "Such a decision is at once super-active *and* suffered, it retains something passive about it, even unconscious, as though the decider were free only to let them-selves be affected by their own decision, and as though the latter came to them from the other. The consequences of such a heteronomy are forbid-ding, but it would be unjust to avoid the necessity." (This sentence is added to the French edition: *Force de loi* [Paris: Galilée, 1994], 58). I would also note that Derrida's attention to the materiality of the human Dasein as it is described in *Being and Time* engages the topic of the bodily character of what Heidegger declares to be the "proper" of the human essence that is appropriated by language (though Derrida does not take it up in these terms and does not discuss this later notion of the "appropriation" of the human to language in *Ereignis*). See the two essays under the title "Geschlecht" in *Psyché*, 395–452.

Do we still "accompany" Derrida by pursuing a path like this one? This might be the point to observe that I have always considered accompaniment to mean working *with* Derrida, not "on" him or simply *after* him. To write "on" Derrida is perhaps the best way to neutralize the deconstructive force of his engagements.

24 *Unterwegs zur Sprache*, 250.

25 Heidegger describes this "powerlessness" in his essay on *"Gelassenheit"* as follows: "The essence of humankind is released into that which regions and accordingly used by it for this reason alone: because humankind for itself has no power over truth and the latter remains in-dependent of it. Truth can only essence independently of humankind because the essence of humankind as releasement to that which regions is used by that which regions in regioning [*Vergegnis*] and for the preserving of determining [*Bedingnis*]. The independence of truth *from* humankind is clearly a relation *to* the human essence, a relation which rests in the *Vergegnis* of the human essence into that which regions" (*Discourse on Thinking*, trans. John M. Anderson and E. Hans Freund (New York: Harper and Row, 1966), 84. I have attempted to work through the implications of this passage in *Language and Relation: ... that there is language* (Stanford: Stanford University Press, 1996) in the course of a lengthy reading of Heidegger's *On the Way to Language*. While I cannot reproduce this analysis here, I would note that it points to the necessity of thinking a fundamental interruption in the relation between Being and humankind. Pushing Heidegger's analysis in this way (which is to say, reading the trace of this interruption in his text), we come into proximity with Derrida's thought of the experience of justice. It is on this basis that I feel it is worthwhile to develop the "schema" of destination in relation to a notion of usage.

26 It would be useful, for our purposes, to review the "quasi-transcendental" status of this "yes" that resembles, as Derrida puts it, "an absolute performative." A careful examination of the manner in which Derrida removes it both from the hold of any linguistic science and from any ontological or transcendental discourse would demonstrate just how great a challenge his thought of "destination" (as it is thought in its linguistic "engagement," or, as I am trying to do, in relation to a notion of "usage") poses to any traditional understanding of the role of philosophy or its relation to other discourses and practices. Here, for example, are the concluding words of his summary ("naive") statement on the status of any discourse addressed to this condition of all discourse (*Psyché*, 649): "And yet, *one must* – yes – maintain the ontologico-transcendental requirement in order to bring forth the dimension of a *yes* that is no more empirical or ontical than it is subject to any science, ontology, regional phenomenology, or finally any predicative discourse. Presupposed by every proposition, it cannot be confused with the position, thesis, or theme of any language. It is through and through that fable which, inasmuch as it is *quasiment* before the act and before the *logos*, remains *quasiment* at the beginning: "With the word *with* this text thus begins ... [*Par le mot par commence donc ce texte* ...]" ("Fable," by Ponge). But to do any justice to the honor paid to Michel de Certeau's memory in this essay, it would be equally necessary to attend to the "quasi-analytic" account of the

necessity of repetition to which I have referred: an extraordinary rendition of the "promise of memory and [the] memory of the promise" (649). Here, Derrida carries forward Heidegger's thought of the multifold character of the engagement with language I have described in an extremely free and compelling manner. (One should also consult, in this respect, the analysis of the promise in Derrida's *Mémoires* – another text that engages at some length Heidegger's meditations on the *Zusage* of language.) Thus, I must reiterate that while Derrida works through the structure of this "originary performative" in a way that is quite consistent with Heidegger (*explicitly* consistent at some points – constant reference is made to Heidegger's thought of language's address and an anticipatory response), his description of the "divided," repetitive character of its "enunciation" clearly departs from the Heideggerian account (which accords its own place to a notion of repetition). Any thought of a Derridean "*Sprachgebrauch*" would have to take account of this thought of a divided enunciation.

27 If "ontological" is understood in reference to "the discourse on the being of a presence" ("Nombre de oui," 648), as it almost always is, then it proves unsuitable here. I use it only to indicate a level of discourse that engages a thought of Being *in its relationality*. "Existential," in its turn, remains burdened by the metaphysics of subjectivity, though it seems to me that Jean-Luc Nancy has done quite a bit to free the term "existence" from that legacy.

28 For Derrida's appeal to a notion of "experience," see, for example, *Specters* ("a certain experience of the messianic experience," 59), ("the experience of the impossible," 65), ("We prefer to say *messianic* rather than *messianism*, so as to designate a structure of experience rather than a religion," 167). In *Force de loi*, Derrida follows Heidegger in thinking the notion of experience from a notion of passage or traversal (see Heidegger's remarks on experience in *On the Way to Language* ([New York: Harper and Row, 1971], 57) and evokes a paradoxical "*experience of the aporia*": "Experience finds its way, its passage, it is possible. In this sense, there cannot be a full experience of the aporia, namely of what does not allow passage. *Aporia* is a non-path. Justice would be, from this point of view, the experience of that which we cannot experience . . . But I believe that there is no justice without this experience, however impossible it may be, of the aporia. Justice is an experience of the impossible. A will, a desire, a demand for justice whose structure was not an experience of aporia would have no chance of being what it is, namely a just *call* for justice" (*Force de loi* [Paris: Galilée, 1994], 38).

29 "The mystical foundation of authority" is a phrase Derrida takes from Montaigne and Pascal to think the performative (and abyssal) character of any institution of law. Pascal's formulation of the notion reads as follows: "Custom is the sole basis for equity, for the simple reason that it is received; this is the *mystical foundation* of its *authority*" (cited in "Force of Law," 939). Taking a freedom similar to the one Derrida claims in his interpretation of the phrase, I cannot help but suggest that a notion of usage (which inevitably evokes a notion of mores or custom) will help us think the "silence walled

up in the violence of the founding act" ("Force of Law," 943). Derrida's own reference to Wittgenstein in this context (to define his understanding of the term "mystical") prompts me here to refer to another, namely Wittgenstein's argument that "meaning is usage." But while Wittgenstein's text actually lends itself in some ways to a thought of the "mystical" along the lines I seek to suggest (a thought of disruptive relation between "Being" and "human being") it remains quite recalcitrant.

30 See *Psyché*, p. 644. I draw this phrase, "silent companion," from the passage by Franz Rosenzweig cited by Derrida.

31 Not to speak of the distinctive cast of his writing – "rhetorical" performative gestures that bear the mark of a singular signature. It is important to recall that the "acts of engagement" I am considering here cannot be thought apart from their occasion and their individual articulation. The "yes" occurs only as it is "drawn out" or "written out," only in its repetition. The same point must be recalled in reference to the notion of "accompaniment," with which I will conclude.

32 *Specters*, 27.

33 Ibid., 67.

34 Ibid., 21.

35 Derrida evokes this Benjaminian notion in *Specters*, 96.

FURTHER READING

Badiou, Alain. *Manifeste pour la philosophie*. Paris: Éditions du Seuil, 1989.

Derrida, Jacques, and Malabou, Catherine. *La contre-allée*. La Quinzaine Littéraire. Paris: Louis Vuitton, 1998.

Derrida, Jacques. *Du droit à la philosophie*. Paris: Galilée, 1990.

Force de loi. Paris: Galilée, 1994.

Parages. Paris: Galilée, 1986.

Psyché: inventions de l'autre. Paris: Galilée, 1987.

"Sendoffs," trans. Thomas Pepper, with Deborah Esch and Thomas Keenan. In *Yale French Studies 77: Reading the Archive: On Texts and Institutions*. Ed. E.S. Burt and Janie Vanpée: 7–43.

Specters of Marx. Trans. Peggy Kamuf. New York: Routledge, 1994.

Fynsk, Christopher. *Language and Relation: . . . that there is language*. Stanford: Stanford University Press, 1996.

"A Decelebration of Philosophy." *Diacritics*, 8:2 (Summer 1978): 80–90.

Heidegger, Martin. "The Anaximander Fragment." In *Early Greek Thinking*. Trans. J. Glenn Gray. New York: Harper and Row, 1973.

Discourse on Thinking. Trans. John M. Anderson and E. Hans Freund. New York: Harper and Row, 1966.

Unterwegs zur Sprache, Gesamtausgabe, vol. XII. Ed. Friedrich-Wilhelm von Hermann. Frankfurt am Main: Klostermann, 1985 [*On the Way to Language*. Trans. Peter D. Hertz. New York: Harper and Row, 1971]].

CHAPTER 7

Derrida and ethics: hospitable thought

Hent de Vries

To situate Jacques Derrida's contribution to the understanding of religion in its complex relation to ethics and politics, one must begin by recalling first Emmanuel Levinas's and then Immanuel Kant's definition of these three terms. Following Derrida's philosophical itinerary, one moves almost invisibly from an engagement with Levinas to a confrontation with Kant. Only by carefully comparing the radically distinct yet intimately related philosophical projects for which the proper names "Levinas" and "Kant" stand can one begin to situate the convoluted thematic and argumentative approach to ethics, politics, and, in particular, religion that Derrida unfolds in increasing detail and consequence in the philosophical trajectory running from his earliest to his latest writings. His discussions, first of Levinas (in "Violence and Metaphysics," arguably the most powerfully argued chapter of *Writing and Difference*, and "At This Very Moment in This Work Here I Am," arguably the most enigmatic essay in *Psyché*) and subsequently Kant (especially in *Truth in Painting, Of an Apocalyptic Tone Recently Adopted in Philosophy, Du droit à la philosophie [(Of the) Right to Philosophy]*, and *Politics of Friendship*), set the tone for a remarkable recasting of our understanding of the ethical and the political in light of the religious, its chances and its perils. Finally, in *Adieu to Emmanuel Levinas*, together with the pamphlet *Cosmopolites de tous les pays, encore un effort! (Cosmopolitans of All Nations, Yet Another Effort!)*, the names – and arguments – of Levinas and Kant are brought together in a single configuration and presented as two complementary views on the same problem. This movement from the concept of the ethical by way of the political to the religious is confirmed by one of the latest of Derrida's sustained discussions of religion, "Faith and Knowledge: The Two Sources of 'Religion' at the Limits of Reason Alone," a study whose subtitle echoes that most Kantian of titles, *Religion Within the Limits of Reason Alone*. Indeed, Derrida's different approaches could be seen as so many endeavors to rewrite Kant's famous essay.

Any such genealogy is inevitably too schematic, however. It suggests a linear development of concepts and themes where there is in fact a far more convoluted trajectory, in which what seems a single leitmotif – unlimited, infinite, or absolute responsibility – is unfolded only to be folded in again, in varying ways depending on the context, the specific occasion of an interrogation, or the urgency of a certain clarification. Derrida insists, time and again, that responsibility, although unrestricted and hence categorical or even transcategorical and excessive, relies on a general structure of iterability in which it is always singularly traced and retraced and only thus attains a certain ideality – qua idea and ideal, in an almost Kantian sense – as well. What might thus be considered Derrida's single most wide-ranging insight – infinite responsibility, as Levinas would have said, and its necessary betrayal in repetition – is presented in an, in principle, incomplete series of "examples" or, better, instantiations whose plurality respects the uniqueness of pragmatically determined situations. The latter also include the idiom of those addressed.

Hence, in a technical sense, the analysis of each of the notions that interest us here – ethics, politics, religion – regardless of (or, rather, thanks to) their conceptual and empirical specificity revolves once again around a critical reassessment of the concept, so central to Derrida's earlier work, of the historical. Ethics, politics, and religion are analyzed neither as transcendental terms (i.e., categories, ideas, or existentials) nor as simple or pure transcendence, but in view of what is called their transcendental historicity. This fundamentally Husserlian concept, studied systematically by Derrida in his introduction to Husserl's *Origin of Geometry* and broached even earlier in his dissertation, *Le Problème de la genèse dans la phénoménologie de Husserl*, forms the interpretive key to the discussion of ethicity (as distinguished from this or that particular ethics or morality), of the political (*le politique*; as opposed to a politics, *la politique*, in the concrete and pragmatic sense of the word), and of revealability or messianicity (as differentiated from the purported revelations and messianisms that punctuate the history of religion, more precisely, the so-called religions of the Book). In all these concepts – which to a certain extent are "non-synonymous substitutions," to cite a helpful formulation from "Différance" – a certain motif of idealization touches upon the realm of the empirical (the world of phenomena, according to Kant; the domain of the ontic, following Heidegger) in the most unexpected of ways. The two extreme poles of our experience and of our language – the ideal and, say, the real – are thereby presented as abstractions from a more complex process of constant resignification (since no signification

was ever first). They are described as being in permanent need of negotiation, as having in fact and for structural reasons been negotiated
from the very outset, and hence as never having been given as such, in
all purity. Responsibility, the whole drama of decision and testimony, of
act and passion, would thus consist in the reiterated engagement of this
very difficulty – or aporia – of engaging (i.e., negotiating, economizing,
betraying, and implicating) the ethical, the political, and the religious.
It consists in compromising the absolute, distributing infinite – yet also
infinitely pervertible (and, one should add, in itself, when left to itself,
also perverse) – justice by translating it into an inescapably limited set of
principles and rules, laws and customs. This translation and consistent
reinscription of ethical responsibility and justice into the realm of *le droit*
cannot be guided or inspired by an ideal of infinite approximation, as
Kant believed. Nor does it obey a Levinasian logic of oscillation between
the invisible and visible, that is to say, between the ethical Saying (*le Dire*)
and the ontological and historico-political Said (*le Dit*), which, again in
Levinas's view, finds its empirical expression in the State and its institutions, Reason and the system. A different, more aporetic relationship
between the infinite and the finite is at work here, one that Derrida spells
out in relentless and increasing consequence. The questions raised in
"Violence and Metaphysics" about a certain residual – radical, some
would say absolute – empiricism, as well as the proposal, made in
"At This Very Moment in This Work Here I Am," to introduce the notion
of seriature (*sériature*), exemplify this concern. They all lead to a formalization of the co-implication of responsibility and ethics, ethics and the
political, the political and politics, politics and religion, regardless of the
no less stringent difference between them. Yet, paradoxically, as soon as
one concept or one realm (ethics, politics, religion) receives its distinctive
articulation, it is folded back into those from which it set itself apart.

TURNING AROUND RELIGION: THE CONDITIONS OF RESPONSIBILITY

In the renewed meditation on Levinas and Kant in *Adieu to Emmanuel
Levinas*, Derrida lets himself be guided by a question that he "will in
the end leave in suspense," if only because it admits no definite answer.
This question concerns "the relationships between an *ethics* of hospitality
(an ethics *as* hospitality) and a *law* or a *politics* of hospitality, for example,
in the tradition of what Kant calls the conditions of universal hospitality
in *cosmopolitical law*: 'with a view to perpetual peace.'"[1] Derrida goes on

to specify at some length the difficulty in thinking and acting upon the complementary relationships between these two meanings and forms of hospitality. As he notes, here we are dealing with relationships whose modality is at odds with those of philosophical (metaphysical, ontological, and transcendental) possibilization, indeed, radically distinct from any form of deduction, empirical causation, and psychological motivation. Even saying that they are complementary would be saying too much or too little, since we are dealing here with relational terms that mutually imply and exclude each other, albeit in an enigmatic and fundamentally aporetic way. To understand what Derrida means by this, it is worth quoting him *in extenso*:

> Let us assume, *concesso non dato*, that there is no assured passage, following the order of a foundation, according to a hierarchy of founding and founded, of principial originarity and derivation, between an ethics or a first philosophy of hospitality, on the one hand, and a law or politics of hospitality, on the other. Let us assume that one cannot *deduce* from Levinas's ethical discourse on hospitality a law and a politics, some particular law or politics in some determined situation today, whether close to us or far away. How, then, are we to interpret this impossibility of founding, of deducing or deriving? Does this impossibility signal a failing? Perhaps we should say the contrary. Perhaps we would, in truth, be put to another kind of test by the apparent negativity of this lacuna, this hiatus between ethics (first philosophy or metaphysics – in the sense, of course, that Levinas has given to these words), on the one hand, and, on the other, law or politics. If there is no lack here, would not such a hiatus in effect require us to think law and politics otherwise? Would it not in fact open – like a hiatus – both the mouth and the possibility of another speech, of a decision and a responsibility (juridical and political, if you will) where decisions must be made and responsibility, as we say, *taken* without the assurance of an ontological foundation? (*AL* 20–21/45–47).

Derrida's hypothesis seems to rest on the very *épokhè* – the same suspension of judgment, an in-decision, if not in-difference, a scruple rather, *Scheu* and *Gelassenheit* – with which "Faith and Knowledge" associates the concept and experience of "religion." What is said of hospitality and its two meanings resembles the characterization of the two sources of "religion" and their relation. All that remains of the religious, apart from the sacrificial, dogmatic, and obscurantist tendencies that animate its historical manifestations, would be the inability or unwillingness to choose which comes first: the transcendental (if not the ideal and pure, then the quasi-transcendental) condition of possibility for responsibility, namely, the ethical and the political qua hospitality, or its empirical and ontic instantiations (which, being conditioned, paradoxically condition their conditions in turn. This hesitation to choose between the most formal and the more concrete features of "religion," between its abstract concept and its material substratum (if not substance), between its idea (or ideality) and its phenomenality (and hence its idiosyncrasies, its idolatries and blasphemies), effectively strips the religious of both its orthodox and its heterodox determinations. Neither faith nor knowledge, neither ethics nor politics, it pervades, inspires, and unsettles both. For good and for ill.

The originality of authors such as Levinas and Kant, in Derrida's view, consists in exposing the concepts of the ethical and the political, in their ancient, modern, and contemporary determinations, to the "religious" tradition, understood against the historical background of the so-called positive religions of the Book, especially Judaism, Christianity, and, more indirectly, Islam. Despite (or thanks to?) this exposure – which is a reinscription, of sorts – these concepts are rethought and rewritten in the most unexpected ways. This paradoxical procedure – a turn at once to and away from religion – forces the notions of the ethical and the political into a relation of simultaneous proximity to and distance from a concept and a phenomenon (namely "religion") that they affirm and generalize or even universalize, but thereby also trivialize, if only by stripping it of its ontological and axiological privilege. To turn around religion here also means to turn religion around.

All this is implied from the outset in the enigmatic title *Adieu*, which Derrida borrows from Levinas, even though he gives it a significant and almost contrary twist of his own ("pronouncing this word of *adieu*, this word *à-Dieu*, which, in a certain sense, I get from him, a word that he will have taught me to think or pronounce otherwise," *AL* 1 / 11). The complexity and aporetic structure of this movement, a conversion and aversion of sorts,[2] is captured by the fact that it evokes the ambiguity of a movement toward God (*à Dieu*), toward the word or the name of God, and a no less dramatic farewell (*adieu*) to at least the canonical and onto-theological interpretations of this notion called "God." As if nothing save its names were untouched, though left all but intact. As if the sacred names were not so much lacking (as Heidegger, misreading Hölderlin, believed), as to be found in the singularity – an absoluteness, safe and sound – of a host of idiomatic, yet infinitely substitutable names.

This turn to – or around – religion should not be confused with the many attempts, old and new, to reduce the problem of ethics and morality to that of articulating a distinct (concrete, empirical, and ontic) conception of the good or the good life, from Aristotle to Hegel, or from Alasdair

MacIntyre to Charles Taylor. Nor should we identify all too quickly the steps taken by Levinas and Kant, as Derrida reads them, with attempts to mobilize a "political theology" of sorts. Their itinerary differs in many regards from that of the historical messianisms and occupies a universe different from that of, say, Carl Schmitt, Walter Benjamin, Jakob Taubes, and the so-called liberation – or genitive – theologies of recent decades. An alternative turn to – and away from – religion is at work in the texts that concern us here.

Their procedure, which I would like to call *reverse implication*, folds the transcendental (albeit the quasi- or simili- or ultra-transcendental) back into the empirical and the historical, in a radical movement whose direction goes against the grain of the phenomenological – and hence transcendental – reduction in its idealist and merely provisional interruption or bracketing of the psychologisms, sociologisms, biologisms, and naturalisms that pervade the realist interpretation of the world and ourselves. Only with this conversion of the gaze does responsibility become possible – and necessary – again.

Husserl and Heidegger compared this turning around of the natural attitude to – or modeled it after? – religious conversion, the kenosis of discourse. Reverse implication converts, and hence doubles, that conversion once again, thereby both intensifying and trivializing the gesture of faith. It multiplies that gesture and folds it back upon itself. The difference is hard to tell. From a Levinasian or Kantian perspective, this would be a disconcerting conclusion. Or so it seems.

To a certain extent, Derrida seems to read these authors against the grain, bringing out a simultaneous allegiance and radical distantiation, contrary gestures that, he shows, are inevitable when dealing with ethics, politics, religion, as well as their traditional resources – gestures, moreover, that cannot be held apart easily, if at all. Any discourse, like those proposed by Levinas and Kant, that would set out to question these notions – the ethical, the political, the religious – would be bound to affirm them all over again; for to engage them is to say the same thing completely otherwise, in a proximity that approaches identification and tautology, yet implies an allegory or heterology as well.

These mutually exclusive yet simultaneous movements are prefigured and formalized in the *terminus technicus* that Derrida introduces and justifies in "Signature, Event, Context," then elaborates in *Limited Inc.*, where he discusses the concept of iterability, and in *Of Spirit*, where he speaks of an originary affirmation, acquiescence, and reiteration at the root of even the most violent negation. Nowhere are these contradictory yet mutually dependent movements expressed more poignantly than in the figure of the *adieu*, whose ambiguity makes all the difference in the world, even though it expresses, repeats, and displaces the function of the more formal term *iterability*.

Why, then, is the reference to religion and to God (*à Dieu*) necessary or useful at all? Why is the analysis of the formal and supposedly universal structure of iterability (paradoxically, aporetically) contingent upon invoking a particular tradition, here that of the religions of the Book, especially since that structure is also held to have made these religions possible in the first place? What are we to make of this circular relation, which seems to undercut what Derrida, in *Aporias*, has called the "logic of presupposition," that is to say, not only foundationalism and reductionism, but, with far more consequence, any assumption of possibilization, of conditions of possibility and the like?

TWO CONCEPTS OF HOSPITALITY

In *Adieu to Emmanuel Levinas*, Derrida rearranges Levinas's reassessment of ethics, politics, and religion around the notion of *hospitality*, a term that is increasingly relevant in the present age. Levinas rethinks these notions in terms of hospitality, Derrida shows, by the qualification, definition, or, rather, infinition of hospitality as absolute hospitality, a welcoming of the other as (the) totally Other, as the other in whose trace, transcendence, and dimension of height we find the sole access to – indeed, the very desire for and fear of – God. The immense relevance of a Levinasian ethics for the most urgent questions dominating contemporary political debates on immigration, globalization, the displacement if not the demise of the nation state, multicultural citizenship, multilingualism, etc., becomes particularly clear, Derrida seems to suggest, if we understand this philosophical thought as an ethics of hospitality, or even ethics as hospitality. What, then, is the relevance of the Levinasian conception of ethics – the relation to the other pure and simple, to the *tout autre* – for questions of politics, rights, and jurisprudence, and especially for all the apparently unprecedented burning issues for which the inherited doctrines of law, recent conventions in international relations, and even the current understanding of cosmopolitanism seem, all of a sudden, so ill-prepared? This question is all the more urgent because the translation from one perspective into the other – or the negotiation of one with the other – seems highly questionable, indeed, impossible.

As Derrida had reminded us in "Violence and Metaphysics" and "At This Very Moment in This Work Here I Am," for Levinas the very notion of ethics is devoid of principles and rules, maxims and practices, and appears to be merely a word – one for which there are an infinite number of substitutes – for the infinitizing relation to the infinite other, the welcome offered to or received from the Other. Derrida's previous readings had shown that for Levinas this relation is one of transcendence, eschatology, and the messianic, of a saintliness that does not even claim to be, that is otherwise than Being, that finds no halt and no limit in beings or in Being. At an earlier stage of his thought, in *Totality and Infinity*, Levinas had conceived of this relation in terms of an infinity of Being in order to stress its exteriority with regard to the finite totality that had been, quite literally, the *idée fixe* of Western ontology. Ethics qua hospitality thus instantiates a relation to the other (*l'Autre* – first of all, the other human being, *autrui*, who comes to me from a dimension of height, as *Autrui*) that does not close itself off in a totality. What is at issue, therefore, is a *relation without relation*, to use a formulation introduced by Maurice Blanchot and echoed by both Levinas and Derrida.

For the Levinas of *Totality and Infinity*, these terms are possible definitions (or, again, infinitions) not only of "religion" but, more specifically, of a "religion of adults," as the opening essay of *Difficult Freedom* has it. This is characterized by a sober rigor that resists not only the conceptual appropriation of the philosophies of the Same and the neuter (from Parmenides through Hegel up to Heidegger), but also the raptures and rhythms of mythico-mystical participation, of diffuse totalities, that encapsulate the self in the other. The later Levinas, however, increasingly characterizes this religious posture in terms of a saintly madness (obsession, trauma, etc.).

Adieu opens with a moving and conceptually astute address spoken by Derrida at Levinas's funeral in 1995, then rereads *Totality and Infinity*, together with some lesser known Talmudic readings and short essays, in view of their contribution to an ethics and politics of hospitality, specifically, to contemporary debates on, for example, "cities of refuge" and the continuing Arab–Israeli conflict. *Adieu* can, moreover, be read as a supplement to Derrida's engagement with the concepts "messianicity" and "friendship" in *Specters of Marx* and *The Politics of Friendship*. It seeks to determine how the politics of friendship – especially as linked to the notion of democracy, in its ancient and modern liberal guises – ties in with the discussion of hospitality, a motif further pursued by the accompanying pamphlet *Cosmopolites de tous les pays, encore un effort!* It is no accident that the notions of hospitality, friendship, and democracy come to surface in a text named *Adieu*, under the heading of this intriguing yet disconcerting turn toward and away from religion, toward and away

from its turns of phrase and everything for which they stand, the best
and the worst. There could be no better entry into the abyssal logics
of this curious phrase – of its semantic potential, where given meanings
and possibilities are charged with unforeseen effects – than an analysis of
the welcome granted to and given by the *tout autre*. *Adieu* draws attention
to the fact that Levinas's *oeuvre*, especially *Totality and Infinity*, is "an immense treatise of hospitality" (*AL* 21/49), indeed, on or of metaphysics
as hospitality. Levinas's book enacts hospitality as much as, or more
than, it thematizes hospitality. It shows certain concepts or notions welcoming each other, signing up with each other, calling each other forth,
and accepting an invitation to enter into a series that is in principle
infinite.

Derrida now sees the absolute and ultimately unphilosophical empiricism that, in the final pages of "Violence and Metaphysics," he had
detected in Levinas's project up to *Totality and Infinity* as giving way to a
different logic and rhetoric – a series of linkages that allows no single
concept or figure of speech to be privileged ontologically, axiologically,
aesthetically, theologically, or ethically and religiously. Instead, in principle if not *de facto*, it treats all alike and "appears to proceed, indeed
to leap, from one synonym to the next" (*AL* 22/50–51). Such a procedure undercuts and outwits both any empiricism, however absolute,
and any insistence on a *primum intelligibile*, any first philosophy, however
ethical. In this more hospitable reading, we are no longer dealing with
an ethical transcendental philosophy or metaphysics but with a mode
of argumentation less reminiscent of the *via negativa* of apophatic theologies than of the hyperbolic affirmations and exaggerations of the *via
eminentiae*, a tradition Levinas invokes in his later writings, especially at
the end of *Otherwise than Being*. One must ask, however, whether these two
theological approaches – which strip dogmatic theology of its metaphysical presuppositions of onto-theology or, what comes to the same thing,
stretch it to its outer limits – do not go hand in hand, historically and
systematically speaking.

In another attempt to explain this peculiar logic, Derrida identifies it
with an "apposition," a "movement without movement" (ibid.), which
could be taken either for no movement at all, for a perpetual movement
on the (one and the same?) spot, or, even more puzzling, for both of these –
movement and stasis, repetition and repetition of the same – at once.
We are dealing here, Derrida continues, with a "play of substitution"
that – paradoxically, aporetically – "would replace the unique with the
unique" (*AL* 65/119); in other words, in Levinas's project, the "thought

of substitution" orients itself toward "a logic that is hardly thinkable, almost unsayable, that of the possible–impossible, the iterability and replaceability of the unique in the very experience of unicity as such" (*AL*70/128). What does this mean? And what would be the consequences of adopting such a model for thought, for ethics, politics, and the like?

Hospitality, we learn, can be neither thematized nor crudely historicized, psychologized, or politicized. Yet it "is," the *concretissimum* par excellence: it unfolds as the openness of intentionality, as the welcome offered to the totally other. As such it is already implied or at work in any account one might want to give of it. What remains or becomes of the welcome and hospitality if its meaning is stripped of its most common familial and juridico-political connotations? When the ethics of pure prescription – originally intended as an ethical first and transcendental philosophy – is identified with the elusive notion of an infinite and absolute hospitality, the homology between the word *hospitality* and its use and abuse in the most pressing institutional and international concerns of our days must give us pause, must make us think, indeed think twice, gesturing in two directions at once. What, precisely, is the relationship between a hospitality vis-à-vis the other that is understood philosophically, whether phenomenologically or not, and politics and law, between an emphatic notion of responsibility and a down-to-earth set of rights and rules, a jurisprudence? This is the problem of *le droit* as opposed to *la justice*, as Derrida has it in *Force of Law*, or of justice as opposed to the wisdom of love, to cite the final chapter of Levinas's *Otherwise than Being*. How can one inspire and enable, orient but inevitably also limit the other? Here we are dealing with two concentric circles that revolve around each other and draw ever closer (the image invoked both by Kant in *Religion Within the Limits of Mere Reason* and in the ancient Stoic conceptions of cosmopolitanism), but also with two focal points that figure as the mutually constitutive poles of a mathematical ellipse, a circle whose center is split down the middle. The question remains: How does one pole affect the other?

In *Adieu*, Derrida explicitly raises this question and reminds us that no unilinear, hierarchical order of foundation, derivation, or causation regulates the relation between these two orders. A completely different logic is at work, one that differs radically from the logic of presupposition Derrida takes to task in *Aporias*, in his discussion of Heidegger's *Being and Time*.[3] Early in *Adieu* Derrida notes that, according to the "canonical" form of philosophical questioning, absolute hospitality, on the one hand, and the hospitality of rights and laws, on the other, must always exist in a relation of subordination, of justification, with one enabling the other. Following the classical and modern schematics, the two orders in question could not be co-originary, co-extensive, co-existent, co-temporaneous, since each is, as it were, the possibility of the other.

By contrast, the other logic that Derrida sees at work in Levinas's thoughts on hospitality leaves in suspense the question of what comes first. It does so in a paradoxical gesture that bears a remarkable resemblance to the classical procedure of the phenomenological *épokhè*. One can thus say of hospitality in its two modes and of their implied ethics and politics what Derrida says of literature in a different context: namely, that it instantiates a "phenomenological conversion of the gaze," a "non-thetic experience, of belief, of position, of naiveté, and of what Husserl called the 'natural attitude.'" In so doing, the language of hospitality, like that of literature, dislodges phenomenology from its supposed "certainties."[4] Levinas's *oeuvre* can thus be read as a phenomenology that liberates itself from all presuppositions: to begin with, the ontological concept of the phenomenon and of logos that Heidegger, faithful and unfaithful to Husserl, develops in paragraph 7 of *Being and Time*, but also from an understanding of the transcendental in terms of conditions of possibility and of the movement of possibilization.

HOSPITALITY AS "CULTURE ITSELF"

Derrida shows that Levinas's conception of hospitality differs radically from the one Kant develops in *Idea for a Universal History with a Cosmopolitan Purpose* and in *Toward Perpetual Peace: A Philosophical Sketch*. Levinas starts out from a nonnatural yet originary – or, better, preoriginary – peace rather than from a natural state of war, as Kant does. Unlike Kant, Levinas does not portray peace as the interruption of war. Regardless of its anteriority and primacy, he insists that this peace still needs to come here and now; it cannot be thought or lived as indefinitely postponed or to be approximated in a distant future, as it would if we were dealing with a regulative idea.

Unlike Kant's cosmopolitanism, which is ultimately based on juridico-political presuppositions and thus limits universal hospitality to a merely (or primarily) juridical, cosmopolitical arrangement of citizens and states (*AL* 68/124 and, notably, 87–88/156), Levinas's notion of hospitality revolves from the outset around a before or beyond of the political. The political is neither its first nor its final point of reference, nor its privileged model. At times it seems that for Levinas hospitality is to be found everywhere but in the political regardless of its conservative or progressive, restorative or revolutionary, anarchist or utopian appropriations. The political seems to be relegated to the realm of a history whose teleology and premature judgment constitutes no more than a finite – or, as Adorno would say, false – totality.[5]

Does Levinas's notion of hospitality, as interpreted by Derrida, allow itself to be transposed to a more pragmatic, everyday politico-juridical context? If so, how? To say that the idea of absolute hospitality serves as a necessary or imperative criterion for the many laws of hospitality is to say too little. It immediately raises the question of when, where, under which circumstances, and in what measure this general principle or rule, if that's what it is, applies. Always, everywhere, immeasurably? Is this all we can say in good faith? Is there nothing more to say from here on, but everything to show, instantly, without any further possible mediation?[6] And should one not raise the same questions when speaking not of hospitality but of friendship and brotherhood, messianicity and democracy to come, all of which hardly differ in their structure or supposed content – since there is none, since their "normativity" (not Derrida's term, to be sure) contains in principle nothing or almost nothing that can be described? In Levinas, Kant, and Derrida, all these notions are formalized to the point of becoming almost pure abstractions, almost substitutable without further remainder. What motivates, justifies, or triggers the emphasis on these figures and privileges them over so many possible, and seemingly equally decisive, others?

The notion of hospitality, like those of the welcome, friendship, eschatology, the messianic, democracy, cosmopolitanism, and, last but not least, religion, schematizes a responsibility that precedes all of its subsequent translations, substitutions, and eventual concretizations. Is this Kantian solution – invoking the mediating function of the schema between form and content – the answer to our question of how the first, absolute or quasi-transcendental mode of hospitality (or all the other notions) relates to its second, empirico-pragmatic counterpart? Not quite; things are more complicated than it would seem at first glance.

A certain revealability (*Offenbarkeit*, as Heidegger would have it) and hence – by reverse implication – the revelations (*Offenbarung*) or accounts thereof in the so-called religions of the Book provide the condition of possibility for the structure and vocabulary of hospitality, but the reverse holds true, as well. Hospitality is made possible by what it makes possible, and vice versa. It is conditioned by what conditions it, in turn. There is no way out of this paradox; indeed, it is an aporia that marks the limit of thought and necessitates and demands a certain suspension or *épokhè* of philosophical or more narrowly phenomenological reflection. In the self-restraint or self-critique that this limit imposes (or enables – and nothing else does), philosophy, responsibility, indeed existence, the experience of factical life – (as the early Heidegger would have said) come into their "own." Yet this pause, halt, reticence, or scruple, Derrida suggests from "Faith and Knowledge" on, might well constitute the very heart and impetus of "religion," "at the limits of reason alone."

As Derrida points out, we can speak of a history of hospitality because of the co-extensiveness, co-existence, and co-implication of ethics and hospitality – as well as of these two and a hospitality to the possibility of the worst. In this emplotment (in French, *intrigue*) or *divina comedia*, an infinite responsibility leaves its mark in the finite according to an infinition, a folding of the infinite into the finite, which at each step emphasizes a positive, superlative excess of meaning or signifyingness at least as much as a certain negation. The "in" in "infinity," Levinas stresses, does not point toward a privation but indicates the place where the other takes hold and hollows one out.

In history, the concepts of hospitality and of ethics, together with their respective socio-political manifestations or instantiations, revolve around each other, correct each other, supplement and at times interpenetrate each other, to the point of confusion. Without this inevitable translation – and betrayal – the very notion of universal hospitality would remain an empty dream. Conversely, if hospitality were reduced to the laws and examples that make up its history, whether individually or as a sum total, then its concept and practical instantiations would lose their critical potential and universalistic import. Neither as an absolute idea nor as a concrete example – neither as the Law nor as a series of particular laws – is hospitality given as such, in its purity or integrity. This is why the relationship between hospitality and all the notions, concepts, rules, and practices of hospitality – including the very concept hospitality – is from the outset aporetic and must irrevocably remain so, if it is thought responsibly – that is to say, hospitably.

The transposition of absolute hospitality into the field of economics (and thereby into its self-contradiction) has to do not only with the inevitable negation and negotiation of an an-archical idea of justice and its betrayal by numbers, in the very distribution and thereby limitation of justice – in virtue, precisely, of its limitless demand. Another ontological interruption of the ethical – in and qua politics and economy in the common meaning of these words – is equally necessary. The unjustifiable mitigation of justice that takes place in the distribution of justice – of rights and the law, permits and goods – finds a partial justification in that it counterbalances the supposed purity and absoluteness of the responsibility toward the one other, who had seemed to come absolutely first. Seen in this light, the figures of the immigrant and the seeker of asylum evoke not only the stranger but also the third, the one who not only deepens my responsibility but also gives me a break and thus makes responsibility, if not bearable or masterable, then at least less violent. The third neither mediates nor mitigates the immediacy of the one for the other, *l'un pour l'autre*, to the point of substitution, which for Levinas constitutes the heart of responsibility – if not of ethics in the traditional and modern philosophical sense, of saintliness and the fear of God. In its interruption of the immediacy of the one for the other, the third is, Derrida notes, itself in turn immediate; it introduces – not after the fact but from the outset of any relation to the other (to *autrui*) qua other – more than one other for the one. Pushing his interpretation beyond commentary, Derrida concludes that it is "as if the unicity of the face were, in its absolute and irreducible singularity, plural *a priori*"(*AL* 110/190). Only by way of this singular plurality in the very heart of singularity does the appearance of the third in principle "protect against the vertigo [*vertige*] of ethical violence itself" (*AL* 33/66). This would be the logic, the argument, or – in Kantian and Husserlian parlance – the "deduction" at work in Levinas's text; without ever being acknowledged, thematized, or formalized as such. To the extent that Levinas offers an "ethical transcendental philosophy" by deducing sociality – the political, laws and rights, the State, etc. – from the structure of "thirdness [*tertialité*]," that is to say, from the one who as a witness (*terstis*) interrupts the complacency of the duality or dialogue of the I–Thou or the obsession-substitution-hostage-taking of the one-for-the-other, his analysis allows for a radical possibility:

The deduction proceeds in this way right up to "the political structure of society, subject to laws," right up to "the dignity of the citizen," where, however, a sharp distinction must remain between the ethical subject and the civic one. But this move out of purely ethical responsibility, this interruption of ethical immediacy, is itself immediate . . . Is he not trying to take into account this hypothesis of a violence in the pure and immediate ethics of the face to face? A violence potentially unleashed in the experience of the neighbor and of absolute unicity? The impossibility of discerning here between good and evil, love and hate, giving and taking, the desire to live and the death drive, the hospitable welcome and the egoistic or narcissistic closing up within oneself?

The third would thus protect against the vertigo of ethical violence itself. For ethics could be doubly exposed to such violence: exposed to undergo it but also to exercise it. Alternatively or simultaneously. (*AL* 32–33/65–66)

This is not all. The interruption of the third, while an interpellation in its own right, given that the third is an other (*autrui*) for me and for my neighbor as well, also constitutes a violation of sorts. It can be treated, judged, and responded to as such. It divides and diminishes – but also intensifies and in a sense exalts – the absolute relationship between the one "me" and the one "other." Both the mediating or mitigating and the hyperbolic effects of "thirdness" (and what other function could *tertialité* have?) violate the purity of the ethical, that is to say, the absolute relationship between uniques or absolutes. The introduction of the third into the one-for-the-other is the drama of this relationship's insufficiency or even exclusivity, and hence, paradoxically, of its being not absolute enough. In and for itself, the ethical relationship could not rest in itself. Even in its obsessive and traumatic structure – substitution and alienation where no identity, no *idem*, but only an *ipse* remains in place or intact – its restlessness would mean too much peace of mind, *égoisme à deux*. And yet in the one for the other, face to face with the other, I am, in a way, facing all others. The introduction of the third – justice in Levinas's sense – is therefore as much the promise and enactment as the interruption and violation (Derrida says "perjury") of ethical responsibility.

The structure of openness, of the welcome, seems premised upon experiences that can be better understood against the backdrop of religious idiom. Levinas inscribes the formal, abstract, and absolute structure of the welcome into a particular (and, in part, inevitably particularist) idiom, that of a revealed, positive, and ontic religion, related to a language, a people, a nation. Likewise, Levinas inscribes the welcome into a phenomenology of femininity; a femininity, Derrida reminds us, that, while taken seriously as a philosopheme, is traditionally and androcentrically defined. Hence this second reinscription demands a double reading – one that at once generalizes or intensifies and trivializes.

Derrida cites some passages from Levinas's early texts in which these two reinscriptions of the quasi-transcendental structure of the welcome into the empirical – here religion and the feminine – go hand in hand. In both instances, we are dealing with a process of folding, of reverse implication, for there is a transformation (one is tempted to say "transsubstantiation") of the empirical into the ontologico-transcendental, following a procedure of phenomenological concretization, on the one hand, and of formal indication, on the other. Are the two instances of equal weight, equally revealing? Or does their respective or simultaneous privileging depend on strategic or pragmatic – more precisely, pragrammatological – considerations alone? No direct answer is given, but clearly neither religion nor femininity – if these two concepts can be clearly separated – is accorded an essential or principal status. They are not written in stone, not based on some *a priori* or anthropological constant. Religion and sexual difference are not mere facts of life, which is not to say that they are mere ideological constructs.

Discussing biblical and contemporary examples of hospitality in Israel's dealings with its neighbors, Egypt in particular – instances that are analyzed by Levinas in *In the Time of the Nations* and in *Outside the Verse* – Derrida reminds us of a similar independence and dependence in the structure of welcome with regard to the Torah and the revelation at Sinai. He notes:

> Levinas orients his interpretation toward the equivalence of *three concepts – fraternity, humanity, hospitality* – that determine an experience of the Torah and of the messianic times even *before* or outside of the Sinai . . .
>
> What announces itself here might be called a structural or *a priori* messianicity. Not an ahistorical messianicity, but one that belongs to a historicity without a particular and empirically determinable incarnation. Without revelation or without the dating of a given revelation. (*AL* 67 / 121–22)

Can the hospitality inspired and dictated by the Torah be recognized before – and, therefore, independently of – the specific historical occurrence of a revelation or account thereof? Can this Torah have any universal meaning for the individuals, peoples, and nations for whom "the name, the place, the event Sinai would mean nothing" (*AL* 65/119)? Can hospitality, or a "structural messianicity," ever stand on its own and be comprehended without the cultural and political instantiations of its historical forms, punctuated by the many names, proper and common, that haunt the religions and the peoples of the Book? This seems to be a decisive and recurring question in Derrida's most recent work on the relation between revelation and revealability, messianism and messianicity, even though it is never answered in any decisive way, since the problem and trial of a certain indecision – yet another *religio*, again interpreted as a halt and scruple – is at stake.

If hospitality situates itself at once inside and outside the ethical relation – along with many other terms, many other synonyms – what, then, constitutes its absolute or relative privilege and priority, here and

now, at this particular juncture in the reception of Derrida's work? Since
we are dealing with a hospitality that is not empirical, visible, or thematic – one that, as Derrida rightly points out, hardly ever occurs literally under this name, whether in the texts under consideration or
elsewhere in Levinas's *oeuvre* – neither historico-political nor philological
nor hermeneutical grounds can be of help. The primacy or prevalence
of hospitality in these readings is not motivated by the current worldwide
tendencies toward globalization, marked by migration, forced displacements, the decline of the nation-state, and "crimes *against* hospitality"
(*AL* 71/132), all of which seem to give the category of hospitality a new
prominence and a new urgency. The notion of hospitality is taken here
(as much as possible, with an unsurpassable analytical gesture) to be a
category beyond all categories, which not only resists definition in common political and juridical terms but, because it is *sui generis*, must in
principle subtract itself from any conceptual determination.

Nonetheless, Derrida suggests that "by means of discreet though transparent allusions, Levinas oriented our gazes toward what is happening
today" (*AL* 70/131). Indirectly, Levinas thus seems to address the present
situation in many modern states, in Europe and elsewhere, in which ever
more refugees "call for a change in the socio- and geo-political space – a
juridico-political mutuation, though, before this, assuming that this limit
still has any pertinence, an ethical conversion" (*AL* 71/131).

COMPLEMENTARY ALTERNATIVES

Derrida distinguishes between two radically different, two opposed and
juxtaposed modes of welcome offered to or received from the other.
For this relation to be what it is – a relation (without relation, again in
Levinas's definition of religion) and not any programmatic exchange of
moves – there must be (*il faut*) at least the possibility that the relation to the
other will pervert itself: "this possible hospitality to the worst is necessary
so that good hospitality can have a chance" (*AL* 35/69). Following the
lines of thought set out in *The Gift of Death*, Derrida analyzes this difficulty
by pointing to the "intolerable scandal" that justice begins with a perjury,
that ethics is violently interrupted by the third – the other of the other,
the other in the other, given with this very other – while this interruption
also interrupts an at least virtual violence of the ethical, which, left to
itself, resembles the worst.

The notion of hospitality thus points both ways. We must attribute to
it a certain transcendental or quasi-transcendental status, but where it is

left to itself and does not translate itself into concrete (empirical, ontic, positive) laws that – inevitably – offer less than the universal or absolute openness it calls for, it betrays itself. Any concrete form hospitality might take is of necessity absolutely distant from the universal and measureless measure, which allows for no gradual approximation. In such form, it resembles and indeed welcomes or solicits the worst. This is why a good conscience, the reluctance to dirty one's hands, to compromise, or to negotiate, is irresponsible. Hospitality, taken in its emphatic, absolute, or all-encompassing sense is caught in a familiar aporetics: rather than give itself in a simple all or nothing, it is all and nothing; it must partition itself in order to remain whole (or wholesome); it must be forgotten and done away with in order to be remembered and lived up to.

The "hiatus" between responsibility and the juridico-political is, Derrida writes, not merely an "empirical contingency" but a fact of reason, in the sense Kant attributes to the word *Faktum*: the "heterogeneity" or "discontinuity" between these "two orders" (*AL* 116–17/201). The distinction, which is not simply that between the Kantian intelligible/noumenal realm of the thinkable and the sensible/phenomenal realm of possible experience, makes the search for schemas at once possible (even necessary or imperative) and, from the outset, impossible. In this difficulty of defining the political in contradistinction to the ethical and the religious (and to hospitality in the emphatic, hyperbolical, and absolute sense of the word), Derrida is at once close to Judaism (in Levinas's sense) and to Christianity (in its early Christian and Augustinian – and perhaps early Heideggerian – determinations). At times Derrida seems to dream of a conception of the political (of a politics of hospitality and of friendship) that situates itself beyond the Greek and modern "post-Hegelian" tradition, just as Levinas is not afraid of espousing, here and there (though never without qualifying the terms involved) a "messianic politics" (*AL* 74/136). In most contexts, however, this beyond of the political becomes more and more difficult to situate. In consequence, Derrida writes, one may ask oneself:

if the alternative between the State of Caesar and the State of David is an alternative between a politics [*une politique*] and a beyond of the political [*du politique*], or an alternative between two politics, or, finally, *an* alternative among *others*, where one could not exclude the hypothesis of a State that would be neither Caesar's nor David's, neither Rome nor Israel nor Athens. (*AL* 74/136)

This unclarity is neither weakness nor deplorable and, in principle, avoidable inconsistency. Levinas's conception of the political, Derrida writes, "seems to defy any topological simplicity" (*AL* 75/138). Like the concept of hospitality (and those of friendship and the messianic), the very idea of the political – and the very practice of politics – can no longer be assigned to a specific place, a topos, a nation, a land. Rather, both are at once within and outside the classical and modern coordinates that determine the realm or the space of the political, especially its connection with the concept of the state or nation. This is clearly expressed in the title of a late Talmudic reading by Levinas, "Beyond the State in the State,"[7] on which Derrida comments: "*Beyond-in*: transcendence in immanence, *beyond* the political, but *in* the political. Inclusion opened onto the transcendence that it bears, incorporation of a door [*porte*] that bears [*porte*] and opens onto the beyond of the walls . . . framing it [*l'encadrent*]. At the risk of causing the identity of the place as well as the stability of the concept to implode" (*AL* 76/138).

Though it is difficult and perhaps impossible to think this tension, we live and instantiate it every day. It is at the heart of each decision and thus of the very structure of everydayness as such. On the one hand, there must be a translation and retranslation of the absolute welcome into the many laws that follow upon it – "*This relation is necessary* [Il faut ce rapport]," Derrida writes – and not every "deduction" is equally responsible or just. Indeed, Derrida insists, "Even in its 'hypocritical' nature, 'political civilization' remains 'better' than barbarism" (*AL* 115/198). On the other hand, only the "*formal* injunction of the deduction remains irrecusable" (ibid.). This means that the ethics of absolute hospitality or ethics qua hospitality demands and implies or even necessitates a politics of sorts, without ever being able to stipulate (let alone deduce) which politics, in whatever particular context, let alone in all possible contexts, this ought to be. In other words, justice (*la justice*) becomes injustice if it does not expose itself to the betrayal of rules and rights (i.e., *le droit*). This being said, however, it must immediately be added that

the political or juridical content that is thus assigned itself remains indetermined, still to be determined beyond knowledge, beyond all presentation, all concepts, all possible intuition, in a singular way, in the speech and responsibility taken (up) by each person, in each situation, and on the basis of an analysis that is each time unique – unique and infinite, unique but a priori exposed to the substitution, unique and yet general, interminable in spite of the urgency of the decision. (*AL* 115/199)

Here two perspectives on the ethical interlock. Being two sides of the same coin, they at once mutually imply and exclude each other. These two perspectives, Derrida writes in *Of Hospitality*, one unconditional or hyperbolical and one conditional (a distinction that roughly corresponds to Kant's distinction between categorical imperatives and hypothetical maxims), form the "two regimes of one law of hospitality," between which the very concept and practice of the ethical and of ethics (one might add, of the political and of politics, of the religious or religiosity and of religion as a historical, positive, ontic phenomenon, of messianicity and of messianism, of christianicity and of Christendom) is permanently "stretched out [*tendue*],"[8] unable to coincide with itself and ever to be just just. In this view, then, there are structural reasons why a good conscience, but also radical idealism and sober or cynical pragmatism, are *ipso facto* signs of bad faith and perhaps are not even possible in full rigor: there are two sources of any action, of any decision, not just of "religion." Put otherwise, the primal, irreducible, or irrevocable duality of the two sources of religion and morality at the limits of mere reason would illuminate (and, in part, obscure) the intelligibility of the structure of experience in general.

This chapter was excerpted from the final chapter of Hent de Vries, *Religion and Violence: Philosophical Perspectives from Kant to Derrida* (Baltimore; London: Johns Hopkins University Press, 2002), forthcoming.

NOTES

1 Jacques Derrida, *Adieu to Emmanuel Levinas*, trans. Pascale-Anne Brault and Michael Naas (Stanford: Stanford University Press, 1999), 19–20; originally published as *Adieu à Emmanuel Levinas* (Paris: Galilée, 1997), 45. Hereafter cited parenthetically in the text with the page number of the French edition following that of the English.

2 Levinas speaks of a *retournement*, that is to say, a "reverting" in *Autrement qu'être ou au-delà de l'essence* (The Hague: Martinus Nijhoff, 1974), 155; trans. Alphonso Lingis as *Otherwise than Being, or Beyond Essence* (Pittsburgh: Duquesne University Press, 1998), 121, cited hereafter – *AL* 58 and 61/108 and 114. The term *aversion* is Ralph Waldo Emerson's (see, for example, "Self-Reliance") and has been analyzed indefatigably by Stanley Cavell. When used in tandem with "conversion," the term reminds us of the doubleness of the turn that resonates through the writings of Paul and Augustine, as read by the early Heidegger, not to mention the deployment of the *à-Dieu* by Levinas and Derrida. The term *conversion* appears in a passage in which Derrida observes that through "discreet though transparent allusions" Levinas draws our attention to the massive displacement of people who in the twentieth century have been forced to seek refuge, to go into exile, to immigrate, etc.; their many examples, he writes, "call [*appellent*] for a change in the socio- and geo-political space – a

juridico-political mutation, though, before this, assuming that this limit still has any pertinence, an ethical conversion" (*AL* 71/131). See below.

3 I have discussed these matters at some length in *Philosophy and the Turn to Religion* (Baltimore: Johns Hopkins University Press, 1999).

4 Jacques Derrida, "Interview," in Derek Attridge, ed., *Acts of Literature* (New York: Routledge, 1992), 46.

5 On these notions, see Hent de Vries, *Theologie im pianissimo: Die Aktualität der Denkfiguren Adornos und Levinas* (Kampen: Kok Publishing House, 1989), English translation forthcoming from Johns Hopkins University Press.

6 The way in which notions like absolute hospitality resist any criteriological interpretation reminds us of the alternative reading that Stanley Cavell has proposed of Wittgenstein's *Philosophical Investigations*. See his *The Claim of Reason: Wittgenstein, Skepticism, Morality, and Tragedy* (New York: Oxford University Press, 1979).

7 Emmanuel Levinas, *Nouvelles lectures talmudiques* (Paris: Minuit, 1996), 43–76.

8 J. Derrida, *De l'hospitalité: Anne Dufourmantelle invite Jacques Derrida à répondre* (Paris: Calmann-Lévy, 1997), 121; English translation forthcoming from Stanford University Press.

FURTHER READING

De Vries, H. *Philosophy and the Turn to Religion*. Baltimore: Johns Hopkins University Press, 1999.

Religion and Violence: Philosophical Perspectives from Kant to Derrida (Baltimore; London: Johns Hopkins University Press, 2002).

Theologie im pianissimo: Die Aktualität der Denkfiguren Adornos und Levinas. Kampen: Kok Publishing House, 1989.

Derrida, J. *Adieu to Emmanuel Levinas*. Trans P.-A. Brault and M. Naas. Stanford: Stanford University Press, 1999. [*Adieu à Emmanuel Levinas*. Paris: Galilée, 1997.]

"Afterword: Toward an Ethic of Discussion." In *Limited Inc.* Ed. G. Graff. Evanston: Northwestern University Press, 1988.

De l'hospitalité: Anne Dufourmantelle invite Jacques Derrida à répondre. Paris: Calmann-Lévy, 1997.

"Interview." In *Acts of Literature*. Ed. D. Attridge. New York: Routledge, 1992.

Politiques de l'amitié. Paris: Galilée, 1994.

Levinas, E. *Autrement qu'être ou au-delà de l'essence*. The Hague: Martinus Nijhoff, 1974. [Trans. A. Lingis as *Otherwise than Being, or Beyond Essence*. Pittsburgh: Duquesne University Press, 1998.]

Nouvelles lectures talmudiques. Paris: Minuit, 1996.

CHAPTER 8

Derrida and politics

Geoffrey Bennington

Which means that, too political for some, [deconstruction] can appear to be demobilizing to those who only recognize the political by means of pre-war signposts.[1]

I believe in the necessity of a certain tradition, in particular for political reasons.[2]

Derrida has never written a work of political philosophy. But given how radical his work appears, how far-reaching in its claims about metaphysics, it is not surprising that the reception of that work, at least in the English-speaking countries, has always involved an expectation or even a demand that it should give rise to a politics or a political philosophy. And although Derrida has been rather more chary than the traditional French Intellectual about taking up political positions, it has always seemed obvious that his work must have, at the very least, "political implications," but less obvious what those implications might be – and it is probably true that Derrida has never been embraced unequivocally by any particular political persuasion, although the political center of gravity of debate (rather than just denunciation or diatribe[3]) around his work has undoubtedly been the Left. Derrida is, obviously and self-proclaimedly, on the Left. But on the Left, there has always been a desire for Derrida to "come clean"[4] about politics, and a lurking suspicion that his (at least apparent) failure to do so was in principle a reason for dissatisfaction. According to a very common mechanism, Derrida's apparent reticence about some forms of political statement and argument led to charges (from the self-appointed guardians of the "Left" tradition in academic politics) of liberalism or even conservatism written into his most general philosophical arguments,[5] while his more obviously "political" texts have given rise to objections on the grounds that they supposedly show no more than a decently liberal attitude, and not the sort of genuine recognizable radicality we might otherwise think it reasonable to expect.[6] Since the late 1980s, the Heidegger and de Man "affairs,"[7] in which Derrida's interest in thinkers seen as tainted by involvement with Nazism was taken by many as a sign of political culpability, have exacerbated a sense of political trouble around Derrida, and it is perhaps not coincidental that most of Derrida's more explicit political reflections have appeared since that time.[8]

There are, however, good reasons for thinking that this configuration of hope, expectation, demand or suspicion subsequently disappointed or confirmed is a poor and naive way of responding to the challenge and radicality of Derrida's work. The reasons for this can be formulated rapidly: it is misguided to expect Derrida's work to answer to the concepts of "politics" or "political philosophy" just because these are metaphysical concepts – and insofar as Derrida's constant concern has been to comprehend and exceed metaphysics, he can hardly be expected to rely simply on metaphysical means to do so.

In this way, the "political" demand on Derrida would fall foul of a structure it is probably easiest to formulate in the context of his discussions, in the 1960s and 1970s, of the then triumphalist discourses of the "human sciences." A number of these discourses (linguistics, poetics, rhetoric, anthropology, sociology, history, even psychoanalysis) appeared to offer powerful ways of reducing traditional philosophical problems to various positive conditions, so that metaphysics might plausibly be seen as no more than a particular use of language, a particular human activity or a conditioned historical practice, always to be finally explained by something else (language, metaphors, human nature, society, relations of production, etc.), that something else being the positive province of the "human science" in question. Derrida's patient interrogation of these discourses involves demonstrating that in every case the very concepts supposed to operate the reduction of philosophy were themselves philosophical (metaphysical). According to a mechanism he would later describe as "transcendental contraband," the very concept supposed to reduce the transcendental claims of philosophy itself comes to occupy a transcendental position which the discourse in question has no further means of understanding, just because it is premised on the claim to reduce the transcendental claims of philosophy to more positive "realities" of whatever order.[9] Derrida's thinking, it now seems reasonably clear, follows a rhythm (now customarily called "quasi-transcendental") which shuttles between what would be traditionally distinguished as transcendental and empirical planes, asserting the priority of neither and the subordination of both to a wider movement neither is in a position to understand.[10]

Although none of Derrida's texts most obviously devoted to exploring this configuration explicitly addresses the attempt at a *political* reduction of philosophy, it seems clear that similar objections obtain. The political demand made of Derrida by a variety of commentators is the demand for the concept "politics" to be placed in the very transcendental position it is self-righteously supposed to reduce and explain, but to which it remains blind, and this, in conjunction with a similar analysis of the role of history, enables convincing refutations to be made of objections to Derrida from authors such as Fredric Jameson, Frank Lentricchia or Terry Eagleton. In many of these cases, the objections were driven at least in part by indignation at what was seen as a perverse or suspect silence on Derrida's part about Marx and Marxism, a silence that *Specters of Marx* can always be thought not to have really or convincingly broken.[11]

The position of transcendental contraband in all of these cases is occupied by a concept or network of concepts that the discourse in question (marked by just this fact as essentially positivistic) cannot understand, which means that those concepts are in fact blindly and helplessly inherited from the metaphysical tradition. In the absence of critical analysis of this mechanism in general, the human sciences remain in thrall to the very metaphysical concepts they think they are reducing, and this affirmation is a constant from some of Derrida's earliest texts. For example, Lévi-Strauss cannot but use traditional concepts:

This necessity is irreducible, it is not a historical contingency; we should carefully consider all its implications. But if no-one can escape it, if no-one is therefore responsible for giving in to it, however little, this does not mean that all ways of giving in to it are equally pertinent. The quality and fecundity of a discourse are perhaps to be measured by the critical rigor with which this relation to the history of metaphysics and inherited concepts is thought through. This is about a critical relation to the language of the human sciences and a critical responsibility of discourse. About posing expressly and systematically the problem of the status of a discourse borrowing from a heritage the resources necessary for the deconstruction of that heritage itself. A problem of *economy and strategy*. (*L'écriture et la différence*, 414 [282])

Of economy and strategy, and therefore, we might want to say, of political calculation. Again, more ambivalently perhaps, the opening of "Freud and the Scene of Writing":

Freudian concepts . . . all belong, without any exception, to the history of metaphysics . . . No doubt Freud's discourse – its syntax or, if you will, its work – is not to be confused with these necessarily metaphysical and traditional concepts. No doubt it is not exhausted by this belonging. Immediate witnesses to this are the precautions and the "nominalism" with which Freud handles what he calls conceptual conventions and hypotheses. And a thought of difference is less attached to concepts than to discourses. But the historical and theoretical meaning of these precautions was never reflected by Freud. (ibid., 294 [197-98])[12]

In *Spectres de Marx* the idea is taken further, in a context which cannot but be perceived as political, and which separates Derrida's understanding of a "politics of memory" from the pieties it often involves:

Let us consider first the radical and necessary *heterogeneity* of an inheritance, the difference without opposition that must mark it, a "disparateness" and a quasi-juxtaposition without dialectic (the very plural of what further on we shall call Marx's spirits). An inheritance is never gathered, it is never one with itself. Its presumed unity, if there is one, can only consist in the *injunction to reaffirm by choosing*. *You must* [il faut] means you must filter, select, criticize, you must sort out among several of the possibilities which inhabit the same injunction. And inhabit it in contradictory fashion around a secret. If the legibility of a legacy were given, natural, transparent, univocal, if it did not simultaneously call for and defy interpretation, one would never have to inherit from it. One would be affected by it as by a cause – natural or genetic. One always inherits a secret, which says "Read me, will you ever be up to it?" (40 [16])

And, a little later:

Inheritance is never a given, it is always a task. It remains before us, as incontestably as the fact that, before even wanting it or refusing it, we are inheritors, and inheritors in mourning, like all inheritors. In particular for what is called Marxism. *To be*... means ... *to inherit*. All questions about being or what one is to be (or not to be) are questions of inheritance. There is no backward-looking fervor involved in recalling this fact, no traditionalist flavor. Reaction, reactionary or reactive are only interpretations of the structure of inheritance. We *are* inheritors, which does not mean that we *have* or that we *receive* this or that, that a given inheritance enriches us one day with this or that, but that the *being* we are *is* first of all inheritance, like it or not, know it or not. (94 [54])

The *explicit* political implications of this situation are, however, most clearly drawn in Derrida's text on Nelson Mandela: having pointed out Mandela's admiration for the European tradition of parliamentary democracy, Derrida goes on:

But if he admires this tradition, does that mean he is its inheritor, simply its inheritor? Yes and no, according to what one understands here by inheritance. One can recognize an authentic inheritor in him who conserves and reproduces, but also in him who respects the *logic* of the legacy to the point of turning it back on occasion against those who claim to be its holders, to the point of showing up against the usurpers the very thing that, in the inheritance, has never yet been seen: to the point of bringing to light, by the unheard-of *act* of a reflection, what had never seen the light. (456 [17]; cf. too 471–72 [34–35], and *Du droit à la philosophie*, 82 and 449)

The point of these gestures seems to be that "politics," so often invoked as though it were *eo ipso* something "radical," remains in just the same position of passive inheritance until its metaphysical genealogy is interrogated, and is to that extent no more promising a candidate for "radicality" than anything else. Political responsibility, on this view, would begin in the *active, critical* memory or reception of an inheritance or a tradition which will remember us if we do not remember it. And this means that Derrida's work will not provide satisfying answers within readily identifiable disciplinary boundaries, nor even (but perhaps this comes down to the same thing) within the domains of philosophy traditionally distinguished.[13] There is no easy way to distinguish logical concerns from epistemological ones in Derrida, nor these from ethical or political ones, simply because Derrida is working at a level that precedes the establishment of such demarcations. Even *Politiques de l'amitié*, Derrida's most sustained analysis of political themes, is focused on the apparently marginal motif of friendship, and is in no easy or obvious sense a work of political philosophy.

* * *

On the other hand, the insistence of this political worry or concern is not neutral or accidental, and it is certainly not in itself illegitimate or foolish to approach Derrida with political preoccupations, nor even to suspect that the *polemical* reactions we have mentioned are not *simply* unfortunate or misguided. The reason for this appears to be a fundamental ambiguity in the inherited philosophical concept of politics, or in the position philosophy can traditionally accord to politics and the thinking of politics. This ambiguity, which might be thought of as an uneasy complicity or a pacified antagonism between metaphysics and politics, can rapidly be illustrated in Aristotle. On the one hand, the *Metaphysics* duly claims that the supreme science of philosophy is the "theoretical science of first principles and first causes" (982b, 9). But that statement is immediately preceded by the idea that "The highest science, which is superior to every subordinate science, is the one that knows in view of what end each thing must be done. And this end is the good of each being and, in a general manner, the supreme good in nature as a whole" (982b, 3–7), and this slight indeterminacy, between "principles" and "causes" on the one hand, and "ends" and "goods" on the other, between arche-ology and tele-ology, between what will later be clearly demarcated as the "theoretical" and the "practical" (no doubt linked here by the value of *freedom*) allows an apparently contradictory claim at the beginning of the *Nicomachean Ethics*, where an apparently identical reasoning leads to a different conclusion:

If, then, there is some end of the things we do, which we desire for its own sake (everything else being desired for the sake of this), and if we do not choose everything for the sake of something else (for at that rate the process would go on to infinity, so that our desire would be empty and vain), clearly this must be the good and the chief good. Will not the knowledge of it, then, have a great influence on life? Shall we not, like archers who have a mark to aim at, be more likely to hit upon what is right? If so, we must try, in outline at least, to determine what it is, and of which of the sciences or capacities it is the object. It would seem to belong to the most authoritative art and that which is most truly the master art. And politics appears to be of this nature; for it is this that ordains which of the sciences should be studied in a state, and which each class of citizens should learn and up to what point they should learn them; and we see even the most highly esteemed of capacities to fall under this, e.g. strategy, economics, rhetoric; now, since politics uses the rest of the sciences, and since, again, it legislates as to what we are to do and what we are to abstain from, the end of this science must include those of the others, so that this end must be the good for man. [trans. Ross, 1094a, 18–1094b, 7]

This tension, according to which the philosophical concept of politics is both subordinate to metaphysics and superior to it, could be followed throughout the tradition in various forms: the relation between law and being, ought and is, theory and praxis, knowledge and action and so on, could be said to derive from this split in philosophy's understanding of itself and its relation to its usually reproachful other. The political demand made of Derrida is a repetition of this long tradition: if Derrida were ever simply to *answer* to that demand, to provide an answer which that demand could hear and accept, then his own thinking could safely be located in the metaphysical tradition he has always claimed to outflank. In this sense, Derrida providing a political answer to his political critics would prove just the opposite of what they would take it to prove, and so we might say that he stands a chance of proposing something radical about the political just to the extent that his texts do not answer simply to that demand.

The fact remains, however, that Derrida himself nowhere produced an analysis of politics in this vein in the 1960s and 1970s. One reason for this may have been itself "political": a sense of political strategy and solidarity may have dictated prudence about criticizing the arguments of the Left. But a more powerful reason lies in just the fundamental ambiguity we have located in the concept of politics itself, which, perhaps more clearly than any other (with the possible exception of "law"[14]) betrays a radical instability in the metaphysical concept of *concept* itself – and one plausible way of reading Derrida's work as a whole is that it shows up an irreducible conceptual politics even in the most theoretical or speculative domains of philosophy. In a way that is not at all a reduction in the sense of the "human science" gestures mentioned earlier, Derrida on this account would liberate a sort of energy in the metaphysical concept of politics, so that *all the conceptual dealings deconstruction has could be taken to be political.*[15] Within this generalized "politics" that deconstruction just is, conceptual dealings with what metaphysics defines as strictly political concepts would have a limited but important, perhaps exemplary, place.

* * *

Politics is the privileged domain of self-importance and self-righteousness for a specific reason: its apparently incontrovertible appeal to reality. The point with politics obviously being to change the world and not just to interpret it, interpreters habitually build the point of changing it into their interpretation as though *that* changed anything at all. At the beginning of Chapter 4 of *Politiques de l'amitié*, Derrida slightly wearily breaks off a discussion of some complicated formulations in Bataille, Blanchot, and Nancy to reflect on this difficulty: might not this patient, prudent way of dealing with the political issues raised by difficult texts appear too slow, too self-indulgent? Is there really time to take this much time in the urgency of contemporary political issues and violences? Following a paradoxical moment in Nietzsche, and aporetical formulations in Blanchot or Nancy, might the reader not become impatient with "relation without relation," "inoperative community," and so on? Might it not be urgent (and just that would be politics) to get on to the "real" issues, with less "bibliophiliac discretion"? This is, of course, not an idle speculation on Derrida's part, but just the reaction his work has most typically aroused, ever since the famous *il n'y a pas de hors-texte* in *Of Grammatology.*

Now, what would a "history", a science and action that wanted to be resolutely and ingenuously extradiscursive and extratextual *do*? What would a finally *realist* history or political philosophy *do in truth* if they failed to take on board, so as to measure up to them, to account for them, extreme normalization, new aporias, semantic instability, all the worrying conversions we have just seen at work in these signals? If it did not try to read all the apparently contradictory possibilities ("relation without relation", "community without community", etc.) these "sophistical discourses" remind us of? Let's say it: very little, hardly anything. They would miss what's hardest, most resistant, most irreducible, most other about the "thing itself". They would dress up as "realism" at the very moment they fall short of the thing – and repeat, repeat, repeat without even the awareness or memory of that repetition.[16]

As with the remarks about the human sciences, where the way to avoid *simply* inheriting from metaphysics was actively to assume (and thereby modify) the heritage of metaphysics, here the chance to engage with reality, with "the thing itself"[17] is given by a rigorous reflection on any possible means of access to that "thing."

The traditional view would be that a certain amount of theorizing or interpretation is no doubt necessary as a preparation for action: Derrida will maintain the paradox that theorizing and interpretation are structurally interminable and can *never* prepare for the interruptive and precipitate moment of decision and action, but that the decisiveness of the decision depends nonetheless on its structural relation to interminable analysis. Traditional political thinking believes it can determine decisions by writing the theory of their practice: Derrida believes that a decision is only a decision to the extent that it cannot be programmed in this manner – as he often repeats, a decision that was determined by prior theories or reasons would not be a decision, but the simple administration of a program, so for a decision to be worthy of its name it must supervene in a situation of undecidability, where the decision is not given, but must be taken.[18]

It is this deceptively simple argument which provides the core of Derrida's thinking about politics, and which will lead to the radical thinking of a "democracy to come." Let us approach it through the analysis of Nietzsche and a certain transcendental "perhaps" in *Politiques de l'amitié*. Derrida is reading a fragment from *Beyond Good and Evil* in which Nietzsche talks about a new type of philosopher capable of thinking the "perhaps," in the context of an attack on so-called "free spirits" and the "taste for democracy," a thought Derrida wants to link to a responsibility toward the future, in a passage I must cite at length to show how these motifs intertwine:

Shall we say that this responsibility which inspires (in Nietzsche) a discourse of hostility about the "taste for democracy" and "modern ideas" is exercised against democracy in general, against modernity in general? Or else does it respond *on the contrary* to the name of a hyperbole of democracy or to the modernity to come, respond *before* it [*devant elle, avant elle*], a hyperbole of which the "taste" and "ideas", in the Europe and America named here by Nietzsche, merely mediocre caricatures, chattering self-righteousness, perversion or prejudice – abuse of the term *democracy*? Are not these lifelike caricatures, just because they are lifelike, the worst enemy of what they look like, whose name they usurp? The worst repression, the very one that must, right up against the analogy, be opened up and really *unlocked*?

(Let us leave this question suspended; it is breathing the *perhaps*, and the *perhaps* which is coming will always have come before the question. The question seconds, it is always tardy and secondary. The moment it is formed, a *perhaps* will have opened it. It will always forbid it from closing, perhaps, at the very place where it forms. No response, no responsibility will ever abolish the *perhaps*. That a *perhaps* forever open and precede questioning, that it in advance suspend – not so to neutralize or inhibit them but to make them possible – all the determined and determining orders that depend on *questioning* (research, knowledge, science and philosophy, logic, law, politics and ethics, language even and in general), that's a necessity we attempt to which we attempt to do justice in several ways.

For example:

1. By recalling that acquiescence (*Zusage*) which is more originary than the question and which, without saying *yes* to anything positive, can only affirm the possibility of the future by opening itself to determinability, and therefore by welcoming what still remains indeterminate and indeterminable. This is indeed a *perhaps* which cannot yet be determined as dubitative or skeptical,[19] the perhaps of what *remains* to be thought, to be done, to live (to death). Now this *perhaps* not only comes "before" the question (enquiry, research, knowledge, theory, philosophy); it would also come, making it possible, "before" the originary acquiescence which in advance engages the question to the other.[20]

Derrida's "political" thinking, explicitly here preceding the *metaphysical* order of the political as determined by the question, will exploit this radical "perhaps," the only condition of possibility for an event of any sort (including an event of decision) to arrive, and the thought of the future it entails, to formulate a notion of democracy which is the closest his thought ever gets to a political projection or program.

This thinking about "perhaps" has some startling consequences. For it is not enough simply to stress that undecidability is a condition of decision, or radical possibility (and therefore unpredictability), for events and decisions nonetheless occur, and must occur, and when they occur they are quite determinate. Derrida will say that an event that occurs out of the condition of the perhaps *lifts* that condition (but remembers it *as* its condition): "If no decision (ethical, juridical, political) is possible without interrupting determination by getting into the *perhaps*, on the other hand the same decision must interrupt the very thing that is its condition of possibility, the *perhaps* itself" (86).[21] Radicalizing this thought about events in general in the context of *decisions* leads to a reinscription of the concept of decision away from the concept of the subject to which it is traditionally bound. For if an event in general has to be thought of in this way, then the traditional way of thinking about decisions can be said to neutralize just what makes the event an event by referring it to the subject:

> The decision makes an event, of course, but it also neutralizes that superven-
> ing that must surprise both the freedom and the will of any subject, in a word
> surprise the very subjectivity of the subject, affect it where the subject is ex-
> posed, sensitive, receptive, vulnerable and fundamentally passive, before and
> beyond any decision, even before any subjectivation, or even any objectivation.
> Doubtless the subjectivity of a subject, already, never decides about anything; its
> self-identity and its calculable permanence turn every decision into an accident
> that leaves the subject indifferent. *A theory of the subject is incapable of accounting for
> the slightest decision* . . . nothing ever happens to a subject, nothing worthy of the
> name "event". (87 [68])

So where the classical theory of the subject (still operating in Schmitt's decisionism, which Derrida discusses at length in *Politiques de l'amitié*) tends to reduce the eventhood of the event of decision by referring it to a subject, Derrida is trying to "eventize" the decision, and this means it can no longer be quite *my* decision. On this view, decisions are taken *by the other*, my decisions, my most sovereign decisions, cannot be decisions if they are taken by some self-coincident agency, but are decisive only if there is a diremption between "me" and the decider (in me):

> The passive decision, condition of the event, is always in me, structurally, an
> other decision, a tearing decision as decision of the other. Of the absolute other
> in me, of the other as the absolute that decides about me in me. In principle
> absolutely singular, in its most traditional concept, the decision is not merely
> always exceptional, *it makes an exception of me*. In me. I decide, I make up my mind,
> sovereignly, would mean: the other than me, the other-me as other and other
> than me, *makes* or *make* an exception of the self-same. This presupposed norm of
> any decision, this normal exception does not exonerate from any responsibility.
> Responsible for myself before the other, I am first of all and also *responsible for the
> other before the other*. (87–88 [68–69])

Now this thought, which is no doubt the key to Derrida's thinking about politics, is in fact a rigorous consequence of the quasi-concept of *différance*, at least as developed through the notion of the "trace" in *Of Grammatology* in 1967. There, Derrida famously claims that "the general structure of the unmotivated trace connects within the same possibility, and they cannot be separated except by abstraction, the structure of the relationship with the other, the movement of temporalization, and language as writing."[22] And the trace-structure of the relation to the other is such that the "presentation of the other as such, i.e. the dissimulation of its 'as such' has always already begun and no structure of beings escapes this" (ibid.). It is just this dissimulated (ghostly[23]) presentation of the other as other in me which determines the analysis of decision we have just seen almost thirty years later.

A further consequence has to do with violence. This description of events and decisions as radically unpredictable arrivals of the other[24] entails a thought that this arrival is irreducibly violent. Reflection on violence has a long history in Derrida's work, and it could be said that in a certain sense violence is the condition of possibility of history and politics. The analysis of Lévi-Strauss in *Of Grammatology*, for example, distinguishes three levels of violence: an originary "violent" non-appropriation (first level) is violently organized into effects of propriety (in this instance by the classificatory system of secret proper names – second level), which can then be violently disclosed (third level) to the guilty ethnographer.[25]

But perhaps more importantly for thinking about politics, "Violence and Metaphysics" establishes, apparently against what can appear too ironic in Levinas, the primordiality of an "economy of violence" (again this flows directly from the thought of trace and *différance*). It also suggests something like a categorical imperative in terms of a "lesser violence in an economy of violence." Positing a primordial "violence" in this way upsets *all* traditional political philosophies, which are bound up in a teleological structure prescribing that *arkhè* and/or *telos* be thought of as peaceful. The metaphysical thought of origin and end entails non-violence, and duly prescribes politics either as the unfortunate and degenerative decline from a peaceful origin (Rousseau), or as the redemptive drive towards an achieved peace (Kant). Even political philosophies which appear in one way or another to give greater thought to violence (Hobbes, Hegel, Marx) cannot think violence other than in the teleological perspective of non-violence. Political philosophy as such is wedded to this metaphysical scheme, and this has the paradoxical consequence that political philosophy is always the philosophy of the end of politics, or that the metaphysical concept of politics is the concept of politics *ending*. Derrida's thinking of primordial violence disallows this teleological scheme, or at least complicates it to the extent that what the remarks about violence amount to is an affirmation of the *endlessness* of politics,[26] and thereby of freedom.

This thinking of violence also has consequences for the political analysis of *foundation* or *institution*. Just because of this originary or pre-originary violence, political institutions are always instituted *in violence* in a way which goes beyond the traditional (Kantian or even Hegelian) recognition of the empirical or contingent violence that *in fact* presides at moments of political foundation or institution. If it is possible to say more generally that institutions, or the institution of institutions, is ("transcendentally") violent, this is because of a formal argument to the effect that, because the institution is, by definition, *not yet* in place at the instant of its institution, it cannot *comprehend* its institution. At its inception, the law of the institution is written, as Joyce has it, in the language of the outlaw.[27] Derrida demonstrates this point not only with respect to an institution such as the University,[28] but more generally and more ambitiously in an extraordinary analysis of the American Declaration of Independence.

This short text, presented as little more than a polite introduction to a lecture on Nietzsche which happens to coincide with a visit to Charlottesville during the bicentennial celebrations of Independence in 1976, shows how the moment of the declaration, by which the "people" who sign it come into existence *as* a people capable of signing, is struck by a necessary undecidability (between the sense that the declaration *describes* a state of affairs and the sense that it produces the state of affairs it appears to describe):

There was no signatory, by right, before the text of the Declaration which remains itself the producer and the guarantor of its own signature. By this fabulous event, by this fable which implies the trace and is in truth possible only through the inadequation to itself of some present moment,[29] a signature gives itself a name. It opens a line of credit *for itself*, *its* own credit, from itself *to* itself. The *self* rises up here in all cases (nominative, dative, accusative) as soon as a signature credits itself, through a single *coup de force*, which is also a writing *coup*, as right to writing. The *coup de force* makes right, founds right, gives right, *gives rise to the law*.[30]

This founding violence, whereby no institution can quite close on itself and integrate all its moments,[31] implies that right will never quite be entirely right, but always opened up by this moment of violence at its foundation. This is not a negative or regrettable situation, however, because if institutions could so close in on themselves in total self-understanding or self-legitimation, then right would simply be transformed into necessity, there could be no question of freedom, and politics as such would simply disappear. The *chance* of politics is given by this founding impossibility at the moment of institution of the institution, which also means that institutions are essentially historical and never entirely stabilized, haunted by the *coup de force* that institutes them. This aporetical moment at the "origin" (what we might call the "absolute past," insofar as this moment cannot be gathered into the form of the present, never really happens as such, precedes the institution as its fabulous dream-time) opens up all institutions in general to time as the radically unpredictable arrival of the event we have described. The absolute past communicates in this way with what we might be tempted to call the "absolute future," which provides the *a-venir* Derrida regularly associates with democracy, and explains Derrida's recourse to the motif of the *promise*.

* * *

It seems just possible to derive from this configuration, which we have seen involves the thought of deconstruction in general, something resembling a politics with which to return to our initial demand. For Derrida indeed attempts, on the basis of just this thinking of other, event and founding violence, to develop a notion of democracy, which runs like the unifying thread throughout *Politiques de l'amitié*, picking up on earlier, more informal developments in *L'autre cap* and *Du droit à la philosophie*. By "democracy" here, Derrida means not so much a particular political regime as a *tension* derived in the first instance from Plato and Aristotle:

> No democracy without respect for singularity or irreducible alterity, but no democracy without "community of friends" (*koina ta philon*), without calculation of majorities, without subjects which are identifiable, stabilizable, representable and equal among themselves. These two laws are irreducible to one another. Tragically irreconcilable and wounding for ever. The wound itself opens with the necessity of having to *count* one's friends, count the others, in the economy of one's own, where every other is entirely other [*là où tout autre est tout autre*]. (40 [22])[32]

Derrida shows at length how the inherited concept of democracy is inseparable from values of nationality and rootedness, and a value of fraternity which excludes (or at least prejudges) the place of sexual difference in politics by normalizing the political relation according to a model of community grounded on the example of the relation between *brothers*. As in every deconstruction (and the case of "democracy" would in that case be exemplary) the point is to exploit other resources in the inheritance, and so the maintenance of an "old word" for a "new concept" requires *strategic* justification:

> If [in Plato's *Menexenus*], between the name ["democracy"] on the one hand, the concept or the thing on the other, the play of a discrepancy gives rise to rhetorical

effects which are also political strategies, what lessons can we draw from this today? Is it still *in the name of democracy* that one will try to criticize such and such a determination of democracy or of aristodemocracy? Or, more radically, closer, precisely, to its fundamental *radicality* (where for example it *roots* in the security of the autochtonic foundation, in the stock and genius of filiation), is it still in the name of democracy, of a democracy to come, that we will try to deconstruct a concept, all the predicates associated in a generally dominant concept of democracy, that in the heritage of which we find without fail the law of birth, natural or "national" law, the law of homophylia or of autochtony, civic equality (*isonomia*) grounded on the equality of birth (*isogonia*) as condition of the calculus of approbation and therefore of the aristocracy of virtue and wisdom, etc.?

What still remains or resists in the deconstructed (or deconstructible) concept of democracy to orient us without end? To order us not only to start a deconstruction but to keep the old name? And still to deconstruct in the name of a *democracy* to come? That is still to enjoin us still to inherit that which, forgotten, repressed, misrecognized or unthought in the "old" concept and in its whole history, would still be awake, delivering up signs or symptoms of survival to come through all its old, fired features? Would there still be in the concept of *eudoxia* (reputation, approbation, opinion, judgment), and in the concept of equality (equality of birth (*isogonia*) and equality of rights (*isonomia*)) a double motif which could, interpreted differently, withdraw democracy from autochtonic and homophyliac rootedness? Is there another thought of calculus and number, another way of apprehending the universality of the singular which, without giving politics over to the incalculable, still justifies the old name "democracy"? Will it still make sense to speak of democracy in a situation in which it would no longer be a question (essentially and constitutively) of country, of nation, even of State and of citizen, in other words, *if at least one still holds to the received acceptation of this word*, in which it would no longer be a question of politics? (126–27 [103–104])

On the one hand, then, this is a specific issue around the specific concept of democracy as it is inherited from the tradition. We shall see in a moment how Derrida develops this deconstruction via the motif of the "to come" we have already noted. But on the other hand, we said that this specific case was *exemplary*. This means, following an ambiguity Derrida himself has often exploited,[33] not only that democracy is one example among others of deconstruction, a sample, but that it is exemplary, the best example, a paragon, for deconstruction in general.[34] Which need not surprise us if we bear in mind our earlier suggestion that one effect of deconstruction was to suggest an irreducible conceptual politics, and that the metaphysical concept of politics carried a privileged ambiguity with it. This is enough to suggest, not just that deconstruction is in one sense a fundamentally political mode of thought, but that it is bound up with this issue of democracy in a more intimate way:

In reaffirming that the maintenance of this Greek name, democracy, is a matter of context, rhetoric or strategy, even of polemics, in reaffirming that this name will last the time it takes but scarcely longer, in saying that things are getting singularly faster these days, one is not necessarily giving in to the opportunism or the cynicism of the anti-democrat not showing his hand. Quite on the contrary: one is keeping one's right to question, to critique, to deconstruction (rights which are in principle guaranteed by every democracy: no deconstruction without democracy, no democracy without deconstruction). One keeps this right in order to mark strategically what is no longer a matter of strategy: the limit between the conditional (the edges of the context and concept of democracy which enclose the effective practice of democracy and feed it on soil and blood) and the unconditional which, from the start, will have inscribed an auto-deconstructive force in the very motif of democracy, the possibility and the duty for democracy to de-limit itself. Democracy is the *autos* of deconstructive auto-delimitation. A delimitation not only in the name of a regulative idea and an indefinite perfectibility, but each time in the singular urgency of a *here and now*. (128–29 [105])

Deconstruction then, on the one hand generalizes the concept of politics so that it includes all conceptual dealings whatsoever, and on the other makes a precise use of *one* particular inherited politico-metaphysical concept, democracy, to make a pointed and more obviously political intervention in political thought. "Democracy" is an old name retained because on the one hand it allows a thought of an endless progress towards a better political state, but on the other, cutting into the teleologism of the structure of the Kantian Idea, obliges an interventionist perception of the here and now, always *in the name* of the democracy-to-come which will never finally arrive, but never claiming to have established a satisfactory democracy. In this way, politics, beginning to drift away from its metaphysical determinations, is projected as *endless* (it never will come to an end, cannot really still be thought within the terms of the regulative Idea, is *perpetually* a promise, never fulfilled), and also endlessly singular (so that politics is happening each time *now*). Derrida's many more or less visible interventions in concrete political situations (most recently, for example, around new immigration laws enacted in France in 1996), are to this extent not merely the circumstantial acts of a philosopher elsewhere, and more importantly, developing theories or knowledge, but continuous with each act of deconstruction from the start, always more or less obviously marked by a strategic event or decision in a given context. This does not provide a theoretical model for politics so much as it strives to keep open the event of alterity which alone makes politics possible and inevitable, but which political philosophy of all colors has always tried to close.

1 Jacques Derrida, "Mochlos, ou le conflit des facultés," in *Du droit à la philosophie* (Paris: Galilée, 1990), 424. [trans. Richard Rand and Amy Wigant, in Richard Rand, ed., *Logomachia: The Conflict of the Faculties* (Lincoln and London: University of Nebraska Press, 1992), 3–34 (23)]. All translations from Derrida in this article are my own.

2 J. Derrida, "Ponctuations: le temps de la thèse," *Du droit à la philosophie*, 397–459 (451) [trans. K. McLaughlin in Alan Montefiore, ed., *Philosophy in France Today* (Cambridge University Press, 1983), 34–50 (42)].

3 See for example Allan Bloom, *The Closing of the American Mind: How Higher Education has Failed Democracy and Impoverished the Souls of Today's Students* (New York: Simon and Schuster, 1987), 379–80. See too Derrida's notes and references in "Les pupilles de l'Université: le principe de raison et l'idée de l'Université," in *Du droit à la philosophie*, 488 n 1 [trans. Catherine Porter and Edward P. Morris, as "The Principle of Reason: The University in the Eyes of its Pupils," *Diacritics* 13 (Fall 1983): 3–20]; and in *Mémoires: pour Paul de Man* (Paris: Galilée, 1988), 34–36 n 2 [trans. J. Culler *et al.*, 2nd ed. (New York: Columbia University Press, 1989), 41–43 n 5].

4 See my analysis of this motif in "Demanding History," in *Legislations: The Politics of Deconstruction* (London: Verso, 1994), 61–73. A notable exception to the schema I am analyzing here is the work of Ernesto Laclau and Chantal Mouffe, which is arguably the only political theory as such to have engaged seriously with Derrida's work.

5 See for example Terry Eagleton, *Walter Benjamin, or Towards a Revolutionary Criticism* (London: New Left Books, 1981), 138; and Frank Lentricchia, *After the New Criticism* (Chicago: University of Chicago Press, 1980). Michael Ryan's *Marxism and Deconstruction: A Critical Articulation* (Baltimore and London: Johns Hopkins University Press, 1982), is a more interesting case: see my analysis of this book in "Outside Story" (*Legislations*, 88–98).

6 There were enough discrete signals and reserves to give this description some plausibility, as for example in the piece on Nelson Mandela which comments on Mandela's admiration for Western parliamentary democracy ("Admiration de Nelson Mandela," in *Psyché: inventions de l'autre* (Paris: Galilée, 1987), 453–75 (455) [trans. Mary Ann Caws and Isabelle Lorenz, in *For Nelson Mandela* (New York: Seaver Books, 1987), 13–42]. See too the objections put forward to "Le dernier mot du racisme" [in *Psyché: inventions de l'autre*, 353–62; trans. Peggy Kamuf, as "Racism's Last Word," *Critical Inquiry* 12 (1985): 290–99], by Ann McLintock and Rob Nixon in "No Names Apart: The Separation of Word and History in Derrida's 'Le dernier mot du racisme,'" *Critical Inquiry* 13: 1 (1986): 140–54; and Derrida's reply in "But, beyond . . . ," trans. P. Kamuf, ibid., 155–70. Alternatively, see Terry Eagleton's review of *Spectres de Marx* (Paris: Galilée, 1993) [trans. P. Kamuf (New York and London: Routledge, 1994)] in *Radical Philosophy*, 73 (1995), 35–37. In this context, see too, more generally, Nancy Fraser's review

of some "Derridean" work on politics: "The French Derrideans: Politicizing Deconstruction or Deconstructing Politics?," in *New German Critique* 33 (1984): 127–54, and Simon Critchley, *The Ethics of Deconstruction* (Oxford: Blackwell, 1992), 200ff.

7 The Heidegger "affair" began in France with the publication in France of Victor Farias's *Heidegger et le nazisme* (Paris: Verdier, 1987), at almost exactly the same time as Derrida published *De l'esprit: Heidegger et la question* (Paris: Galilée, 1987), which explicitly analyzes Heidegger's Nazi involvement. Numerous polemical pieces and books followed in France (by, among others, Bourdieu, Lyotard, Ferry and Renaut, Janicaud), with much discussion in the press. The American side of this "affair" was concentrated around a book edited by Richard Wolin, *The Heidegger Controversy* (New York: Columbia University Press, 1991), and Derrida's disagreement with the publication of one of his interviews in it. The de Man affair began with the discovery by the Belgian scholar Otwin de Graef of a large number of newspaper articles (some of an apparently anti-Semitic nature) the young Paul de Man had written for the Nazi-controlled Belgian newspaper *Le Soir* during the occupation. See the two volumes devoted to these pieces: W. Hamacher, N. Hertz and T. Keenan, eds., *Paul de Man: Wartime Journalism 1939–45* (Lincoln and London: University of Nebraska Press, 1988), and *Responses: On Paul de Man's Wartime Journalism* (Lincoln and London: University of Nebraska Press, 1989). See especially Derrida's piece "Like the Sound of the Sea deep in a Shell: Paul de Man's war," trans. P. Kamuf, *Critical Inquiry* 14 (Spring 1988): 590–652, reprinted in *Responses*, 127–64, and the issue of *Critical Inquiry* 15 (Summer, 1989) devoted in part to responses to this piece and Derrida's further reply, "Biodegradables: Seven Diary Fragments" (812–73). What is striking about these two "affairs" is on the one hand the alacrity with which supposedly serious scholars were often prepared to make gross and unsubstantiated accusations and assimilations, and on the other Derrida's patience and appetite for arguing with unworthy opponents, for reasons it is hard not to see as political. It is also worth noting that already in the late 1960s Jean-Pierre Faye had (incorrectly and indeed scurrilously) already suggested that Derrida was urging an espousal of mythos over logos, as had been the case with Nazi philosophers. See the account in Elizabeth Roudinesco, *La bataille de cent ans: Histoire de la psychoanalyse en France*, vol. II (Paris: Éditions du Seuil, 1986), 542, and Derrida's comments in *Positions* (Paris: Minuit, 1972), 75–76 [trans. Alan Bass (Chicago: University of Chicago Press, 1981), 55–56, and Bass's helpful note, 103–104 n 28].

8 See especially *L'autre cap* (Paris: Minuit, 1991) [trans. M. Naas and P.-A. Brault, *The Other Heading* (Bloomington: Indiana University Press, 1992)], *Spectres de Marx*, and *Politiques de l'amitié* (Paris: Galilée, 1994) [trans. George Collins, *Politics of Friendship* (London: Verso Books, 1997)].

9 The confusion of levels of analysis that this involves is explicitly pointed out in "Violence et Métaphysique": see *L'écriture et la différence* (Paris: Éditions

du Seuil, 1967), 117–228 (189 n 1) [trans. Alan Bass, *Writing and Difference* (Chicago: University of Chicago Press, 1978), 129 n 46].

10 For a fuller explanation of this pervasive structure of Derrida's thinking, first clearly brought out by Rodolphe Gasché in *The Tain of the Mirror: Derrida and the Philosophy of Reflection* (Cambridge, MA: Harvard University Press, 1986), see my "Derridabase," in G. Bennington and J. Derrida, *Jacques Derrida* (Paris: Éditions du Seuil, 1991), 248–63 [English translation, *Jacques Derrida* (Chicago: University of Chicago Press, 1993), 267–84].

11 The history of Derrida's "silence" about Marx would merit treatment in itself, starting with what is now quite a complex job of decoding the third of the interviews collected in *Positions* (see especially pp. 85 ff [62 ff], where Derrida famously suggests that his reading of Marx is "still to come" (85 [62]). That *Specters of Marx* always might be taken to maintain rather than dissipate Derrida's silence about Marx was illustrated at the 1995 "Applied Derrida" conference in Luton, where, in a general discussion with Derrida, an irritated participant demanded that Derrida say "what he really thought" about Marx; when politely pointed by Derrida to *Specters of Marx*, the now angry participant replied that he'd read that, but wanted to know what Derrida *really thought* about Marx.

12 See my detailed discussion of this gesture with respect to Freud in "Circanalyse: la chose même," in P. Guyomard, ed., *Depuis Lacan*, forthcoming.

13 In a companion piece to this, I try to take up some of these issues with respect to the traditional philosophical domain of "ethics." See "Deconstruction and Ethics," in Nicholas Royle, ed., *Deconstructions: A Critical Reader* (London: Macmillan, 2000).

14 See *Force de loi* (Paris: Galilée, 1994) [trans. Mary Quaintance, "Force of Law: The 'mystical foundation' of authority," with original French text in *Cardozo Law Review* 11, 5–6 (1990): 920–1045], in the course of which Derrida makes the startling claim that justice (always prior to its formulation as law) is the undeconstructible condition of deconstruction (35 [945]), or that deconstruction *is* justice.

15 I have elsewhere attempted to derive the necessity of this conceptual "politics" from temporal finitude: see "Contre (le) temps, pour (le) temps," at http://www.sussex.ac.uk/Users/sffc4; and pursued an analysis of the appeal to urgency as a mark of the political in "Emergencies," *Oxford Literary Review* 18 (1997): 205–46. Richard Beardsworth's important and challenging book *Derrida and the Political* (London: Routledge, 1996), reviewed in "Emergencies," attempts more ambitiously to derive "the political" in general from what he calls "the aporia of time."

16 *Politiques de l'amitié*, 99–100 [81].

17 This is still consistent with the closing sentence of *La voix et le phénomène* (Paris: PUF, 1967) [trans. D. Allison, *Speech and Phenomena* (Evanston: Northwestern University Press, 1973)], "La chose même se dérobe toujours" [the thing itself always escapes].

18 Derrida's "early" work appeals to the notion of the undecidable (see for example "La double séance," in *La dissémination* [Paris: Éditions du Seuil, 1972], 199–308 [240, 248–49] [trans. Barbara Johnson, *Dissemination* (Chicago: University of Chicago Press, 1982), 173–286 (211, 219–20)], where Derrida insists that this term is being used *analogically*). The explicit claim that undecidability is a positive condition of possibility of decision comes later: see, for example, in Introduction to *Parages* (Paris: Galilée, 1986), 15: "But the event encounter, decision, call, nomination, initial incision of a mark – can only come about from the experience of the undecidable. Not the undecidable which still belongs to the order of calculation, but the other, the one no calculation could anticipate."

19 [Derrida's note:] see *De l'esprit: Heidegger et la question* (Paris: Galilée, 1987), 147 [trans. G. Bennington and R. Bowlby, *Of Spirit: Heidegger and the Question* (Chicago: University of Chicago Press, 1989), 94 n 5] and especially "Nombre de Oui," in *Psyché*, 644–50 [trans. B. Holmes, "A Number of Yes," *Qui Parle*, 2, 2 (1988): 120–33]. The analysis of the *Zusage* to which Derrida refers occurs in an enormously long footnote to *De l'esprit*, which appears to have been added as something of an afterthought to the original text.

20 *Politiques de l'amitié*, 58–59 [38].

21 This sketch of a notion of self-interrupting structures is carried further in "Le mot d'accueil," in *Adieu: à Emmanuel Lévinas* (Paris: Galilée, 1997), 38–211, especially 95–98, 117, 146, and is implicit at least since "Le sans de la coupure pure," in *La vérité en peinture* (Paris: Flammarion, 1979), 95–135 [trans. G. Bennington and I. McLeod, *The Truth in Painting* (University of Chicago Press, 1987), 83–118].

22 *De la grammatologie* (Paris: Éditions de Minuit, 1967), 69 [trans. Gayatri Chakravorty Spivak, *Of Grammatology* (Baltimore: Johns Hopkins University Press, 1976), 47].

23 The thematics of the ghost in *Spectres de Marx* (as in the earlier improvisations in Ken McMullan's film *Ghost Dance* (1983)) are a further ramification of this trace-structure of alterity, giving rise there to the proposition of a "hauntology" prior to any ontology.

24 See too *Apories*, 66 ff [33 ff], for an analysis of the figure of the *arrivant*.

25 *De la grammatologie*, 149–202 [101–40], and especially 164–65 [112–13].

26 This affirmation of endlessness is not, as might appear, an affirmation of what Hegel would call a "bad infinite," but grows very specifically from a non-Hegelian (and non-Husserlian) understanding of the Kantian notion of the Idea of Reason, which functions in Kant as a way of organizing future progress towards something which may well be empirically unrealizable as such, but to which an asymptotic approach is obviously recommendable. Derrida's suspicion of this Kantian motif goes back to his earliest work: see for example "Introduction" to Husserl's *Origine de la géométrie*, 150–55 [trans. John P. Leavey, Jr. (Stony Brook: Nicholas Hays, 1978), 134–41]. This is rigorously consonant with the view of the event and the decision

we have outlined, and with earlier formulations as to the "monstrosity" or "formlessness" of the future.

27 James Joyce, *Ulysses* (Harmondsworth: Penguin Books, 1968), 144.

28 See "Mochlos ou le conflit des facultés," 435 [31].

29 In *Spectres de Marx*, this will become the text's major motif, borrowed from *Hamlet*, that of the "time out of joint" (see especially 43 ff [18ff]). See too *Politiques de l'amitié*, 126 [103], and "Le mot d'accueil," 200.

30 *Otobiographies: l'enseignement de Nietzsche et la politique du nom propre* (Paris: Galilée, 1984), 23 [trans. T. Keenan and T. Pepper, "Declarations of Independence," *New Political Science* 15 (1986): 7–15].

31 See too the comment from one of Derrida's earliest papers: "Ce que je ne peux jamais comprendre, dans une structure, c'est ce par quoi elle n'est pas close," " 'Genèse et structure' et la phénoménologie" [1959], in *L'écriture et la différence*, 229–51 (238) [160].

32 This formula, which can still be read as an elaboration of the remarks on the trace from *Of Grammatology*, is first developed in "Donner la mort" (in Derrida *et al.*, *L'éthique du don* (Paris: Métailié-Transition, 1992), 11–108 [trans. David Wills, *The Gift of Death* (Chicago: University of Chicago Press, 1995)]) in the context of a questioning of the distinction made by Kierkegaard between ethics and religion. Wills comes to the inevitably compromising translation: "Every other (one) is every (bit) other."

33 See *Passions* (Paris: Galilée, 1993), 42–43 [trans. D. Wood in D. Wood, ed., *Derrida: A Critical Reader* (Oxford: Blackwell, 1992), 5–35 (15).

34 I attempt to follow this logic of exemplarity a little further in "Derrida's Mallarmé," in Michael Temple, ed., *Meetings with Mallarmé* (Exeter: Exeter University Press, 1998), 126–42.

FURTHER READING

Beardsworth, Richard. *Derrida and the Political*. London: Routledge, 1996.
Bennington, Geoffrey. *Legislations: The Politics of Deconstruction*. London: Verso, 1995.
Laclau, Ernesto, and Mouffe, Chantal. *Hegemony and Socialist Strategy: Towards a Radical Democratic Politics*. London: Verso, 1985.

CHAPTER 9

Derrida and law: legitimate fictions

Margaret Davies

Three texts, one law. Or equally, three texts, no founded law, or an unfounded law of anti-foundation. The three texts of Derrida's I am going to base my comments upon are some of those which most overtly, or most directly deal with the question of law. I make this distinction between texts simply for the sake of convenience, since in my view many of Derrida's works in one way or another deal with the question of law.[1] However, those I am here concerned with all *name* law – "Devant la loi," "The Law of Genre," "Force of Law"[2] – and this naming of law has a special significance in the context of this chapter. In its naming, the text proclaims itself and authorizes its legal content: as Derrida comments in "Before the Law": "A sort of intrigue is already apparent in a title which names the law... a little as if the law had entitled itself."[3] This comment goes to the very core of the jurisprudential problematic which is my concern here. Self-entitlement of the law is nothing more than a parental "because I say so" translated into a constitutional mandate, and – as the guardian and apologist for legitimacy – mainstream legal philosophy has struggled to escape such arbitrariness by attempting to discover or describe an absolute source of legitimacy. This "law of law" or "source of authority" not only preoccupies legal philosophers, it is presumed to have real force by citizens and legal officials alike, and for those who do not accept a particular legal regime, it represents a refusal to negotiate, compromise, or reconcile on the part of those who uphold and administer the law.

As I will explain, the philosophical project of discovering the source, nature, or law of law has been plagued by some unresolvable contradictions and paradoxes. Derrida's work on law is not about resolving these theoretical difficulties, nor does it necessarily entail a wholesale rejection of traditional legal theory for failing to develop a conceptually unified or coherent picture of law. Derrida's work in relation to law allows us to see the contradictions and paradoxes of legal thought not as conceptual failures (except, perhaps, as a failure in self-reflectiveness), but rather as systemic philosophical matters which go to the heart of any question of meaning (and thus normality, authority, and understanding). In other words, the gaps and contradictions of legal philosophy and legal systems are also the gaps and contradictions of philosophical systems generally.

Several further introductory points perhaps need to be made for those who approach this chapter with a background in legal theory. First, there is the issue of what is the "law" which is raised here. Mainstream legal philosophy – for obvious reasons – tends to concentrate on positive institutionalized law, and not upon the multitude of other types of prescription which inform our existences, such as the norms of sexual identity, of social customs, or of writing a literary work. Indeed John Austin said that many of these norms were "law" only in an improper or sometimes metaphorical sense,[4] and Anglo-American legal theory has tended to accept this characterization. Of course, this is not the only way that the term "law" can be used, and Derrida's writing on law, as on other topics, works on several layers, so that the ambiguities and intersections may more readily be identified. This is most evident in "Before the Law," where the "law" is at once the institutionalized positive law, the laws of psycho-social development as articulated by Freud, the moral law, and the laws of literary production. Having said that, in this chapter I have deliberately confined myself to an analysis of the more traditional subject matter of legal theory, attempting, however, to indicate its ultimate inseparability from Austin's "metaphorical" law.

Secondly, within this multiplicity of the possible dimensions of "law," it seems to me that when Derrida *does* focus upon the institutional law, he takes as his point of departure the positivist view, which states essentially that law is separate or separable from its "other," non-law (often characterized by legal philosophy as a nebulous set of norms called "morality"). This emphasis upon the traditional concept of "law" is particularly evident in "Force of Law." It is important to emphasize this, and to point out that Derrida's approach does not take the form of either an internal or an external critique of law or legal positivism, but rather an interrogation of the conceptual frontiers of the idea of law. Therefore it is not possible to state unequivocally that Derrida accepts or rejects positivism as a theory of law: rather the point of these texts is to deconstruct or "de-sediment" the positivist notion of law, in the process revealing its conceptual limitations and suggesting an alternative place for ethical or political questions to arise – as neither external to nor internal to law, but at the limits of law. Interestingly, many of these conceptual limitations have been recognized in various ways by positivist thinkers, but are frequently glossed over or underemphasized.

BEGINNING LAW

Let me begin, then, by making several observations about the structure of legal or normative systems as envisaged by orthodox legal theory. I will return to these matters later, but wish to raise them as a straightforward way into the more complex Derridean problematic. These introductory points can be stated relatively succinctly.

First, mainstream legal theory of the past two hundred years or so has been shaped by the modernist desire to ground knowledge about law in some objective or absolute fashion. Modernist legal thinking, driven by certain enlightenment and liberal ideals – such as equality before the law and the desirability of a rational basis for government – has attempted to identify a foundation for legal authority and for authoritative knowledge about law which avoids the unequal and seemingly irrational practices and beliefs of earlier legal doctrine. Modernist legal thought puts the law firmly above individual human persons, meaning that the source of legal authority must have some superior or transcendent existence, at least an existence which is objectively identifiable and certain. In this way, contemporary natural law thought has tended to retreat from the possibly whimsical and in any case infinite and unknowable god as the author of law, preferring in her place more scientifically grounded principles such as "practical reason"[5] or even in a popular version, natural physical laws.[6] Similarly, the growth and present dominance of legal positivism is based on the notion that law is describable, indisputably grounded in some elementary principle, and conceptually (though not practically) separate from all of the human politics and instabilities which might threaten law's neutrality.[7] Kelsen's idea of a "pure" theory of law, which would be uncontaminated by non-legal influences,[8] provides an informative and rigorous approach to this matter, and his work will provide the basis for several aspects of my comments about positivist thought.

Second, clearly none of these modernist attempts to secure a foundation for legal authority has succeeded in satisfactorily identifying a basic principle which coheres with the desire to provide a pure description of law. The philosophical reasons for this failure can be stated reasonably simply, although the implications are far-reaching, as Derrida's work indicates. To understand the general dimensions of the problem with positivist foundationalism, we need turn only briefly to Wittgenstein, who imagines that the search for normative authority is like digging for reasons. When I am faced with a rule or a law, I ask, "why should I follow this rule?" (Wittgenstein is more concerned with the question: "how do I know what this rule means?" Ultimately, however, knowing what a rule means, and knowing what authority lies behind it are intimately connected questions: again, Derrida's linking of the performative with the interpretative basis of the law, which I will discuss below, clarifies this point.) Thus I look for some justification for the rule – for instance a more basic rule – and then I look for a justification for that more basic rule, and so on: "If I have exhausted the justifications I have reached bedrock, and my spade is turned. Then I am inclined to say, 'This is simply what I do.' "9 We are therefore faced with a problem. The potentially infinite regress of reasons underlying our rules must stop at some point, but it does not stop at a place where we can be satisfied that we have reached a rational origin, or an origin which clearly demarcates the inside from the outside of law. It is just there, an assumption or premise which can be subject to no further scrutiny.

This is precisely the problem faced repeatedly by Hans Kelsen in his attempt to identify a basic principle which authorizes all law, and separates legal from non-legal norms. Kelsen said that each norm in a legal system is authorized by a norm which has a higher authority within that system. For instance, when you are fined for speeding on the road, according to Kelsen you are subject to an individual norm (a norm applying only to you).10 You may ask where the police officer gets the authority to impose such a fine, and you will find that there is an Act of Parliament (or in the common-law system, a precedent) which lays down a general norm prohibiting travelling over a certain speed and conferring the authority to impose penalties on certain persons or institutions. If you are very persistent, you will ask where that Act of Parliament gets its validity, and you will find that there is a body of constitutional law, if not a written constitution, which gives Parliament the authority to create such rules for society. Kelsen says further that the present constitutional order is authorized by the prior constitutions (if such exist) and that finally you will find a "historically first constitution," prior to which there was a revolution or some radical breach of the previous legal order.11 However, naturally it is still possible to ask what validates that constitution, and this is where Kelsen hits bedrock.

Kelsen's solution was to propose a "basic norm," which he described variously as a hypothesis, a presupposition, and finally as a fiction.12

In itself, Kelsen's basic norm is neither valid nor invalid: it cannot be valid because there is no further place to ask questions about validity, and it cannot be invalid because it is itself the source of all validity. It is beyond questions about validity. Thus, according to Kelsen, it is a fiction, or rather a "proper" fiction, because it contradicts reality (it does not exist as law, but is merely a conceptual construct), and because it contradicts itself (as authoritative of law but not itself authorized in a way which would give it this authority).[13] Moreover, the basic norm or "fiction" is not an institutional foundation of authority which can be empirically discerned, but rather the conceptual condition upon which acceptance of any norm as a legal norm is based. In other words, it is a condition of a transcendental mind which makes a norm into law, not a concrete source of law. However, it *is* a source of law in the sense that it is the condition for any otherwise completely "subjective" order or norm to be "objectively" understood as a norm.[14] The basic norm is the condition for the construction of objectivity in the legal system: in other words, it is what ensures that law is regarded as superior to human will.

This paradox or uncertainty at the heart of law is evident not only in Kelsen's thought, but also in the work of other legal theorists such as H.L.A. Hart, and in various legal puzzles, most notably the paradox of parliamentary sovereignty.[15] Clearly the attempt at legal self-justification is bound to fail at some point in the structure. The way out of these puzzles is to locate the source of authority strictly *outside* the legal system, in some social, political, or moral order. For instance, the contemporary positivist thinker, Tom Campbell, argues that there are sound *ethical* reasons for adopting the positivist approach to law.[16] This does not give us a source of authority, simply a moral argument about why it is necessary to have a separation between law and non-law. It could be demonstrated that the argument in favor of separation sets up a limit which is not only incapable of achieving the project of certainty in law, but also has an inherently exclusionary and potentially oppressive impact. The reasons for this lie in the inherent undecidability of the limits of law, and will become clearer shortly.

Finally, legal thought has tended to assume that there is a singular and linear relationship between the structure of norms which forms the legal system, and the acts and decisions which take place "within" the system. It is assumed that the rules, doctrines, or principles are the primary legal sources or materials, and that decisions flow from this conceptual basis. Part of this mode of thought is that there are clear cases – which fit easily within a particular rule and do not require any active construction by the judge – and hard cases – which require the judge or decision-maker to reflect and construct in relation to the existing rules in order to arrive at a coherent solution. Positivist thought places the performances of the law below any relevant norm, regarding established rules and other norms as the primary material of law. Thus, parliamentary performances are subject to the constitution, judicial and other performances are determined by legal principle. Certain legal realists reversed this order, arguing instead that the actions of judges constitute the law. However, it is no exaggeration to say that mainstream legal thought still assumes that rules and other ideational creations are primary – they are, in fact, the law itself – while legal "performances," such as the signing of a contract, the celebration of a wedding, or the making of a decision "in accordance with" the law, are merely the exercising of already existent legal powers. The performative aspects of judgment (that it carries consequences for the parties to a dispute and may create new law) are regarded as subordinate to general legal principle. This explains why a great deal of anxiety is felt by lawyers at the appearance of an "activist" court or judge: it is as though the decision-maker places its own performance above the transcendent principles of the law.

THE LAW OF THE LAW OF LAW

Bearing these introductory points about Western legal theory in mind, I now wish to elaborate on Derrida's reflections about law, beginning with a fiction (*the* fiction, perhaps). At the beginning of "Devant la loi" Derrida quotes Montaigne: "our law, it is said, even has legitimate fictions on which it bases the truth of its justice."[7] The enigma of the legitimate fiction is one to which Derrida returns in "Force of Law." (Remember here that Kelsen also described the basic norm which legitimizes the entire legal order as a fiction, a proper fiction.) The legitimate fiction, we might say, fills the aporia of legal authority.

In order to explain this, I need at least to attempt to start at the beginning, the place where legal authority would find itself. Indeed Derrida says that this compulsion for origins and for law itself is irresistible (and far be it from me to resist an irresistible compulsion). In the tale which is the object of Derrida's reading, Kafka's man from the country stands before the law, seeking access, while the gatekeeper says "not yet." Entry is not absolutely forbidden, but it is deferred, and – as it turns out – deferred forever. Derrida says:

> What remains concealed and invisible in each law is thus presumably the law itself, that which makes laws of these laws, the being-law of these laws. The question and the quest are ineluctable, rendering irresistible the journey towards the place and the origin of law.[18]

There are several strands to this irresistible journey, and the impossibility of its fulfillment, which need unraveling here. First, for the man from the country, the law just is: it presents itself, as Derrida says, as "an absolutely emergent order, absolute and detached from any origin."[19] When it recognizes us as legal persons, the law does not give us any choice about accepting it: we stand before it, but are not empowered to see behind it, or to question its history, its source, or its authority. Although it may hold out a promise of transparency and accessibility, the authority of law is absolutely beyond criticism, meaning that in all practical instances it is pointless to question any law without passing through the channels of reform which the law itself lays down: if we find the law unreasonable, unfair, or irrational it is, nonetheless, the law. Perhaps, standing before the law, one would find this recognition (determining, seeing-through) of oneself, together with the deferral (or sometimes outright refusal) of any request for the law to justify itself transparently, somewhat strange, unsettling. None of which matters to the law, of course. Within its own institutions, the law forecloses such close inspection of its foundation and this is one reason why – outside the courts and parliaments – historical, indigenous, feminist, racial, and class critiques of law have had such a negative impact on the standing of law: they expose its ahistorical and acontextual pretences as completely fraudulent. *Every* moment of founding and conserving law is politically charged, and has implications for power relations in society, despite law's claim to a grounded neutrality. In this way, the question of what the law is, and the quest for the law itself are irresistible, yet their fulfillment is endlessly deferred and ultimately impossible.

The second aspect of this irresistible journey to the place and origin of law is that practiced by the legal philosophers and, indeed, by all logocentric thinkers whose aim is to solidify theory into a unified whole or a fundamental explanatory principle. The quest of legal philosophy is for the law of law, for some fundamental criterion or principle of legitimacy. As I have indicated, the stopping point entailed by the idea of a closed system of law has always been undermined by tautologies or contradictions.

To understand why this is the case we can briefly consider an argument presented in "The Law of Genre." In literature a "genre" is a type or mode of expression which is conceptually separate from another type or mode. The idea of the novel is conceptually separate from the idea of the poem. As Derrida explains, the separateness implies a limit, which implies a law of demarcation: "As soon as the word 'genre' is sounded, as soon as it is heard, as soon as one attempts to conceive it, a limit is drawn. And when a limit is established, norms and interdictions are not far behind."[20] The law of genre as interpreted by Derrida states that the genre has some unity, that it is not to be mixed up or confused with other genres. Remember at this point that the entire project of positivist theories of law is to establish separateness or separability of law, to establish, that is, that law is separate or separable from non-law, that it is in a genre of its own. Joseph Raz, for instance, has made it clear that this separateness requires some method of ensuring classification of law as law: "By the thesis of the 'limits of law' I mean the position that there *is a test* which distinguishes what is law from what is not."[21] Like any genre, the separateness of law must be established and maintained by a limit, a law of demarcation. It is precisely this limit which Derrida refers to as the "law of law" or the "being law of the law."

Now, Derrida proposes that the law of genre has its own law ("the law of the law of genre"[22]), which can be schematically described, even though its consequences cannot be so easily contained. Each genre must have at least one defining characteristic or mark just as each law must, according to the thesis of the limits of law, satisfy a criterion which brings it into the category "law." However, the mark which defines what is within a genre is not itself within that genre: whatever it is that makes a scholarly article within that genre is not itself a scholarly article. Whatever makes a law legal is not itself a law (it is, for instance, a presumption), but rather the conceptually prior condition of law, the limit of law which polices the boundary between law and non-law. The mark is therefore "remarkable" for its absence from the category which it defines. However, although it is absent in this way, it is also present, because *each* object within the genre is marked by it. It leaves its trace, to use another Derridean term, in every object within the genre. It is not only an outer edge, but an internal imprint, meaning that there is never a clear distinction between the outside and inside of a category or system, because the inside carries through it the trace of the other. Thus "the remark of belonging does not belong. It belongs without belonging."[23] Embedded in the law of genre, therefore, is another law, a law which is at once present and absent, same and other, and it is this "law of impurity" which engenders the very possibility of law, of genre, and of taxonomy.

Without this impure law to determine what is purely law, there would be no law.

ABOUNDING, EXCESS, IMPURITY, CONTAMINATION

Are we then confronted with a basic law, a law which not only informs the positive legal system, as Kelsen's did, but rather a law of everything which is knowable, identifiable, or textual? Again, in "The Law of Genre," Derrida comments:

> Here now, very quickly, is the law of abounding, of excess, the law of participation without membership, of contamination etc., which I mentioned earlier. It will seem meager to you, and even of staggering abstractness. It does not particularly concern either genres, or types, or modes, or any form in the strict sense of its concept. I therefore do not know under what title the field or object submitted to this law should be placed. It is perhaps the limitless field of general textuality.[24]

A law which abounds and exceeds the field which it determines, whether that is a genre, a legal system, or a field of knowledge. A law which establishes the norms of participation, without itself belonging. A law which thus sets the limits and secures purity while entrenching its otherness at the heart of every law – thus, a law of impurity or contamination of the pure. Such a law cannot itself be foundational, because it is never confined to the foundation (I will come back to this point), and because it is always other to any system or taxonomy. At the same time it is the condition upon which any foundationalism rests: the law of impurity is a necessary element of any separation of categories, or imposition of form on a class of objects.

The comparison with Kelsen's legal philosophy is simplistic in many ways, but it is nonetheless illuminating: we could say that the basic norm is not simply a foundation for the legal system, but rather a rupture or limit which makes the legal system possible. The "pure" theory of law, wholly reliant on self-legitimation through *exclusion* of an other, at this point *becomes* the other: the inside and the outside are undecidable, and we have a limit of impurity. And if the condition for purity and legitimacy is itself a "law of impurity," then is not every law also marked by impurity? Beyond Kelsen, we could say simply that what the notion of a limited law represses is that each law, and the entirety of the legal system, *is marked by the otherness which it excludes.* Although such a lack of closure may in fact be recognized to some degree by positivist legal thought, it is usually relegated to the question of the penumbra, the open-texture, or the hard cases at the edges of law, rather than recognized as internal to the structure of law. And therefore as marginal, rather than 'core', it is not accorded a great deal of significance. This is not to argue that positivism can or must be rejected because it results in an impure theory of law. I take the implication here, as in other areas of Derrida's work, to be that this conceptual impurity is the condition for the claim of purity, and that it is important to understand this and to think about its political and ethical consequences. If general acceptance of law rests upon the assumption that its claim to limitedness (objectivity, wholeness, neutrality) is in some sense justified, and if this claim can be shown to rest upon an act of exclusion, forgetting or repression, is it not then crucial to highlight rather than repeat this ideological and theoretical act of foreclosure?

It ought to be reasonably evident at this point that this law of the law of genre, or law of impurity, is not something which is confined to any strictly legal analysis, but goes to the heart of the constitution of any category, and thus of philosophy, and meaning itself. It is another moment of the *différance* which in Derrida's thought precedes and sets the conditions for signification: *différance* names the differing and deferring, the "spacing" and "temporization,"[25] which enables the construction of meanings. Any meaning is defined and sustained differentially, in contrast to its other(s): the meaning "cat" has to be held apart from the meaning "bird" – it is not just different, but is maintained as different by the process of meaning.[26] Similarly, as I will explain shortly, the positivist insistence on the thesis of the limits of law requires not only that law just *is* different, but that it be constructed as different and that this difference is maintained through legal processes. Secondly, *"différance"* refers to the process where complete, absolute, authoritative meaning is *deferred* as the "not yet" to our desire to obtain closure.[27] It is always possible and necessary to ask further questions about meaning, just as it is always possible and necessary to ask further questions about the authority of law, even though any such quest is continually foreclosed by legal, literary, scientific, or philosophical "discipline(s)." In this way Derrida's law of impurity and his notion of *différance* both suggest a structure where any closure is conditional upon a force maintaining space between same and other, and suspending forever the presence of meaning. In relation to the positive law, this work of maintenance is undertaken daily by the judges, legal officials, and legal persons who assume and therefore practice the separateness of law.

Since we are here concerned with a *law*, and with the structure of signification in a sense *as* the structure of law, it is clearly the case that any legal analysis cannot be confined to that which lawyers and legal philosophers would ordinarily assume to be their proper object – positive law. Law cannot escape the fact that it is subject to questions about the meaning of meaning, even though it is empowered to some extent to legislate its own meanings. Conversely, however, meaning itself rests upon the issue of legitimacy, and upon a "law" which explains it.[28] We cannot say that the "law" is a question internal to signification, or discourse, since signification and discourse themselves are conditioned by a species of law. Therefore, Derrida remarks in "Force of Law" that it "was normal, forseeable, desirable that studies of deconstructive style should culminate in the problematic of law (*droit*), of law and justice . . . It is even the most proper place for them, if such a thing exists."[29]

What does it mean to say that there is a "law" of impurity, contamination, excess? Does it not imply a singularity or homogeneity that is precisely the opposite of Derrida's argument, which is to show that singularity and homogeneity rest on a non-singular and heterogeneous condition or moment? Ordinarily, when speaking of "law" we might assume such singularity: that of the uncrossable frontier, the simple limit, or clear line which separates the legitimate from the illegitimate, or the legal from the non-legal. However, the *limit* in Derrida's thought never assumes such a singular and simple existence, but is rather a place of paradox, contradiction, or silence. The limit is never a line of delineation separating an outside from an inside, but rather a mark which exceeds the distinction between outside and inside – an internal other.

Thus to articulate the nature of the "law" in certain instances as a *limit* is to say that it is a place where logic fails, not a place where logic is supreme. And such an understanding of law foreshadows a challenge of a massive order to established legal assumptions and practice, for it leads us towards a conclusion, or rather a starting point, of the arbitrariness, the violence, and the deconstructible nature of law. And therefore, I would add, the supremacy of the singular, homogeneous law which is defined by a conceptually impermeable frontier cannot be sustained except by force, and there is *no* ethical basis for protecting it from the challenge to its status made by feminist, indigenous, and other activists. In fact, justice demands that it undertake the self-reflection and consequent transformation required by these "others."

As I have indicated, however, having undertaken the quest for the law of law, mainstream legal theories have become the apologists rather than the critics of the legal (af)front which forbids challenges to the sovereignty or ultimacy of law. In attempting to locate and describe the absolute authority of law, rather than confront uncertainty and paradox, legal philosophy has tended to maintain legitimacy: in the name of a neutrality worthy of law, and having undertaken the journey towards the "being-law of law," philosophy has fictionalized the end of the journey which is the beginning of law, the result being a mystification of the legality of law. Not surprisingly, the nature of the supposedly universal law which has been discovered and described bears striking similarities to the legal regimes of the "democratic" West.[30] In order that these possibly intemperate claims may be more fully elaborated, let me now look more closely at the supposed place of origin of the law.

AN "EXTRAORDINARY PERFORMATIVE":[31]
THE FORCE OF LAW

It is in "Force of Law" that Derrida is most explicit about the law itself, positive law, or law "properly so called." (I should add that most of my comments will be drawn from the beginning of this work, from the place which Derrida implies is not entirely a beginning.)

After commenting on the law which requires him to speak in English and his position as subject of this law (an introductory gesture which characteristically reflects the themes of the paper), Derrida begins "Force of Law" with some observations about the phrase entitling the work. To say that a norm has the "force of law" means not only that it is legally prescribed, but that it can be backed up by legal force: "law is always an authorized force."[32] A legal norm is enforceable, even though it may not in fact be enforced.

This gives rise to several issues about the relationship between force and law, however I wish to deal with only one at this point: how can the legitimate force of the law be distinguished from the violence or force which originates the law?[33] In the first place, it is to be noted that Derrida emphasizes the original *violence* of the law, a violence which cannot be mandated by law. Derrida's raising of violence as something which is of the law rather than something forbidden by law is perhaps somewhat startling or confrontational in the context of our expectations of a positivist law and legal theory which is dedicated to maintaining its legitimacy. A law based on illegitimate violence would not live up to its own standards of legitimacy. However, clearly in Western regimes of positive law, there is no avoiding the fact that at some point the law fails in its own justifications, which is where we reach the limit of law, the place where legal justifications simply run out. This place has both a historical and a conceptual existence. The legitimate history of a legal system has a stopping point where the legality or illegality of a particular act is undecidable. For instance, a successful *coup d'état* is defined by the fact that an act which is illegal under the pre-existing legal order retrospectively becomes the source of all legality.[34] The act which is illegal now (i.e. at a revolutionary moment), at some time in the future will be interpreted as having been the source of all legitimacy: this is the "legitimate fiction." Similarly, as I explained above, the conceptual system of Kelsen is framed by the basic norm, the fiction of legitimacy which essentially dictates that citizens must behave *as if* the law has legitimacy. The basic norm constitutes a conceptual or interpretative violence, insofar as it demands that the otherwise "subjective" acts of will of the legislature, judges, or officials, be accorded "objective" legal status.[35]

For these reasons, there is a violence or force at the conceptual and historical origin of law. It is violence which demands that the norms it defines are accorded legitimacy, and that challenges to law's sovereignty and questions over its rationale must simply stop. Derrida emphasizes that we are not here speaking of law simply as the agent or creation of a particular dominant ideology or power: it is not a question of law as subordinate to an overarching cultural or political force, but rather a relationship which is "more internal, more complex."[36] Force does not simply give authority to the law which would remain otherwise self-contained. Like the element of force implicit in the differentiation of *différance*, the force of law *establishes and maintains the spacing between law and non-law* which is so crucial to its identity. Furthermore, any legal theory which takes this spacing as a pre-given fact about law is complicit in the work of maintenance, complicit, that is, in the enforced distance between law and its moral, social, or political environment. (As we will see, Derrida is speaking not only of a founding violence of law, but also of a violence which conserves law: ultimately the two are indistinguishable.) The moment of foundation is undecidable, neither legal nor illegal:

Its very moment of foundation or institution (which in any case is never a moment inscribed in the homogeneous tissue of a history, since it is ripped apart with one decision), the operation that consists of founding, inaugurating, justifying law (*droit*), making law, would consist of a *coup de force*, or a performative and therefore interpretative violence that in itself is neither just nor unjust and that no justice and no previous law with its founding anterior moment could contradict or invalidate.[37]

There is no continuous historical development to be described at the origin of a legal system, but rather a rupture with the practices of the past, a rupture which inaugurates the new system. Note that Derrida says here that it is a *performative and interpretative* violence: the force which establishes law is constituted by performative acts of, for instance, declaring and instituting new law, but it is also an interpretative force in that it dictates certain interpretations of itself and of the law generally, primarily the interpretation that it is legitimate. A *logos* is established by an interpretative force which negates interpretative undecidability.[38] Derrida continues by saying that it is here where we find a limit (to questions) and a silence, saying, "It is what I here propose to call the mystical."[39] This is not a limit or a silence which is simply external to law, because it is *of* the law, "Walled up, walled in because silence is not exterior to language"[40]: it is what makes the law law.

CONSERVING VIOLENCE

The silence or mystical element which is thus embedded in law marks a moment of undecidability in law. I will explain this further shortly, but first it is very important to recognize that this is not something which simply affects the origin of law: it is not simply an exterior force which determines law, but rather a force internal to law. This is a matter considered at length in the second part of "Force of Law" where Derrida deconstructs Benjamin's distinction between these two types of law-related violence. The central point here is that in order for law to have an ongoing legitimacy, the violence of the foundation must be repeatable, or rather iterable:

A foundation is a promise. Every position [i.e. positing – of law] . . . permits and promises (*permet et pro-met*), it positions [posits] *en mettant et en promettant*. And even if a promise is not kept in fact, iterability inscribes the promise as guard in the most irruptive instant of foundation. Thus it inscribes the possibility of repetition at the heart of the originary. With this, there is no more a pure foundation or pure position of law, and so a pure founding violence, than there is a purely conserving violence. Position is already iterability, a call for self-conserving repetition. Conservation in its turn refounds, so that it can conserve what it claims to found.

If the foundation is to found anything, it must be repeatable, since every law contains the origin in order to be law. (The mark of the genre appears in every example of the genre, as the defining feature of its classification.) In fact, the foundation is not only repeatable, but *iterable*, since it is repeated as an *other* to itself, for instance in every law, and because it holds the undecidability of same and other within itself. Thus to posit law is to posit that law may be iterated, and thus conserved: "Position is already iterability." At the same time every conservation of law is a return to the foundation of law: every time a judge or legal official applies the law, implicit reliance is placed on the authority of law, and thus on the foundation of law. Thus law continually pulls itself up by its bootstraps, because every decision is a reassertion of the authority of law.

Thus there can be no absolute distinction between the originating violence of law and the violence which is needed to conserve law. Derrida's analysis therefore provides an interesting contrast to that of Kelsen, who, as we have seen, identifies a single, though contradictory, stopping point to questions about validity. Kelsen's description of the legal system comes to rest on the fiction of a basic norm, which is the source of validity for all law, a fiction which requires a "subjective" act of will to be interpreted as an "objective" law. Although logically Kelsen's basic norm must inform each and every norm in the legal system, he does not regard this as an *internal* rupture: the contradiction for Kelsen appears only at the level of the basic norm. However, it is clear that the assumption of a unified legitimacy and therefore the paradox which it entails can not exist in only one place, but must be repeated throughout the system, meaning that the price of identity (or separation) is disunity, contradiction, and a repression of the force which maintains separation.

Finally on this point, it must be remembered that to articulate the foundation of authority in this way does not amount to a celebration of violence or of force.[41] I understand it more as a *revelation* or *exposure* of the fact that law as we know it is not ultimately justifiable, and a reminder that positive law masks its own violence by reference to some justification which it can never find. Therefore, Drucilla Cornell says: "When there is not peace, we should not pretend there is. Certainly the patriarchal order does not provide a 'peaceful' world for women. The very recognition of the violence, then, can be understood as a step towards its mitigation."[42] The arguments that gender is a violent hierarchy, or that heterosexuality is compulsory, do not amount to an approval of force but rather a revelation of the fact of violence in the very concept (and therefore the practice) of sexual relationship as traditionally understood. Similarly the argument that law is based upon a violent rupture demystifies the legal orthodoxy that law is a neutral and peaceful arbitrator, or means of achieving social order, but does not necessarily posit a universal conjunction of law and violence: the central point is that the thesis of the limitedness of law owes its existence to a formal and conceptual force, which is repeated in the actual decisions of legal functionaries. Understanding the violence of Western and neo-colonial positivist conceptions of law provides space for reconceptualizing and reliving the relationship between homogeneous law and the others which it presently excludes.

(UN)DECIDABLE LAW

The law, therefore, is conditioned or preceded by a moment of undecidability: the foundation of authority is "neither legal nor illegal" and exceeds "the opposition between founded and unfounded, or between any foundationalism or anti-foundationalism."[43] Moreover, as we find later in "Force of Law," the founding violence or force is not simply a foundation, but comprehends all law – it is repeated in each law as a conserving force, meaning that each law and each moment of application or decision of law, must come up against this limit. In this way, the law of impurity, which, as we have seen, is the condition for any textuality, resurfaces as the structure of law itself. Law is a system of limits and differences which, like any textual phenomenon (i.e. any *significant or signifying* phenomenon), is inaugurated by a law which ensures the impurity and aporetic nature of all law, all texts, all classification.

Therefore, it is not surprising to read Derrida's claim that "The structure I am describing here is a structure in which law ... is essentially deconstructible."[44] Law is deconstructible because it is "constructed on interpretable and transformable textual strata" and because its "ultimate foundation is by definition unfounded."[45] The point is worth repeating then, that law is not only deconstructible because of its textuality but also because the very notion of law is based upon the differential between the legal and the non-legal, and between the legal and the illegal. At the same time, as we have seen, deconstruction itself proceeds upon the recognition of a law, the "law of impurity" or the "law of differential contamination" and therefore we can begin to see the meaning of Derrida's claim that "it is this deconstructible structure of law ... that also insures the possibility of deconstruction."[46]

The fact that law is "essentially deconstructible" leads us into difficulty if we wish to insist upon a legal structure which at some point is absolutely defensible in social, philosophical, political, or other normative grounds. If the foundation of law is undecidable, how can any decision, any law, or any legal system, be judged as being more just, or more justified, than any other? Even if the foundation of law is linked to a particular ethics, it will always rest on a fundamental exclusion and force, which cannot be justified once only in the manner of a social contract, but which needs continual reconsideration. At this point I should add that it is my view that both the deconstructibility of law, in the way it is articulated in "Force of Law," and any problems about external normative grounding for law arise from the context of the Western positivist separation of law from politics, morality, and culture. The situation would be entirely different where law did not insist on its separate existence but was joined to a religion, a culture, a politics, or an accumulation of custom. This is not to underestimate the importance of the argument because, as I have said, positivist presuppositions largely account for Western and neo-colonial systems of law.

The deconstructibility of law may also appear to pose some practical problems for legal decision-makers for whom the urgency of deciding what the law is, and how it applies to a particular case, is completely unavoidable. A judge who refused to make a decision would not be fulfilling her legally designated function. Therefore, although the foundation of law, and therefore the law itself, is ultimately undecidable, any case which is subject to law must be regarded as completely decidable. In the face of undecidability, a decision must be made, a settlement must be reached. As I have indicated, the imperative to decide ensures that the force of law is continually repeated. The decision that a particular norm represents the law is not made just once, at the founding moment of legality, but every time a decision is made, whether that decision merely applies an existing legal norm, or creates a new one.

JUST DECONSTRUCTION

The question arises, then, as to the relationship between law and justice, bearing in mind that law is deconstructible. In the positivist legal philosophy which I have been concentrating upon here, justice is figured as external to law. Because the positivist understanding of law insists that law is simply law, regardless of its justice, there has been a tendency either to eliminate the term "justice" altogether, or to reduce it to law, for instance in such terms as "access to justice" (by which we generally mean "access to law"), or "administration of justice" (which is nothing more than "administration of law"). Juridically, law is not measured by its justice, but rather by its validity. Law is its own measure, and although law may be criticized for being unjust, any such criticism emanates from a position strictly outside law, and usually irrelevant to its existence.

However, the reason for the distinction between law and justice in positivist thought is the conceptualization of justice as an idealized normative order, a conceptualization which arises from established philosophical approaches to justice. Justice is like law, but it exists in a different space: although the law may or may not reflect this order, any intersection does not affect the structure or existence of law or justice, only their respective qualities.

Now, Derrida has articulated a somewhat different relationship between law and justice that cuts through this notion of parallel but intersecting normative orders, and at the same time clarifies the relationship between deconstruction and ethics, politics, and justice. This latter clarification was perhaps somewhat overdue, given that so many commentators had already rejected deconstruction as an approach which was devoid of any moral or political implications. I will come back to this in a moment.

As I have explained, Derrida has said that law is deconstructible, that the foundation for its authority is mystical, and that it is force which is both original and conserving which maintains the differentiation (or spacing) necessary for law to preserve its identity. Law is deconstructible, but that does not mean that its boundaries or frontiers disappear into nothingness. This would be to misunderstand deconstruction as destruction. Law is deconstructible precisely *because* it has this legal/illegal, founded/unfounded structure, and because by interpretative force it maintains its boundaries as the limits of law. As part of this maintenance of limits which is so characteristic of law, and as a result of it, law is represented by that which is calculable. Thus, Derrida says, "Law . . . is not justice. Law is the element of calculation, and it is just that there be law, but justice is incalculable."[47] This may appear to be contradictory – law is "essentially deconstructible" and at the same time it is "the element of calculation." However, it is precisely because it represents the calculable that law is deconstructible. Law can only come to represent the calculable because of the force which originates and conserves it as having a particular limited identity, and it is because of this force that law is deconstructible.

Thus law is the calculable, and justice is incalculable. What does this mean? To summarize a complex and detailed argument, justice is what takes place in the gaps or aporia of law. There "is no justice without this experience, however impossible, of aporia."[48] The experience of aporia is impossible because "an aporia is a non-road" and because an experience is "something that traverses and travels toward a destination."[49] Law is the attempt at calculation, but it is always deconstructible, meaning in this context that it is always possible to question, examine, or demystify its foundation, its authority, its identity, and its applicability. Justice is the incalculable, meaning that it is not possible to calculate or normalize justice in advance. Derrida says that justice is *à venir*, to come, in the future.[50] Having said that, justice does not take place in a vacuum: like deconstruction, justice is a kind of attitude or response to a normalized state of affairs, in this case, the law. Therefore justice and law are not opposed:[51] rather justice is a noncalculable response to the law in a particular case.

Derrida notes three examples or moments of *aporia* which are of interest to this question of the relationship between law, deconstruction, and justice, and which suggest the place or position of justice (even though it has no place, and is not a position). First, the otherness of any case is not accounted for by a rule, and justice demands some reconciliation between the rule and the other:

for a decision to be just and responsible, it must, in its proper moment if there is one, be both regulated and without regulation: it must conserve the law and also destroy it or suspend it enough to have to reinvent it in each case, rejustify it, at least reinvent it in the reaffirmation and the new and free confirmation of its principle. Each case is other, each decision is different and requires an absolutely unique interpretation, which no existing, coded rule can or ought to guarantee absolutely.

Justice is not achieved simply by applying the law as though it were a formula. Justice is a deconstructive attitude to law: it is a transgression of law, which nonetheless reinvents the law. Justice is the opportunity to reconstruct the law, having regard to the singularity and otherness of the case. Secondly, as we have seen, the foundation of law is undecidable, and if a decision is to be just according to Derrida, it must come up against this undecidability which cannot be resolved, sublated, or surpassed, but – like *différance* – is forever suspended in meaning. Thus justice cannot be encapsulated and is infinite, even within a decision, for its encapsulation would be to freeze it or stabilize it in a denial of otherness and undecidability (and therefore a denial of justice). Thirdly, in the face of the undecidability of law and the fact that justice is always deferred, there is nonetheless the need for decisions to be made. In law, decisions are completely unavoidable. (This is a feature of law which in some ways appears to set it apart from literary or philosophical analysis, where the need to settle meanings is neither as urgent nor as

consequential as it is in law. I'm sure this point could be argued, however.)
The decision is finite, urgent, and "always marks the interruption of the
juridico- or ethico- or politico-cognitive deliberation that precedes it."[52]
A decision puts a stop to any further questions or rationalizing. (Raz
calls the decision an "exclusionary reason, because it is there to prevent
further reasons being weighed in consideration of an issue or a case."[53])
And therefore, finally, because it interrupts the flow of reasons, a decision
is "a madness," meaning simply that it cannot be accounted for within
the calculable, the rational, or the order of ethical reasons.[54]

These reflections bring us finally to a critical aspect of Derrida's argument, which is that "deconstruction is justice."[55] Justice is the relationship to the other which cannot be determined or simply mediated
by the construct of law, but which reaches out to the other through an
experience of the failure, instability, inadequacy, and unfoundedness of
law. Deconstruction is an intervention in the law which reveals both the
embeddedness of otherness within the law and the impossibility of purity.
Deconstruction and justice are impossible, but necessary.

THE POLITICS OF LAW

I wish to conclude with a few brief remarks about some of the broader
implications of Derrida's work on law.

First, as I have indicated above, to speak of the force of law does not
necessarily suggest the inevitability, much less an affirmation, of force.
Rather, it exposes a juncture between politics and law which is commonly
erased in legal thinking, and allows us to see the connection between the
question of the validity and ultimate authority of law and the everyday
exclusions and impositions which law practices upon its subjects. I am
not speaking here of the arguably benign requirements of law which
are "imposed" in order for a society to achieve a measure of order.
Rather I am speaking of the violence disguised as equality which law
does to women, to indigenous people, to lesbians, bisexuals, transsexuals,
gay men, and to many others. I am speaking of the violence disguised
as neutral principle which law does in shaping and determining social
relationships.

In my view, the fact that law is able to mask its role in determining and
maintaining relationships of power is directly due to the legal erasure of
the force of law. Violence is systemic and structural in our conception of
law, but this violence is masked by legal ideologies of equality, neutrality,
objective principle, and so on, self-justifications which *in the one moment*

erase the everyday violence of law as well as its ultimate force. The force of law which, for instance, posits the white adult male as the legal person is conditioned by the force of law which founds and conserves the legal system.[56] In other words, the political inequalities of law which are increasingly being exposed by critical theorists are not matters internal to law and which can be solved by law, or by a better articulation of otherwise sound legal ideals. The whole structure of law as a fundamentally separate order is implicated in the violence.

Secondly, Derrida's work on law has an oblique relationship to mainstream positivist accounts of law. As I indicated at the beginning, much of what Derrida says about the structure of law can be accommodated, and has been acknowledged, by positivist theory. So where are the differences, and why is this so important? In the first place, unlike many legal philosophers, Derrida refuses to forget or gloss over the significance of legal force: in repeatedly stressing that the law/non-law distinction is a violent distinction, not internally peaceful or neutral, the ideological power of the story of self-justification is uncovered. Moreover, the emphasis upon the conserving force of law reveals both that the performative dynamic of legal decision-making is fundamental to the ongoing existence of law, and that the ethical, political, or social are ultimately not separable from the internal structure of law. Finally, therefore, justice is not simply the same or the other of the existence of law, never simply internal nor external, as the natural law/positivism debate would suggest: like deconstruction, justice is *of* the law, but not reducible to law.

NOTES

1 See the comments of Derrida's quoted at the beginning of S. Weber, "Deconstruction Before the Name: Some Preliminary Remarks on Deconstruction and Violence," *Cardozo Law Review* 13 (1991): 1181. These remarks suggest that there is a theme, the "law of differential contamination," which arises in much of Derrida's work, and that this law is itself at the heart of law, embedded in and encircling law. In "Force of Law" Derrida says, "it was normal, forseeable, desirable that studies of deconstructive style should culminate in the problematic of law (*droit*), of law and justice. . . . It is even the most proper place for them, if such a thing exists." *Cardozo Law Review* 11 (1990): 929. See also Margaret Davies, *Delimiting the Law: Postmodernism and the Politics of Law* (London: Pluto Press, 1986).

2 Jacques Derrida, "Before the Law," in *Acts of Literature*, ed. Derek Attridge (London and New York: Routledge, 1992), 181–220; "The Law of Genre" in *Glyph* 2 (1980): 202; "Force of Law: The 'Mystical Foundation of Authority'" *Cardozo Law Review* 11 (1990): 919; also published in D. Cornell

et al. (eds.), *Deconstruction and the Possibility of Justice* (New York: Routledge, 1992). My text refers to the version published in the *Cardozo Law Review*. See also Derrida, "The Laws of Reflection: Nelson Mandela, In Admiration" in Jacques Derrida and Mustapha Tlili (eds.), *For Nelson Mandela* (New York: Henry Holt and Co., 1987).

3 Derrida, "Before the Law," 189.

4 See John Austin, *The Province of Jurisprudence Determined* (London: Weidenfeld and Nicolson, 1954), 10–12.

5 See Finnis, *Natural Law and Natural Rights* (Oxford: Clarendon Press, 1985).

6 For instance, the ethos of the Natural Law Party as a minor political party is that we ought to live in harmony with nature.

7 See Austin, *Province of Jurisprudence*; H.L.A. Hart, *The Concept of Law* (Oxford: Clarendon, 1961); Hans Kelsen, *The Pure Theory of Law*, trans. Max Knight. (Berkeley: University of California Press, 1967). The form of the elementary principle has varied with different theorists. For a recent defence of the positivist tradition see Tom Campbell, *The Legal Theory of Ethical Positivism* (Aldershot: Dartmouth, 1997).

8 See Iain Stewart, "The Critical Legal Science of Hans Kelsen," *Journal of Law and Society* 17 (1990): 273–308, for a succinct and thorough account of Kelsen's legal thought. See also Iain Stewart, "Kelsen Tomorrow," *Current Legal Problems* 51 (1998): 1–16.

9 Ludwig Wittgenstein, *Philosophical Investigations* (Oxford: Basil Blackwell, 1958), § 217.

10 Kelsen, *Pure Theory of Law*, 199–200. I have changed Kelsen's example from an execution of the death penalty, to something much more mundane.

11 Ibid., 200.

12 Kelsen, *General Theory of Norms*, trans. Michael Hartney. (Clarendon Press: Oxford, 1991), ch. 59, "Logical Problems about Grounding the Validity of Norms." See Stanley L. Paulson, "Kelsen's Legal Theory: The Final Round," *Oxford Journal of Legal Studies* 12 (1992): 265–74.

13 The basic norm "is a genuine or 'proper' fiction (in the sense of Vaihinger's philosophy of As-If) whose characteristic is that it not only contradicts reality, since there exists no such norm . . . but is also self-contradictory"; ibid., 256.

14 cf. Iain Stewart, "Kelsen Tomorrow," 6–7.

15 Davies, *Delimiting the Law*.

16 Campbell, *Legal Theory of Ethical Positivism*.

17 Montaigne, *Essays II*, 12, as quoted in Derrida, "Before the Law," 183.

18 Derrida, "Before the Law," 191–92.

19 Ibid., at 135.

20 Derrida, "The Law of Genre," 203.

21 Joseph Raz, "Legal Principles and the Limits of Law," *Yale Law Journal* 81 (1972): 823, 842.

22 Derrida, "The Law of Genre," 206.

23 Ibid., 212.

24 Ibid.

25 Derrida, "Différance" in *Margins of Philosophy* (Brighton: Harvester Press, 1982), 7–8.
26 The force which maintains spacing between signifying terms is emphasized and explained by G. Bennington in "Derridabase" in G. Bennington and J. Derrida, *Jacques Derrida* (Chicago University Press, 1993), 71.
27 Derrida, "Différance," 8.
28 The name of a book may help to illustrate this point. *Postmodern Jurisprudence* (London: Routledge, 1991), by Costas Douzinas, Ronnie Warrington, and Shaun McVeigh is subtitled *The Law of Text in the Texts of Law*. This suggests the textuality of law, and the fact that law texts are subject to textual laws. However, because texts are also subject to a law, it is not possible to conceptualize the relationship simply as one of law being encapsulated by textuality.
29 Derrida, "Force of Law," 929.
30 This is particularly so in the work of H.L.A. Hart, whose description of "civilized" law relied upon differentiating it from "primitive" law. See Hart, *Concept of Law*, ch. 5.
31 Elsewhere Derrida says: "This fundamental law cannot, either in law or in fact, simply precede that which at once institutes it and nevertheless supposes it: projecting and reflecting it! It can in no way precede this extraordinary performative by which a signature authorizes itself to sign, in a word, legalizes itself on its own without the guarantee of a preexisting law." Derrida, "The Laws of Reflection: Nelson Mandela, In Admiration," 20.
32 Derrida, "Force of Law," 925.
33 Ibid., 927.
34 In a number of cases a court has been called upon to determine the validity of laws created by a revolutionary regime. These cases, and the difficulties arising from the extra-legal origin of law, are described and discussed extensively in a case arising out of the 1979 coup in Grenada, *Mitchell v. DPP* (1986) LRC (Const) 35. See also Derrida, "Force of Law," 993.
35 Kelsen, *General Theory of Norms*, 254–55.
36 Derrida, "Force of Law," 941.
37 Ibid., 941–3.
38 See Derrida, "Plato's Pharmacy," in *Dissemination* (London: Athlone Press, 1981).
39 Ibid., 943.
40 Ibid.
41 See, for instance, Seyla Benhabib, "Some Comments on Deconstruction, Justice, and the Ethical Relationship," in *Cardozo Law Review* 13 (1991): 1219, 1221.
42 Drucilla Cornell, "Civil Disobedience and Deconstruction," in *Cardozo Law Review* 13 (1991): 1309, 1314.
43 Derrida, "Force of Law," 943.
44 Ibid.
45 Ibid.

46 Ibid., 945.
47 Ibid., 947.
48 Ibid.
49 Ibid.
50 Ibid., 969.
51 Ibid., 959.
52 Ibid., 967.
53 J. Raz, *Practical Reason and Norms* (Princeton, NJ: Princeton University Press, 1990), ch.1, "On Reasons for Action."
54 Derrida, "Force of Law," 969.
55 Ibid., 949.
56 I am responding in part to an argument presented by Nancy Fraser in "The Force of Law: Metaphysical or Political?," in *Cardozo Law Review* 13 (1991): 1325.

FURTHER READING

Benhabib, S. "Some Comments on Deconstruction, Justice, and the Ethical Relationship." *Cardozo Law Review* 13 (1991): 1219–21.
Cornell, D. "Civil Disobedience and Deconstruction." *Cardozo Law Review* 13 (1991): 1309–15.
The Philosophy of the Limit. New York: Routledge, 1992.
Cornell, D., Rosenfeld, M., and Carlson, D.G., eds. *Deconstruction and the Possibility of Justice*. New York: Routledge, 1992.
Dallmayr, F. "Justice and Violence: A Response to Jacques Derrida." *Cardozo Law Review* 13 (1991): 1237–43.
Davies, Margaret. *Delimiting the Law: 'Postmodernism' and the Politics of Law*. London: Pluto Press, 1996.
Derrida, Jacques. "Before the Law." In Derek Attridge, ed. *Acts of Literature* (London and New York: Routledge, 1992), 181–220.
"Force of Law: The 'Mystical Foundation of Authority,'" *Cardozo Law Review* 11 (1990): 919–1045. Also published in D. Cornell *et al.*, eds. *Deconstruction and the Possibility of Justice*. New York: Routledge, 1992.
"The Law of Genre" *Glyph* 2 (1980): 202.
"The Laws of Reflection: Nelson Mandela, In Admiration." In Jacques Derrida and Mustapha Tlili, eds. *For Nelson Mandela*. New York: Henry Holt and Co., 1987.
Douzinas, C. and Warrington, R. "A Well-Founded Fear of Justice: Law and Ethics in Postmodernity." *Law and Critique* 2 (1991): 115.
Douzinas, C., Warrington, R., and McVeigh, S. *Postmodern Jurisprudence: The Law of Text in the Texts of Law*. London: Routledge, 1991.
Fraser, Nancy. "The Force of Law: Metaphysical or Political?" *Cardozo Law Review* 13 (1991): 1325–31.
Gasché, Rodolphe. "On Critique, Hypercriticism, and Deconstruction: The Case of Benjamin." *Cardozo Law Review* 13 (1991): 1115–32.

Litowitz, D. "Derrida on Law and Justice: Borrowing (Illicitly?) From Plato and Kant." *Canadian Journal of Law and Jurisprudence* (1995): 325–46.

Rosenfeld, M. "Derrida, Law, Violence and the Paradox of Justice." *Cardozo Law Review* 13 (1991): 1267–72.

Weber, Sam. "Deconstruction Before the Name: Some Preliminary Remarks on Deconstruction and Violence." *Cardozo Law Review* 13 (1991): 1181–90.

Wolcher, L. "The Man in the Room: Remarks on Derrida's *Force of Law*." *Law and Critique* 7 (1996): 35.

See also generally "On the Necessity of Violence for Any Possibility of Justice." Conference Publications. *Cardozo Law Review* 13 (1991): 1081–53.

CHAPTER 10

Derrida and technology: fidelity at the limits of deconstruction and the prosthesis of faith

Bernard Stiegler

It could be argued that since 1967 Jacques Derrida has elaborated deconstruction within the context of an unprecedented development in technology – the development, that is, of the amalgamation of technics with science in the field of industry. A context in which "the future can only be anticipated in the form of an absolute danger and can only be proclaimed as a sort of monstrosity."[1] And a technology that constitutes something like an "objective" – that is to say, factual – "deconstruction." In 1967 the world, divided between "East" and "West," was still in the process of enjoying the post-war years of prosperity; and the "movement" of 1968 that was to disturb the apparent harmony of this economic growth continued to affirm, ultimately, a basic trust in the emancipatory power of social history.

In 1997 it is loss of trust and "monstrosity" that now dog the most routine experience. Many ghosts haunt the world, but one is more haunting than all the others: the crisis in faith, loss of "credit," an experience of "kenosis" – that is, the emptying out of God in the incarnation and the experience of emptiness, in turn, that this emptying induces – pushed to the limit, and what tries to answer this crisis in the way of "belief" or "fidelity."[2] And yet belief and fidelity today assume such a convulsive form as to do nothing but announce the imminent advent of total incredulity and infidelity. This imminence is as much masked as marked by the repetition, disseminated throughout the planet, of ritual automatisms and reflex behavior, behavior that characterizes the various figures of fundamentalist movements emerging from monotheism (not to mention apocalyptic sects) as well as re-emergent nationalisms, and even a certain *secular faith* – the "promise" of an absolutely clear future – one that does not escape, either, the dark mechanisms emanating from the same compensatory reaction to the loss of the proper.

It is a situation of extremity and disarray, one of disinheritance and disorientation. A situation in which the world as a whole is so affected by political impotence that even the concept of "crisis" is now inadequate to describe what is happening (a "crisis which is more than a crisis"[3]), and one in which the media, a major factor in "globalization,"[4] is playing a structural role.

During the thirty years between 1967 and 1997 the thought of Jacques Derrida has not stopped announcing what is happening as, precisely, what cannot simply be announced, as always exceeding the possibility of announcement and yet demanding the (performative) responsibility of an announcement. From the thinking of the trace and *différance* to the more recent themes of the "promise," the "messianic," "faith" and "hospitality," the same question is deployed and broken down again and again – a highly consistent movement of thought that pays the greatest attention to what, in its accidental essence (a radical paradox that deconstruction, precisely, endures), comes [*advient*] as an improbable event, one that is always singular, impossible to anticipate, and thereby monstrous in its very structure.

This itinerary is an assumed paradox: open constantly to what can surprise it, while always having already announced the possibility of the surprise. I will try to account for this itinerary by briefly surveying what goes on between *Of Grammatology*, published in 1967 – the concerns of which are in preparation as of 1953 – and "Faith and Knowledge" which appeared in 1996 in the collective volume *La religion*. I wish to show that deconstruction, understood in terms of the problematic of "hypomnesis" (as it is defined in the commentary on Phaedrus in "Plato's Pharmacy"[5]), is both:

- a thinking of technics, of tele-technologies, and, as a thinking of tele-technologies, of the "media" in all its guises – beginning with the most primal traces that launch the process of hominization (the emergence of the human species), and extending as far as the Web and all forms of technical archiving and high-fidelity recording, including those of the biotechnologies. All are figures, in their singularity, of the originary default[6] of origin that arche-writing constitutes;
- a thinking of *fidelity*, of fidelity to the past, of memory and of heritage – that is, fidelity in the Law. And, in this sense, a thinking of faith, of truth and religion.

* * *

At the origin of deconstruction lies the *aporia* of *passive synthesis* to be found in the work of Edmund Husserl.[7] Derrida explores the aporia in his MA dissertation of 1953, *The Problem of Genesis in Husserl's Philosophy*, published in 1990.[8] In this text he describes the aporia as a structure that already evokes what will later become the "inverting" logic of the supplement [*la logique renversante du supplément*]. Phenomenology is caught in a dual, contradictory ambition. From the very beginning of Husserlian thought the issue is, on the one hand, accounting for the *genesis* of ideal concepts, and, on the other, affirming their *transcendental* character (ideal, these concepts cannot be engendered by experience). The difficulty of this transcendental genesis is that:

> the absolute foundation itself must be described in its genetic appearing; implying its past, being implied in its past, it must neither be reducible to it, nor must it be dependent upon it (in the sense of a conclusion depending upon its premises or of an effect depending upon a cause). Here it is the effect which constitutes the meaning of the cause as such.[9]

The question is that of time:

> A genetic conception ruins the foundations of any intelligibility in general . . . if it reverts back to a causal explanation or analysis in which temporality is integrated as a simple "element."[10]

The problem confronting phenomenology – together with all its developments in the work of Husserl – is explored as the aporia of a synthesis brought about passively as the *condition* of the active synthesis of the transcendental subject. In *Of Grammatology*, via *Speech and Phenomena*,[11] this passive synthesis will become a "logic of the supplement." That said, what emerges from this analysis in 1953 is not yet a thinking of *différance* and supplementarity, as is clear from the nature of the reading of Husserl's essay "Origin of Geometry" in the last chapter of *The Problem of Genesis*. It is Husserl's *Origin of Geometry: An Introduction*,[12] published in 1962, that will make the transition to a thinking of *différance* possible. Since the conclusions of the 1953 dissertation are the very *inverse* of those of the later *Introduction*, *The Problem of Genesis* highlights the fact that Derrida's thought only constitutes itself as such once its analysis of *technology* (qua Husserl's ultimate theme before the question of passive synthesis, of, that is, time) is radically rethought.

For the young Derrida, Husserl accounts for the genesis of idealities in "The Origin of Geometry" through an unacceptable, indeed "derisory", "technological explanation"[13] – a sleight of hand that appears to abandon everything that phenomenology always, and unconditionally, seemed to want to maintain. Derrida is quick to condemn in 1953 what in the Husserlian position will become after several years of reflection the very source of Derrida's own thought:

It is then it seems that the transcendental intentional analysis subsides into a surprising interpretation the poverty of which holds together in somewhat derisory manner all the inadequacies of a bold hypothesis of explanation, a muddled probabilism and a pre-philosophical empiricism: "In the first oral cooperation of the beginning geometers, the need was understandably lacking for an exact fixing of descriptions of the prescientific originary material and of the ways in which, in relation to this material, geometrical idealities arose together with the first 'axiomatic' propositions."[14]

The explanation, Derrida continues, "locks us into the domain of a purely empirical facticity, one that one wished precisely to 'suspend'."[15] As the following quotation makes clear, it is a *technological* explanation. The genesis of originary idealities presupposes, for Husserl, "the rigorous measurability [that] emerges from the world of spatio-temporal things," and:

its origin in human activity is purely technical; it is a process of "polishing" that gave us the pure idea of surface; starting from "more or less pure" lines and points there emerged geometrical lines and points. Similarly the empirical, technical and psychological act of "comparing" gave rise to identity. Every detail in this curious analysis describes a purely technical genesis.[16]

In *An Introduction to Husserl's "Origin of Geometry"* the question will become, for Derrida, that of writing: writing understood in the normal sense of the term, but one which will set his thinking upon the path of "arche-writing."[17] It is along these lines that the thinking of deconstruction is formed. Now, the *technological* question posed by "The Origin of Geometry" is not restricted to that of writing in the normal sense. What implications this point carries for the concept of arche-writing, just as for the thinking of the trace and *différance*, is, as we will see, important. For once Derrida has crossed the threshold of *An Introduction to Husserl's "Origin of Geometry,"* a hesitation remains as to the "technicity" of writing and arche-writing, that is, as to the technical "essence" of both writing and arche-writing – a hesitation that continues, perhaps, even to the present. The stake of fidelity, of credit, credence, trust, and of faith lies, I would argue, in this "break" [*brisure*].[18]

* * *

The question of passive synthesis is that of time (since time is not a "simple element"). In this context, all of Derrida's work passes through his reading of Husserl's *On the Phenomenology of the Inner Consciousness of Time*

(1893–1917).[19] Let me briefly recall what makes up the phenomenological kernel of this work in which Husserl analyses the way in which a "temporal object" (melody is his example) is constituted for a consciousness, thereby bringing to light the phenomenon of primary retention.

Husserl argues that, as regards a temporal object, it is clear that attached to the "now" of the object passing or flowing by – at the same time as the time of the consciousness of the object flows by – there is a "primary retention." Primary retention unifies (*intègre*) the now, is unified by it; it does not pertain to the past, but to the passing presence of the past. This "just past" that is maintained in the passing now – constituting the present of what Gérard Granel has called the "large now" (*le grand maintenant*)[20] – is not of the order of a past added by the imagination to perception, as Brentano believed; it is, for Husserl, the very phenomenon of the perception of time. For, otherwise, perception could not be distinguished from imagination, nor reality from fiction, and one would be forced to argue that time is an illusion of the imagination.

It is for this reason that primary retention is to be distinguished from secondary retention, or recollection (the repetition through the imagination of a present become past). Husserl argues:

> We characterized primary memory or retention as a comet's tail that attaches itself to the perception of the moment. Secondary memory, recollection, must be distinguished absolutely from primary memory or retention. After the primary memory is over with, a new memory of this motion, of that melody, can emerge. The total memory of the melody consists in a continuum of such continua of temporal fringes, and, correlatively, in a continuum of apprehension-continua of the kind described. The temporal present in recollection is a remembered, re-presented present; and the past too is a remembered, re-presented past, not a perceived past, not a past primarily given and intuited.[21]

From 1953 Derrida is concerned with breaking down the separation between the primary and the secondary, thereby bringing into question the very possibility of suspending objective time (maintained as a principle by Husserl at the beginning of the book). The critique will only be firmly established in *Speech and Phenomena*, once the decisive passage through *An Introduction to Husserl's "Origin of Geometry"* has been made. As Derrida says:

> The presence of the perceived present can appear as such only inasmuch as it is *continuously compounded* with a nonpresence and nonperception, with primary memory and expectation. We might suspect that if Husserl nonetheless calls

[retention] perception, this is because he holds to establishing a radical discontinuity between retention and reproduction, between perception and imagination, etc., and not between perception and retention.[22]

He continues:

The difference between retention and reproduction, between primary and secondary memory, is not the radical difference Husserl wanted between perception and nonperception; it is rather a difference between two modifications of nonperception. Whatever the phenomenological difference between these two modifications may be, and despite the immense problems it poses and the necessity of taking them into account, it only serves to separate two ways of relating to the irreducible nonpresence of another now. This relation to nonpresence neither befalls, surrounds, nor conceals the presence of the originary impression; rather it makes possible its ever renewed upsurge and virginity.[23]

[Husserl] is trying to retain two apparently irreconcilable possibilities: (a) the living now is constituted as the absolute perceptual source only in a state of continuity with retention taken as nonperception. Fidelity to experience and to "the things themselves" forbids it be otherwise. (b) The source of certitude in general is the originary character of the living now; it is necessary therefore to keep retention in the sphere of originary certitude and to shift the frontier between the originary and the nonoriginary. The frontier must pass not between the pure present and the nonpresent, i.e., between the actuality and the inactuality of a living now, but rather between two forms of the re-turn or re-stitution of the present: re-tention and re-presentation.[24]

It should be more than clear from the above that it is first reflection upon, then the inversion (*le renversement*) of, the Husserlian expansion of the present to the "large now" of the temporal object that leads to the Derridean thinking of the trace:

The possibility of repetition in its most general form, that is, the constitution of a trace in the most universal sense is a possibility which not only must inhabit the pure actuality of the now but must constitute it through the very movement of *différance* it introduces.[25]

An absence *constitutes* the heart of the presence of the Living Present: contrary to what Husserl is seeking, the difference between primary and secondary is not, as Derrida says, "between perception and nonperception; it is rather a difference between two modifications of nonperception." Now, Derrida can only attain such an "inversion" (*renversement*), however, by reversing (*renversant*) his own position regarding "The Origin of Geometry" in 1953. From which it also appears that the constitution of presence by an absence is in fact always already a re-constitution.

This will also mean, as we shall see, that the synthesis of judgment, that is to say, belief, always already forms the doubling/lining (*la doublure*) of a *techno-logical synthesis*: a passive synthesis that also makes up the *prosthesis of faith*.

*　*　*

Lying at the heart of the present of perception is the nonperceived; the difference between the primary and the secondary is not radical. Since the Living Present is marked by traces, by nonpresence, this present is not *purely* living – neither fully "present to itself" nor certain of itself. The truly "Derridean" problematic is not opened up, however, in *Speech and Phenomena* but in *An Introduction to Husserl's "Origin of Geometry."* In this text the issue is not one of either secondary or primary memory, but of a *third type of memory* – the technical and/or written trace, what pertains to what Husserl calls an "image-consciousness" (*Bildbewusstsein*).

A painting or a bust can be an object, Husserl says, of "image-consciousness." The object of an image-consciousness, even if it commemorates what it figures, is not a memory of consciousness: it has been neither perceived nor lived by consciousness. For example, it would be wrong to say of a nineteenth-century painting that it is a question of the memory of the person who is looking at it. Rather, it is a question of the trace of a memory of the person who painted it, a trace which has in a sense exteriorized and fixed the person's memory, allowing a century later for another consciousness to come and study it as an image of the past (not, however, as a memory of its own lived past). For Husserl, this "pictorialization" plays no role whatsoever in the constitution of a temporal object – neither in the constitution of the stream of consciousness, nor, consequently, in the maintenance (nowness) of the Living Present. Not only does this third type of memory not pertain to perception – the case, already, of secondary memory – in contradistinction to secondary memory, it does not even pertain to the past stream of consciousness, inscribed in this stream's past and pertaining to this living consciousness as its past *because it has been perceived*. To summarize, then, Husserl brings to light two types of retention which he distinguishes and which he calls "primary" and "secondary" retention. He opposes to these two forms of retention a third type of memory (what was called above "image-consciousness") which I have called for this reason "tertiary memory."[26]

Now, and in tension with the general movement of Husserl's own thought, it is this tertiary memory that is placed, precisely, at the heart of the origin of geometry qua writing. For it is writing that allows the *retentional finitude* of the consciousness of the protogeometrician to be exceeded.[27] What is exceeded is the essential fallibility of a person's *memory* that, as living, is mortal; the supplement of writing allows that person to confide the trace of his or her intuitions, which become as a result transmissible, to future generations of geometricians. It is here that Husserl inscribes within the constitutive genesis of idealities an essential articulation between the living and the dead – an articulation of which Derrida will, of course, make much. Deconstruction can from this moment begin to put in question self-presence by showing that, in every case, the living of consciousness, given its retentionally finite structure, is compounded with the dead.

It is, then, the problematic of tradition – and of transcendental history – that leads Husserl to revise his categorical exclusion of tertiary memory from phenomenological concern in 1905 and declare it to be *constituting (constituant)* in 1937. Derrida was himself aiming at a problematic of tradition from 1953, although the text that concerned him was Husserl's *The Inner Consciousness of Time*. Commenting upon a text that will be quoted again in *An Introduction to Husserl's "Origin of Geometry," The Problem of Genesis* actually sketches out – be it in metaphorical terms – the first decisive step leading from retention to tradition. If decisive, it will only be exploited, however, much later. I quote:

The originary and constituting present is only absolute in its continuity with a "non present" that is at the same time constituted before, through and in it. The originary synthesis is precisely that of the constituted and constituting, of the present and nonpresent, of originary temporality and objective temporality. It is crucial for the temporality of an immanent lived experience to be the absolute beginning of the appearance of time, and yet it only appears to itself as an absolute beginning thanks to a "retention"; *it only inaugurates within tradition*; it creates precisely because it has *a historical heritage*. It seems illegitimate, then, to exclude from the beginning of reflection all temporal transcendence and any constituted unity of time. The act of exclusion cannot be pure; it is originarily retentional.[28]

Husserl had already responded to this problematic of tradition in 1937, a response that Derrida fails to see in 1953, but one from out of which and to which he responds in turn in 1962, reversing [*renversant*] in so doing his first analysis by setting out the literally *inverting* [*renversant*] logic of the supplement. The jump made in 1962 brings to the foreground of the analysis the conditions for passing from retention to tradition: namely, the presence of a *documentary* element, in other words, a *tertiary memory* pertaining to what will end up being a logic of the supplement. And yet, the logic of the supplement in Derrida's work does not identify this memory as tertiary.

* * *

The issue is that of the already-there of the world qua sedimented memory, objectivated "secondary" memories, memories, in other words, that have become "tertiary." This already-there can only be reactivated through the presence of a support that is itself present. This there is the present synthesis of a memory synthesis capable of being reactivated within a living present. That which, at the origin of geometry, first concerns writing is also affected by the supports that one polishes, with which one surveys, and that themselves make spatiotemporality protogeometrical. Writing alone, however, allows for the constitution as well as the transmission of the intuition of ideality. At the origin of geometry there is the fact, brought about by the existence of orthographic writing (that is, alphabetic writing, in the sense of writing that records exactly the past of discourse) that "after quick and transitory evidence, after a finite and passive retention vanishes, its sense can be re-produced as the 'same' in the act of recollection; its sense has not returned to nothingness."[29] This means that recollection, *in so far as it depends upon the durability of tertiary memory*, becomes the *constitutive* possibility of the *collective* large now of geometry, of the historical present qua retentional maintenance (nowness). The same is also true for the intimacy of egological consciousness – before this consciousness' teleologico-transcendental truth is retrospectively filled out in the community of geometric "I"s.

Before being the ideality of an identical object for other subjects, sense is this ideality for *other* moments of the same subject. In a certain way, therefore, intersubjectivity is first the nonempirical relation of ego to ego, of my present present to other presents as such; i.e., as others and as presents (as past presents).[30]

The memory support is what gives one the possibility of *resuming* an interrupted piece of work: which, for the phenomenologist, is always the work of the time of "filling-in" on the part of an intention intending an *eidos*.[31] It gives one the possibility of beginning again where things stood (where things already stood), of becoming autonomous, in this sense, from the normal stream of life. The possibility of resuming (work) from out of the support of a "tertiary memory" constitutes the suspension of the law of impressional consciousness, an exit from retentional finitude. It forms the real *épokhè*[32] of so-called "objective" time, since a unity such as geometry, something like a very large now, constitutes itself within it.[33] It is, as

Derrida suggests, the opening of a transcendental epochality, resuming the hypothesis, proposed by Hyppolite, of "a subjectless transcendental field."[34] However, this epochality appears here not only as writing, but as *"transcendental" technicity*, or rather as *"quasi-transcendental"* technicity. *The whole question is, for us, the nature and status of this "quasi."*

For if "the volume and duration are neither purely sensible phenomena, nor purely intelligible noumena",[35] must one then not question, as Husserl's analyses of "objects invested with spirit" invite one moreover to do,[36] the "ontological" status of *all* technical entities – or the crisis of all ontology that *they* imply? The ideality of geometry – its unity – is a unique very large now that unfurls from Greece. In this very large now, the structure of science appears to be essentially documentary; the document becomes, in other words, *constitutive*. Now, this constitutivity should be widened out to include tertiary memories in all their forms in *every* apprehension of a temporal successivity.

The *limited* character of the temporal field, both announced by Husserl and paradoxically dismissed *idealiter* by him in the 1905 lectures *The Inner Consciousness of Time*, is broadened out in 1936 in the "Origin of Geometry" by the third type of memory. The latter opens the past to the future of an infinite task in so far as the "retentional finitude" of the egological sphere spreads out to include, qua the possibility of geometry, the "in-finitude" of a transcendental community of "I"s. Inversely, this broadening out, by having documentarity – in other words, the *technical* possibility of sedimentation which alone makes possible reactivation – as its condition, makes the field at the very same time vulnerable to the imminent possibility of the *destruction* of its sediments, affects it, that is, with an improbability that could always become possible. The transmission process of science and philosophy has thus become

analogous to, if not identical with the processes of the inner consciousness of time. The present does not appear to itself either as rupture or as the effect of a past, but as the retention of a past present, that is to say, as the retention of a retention, etc. Since the retentional power of a living consciousness is finite, this consciousness keeps meanings, values and past acts in the form of habits and sediments.[37]

Husserl's point is crucial. For exactly where the stakes are those of the time of the origin of geometry, it presupposes that tertiary memory has not only entered the transcendental field, but in fact *institutes* it *as* transcendental, or, more properly, as "quasi-transcendental" given that this field is irreducibly empirico-worldly – that is, *hypomnesic* and, accordingly, *technical.*[38] Documentarity is originary to the extent that language itself already pertains to it, if it is true, following upon the *Logical Investigations* in the light of the "Origin of Geometry," that:

Linguistic ideality is the milieu in which the ideal object settles as what is sedimented or deposited. But here the act of primordial *depositing* is not the recording of a private thing, but the production of a *common* object; i.e., of an *object* whose original owner is thus dispossessed.[39]

Qua hypomnesic and documentary, the inverting *logic* of the supplement outlined here requires a *history* of the supplement, one *which is also a history of technics* [*les techniques*]. Now, this history poses a real problem for deconstruction.

* * *

The history and logic of the supplement make up the concerns of *Of Grammatology*. As the preface to the book recalls, its first part "Writing before the letter" was sketched out in the journal *Critique* on the occasion of a review in 1965 of, among two other books, André Leroi-Gourhan's *Gesture and Speech*.[40] Let me quickly recall here that in Husserlian thought three types of memory have to be distinguished, the first two of which pertain to consciousness, the third constituting an external trace, something like an "objective" memory. It is in the work of the French paleontologist Leroi-Gourhan that this problematic of the exteriorization of memory, that is of a non-psychological memory, one that is neither psychological nor biological, is taken up. Thus, just as Leroi-Gourhan will place at the center of his analyses of hominization the concepts of "program" (organizations of memory) and processes of "exteriorization," so these concepts will to a large extent release the next stage in Derrida's thought represented by *Of Grammatology*. Leroi-Gourhan shows:

- that it is impossible to dissociate anthropogenesis from technogenesis,
- that technogenesis pursues the conquest of mobility, that is, of life, by means other than life,
- that, accordingly, the difference between human- and animal-kind is to be rethought,
- that the technical exteriorization of the living marks the origin of humanity,
- that the technical object constitutes as such a memory support (as well as the condition of what Plato calls "hypomnesis"),

- that, for these reasons, language and instrumentality are two aspects of the same phenomenon.[41]

When exploring the concepts of trace and arche-trace, Derrida refers directly to these theses. He also refers to their further elaboration when Leroi-Gourhan analyzes electronic, computer, and audiovisual informational technology in terms of reading machines and the industrial *dispositif* of an enormous magnetic library that constitutes the most recent stage of the exteriorization of memory.[42] In 1965 the anthropologist together with his philosophical reviewer anticipate the reality which has today led most notably to hypertext, e-mail, and the World Wide Web.

When it becomes "conscious of itself" at the least, the history of the supplement is both one of retentional finitude and of the programs that this finitude develops to supplement [*suppléer*] its default.[43] It is the history of a writing of programs that is pursued beyond genetic differentiation through the "process of exteriorization." This process can be considered as the technical conquest of mobility, amounting to an ever-growing power in formalization, abstraction, and deterritorialization. Mobility, that is, speed, that is, spacing and tempor(al)ization – *différance* as the technical constitution of time and space [*Mobilité, c'est-à-dire vitesse, c'est-à-dire espacement et tempor(al)isation – différance en tant que constitution technique de l'espace et du temps*].

The "logic of the supplement"[44] – as a logic of prosthesis that shows the "truth" of the "inside" to be (in) the outside in which it exteriorizes itself – makes the opposition inside/outside redundant. Leroi-Gourhan can only speak of "exteriorization" to the extent that what exteriorizes itself (the "interior," "life becoming conscious of itself") is *constituted* by its very exteriorization. This is something that the reading of Plato's *Phaedrus* also elaborates in terms of the logic of hypomnesis and is already made explicit in "Freud and the scene of writing"[45] as the indissolubility of memory and technics.

Here the question of technics [*la technique*] (a new name must perhaps be found in order to remove it from its traditional problematic) may not be derived from its assumed opposition between the psychical and the nonpsychical, between life and death. Writing, here, is *techne* as the relation between life and death, between present and representation, between the two apparatuses. It opens up the question of technics: of the apparatus in general and of the analogy between the psychical apparatus and the nonpsychical apparatus.[46]

Deconstruction is a thinking of *composition* in the sense that composition is "older" than opposition (what Simondon would have called "a transductive relation": that is, a relation that constitutes its terms, the terms not existing outside the relation).[47] It is a relation that is the vehicle of a process (that of *différance*), one very close, I would argue, to what Simondon also elaborates in terms of a "process of individuation."[48]

* * *

The themes of life, understood in terms of *différance* and of arche-writing (as the "movement of *différance*, an irreducible *arche-synthesis*, opening in one and the same possibility, temporalization, the relation to the other and language"[49]) continue to explore the aporias of passive synthesis and refer back to questions of retention and protention. The notion of "program," taken up from Leroi-Gourhan, must be understood:

in the cybernetic sense, but cybernetics is itself intelligible only in terms of a history of the possibilities of the trace as the unity of a double movement of protention and retention. This movement goes far beyond the possibilities of "intentional consciousness." It is an emergence that makes the *gramme* appear *as such* (that is to say according to a new structure of nonpresence) and undoubtedly makes possible the emergence of the systems of writing in the narrow sense.[50]

The *gramme* and arche-writing are not anthropological: arche-writing is older than the epoch of the "gramme as such," and

if the expression ventured by Leroi-Gourhan is accepted, one could speak of a "liberation of memory," of an exteriorization always already begun but always larger of the trace which, beginning with the elementary programs of so-called "instinctive" behavior up to the constitution of electronic card-indexes and reading machines, enlarges *différance* and the possibility of putting in reserve.[51]

That said, did not Derrida write a year earlier in "Freud and the Scene of Writing" that writing and *techné* had to be thought together? What type of writing is it, then, a question of? What happens in the *history* of the supplement that comes to enrich the *effectivity* [*l'effectivité*][52] of the *essentially accidental logic* of the supplement?

   The analysis of the protentional/retentional structure of *différance* is that of an economy of death. This economy inherits from Heidegger's *Being and Time*[53] the problematic of being-towards-death (of, in other words, an "ipseity") while subverting it, since the movement of *différance* constitutes calculability as much as the experience of incalculability. With the program and with what Derrida will later call the "promise" being mutually conditioning, *différance* is both the opening to the possibility of the singular and what always already condemns this singular to be composed with that which reduces it.[54] Derrida explores this stricture of *différance* in particular in the question of the idiom. The idiom is always both an expression of the unique exceeding any program and an expression that must submit, in its idiomatic singularity, to the possibility of its expression, of, that is, its programmatic iterability. Pursuing the Heideggerian question of time at the same time as conserving and criticizing the Husserlian thematic of passive synthesis, arche-writing radically undermines at one and the same time the Heideggerian discourse on the proper, Heidegger's *trust* in the authenticity of originary time, and phenomenology's *trust* in the Living Present, thereby removing the possibility of an originary non-trace, of an absolute presence of origin.

To wrench the concept of the trace from the classical scheme, which would derive it from a presence or from an originary nontrace and which would make of it an empirical mark, one must indeed speak of an originary trace or archetrace. Yet we know that that concept destroys its name and that, if all begins with the trace, there is above all no originary trace.[55]

The trace is not, then, an empirical mark. We must now explore more deeply this non-empiricity in order to see how the question of the relation between technics and arche-writing is set up. Let us first return to the aporia of this relation.

* * *

Bringing the logic of the supplement together with its history, the relation between technics and arche-writing brings back the question of genesis that marked the beginning of Derrida's thinking in 1953, re-opening the whole difficulty of the status of technics and sending us back, as we shall see, to the question of tertiary memory. With *différance* making up the play between protention and retention, *tertiary memory, articulated with primary and secondary retention*, is – although it is never analyzed by Derrida in these terms – *the condition of the possibility and impossibility of having access to the gramme "as such."*[56] In other words, although the logic of the supplement is nothing but the question of passive synthesis, and although tertiary memory is indeed the *effectivity* [*l'effectivité*] of this passive synthesis for living beings that can accede to the gramme as such, arche-writing cannot for all that be reduced to this effectivity, to, that is, technicity.

One might feel justified in thinking that the logic of the supplement developed by *Of Grammatology*, together with the outlines of a history of the supplement to be read both in the commentaries of Leroi-Gourhan and of the historians of writing that *Of Grammatology* works with, establishes that the grammatological supplement is nothing but a new name to designate the technicity of the living. We have just seen, however, that arche-writing is not reducible to the technical epoch of the gramme: which means that, insofar as there is no originary arche-trace, there is neither pure (transcendental) presence, nor full empirical facticity. This is the reason why the trace/writing has the *quasi-transcendental* character of what must also for this reason be called *arche*-writing. So, how, in this context, is the technicity of tertiary memory not to be reduced to a merely *empirical* technicity?

Derrida forewarns us that a purely technical understanding of writing would be instrumentalist and would reduce writing to an instance derived from speech. This would amount, precisely, to the way in which logocentrism reduces writing, expelling it from out of "full speech"[57] and thereby confining it to "a secondary and instrumental function: translator of a full speech that was fully *present*."[58] The question, then, is that of *thinking technics otherwise*, on the basis of a new conception of writing. And/or, inversely,

> a certain sort of question about the meaning and origin of writing precedes, or at least merges with, a certain type of question about the meaning and origin of technics. That is why the notion of technics can never simply clarify the notion of writing.[59]

"Simply" would seem the operative term. For the notion of technics *can* clarify the notion of writing *if* our understanding of the former is heavily revised. For this to be done, the two notions of technics and writing need to be carefully analyzed in relation to each other, and analyzed in the context of the crisis of the *logos* that they bring about. This crisis should be seen, accordingly, as an "objective deconstruction" that comes to a head through a certain technicity. One also needs to think a new instrumentality as such.

> Martinet exploits and develops at length the definition of language as "instrument", "tool", etc., whereas the "metaphoric" nature of this definition, recognized by the author, ought to have made it problematic and to have *renewed the question of the meaning of instrumentality*, of the meaning of functioning, and of the functioning of meaning.[60]

Everything seems to confirm here Derrida's positing of a quasi-similarity between technics and writing. But this is not the case, indeed it cannot be the case since the trace, as arche-trace, "does not depend on any sensible plenitude, audible or visible, phonic or graphic. It is, on the contrary, the condition of such a plenitude."[61] The statement is a somewhat surprising declaration of *independence* which is problematic (because it effaces the *fallibility* on which the trace "depends" qua its *necessity*) and ultimately *risky*. It indicates, nevertheless, that, if deconstruction intends to undermine radically phenomenology's confidence in the Living Present, this does not mean that, in doing so, *it effaces the phenomenological necessity of the épokhè and sacrifices what was gained out of the Husserlian critique of the natural attitude.* Derrida stresses this crucial point when criticizing the Copenhagen School.

> The bracketing of regions of experience or of the totality of natural experience must discover a field of transcendental experience. This experience is only accessible in so far as, after having, like Hjelmslev, isolated the specificity of the linguistic system and excluded all the extrinsic sciences and metaphysical speculations, one asks the question of the *transcendental origin* of the system itself, as a system of the objects of a science, and correlatively of the theoretical system which studies it: here of the objective and "deductive" system which glossematics wishes to be.[62]

This reference to the *transcendental* will appear paradoxical unless it is understood that to proceed according to phenomenological exigency is a precondition for *opening up* the question of the *quasi-transcendental* to which the path analyzing the possibility of writing necessarily leads. It is not a question, then, of taking leave of the difference between appearing as in the "appearing [*apparaître*] of the sound" and appearing as in "the sound appear-ing [*apparaissant*]." To do so would lead "to the worst and the most prevalent of confusions."[63] Nor, therefore, is it a question of simply effacing the difference between the empirical and the transcendental. Rather it is a question of deconstructing a play of *oppositions* (including that between the empirical and the transcendental) in such a way that the differences are not effaced. But *how* and *why* must one *both* distinguish and *not* oppose quasi-transcendental arche-writing and writing in the current sense that is, also, writing and technics?

Arche-writing is not writing: it is the structure of elementary supplementarity. This structure is not a supplement in particular, one that is historically constituted (as, for example, the phenomenon of writing); it is the quasi-transcendental necessity of filling in retentional finitude with a *pharmakon*, a remedy, an expedient that is always technical. At the same time this expedient can only serve to worsen the situation, aggravating, necessarily, the default to which it responds. As the movement of *différance* qua ex-appropriation,[64] arche-writing means that what is alive cannot be sufficient unto itself: which is why the illusion of self-presence must be deconstructed. "Quasi"-transcendental (and not transcendental) because the inscription of elementary supplementarity in the empirical is originary (it is precisely the reason why the origin – necessarily full – is lacking [*faut défaut*]); "quasi," in other words, because:

- there is no origin,
- the supplement is always already *materialized*, while never simply being *material*. It is impossible to suspend the thesis of the world since the "constituted" always already affects, but after the event [*après coup*], the "constituting".

We will return to this *après coup* at the end since it constitutes the stricture of the technological and of the "mystical," the stricture of prosthesis and faith.

The difference between appearing and appear-ing must be kept while the inside/outside opposition, where it takes form, must be refused.[65] A grammatology can, therefore, be neither empiricist nor transcendental: it privileges neither the inside nor the outside, but analyzes what constitutes the very possibility of these oppositions by placing the opposites back into the transductive relation in which they are compounded with one another.

In the originary temporalization and the movement of the relation with others, as Husserl actually describes them, non-presentation or de-presentation is as "originary" as presentation. That is why a thought of the trace can no more break with a transcendental phenomenology than be reduced to it.[66]

* * *

And yet, nothing has been said as long as the history of the supplement is actually *carried out*. For if the question is that of *quasi*-transcendentality (rather than transcendentality), an originary accidentality forbids one from saying anything *tout court* about the originary (elementary supplementarity) since it never "presents itself" *except* in the occurrence (always singular) of an effective supplementarity, of a paradoxical "artifactuality," one in which the artifact becomes "essential." In order, then, not to fall into either an empiricism or a transcendentalism of the trace the following must be held together:

- one must deal with the past *that has been present*, but has not been lived by the person to whom it is now re-presented, this past having been present for someone dead who is now absent: this is the way in which the possibility of geometry, exceeding every Living Present, is constituted and yet:

- this non-lived past that has nevertheless been present (that is to say, "lived") refers to an "originary trace," to, in other words, *a past that has never been present and never lived*, that *does not exist.*[67]

This is why the concept of the originary trace or arche-trace "destroys its name" and "if all begins with the trace, there is above all no originary trace."[68] There is no origin, it is impossible to begin absolutely: there is the already-there (*il y a du déjà-là*). Grammatology here inherits the Heideggerian problematic of Da-sein. *Two dimensions of the already-there* must nevertheless be distinguished:

- the already-there of what was lived by others whose supplementarily en-grammed experience can be reactivated, which presupposes the trace "articulating the living upon the nonliving in general, origin of all repetition, origin of ideality,"[69] which presupposes in turn
- the already-there of "a past that has never been present"[70] which looks upon every lived experience as a phantom:

This passivity is also the relationship to a past, to an always-already-there that no reactivation of the origin could fully master and awaken to presence. This impossibility of reanimating absolutely the manifest evidence of an originary presence refers us therefore to an absolute past. That is what authorized us to call *trace* that which does not let itself be summed up in the simplicity of a present. If the trace refers to an absolute past, it is because it obliges us to think a past that can no longer be understood in the form of a modified presence, as a present-past. Since past has always signified present-past, the absolute past that is retained in the trace no longer rigorously merits the name "past."[71]

It is not enough to say, then, that "quasi-transcendental" would imply the invariability of the (technical) *fact* of retentional finitude: which is why Derrida says that "*différance* is also something other than finitude."[72] If arche-writing and the logic of the supplement are to be distinguished from the history of empirical supplements, it is primarily because an *absolute past* constitutes the impossibility of approaching the trace in terms of a mark, the impossibility of folding arche-writing back upon its irreducible empiricity (made concrete in the history of the supplement). Blanchot would call this impossibility a "curve,"[73] one in which the Other in general is constituted – a dissymmetry that also opens up Levinas's ethics. It is this absolute and unnameable past that forbids one (it is the *law* – and the *undeconstructible* justice beyond law (*le droit*)) from reducing [*arraisonner*] *différance* to technics. And yet, at the same time, it is the technicity of the trace which *supports* the *synthesis* of *faith*.

For it is a question of faith. And of the (theologico-political) question of the articulation of the *program* with the *promise*. No trust, no belief, however secular they are, are possible *as effects* [*en effets*] without this curve before the law that the absolute past constitutes. And no empirical supplement (no "effectivity" of "tertiary memory") is possible without there being trust in its power to *synthesize effectively what has happened and what has been lived on from out of* [*depuis et à partir de*] *this absolute past that has never been present, lived or effective* [*effectif*].

* * *

The question of the program and of the promise is therefore that of a *double synthesis*. A passive synthesis, handed down by the *effectivity* of an already-there itself referring to an *ineffective* already-there (the absolute past), must precede the synthesis of judgment – the judgment of the subject constituting the object of its belief, of the belief according to which, always, one judges. The point is not understood by those who denounce in the deconstruction of the subject its destruction. Derrida does not destroy the subject (to do so would be absurd): he deconstructs the metaphysics of subjectivity insofar as it ignores the irreducibility of passive synthesis – and of the already-there qua the ground of *all* belief. He thereby sets out the *fallibility* of the subject, putting in question both the "trustworthiness" [*fiabilité*] of its "en-gagement" ["*fiance*"] and the conditions of that trust [*confiance*] without which there would no longer be life (or *différance*). The living is what *wants* to live, and, wanting to live, what *believes unconditionally* in life in that, having access to the "gramme as such," it only believes in life insofar as it is haunted by the dead qua the non-living, by the dead in the sense of those who have lived, and by death as that to which life testifies. This haunting is only possible as the technicity of life.

In what respect do the media say the truth, do they give the possibility of truth (there is no belief possible unless it is in *one* truth)? And, inversely, whatever form the media assumes, in what respect do they actually distance the true, "reporting" it only insofar as they reduce, fictionalize, and sensationalize it? These questions have everything to do, of course, with the economy (there is no industrial investment that, of a financial nature, does not call upon trust and the media). They emerge today at a moment when, in *kenosis* and under the form of "monstrosity," religion is also becoming a question. The question is one of possible belief in the media and in mediation, supplementarity – whether it be, for example, in the materialized textuality of *Phaedrus* or in biblical or evangelical textuality. The question of passive synthesis is immediately that of the trustworthiness of the message and of the messenger, of news and media, of belief and credit – a question, at one and the same time, of fiduciary capital, of tele-technologies, of faith and incarnation.

As a reflection upon the logic of the supplement, deconstruction is thus a thinking of mediation, of non-immediacy, and, consequently, of the *trust* that one must have in truth, a trust that always rests on the ground of an "already-there" (for example, that of alphabetic writing supporting the history of the development of geometric thought). The nature of this trust means also, at one and the same time, that truth must call upon that which will have always already exceeded any calculation, any program, that to which the Law *obligates us*, always referring to the absolutely non-lived made up by the absolute past. This inscription of every faith and every form of knowledge in the *double already-there* orients Derrida's recent article "Faith and Knowledge."

What is to be said of religion? What is to be said of religion today? And what does one say as a philosopher?

The Enlightenment is supposed to have handed down to us a philosophical discourse on religion that opposes the clarity of knowledge to the obscurities of faith. "Faith and Knowledge" calls upon and testifies to that which precedes science and religion qua their common possibility of believing – in the truth. The possibility of believing common to faith and knowledge is that of an initial *yes* contained in every assertion, in every word which promises. This *yes* always takes as *witness* an *absolute elder*, someone *who is not yet born*.

Presupposed at the origin of every address, come from the other *at his address*, the wager of some sworn promise cannot not, taking God immediately as witness, have already so to speak engendered God quasi-mechanically. A priori inevitable, God's *ex machina* descent could be seen to put on stage a transcendental machine of address. One would have thus begun by retrospectively laying down the right of absolute antecedence of a One who is not yet born. Taking God as witness, even when he is not named (as in the pledge of the most secular engagement), an oath cannot not produce, invoke or convoke God as already-there, unengendered and unengenderable – before being itself: unproduce-able. And absent at its place. Everything begins with the presence of this absence. The unengenderable thus engendered – this is the empty place.[74]

This absolute elder of the past that has never been lived is also the promise of an absolute future, a future intended by *any* truth statement, any judgment of truth, quite simply any judgment, since *no* judgment can take *place* except under the condition of the possibility of an oath. The absolute future qua the very messianicity of the messianic. This infinite promise is to be seen as the waiting on the part of an invincible desire for justice that:

is not and cannot be assured of anything, whether it be through knowledge, consciousness, predictability or any program as such. This abstract messianicity belongs to the experience of faith, of belief, of a credit irreducible to knowledge and of a trustworthiness [*fiabilité*] that "grounds" any relation to another in testimony. This justice alone allows one, beyond all "messianisms," to hope for a universalizable culture of singularities . . . in which the abstract possibility of the impossibility of translating can at least be announced. It is inscribed in advance in the promise, in the act of faith or in the call to faith that inhabits every act of language and every address to the other. The universalizable culture of *this* faith, and not of another or before any other, allows alone a "rational" and universal discourse on the subject of "religion."[75]

This understanding of messianicity is not accounted for by the opposition between reason and the mystical.

The foundation of the law is a "performative" event which cannot belong to the ensemble that it founds "indisputable mystical foundation of authority."[76]

If, therefore, the absolute past, constituted by the trace and constituting it as arche-trace, the possibility of every empirical trace, to which every empirical trace refers, is grammatological, that is, programmatological, the infinite promise to which this infinite past refers is assured of "no program as such," no calculation, and no predictability. Equally – indeed for this very reason – this infinite promise is untenable: it can never be freed from a calculation.[77] The incalculable, the improbable, God, what can only become the object of a faith, is always already and ever compounded with calculation, the program, etc. Inversely, every program, qua tertiary memory, that is, as the tertiary "retention" of a living being haunted by death, in the first and last instance calls upon an absolute past which is *also* an absolute future: the absolute future which is held in every promise, and which no promise can ever hold. The absolute future is the reflection of this tainless mirror out of which the absolute past looks at me.

At the very heart of the question of synthesis, of the question of time, there is belief qua an initial yes. Reason is referred to the faith that sustains it, to a faith older than that which distinguishes science and religion. But what of technics in all this? The article "Faith and Knowledge" seems with regard to such a question simply to associate science and technics in the technoscience of the industrial tele-technologies. Derrida comments at one point:

Perhaps we could try and "understand" in what respect the imperturbable and interminable development of critical and techno-scientific reason, far from being opposed to religion, bears it, supports it, presupposes it. One would have to show – it will not be simple – that religion and reason have the same source. Religion and reason develop together, starting from this common resource: the testimonial pledge of every performative engaging one as much to respond *before* the other as to answer *for* the performing performativity of techno-science.[78]

"Faith and Knowledge" also develops an analysis of the media as tele-technologies.

In the end we would like to tie the question of religion to that of the ill of abstraction [*mal d'abstraction*]. To radical abstraction. Not to the abstract figure of death, of evil/ill or the illness of death, but to forms of evil that are traditionally linked with radical upheaval and, therefore, the uprooting of abstraction, analyzing on the way places of abstraction like the machine, technics, techno-science and, above all, tele-technological transcendence. "Religion and mekhanè," "religion and cyberspace," religion and the numeric," "religion and digitality," "religion and virtual time-space."[79]

The "tele-technologies" Derrida alludes to – a particular epoch of supplementarity – are, however, neither science nor reason. *Technics cannot simply be reduced here to science or to knowledge.* Nor inversely. *Technics is the condition as much of science and knowledge as of religious faith. The issue continues to be that of tertiary memory.* Now it is here that the relation between the promise and the program holds. It is, in other words, a *theologico-political* relation.

* * *

God, or the absolute past, or everything that bears witness cannot be reduced to calculation, to the probable; it exceeds every program, every form of knowledge. And yet:

1. The absolute past and the past that has been present, the absolute already-there and the relative already-there are in transductive relation to one another. One past does not come without the other: the absolute (that which is *absolutely* lacking [*ce qui fait absolument défaut*]) is "constituted" retrospectively, in an *après coup*, in so far as the past that has been lived always refers to what will have never been lived, to, that is, what cannot be "constituted" as such.

2. The prosthesis of the past made up by tertiary memory as the mark of passive synthesis configures historically, that is, as a history of the supplement, the *conditions of inaccessibility* to the absolute past. The already-there of what is lacking [*fait défaut*], of this unnameable De-fault [*ce Défaut innommable*] (whether one names it God or not) *passes* through the unlived already-there of those who once lived and bore witness.

In other words, this "past" that has never "gone past," that never stops passing, passes through tertiary memory without passing through it. Quasi-immortal. Quasi-transcendental. But *through* empiricity. Empiricity "invested with spirit," with the spirit, for example, of the *letter*: the empirical mark of the trace common to geometry, the *Bible*, the *New Testament* and the *Koran*.

If an arche-belief, common both to the Enlightenment and to religion that echo it, therefore swears to the improbable of the absolute past and the absolute future, this arche-belief is grammatological. Constituted through the play of primary, secondary, and tertiary retentions and protentions, the improbable only takes place *effectively* [*en effets*] on the condition of supplementary exteriorization. It only takes place on the condition that technicity opens up the possibility of calculation qua the experience without evidence [*l'épreuve sans preuve*] of the incalculable to which it is only possible to bear witness under oath. Technicity unfurls as the process of *différance* and as the conquest of time and space. It is thus that which uproots from the ground, that which does violence to one's home, that which thrusts outwards the intimate, and that which corrodes idiomatic differences. But this violence is also the very possibility of idiomatic differentiation, that which *constitutes* one's home in the first place by opening it to what is other than oneself:[80] a process of ex-appropriation in which desire becomes all the more intense the more it is satisfied. For the supplement, marking the default of origin, does nothing but try and fill this default in; and yet, in doing so, it can only affirm it as necessary in a

double movement of abstraction and attraction that both tears away from and attaches back to the land, to the idiom, to the literal, to everything that is somewhat unclearly brought together under the name of "identity" [*l'identitaire*]: in short, what both ex-propriates and re-appropriates, uproots and re-roots, ex-appropriates according to a logic of self-immune self-indemnification [*auto-indemnisation auto-immune*].[81]

It is within the process of exteriorization that the ground, "grounding as it collapses," opens the desire that both binds and unbinds, *referring* as much to the absolute past as to the absolute future – exteriorization (the technicity of the living), that is, tertiary memory, an archival memory that calls for a witness.

The default produces defaults [*fait défauts*]: defaults of pronunciation, for example – the "babelization" in which the idiomatic sense of home is constituted in the structure of the *schibboleth*.[82] "The" default produces defaults: the unpronounceable default, what was never and will never be effective, another name for God. This improbable, *constituted* by the program, exceeds all programs. Witnessed on the unique occasion of the idiom, in utter singularity, it ensures, guarantees, and protects, *but only as a trace*, the possibility of its return, of its repetition. It guarantees as much the presence of ideality in the Living Present as its iterability.

A politics of memory and hospitality – of heritage, adoption and grafting – must consequently be a politics of the supplement, that is, of technics. To speak of prostheses of faith is in fact to speak of the *graft* and *adoption*. What Derrida thinks through the supplement is the originary graft. Not a supplementarity which could be produced in any conditions whatsoever, as if nothing was to be found under the name of the "proper." On the contrary, the question is that of accounting for attachment to the supplement. Everything is supplementary, and yet no supplement can stand in general for what is supplemented and what supplements. There are immune systems which are always also self-immune: they can never go on resisting forever supplementation. This is the reason why faith has a history: the alphabetic support does not give access to the same regime of belief as hieroglyphic writing, or indeed any other form of trace. Every trace calls for a witness, supports a belief, but all traces do not make possible the same beliefs, *even if every belief calls upon the absolute past*: which is why universalizing reason is required and promised as the absolute of any faith.

Only the program – supplementarity – can *give* the necessity, after the event [*après-coup*], of the absolute past and the absolute future; only the program can both compel and interrupt belief just as it can both compel and forbid the calculation of belief. This "both" has a history, it is never given except in the singularity of epochs that are traced by the history of supplementary specificities, notably those of contemporary technology. The improbable cannot be reduced; there is always an excess over the programmatic, an excess that *animates* it in the first place. This is why testimony is always testimony of the living insofar as it is living. But let us remember that the inverse is true as well. The living witnesses *because it is prosthetized*. Let us remember that. Otherwise all is lost.

* * *

Of Grammatology elaborated, we saw, a quasi-transcendental discourse, referring to the linguistic school of Copenhagen, particularly to H. J. Uldall, whom at one moment Derrida quotes:

> It is only through the concept of a difference between form and substance that we can explain the possibility of speech and writing existing at the same time as expressions of one and the same language. If either of these two substances, the stream of air or the stream of ink, were an integral part of the language itself, it would not be possible to go from one to the other without changing the language.[83]

The fact that speech is always already writing shows itself in the very possibility of writing language down: speech and writing form nothing but two singular modalities of an "exteriorization" in which the interior does not precede the exterior, the unity of the two, their co-possibility being the arche-trace, precisely, the arche-trace as the movement of *différance* in terms of spacing and temporalization. Wherein Derrida's criticisms of Uldall, or rather, his limitation of the horizon of the linguist's remarks:

> It is clear that if the phonic substance lost its privilege, it was not to the advantage of the graphic substance, which lends itself to the same substitutions. To the extent that it liberates and is irrefutable, glossematics still operates with a popular concept of writing. However original and irreducible it might be, the "form of expression" linked by correlation to the *graphic* "substance of expression" remains very derivative with regard to the arche-writing of which I speak. This arche-writing would be at work not only in the form and substance of graphic expression but also in those of nongraphic expression.[84]

What Uldall confuses is certainly to be separated out. And yet, if the tertiary, here, the graphic, is granted a constituting role [*une constituance*], one cannot simply argue this by referring the materiality of the graphic and the phonic to their equivalence under the authority of arche-writing. Whenever language is inscribed, written down, another language is formed, contaminating the first, grafting itself upon it and that it adopts with more or less consent. This violent play that sets to work a politics of language – making possible what "Faith and Knowledge" calls "mondiolatinization"[85] – is nothing but the history of the supplement. Language "as such" changes with its supports. There is, in other words, neither language nor linguistic competence, but a graphematic, or grammatological, or prosthetic competence – one that calls for a genealogy (of the supplement), in which *every bifurcation in supplementarity counts*. This is another reason why the "transcendental origin of the system itself" is nothing but quasi-transcendental, that is, accidental.

If, on the one hand, a history of the supplement *cannot not account* for the *possibility of accounting* for a history of the supplement, deconstruction, on the other hand, shows that fidelity to the logic of the supplement makes such a history *stricto sensu* impossible. For one cannot *calculate* [*compter*] with the absolute past; the history of the supplement refers necessarily to belief in this history, that is, *in effect(s)*, to the absolute past which it can do nothing but witness. Deconstructive grammatology cannot for this reason be a "positive science."

The question of belief is, that said, the question of belief in the fidelity of tertiary memory. And that is why Uldall's analysis cannot be accepted. It is tertiary memory which accounts for the possibility of accounting faithfully at the same time as suspending any possibility of accounting for fidelity as such, that is, for the gramme as such.

An intelligence of faith – which is impossible, which we can do nothing but promise, which we have to promise in its very default – must/fails to account each time for the conditions in which faith yields to the trust that we have or do not have in tertiary memory.[86] No politics of memory or of the archive, of hospitality or of home, no future is, perhaps, promised outside this "must/failure" of life that the dead haunts *in life's technicity*.

The tertiary trace refers to the arche-trace, older than any empirical or meta-empirical trace; it refers always to the absolute past. But the absolute past only constitutes itself "as such" *through* this referral. It is why a logic of the supplement, without ever simply being such a history, must also be a history of the supplement in its epochs, epochs that are each time singular and must each time form the object of a technical history constantly *renewed*. Faith and tele-technology are for this reason mutually insoluble and mutually inseparable – transductively (re)constituted by each other. It is why, finally, fidelity is always at the limits of deconstruction qua undeconstructible justice. Such would be faith: at the limits of deconstruction. Such would be faith at the limits of deconstruction.

Translated from the French by Richard Beardsworth

NOTES

1 Jacques Derrida, *Of Grammatology*, trans. Gayatri Chakravorty Spivak (Baltimore: Johns Hopkins University Press, 1976), 5.

2 On the "kenotic horizon" and the death of God, compare "Foi et savoir: les deux sources de la 'religion' aux limites de la simple raison," in *La religion*, ed. Jacques Derrida and Gianni Vattimo (Paris: Éditions du Seuil, 1996), 9–86, and especially 27–28.

3 Jacques Derrida, "Quelqu'un s'avance et dit," in *Autour de Karl Marx Théâtre inédit* (Éd. Théâtre Nanterre-Amandiers, 1997), 4.

4 A concept that is itself problematic. As Jacques Derrida puts it, "globalization does not globalize itself globally, so to speak, nor equally for everyone – which makes this new notion, as well as the rhetoric exploiting it, suspect" (ibid.).

5 In Jacques Derrida, *Dissemination*, trans. Barbara Johnson (Chicago: University of Chicago Press, 1981), 61–172, esp. 106–16. For Plato, there are two kinds of memory: *mneme* and *hypomnesis*. The first is within the psyche, is active, and alive, and characterizes the type of questioning and reflecting that, for Plato, marks proper knowing; the second is a type of rememoration dependent on external supports and supplements (a clay- or wax-board, a scroll, a blackboard, a computer, or a handkerchief) that characterizes the type of knowing that is secondary and technical and, ultimately, haunted by death. For Plato, this opposition is eminently an ethical one between two types of responsibility, the one active and autonomous, the other passive and heteronomous: for Derrida, this opposition is the very institution of metaphysical philosophizing and constitutes the site of a violent desire to remove from the structure of the psyche the trace of supplementarity. Hence the importance of this text for understanding the reach of Derrida's philosophy and the interest of Stiegler's intense focus on this instituting moment. – Trans. note.

6 The term "default," or better "de-fault" [*le défaut*], while in part consonant with the problematic of the radical lack of origin in Jacques Derrida's work, is one nevertheless particular to the work of Bernard Stiegler on technical supplementarity. Initially following Derrida, Stiegler argues that technical supplementarity is the originary "default" of life: a default explicitly marked by hominization; Stiegler stresses nevertheless the historical and contingent nature of this supplementarity in terms that lead, as the reader will see, to an important disagreement with Derrida concerning the relation between arche-writing and technicity. It is this relation with which Stiegler is here concerned. For a prolonged elaboration of Stiegler's understanding of "originary de-fault," see his *La technique et le temps. Tome 1: La faute d'Epiméthée* (Paris: Galilée, 1994), English trans. Richard Beardsworth and George Collins, *Technics and Time. Volume 1: The Fault of Epimetheus* (Stanford: Stanford University Press, 1998) – Trans. note.

7 Passive synthesis consists in the fact that consciousness, in principle constitutive of its objects, finds constituted before it a horizon (the already there of its constitutivity) – what Heidegger calls "Dasein's facticity." The metaphysics of consciousness posits consciousness as an active synthesis, that is, as master of its judgment. Passive synthesis refers, therefore, and as we shall see, to the

aporia of an absolute past that precedes and reorganizes this metaphysics. The detail of these terms will be discussed in what follows.

8 Jacques Derrida, *Le problème de la genèse dans la philosophie de Husserl* (Paris: Presses Universitaires de France, 1990).

9 Ibid., 14.

10 Ibid.

11 Jacques Derrida, *Speech and Phenomena*, trans. David B. Allison (Evanston: Northwestern University Press, 1973).

12 Jacques Derrida, *Husserl's Origin of Geometry: An Introduction*, trans. John P. Leavey, Jr. (Nebraska: University of Nebraska Press, 1989). Henceforth, the text will be referred to by the more convenient title *An Introduction to Husserl's "Origin of Geometry"* or, where the context is clear which work is being referred to, simply *An Introduction*. – Trans. note.

13 Derrida, *Le problème de la genèse*, 267 and 269. Before laying down the terms of this general problematic Derrida adds in a note of 1990 (*Le problème de la genèse*, 264 n 12): "a short time after, I put in the margin of these lines 'No! To be reconsidered.'"

14 Ibid., 267.

15 Ibid., 270.

16 Ibid.

17 Derrida shows, with particular reference in the 1960s to Saussure and Freud, that language is "always already" a *dispositif* of differential marks and, in this sense, always already a "writing." That said, writing in the normal empirical and phenomenal sense cannot be confused with this differential or "arche"-writing. Here Derrida directly refers to the structure of protention and retention in Husserl.

18 On the various meanings of the term "brisure," see *Of Grammatology*, 65–73.

19 Edmund Husserl, *On the Phenomenology of the Consciousness of Internal Time (1893–1917)*, trans. John Barnett Brough (Dordrecht, Boston, London: Kluwer Academic Publishers, 1991). In accordance with the original German (*Zur Phänomenologie des inneren Zeitbewusstseins (1893–1917)*) the more appropriate title *On the Phenomenology of the Inner Consciousness of Time* (cited hereafter in the text as *The Inner Consciousness of Time*) has been preferred. – Trans. note.

20 See Gérard Granel, *Le sens du temps et de la perception chez E. Husserl* (Paris: Gallimard, 1968).

21 Husserl, *On the Phenomenology of the Inner Consciousness of Time*, 37–38.

22 Derrida, *Speech and Phenomena*, 64.

23 Ibid., 65–6.

24 Ibid., 67.

25 Ibid.

26 See Stiegler, *La technique et le temps. Tome 1*, 250–62 and, specifically, *La technique et le temps. Tome 2: La désorientation* (Paris: Galilée, 1996), 54–56 and ch. 4.

27 "Retentional finitude" designates the fact that all psychological and biological memory is limited, having to acquire memorial prostheses to supplement its finitude.

28 Derrida, *Le problème de la genèse*, 123–24.

29 Derrida, *An Introduction to Husserl's Origin of Geometry*, 85–86.

30 Ibid., 86.

31 Intentionality is the major concept of phenomenology. All intention aims at an ideal object that it attempts to reach – what Husserl calls "filling-in." In this respect, the *eidos* constitutes the essence of the object aimed at; it is in a sense an equivalent of the Platonic idea.

32 *Épokhè* is the determining concept of the phenomenological method which affirms the necessity of reversing our normal way of looking at things, of abandoning, that is, what Husserl names the "natural attitude." This attitude takes for granted that the world is a constituted world outside itself while phenomenology argues that consciousness posits the world. (The *épokhè* becomes, specifically, the reduction of the world that allows for the movement of transcendental consciousness to be analyzed as such. The above argument not only rehearses why this suspension is radically impossible within its very possibility, but shows why this aporia is to be thought in terms of technics. – Trans. note.)

33 This extends a point that is elaborated in much greater detail in the last chapter of Stiegler's *La technique et le temps. Tome 2: La désorientation*.

34 Derrida, *An Introduction*, 88.

35 Ibid., 91.

36 See Edmund Husserl, *Ideas Pertaining to a Pure Phenomenology and to a Phenomenological Philosophy. Book 2: Studies in the Phenomenology of Constitution* (Dordrecht: Kluwer, Imprint, 1989), 224.

37 ibid., 45.

38 Compare again "Plato's Pharmacy," in Derrida, *Dissemination*. – Trans. note.

39 Derrida, *An Introduction*, 78.

40 André Leroi-Gourhan, *Gesture and Speech*, trans. Anna Bostock Berger (Cambridge, MA: MIT, 1993).

41 Leroi-Gourhan's analyses are not free of several important contradictions. I have proposed a commentary of them in *Technics and Time. Volume 1: The Fault of Epimetheus*, part 1, ch. 3.

42 Leroi-Gourhan, *Gesture and Speech*, 264–66.

43 See note 6.

44 See, for Derrida's elaboration of this logic, "This Dangerous Supplement," *Of Grammatology*, part II, ch. 2, 141–64. The oppositional logic of metaphysical thinking places one term of an opposition as the external supplement to the other: culture is added, from outside, to nature, technics is added, from outside, to culture, and so forth. In such thinking, this addition can only be an act of God, a miracle, a catastrophe, or an act accounted for from within a mythical and/or narrative understanding of the world. That said, the logic of the supplement is a radical structure, developed in Derrida's reading of

Rousseau's texts, that shows, contra the oppositional logic of metaphysical thinking, that the supplement is a necessary addition to the first term for this term to work in the first place. If, therefore, there is no nature without culture, no culture without technics, what is supplementing is more internal to what is being supplemented than what is being supplemented: in which case, what is more interesting than either term is the very logic of supplementation itself, accounting, for example, for the fact that supplementarity is the "truth" of all transcendental or originary concepts (God, Truth, Nature, Consciousness, etc.). Stiegler is therefore arguing that technics is the vehicle through which this logic can be best thought, all the while maintaining that this does not reduce *différance* to technics. – Trans. note.

45 Jacques Derrida, *Writing and Difference*, trans. Alan Bass (London and New York: Routledge, 1990), 196–231.

46 Ibid., 228.

47 See Gilbert Simondon, *L'individu et sa genèse physico-biologique* (Paris: Presses Universitaires de France, 1964), 18.

48 Ibid.; the concept is equally developed in *L'individuation psychique et collective* (Paris: Aubier, 1981).

49 Derrida, *Of Grammatology*, 60, my emphasis.

50 Ibid., 84.

51 Ibid., translation modified. – Trans. note.

52 This effectivity designates the historical and contingent unfolding of the effects of supplementarity.

53 Martin Heidegger, *Being and Time*, trans. John Macquarrie and Edward Robinson (Oxford: Blackwell, 1967).

54 A "program" can perhaps best be understood here as any determination of memory, from the organization of the nervous system to the memories of informational technology. For Stiegler, following his reading of *Of Grammatology*, programs are supplementary effects of a radical absence, or default in his terms, which absence determines both their necessity and their indefinitely supplementary nature. It is within this radical absence, within this absolute past, that indeterminacy is to be understood, and, therefore, that something like the "promise" of an unprogrammable future is held.

To situate further the terms Stiegler is using: this radical structure of the promise – developed from out of religious discourse, but also inscribed behind it as its condition of possibility – is first developed by Jacques Derrida in relation to negative theology in "Comment ne pas parler: dénégations," in *Psyché* (Paris: Galilée, 1987), 555–96; to the Heideggerian problematics of debt and engagement in *De l'esprit: Heidegger et la question* (Paris: Galilée, 1987), note 1: 147–54 [trans. G. Bennington and R. Bowlby, *Of Spirit. Heidegger and the Question* (Chicago: University of Chicago Press, 1989), note 2: 129–36]; and to Paul de Man's reading of Rousseau's *Social Contract* in Jacques Derrida, *Mémoires: pour Paul de Man*, trans. Cecile Lindsay, Jonathan Culler, and Eduardo Cadava (New York: Columbia University Press, 1986). The distinction that Stiegler will allude to later between the "messianic" and messianism in the context of the promise is first fully developed by Derrida in relation to Marxian thought and its modern and contemporary fates in Jacques Derrida, *Spectres de Marx* (Paris: Galilée, 1994), especially 56, 111–12, 124–26 and 265–68 [trans. Peggy Kamuf, *Specters of Marx: the State of the Debt, the Work of Mourning and the New International* (London and New York: Routledge, 1994), 28, 65–66, 73–75, 167–69]. The relation between the promise, the messianic, religion and technology with which *Spectres de Marx* ends is elaborated in detail in Derrida's "Foi et savoir: les deux sources de la 'religion' aux limites de la simple raison," in *La religion* (translated by Sam Weber as "Faith and Knowledge: The Two Sources of 'Religion' at the Limits of Mere Reason," in J. Derrida and G. Vattimo (eds.), *Religion* (Stanford: Stanford University Press, 1998), an important text to which Stiegler refers at the beginning and towards the end of this article. (Renderings here of "Faith and Knowledge" are mine since Sam Weber's text appeared after the translation of this piece.) – Trans. Note.

55 Derrida, *Of Grammatology*, 61.

56 Derrida also explores this impossibility in *Aporias*, trans. Thomas Dutoit (Stanford: Stanford University Press, 1993).

57 Derrida, *Of Grammatology*, 7.

58 Ibid., 8.

59 Ibid.

60 Ibid., 332, n. 26, my emphasis.

61 Ibid., 62.

62 Ibid., 61, my emphasis.

63 Ibid., 64.

64 This term marks for Derrida the process of desire itself where the "appropriation" of the other is also immediately the desire of the alterity of the other, that is, its irreducibility and extraneousness. The desire of appropriation is thus also the desire of expropriation – a tension which Derrida appropriately calls "ex-appropriation."

65 Concerning this difference between the appearing and the appear-ing, Husserlian phenomenology shows how important it is to distinguish the object that appears from the process by which it appears, that is, by which it is constituted for consciousness. This distinction is also what distinguishes the constituting consciousness from the constituted world, and the transcendental from the empirical.

66 Ibid., 62.

67 The question of inexistence and spectrality as the question of the *eidos* constantly returns in Derrida's *Specters of Marx*.

68 Derrida, *Of Grammatology*, 61.

69 Ibid., 65.

70 Ibid., 66.

71 Ibid.

72 Ibid., 68.

73 Maurice Blanchot, *L'entretien infini* (Paris: Gallimard, 1969), 104.

74 Derrida, "Faith and Knowledge," 39.
75 Ibid., 28.
76 Ibid., 29.
77 See Jacques Derrida, *Given Time. 1: Counterfeit Money*, trans. Peggy Kamuf (Chicago: University of Chicago Press, 1992).
78 Derrida, "Faith and Knowledge," 41.
79 Ibid., 10.
80 J. Derrida and B. Stiegler, *Echographies de la télévision* (Paris: Galilée-INA, 1996), 91–92.
81 Derrida, "Faith and Knowledge," 56.
82 On Derrida's use of this term, see *Schibboleth, pour Paul Celan* (Paris: Galilée, 1986). Translated by Joshua Wilner as "Shibboleth", in *Word Traces*, ed. Aris Fioretes (Baltimore: Johns Hopkins University Press, 1994).
83 Derrida, *Of Grammatology*, 58.
84 Ibid., 60.
85 Derrida, "Faith and Knowledge," 58.
86 Given the play on "faut" in this sentence (the verb "falloir" is being used here both in the old sense of "faillir" [to fall, and, therefore, to fail] and in the current sense of expressing an obligation), the reader might find it useful to have the French sentence in full: "Une intelligence de la foi, qui est impossible, que nous ne pouvons que promettre, qu'il nous faut promettre dans son défaut même, *faut* de rendre compte chaque fois des conditions dans lesquelles la foi se rend à la confiance que nous faisons ou ne faisons pas dans le souvenir tertiaire." – Trans. note.

FURTHER READING

Derrida, Jacques. "Foi et savoir: les deux sources de la 'religion' aux limites de la simple raison." In *La religion*. Ed. Jacques Derrida and Gianni Vattimo. Paris: Éditions du Seuil, 1996.
"Freud and the Scene of Writing." In *Writing and Difference*, trans. Alan Bass. New York: Routledge, 1990.
Husserl's Origin of Geometry: An Introduction. Trans. John P. Leavey, Jr. Nebraska: University of Nebraska Press, 1989.
Of Grammatology. Trans. Gayatri Chakravorty Spivak. Baltimore: Johns Hopkins University Press, 1976.
"Plato's Pharmacy." In *Dissemination*, trans. Barbara Johnson. Chicago: University of Chicago Press, 1981.
Le problème de la genèse dans la philosophie de Husserl. Paris: Presses Universitaires de France, 1990.
Speech and Phenomena. Trans. David B. Allison. Evanston: Northwestern University Press, 1973.
Husserl, Edmund. *Logical Investigations* (2 vols., based on revised Hallé editions). Trans. J.N. Findlay. New York: Humanities Press, 1970.

On the Phenomenology of the Consciousness of Internal Time (1893–1917). Trans. John Barnett Brough. Dordrecht, Boston, London: Kluwer Academic Publishers, 1991.

"The Origin of Geometry." In Derrida, *Husserl's Origin of Geometry: An Introduction* (above).

Leroi-Gourhan, André. *Gesture and Speech*. Trans. Anna Bostock Berger. Cambridge, MA: MIT, 1993.

Simondon, Gilbert. *L'individu et sa genèse physico-biologique*. Paris: Presses Universitaires de France, 1964.

L'individuation psychique et collective. Paris: Aubier, 1981.

Stiegler, Bernard. *Technics and Time. Volume 1: The Fault of Epimetheus*. Trans. Richard Beardsworth and George Collins. Stanford: Stanford University Press, 1998.

La technique et le temps. Tome 2. La désorientation. Paris: Galilée, 1996 [translation forthcoming: Stanford University Press].

CHAPTER 11

Derrida and history: some questions Derrida pursues in his early writings

Peter Fenves

History entered into the domain of philosophical inquiry once philosophers had exhausted other responses to a question they cannot fail to pose: under what conditions does philosophical inquiry begin? Because one cannot know these conditions unless one is a philosopher and one cannot become a philosopher unless one is aware of these conditions, the question issues into an aporia. The aporia may be called "meta-philosophical," since it is less concerned with specific philosophical questions than with the moments at which questions first become philosophical. If the conditions under which philosophical inquiry takes place are not supposed to remain a mysterious gift, and if philosophers are not supposed to reconcile themselves to the mystery at the inception of their questioning but are, instead, under an obligation to inquire into its enabling conditions, then these conditions must themselves be available for inquiry (in Greek, *historein*). The term *history* thus opens a way out of an otherwise intractable aporia: it allows philosophers to speak of the conditions that give rise to the questions they pose without having to invoke categories such as the ineffable or indescribable. As long as philosophers can appeal to history in response to the question "how does philosophical inquiry begin?" they need not repeat the traditional Platonic-Aristotelian answer: under the miraculous, mysterious, or in any case indescribable condition of "wonder" (*thauma*).[1] And this appeal to history has a similar function for those who wish to reveal the faultiness, failure, or poverty of philosophy, for it can also express itself in the contention that the study of historical conditions – rather than any supposedly autonomous reflection – grants access to the origin and significance of philosophical questions, methods, and movements.

From his earliest writings onward Derrida has wondered about this appeal to history as a way out of a "meta-philosophical" aporia. Wondering about history precludes celebrating it as the solution to every – or any – philosophical problem. Celebrations of this sort were common during the years in which Derrida began his work, especially among philosophers who, like Kojève and Sartre, aligned themselves with various versions of Hegelianism.[2] But wondering about history does not mean rejecting it as unworthy of attention. The blanket dismissal of history is a gesture that links classical forms of rationalism with certain versions of structuralism that have exercised considerable influence on scholarly inquiry in France since the publication of Saussure's lectures.[3] Wondering about history means asking whether the appeal to history can lead out of a "meta-philosophical" aporia and, more importantly, whether a way out of this – or any other – aporia ought to be forged in the first place. Because Derrida, from the inception of his work, does not conceive of aporias as disabling, he does not seek to avoid them as obstacles to the progressive accomplishment of tasks or programs, and his work can even be said to welcome aporias as chances to alter tasks or programs – or for something other than tasks and programs altogether. Derrida evades, in short, a facile alternative between historicism and rationalism: he presents history neither as the solution to, or dissolution of, philosophy nor as an incoherent concept or extraphilosophical concern. What Derrida writes at the beginning of his first major essay could apply with certain modifications to the "attitudes" and "postures" he analyzes in the course of his subsequent work: "The structuralist attitude and our posture today in view of or within language are not only moments of history. Astonishment, rather, by language [*langage*] as the origin of history. By historicity itself."[4]

Once philosophers begin to rely on the idea of history in response to a "meta-philosophical" aporia, they cannot fail to ask questions such as "what makes something historical?" and "what makes history possible?" Such questions are attracted to the term *historicity*, for the historicity of something is whatever makes it historical – in both senses of the term: dated (even if the precise date can never be determined) and capable of entering into public memory (even if it is only the most rudimentary calendar). Hegel, who first made history into a major philosophical concern, revels in the ambiguity of the term: "The word *history* in our language unites the objective and the subjective sides and means both *historiam rerum gestarum* and the *res gestas* itself; it is the event no less than its narrative. This union we must regard as of a higher order than mere outward accident."[5] According to Derrida's first major essay, it is language that inaugurates history in both senses of the word, and this is cause for astonishment. But the word *language* is even more ambiguous than the term *history*, and its ambiguity cannot be resolved by invoking the distinction between subjective and objective "sides." The astonishment to which Derrida refers – an astonishment without a grammatical subject and perhaps without a subject at all – can be understood as a philosophical "posture" only if it issues into an investigation into the precise manner in which language is "the origin of history." Derrida does precisely this in his early writings.

The following essay is historical in a narrow sense: it is not concerned with the genesis of deconstruction, or even with a description of the original contexts in which Derrida's early writings might be understood, but with two apparently opposing projects through which Derrida begins to elaborate his own. These two projects, perhaps more than any others, circumscribe "our posture today": the situation of philosophical inquiry in France during the years Derrida began to publish his writings. Both of these projects attempt to do away with all constructions of history and to retrieve certain events through which both the possibility of historiography and the experience of history are first disclosed. One of these projects aims for an "archeological" history of madness, the other for a "teleological" history of reason. Derrida's analyses of these two modes of historical inquiry can be seen to mark out the extremes within which historiography in general operates. The essay concludes with certain consequences Derrida draws from his discovery that, for all their differences, the historical inquiries of Foucault and Husserl share a common requirement: that, for history to be possible, the danger to meaning must be arrested – if only in the historiographic act of recounting and thus accounting for such danger.

THE HISTORY OF MADNESS

Derrida begins an early essay entitled "Cogito and the History of Madness" (1963) by noting the inevitable result of any attempt on the part of disciples to speak with their teachers: the dialogue will be interpreted as a challenge. And Derrida does seem to issue a challenge to his former teacher, Michel Foucault, that strikes at the root of the project the latter pursues in *The History of Madness*[6]: the history Foucault wishes to write cannot be written; historiography can only make sense of historical events, including the decisive event – "decision" being Foucault's word – in which the mad were interned, reason authorized itself to speak *about* madness, and the classical age was firmly established. Derrida does not simply say this, nor does he challenge Foucault's interpretation of specific historical events, including the "great internment" of the mad, and indeed his essay is less a challenge to Foucault than an occasion to raise certain questions, to admire the intricate design of *The History of Madness*, and to wonder about "the possibility of history." This phrase is also Foucault's, and it is closely related to his account of the "decision" in which reason and madness break off their erstwhile "dialogue." But as Derrida emphasizes, Foucault touches on the question of the possibility of history without seeming to recognize the extent to which it threatens his own enterprise and, more generally, without acknowledging a grave threat to the idea of history as such.[7]

By describing his endeavor as "a history of madness *in* the classical age," Foucault indicates from the start that the conception of reason under discussion is only one version of reason: there must be other ones, some of which are older than that of the classical age. At least one of these earlier versions must have been capable of conducting a conversation with – and not simply authorizing itself to speak about – what would later be called "madness": "The issue is therefore to reach the point at which the dialogue was broken off, dividing itself into two soliloquies – what Foucault calls, using a very strong word, the *Decision*. The Decision, through a single act, links and separates reason and madness, and it must be understood at once both as the original act of an order, a fiat, a decree, and as a schism, a caesura, a separation, a dissection" (*WD*, 38). Attempting to reach this point gives rise to certain dangers, especially if an historian tries to pinpoint this decision and identify it with a specific historical event; the decision then appears as though reason were at first untroubled about its own rationality and could therefore afford to engage in a lively dialogue with madness. Once the decision is identified with a specific historical event or structure, a basic idea of classical metaphysics is reinvigorated – that of the original unity of reason: "The attempt to write the history of the decision, division, difference runs the risk of construing the division as an event or a structure subsequent to the unity of an original presence, thereby confirming metaphysics in its fundamental operation" (*WD*, 40).

Derrida does not, then, abandon Foucault's project of reaching the point at which reason and nonreason, *raison* and *déraison*, or meaning and nonmeaning meet; but he does not identify this meeting point with an identifiable historical event within an already constituted history. Following Foucault's lead, he links it, instead, to the *possibility* of such events. After citing a passage where Foucault proposes such a linkage, Derrida poses a series of questions that, as he writes, "haunt" any attempt to write a history of an historical event that makes history possible:

"*The necessity of madness*, throughout the history of the West, is linked to the deciding gesture which detaches from the background noise, and from its continuous monotony, a meaningful language that is transmitted and consummated in time; briefly, it is linked to the *possibility of history*." [Derrida's emphasis]. Consequently, if the decision through which reason constituted itself by excluding and objectifying the free subjectivity of madness is indeed the origin of history, if it is historicity itself, then ... the "classical" moment of this exclusion described by Foucault has neither absolute nor archetypal exemplarity... [I]f this great division is the possibility of history itself, the historicity of history, what does it mean, here, "to write the history of this division"? To write the history of historicity? (*WD*, 42–43)

When Derrida turns toward Foucault's exposition of Descartes's part in the "great internment," he does not deny that the *Meditations* belongs to one of the "determined figures" of reason, and he does not undertake an "analysis of [Descartes's] manifest intentions" (*WD*, 45) in order to correct Foucault's error and restore what the philosopher wished to say. On the contrary, he proposes a "classical" reading of Descartes's work in order to disengage a project in which the Cogito takes part – "the project of exceeding the totality of the world, as the totality of what I can think in general" (*WD*, 56) – from the program Descartes intends to pursue and, more generally, from every intention to make sense of things. The *Meditations*, in other words, belongs to one of the determinate figures of reason and is comprehensible as an event within a determinable historical context only under one condition: the project of exceeding the totality of the world is forgotten, and the Cogito is understood simply as a rational statement or a reassurance of rationality. Foucault's contention that the opening sections of the *Meditations* participate in the "act of force" by which the mad were interned depends, according to Derrida, on such an understanding. If the Cogito is understood otherwise; if it is understood as an event that threatens meaning and cannot therefore be understood – not even as *an* event – then it is not a determinate figure of reason. And Derrida claims the Cogito demands to be read in this manner: "The hyperbolical audacity of the Cartesian Cogito, its mad audacity ... would consist in the return to an original point which no longer belongs to either a determined reason or a determined unreason, no longer belongs to them as opposition or alternative. Whether I am mad or not, *Cogito, sum*.... It is therefore a question of drawing back toward a point at which all *determined* contradictions, in the form of given, factual historical structures, can appear, and appear as relative to this zero point at which determined meaning and nonmeaning come together in their common origin" (*WD*, 56).

The audacity of Derrida's own project can be located in this gesture toward a "zero point" in relation to which historical events and structures as such appear. This point is not a "logical origin," an *a priori* form or category from which the empirical world is supposed to originate, for it precedes the division between reason and nonreason, the *a priori* and the *a posteriori*. Nor can this zero point simply be seen as a determinable phenomenon, for, as a null-point, it is nothing in its own right – not even a point: "it is less a question of a point than of a temporal originarity in general" (*WD*, 309). The zero point presents itself as the occurrence of certain punctuation, and in the case of the *Meditations*, it punctuates the rationalist program that, for its part, unambiguously belongs to a specific historical structure: "The extent to which doubt and the Cartesian Cogito are punctuated by this project of a singular and unprecedented excess – an excess in the direction of the nondetermined, Nothingness or Infinity, an excess that overflows the totality of that which can be thought, the totality of beings and determined meanings, the totality of factual history – is also the extent to which any effort to reduce this project, to enclose it within a determined historical structure, however comprehensive, risks missing the essential, risks dulling the *point* itself" (*WD*, 57). This risk is similar to the one Derrida describes when he discusses Foucault's decision to identify the decisive moment when reason distinguishes itself from nonreason with specific events and determinate structures: it is the risk of reinvigorating metaphysics – not now under the category of unity but under that of totality. Derrida does not counter this risk with certainties, least of all the certainty that his own thoughts somehow exceed metaphysics; on the contrary, the risk he proposes – drawing toward a "zero point" – invites the accusation that Foucault, among others, will later level against him: that his work preserves metaphysics.[8]

Parodying the very words he wishes to free from historicist reduction, Derrida lays out the terms in which a hyperbolic project poses a grave threat to every representation of history: "I think, therefore, that (in Descartes) everything can be reduced to a determined historical totality except the hyperbolic project. Now, this project belongs to the narration narrating itself and not to the narration narrated by Foucault. It cannot be recounted, cannot be objectified as an event in a determined history" (*WD*, 57–58). If historicism consists in the thesis that there is no point outside the totality of history, least of all a perspective of "pure reason," then it not only misses the project in which, according to Derrida, the

Cogito is enlisted; it also *interns* this project by declaring it impossible. The edict of internment runs like this: nothing can puncture the complete and in principle closed context to which all historical events and structures belong. Derrida likens this edict to the "act of force" on which, according to Foucault, the classical age was founded. As long as Foucault accepts the historicist tenet of totality, he will never be in a position to recognize Descartes's fictional war with the specters of generalized falsity, unrestrained fictionality, and sheer nonmeaning. But the Cogito occurs, if it ever occurs, only in the "context" of this war – "context" in scare quotes because such a war is not only fictive, it knows no limits and cannot therefore settle into any horizon of sense-making.

As he closes his essay, Derrida insists on almost the opposite point, however: it is philosophy itself – and first of all Descartes's – that interns the Cogito. The internment takes place at the very moment the Cogito is generally communicated, for communication can take place only under the condition that the Cogito is meaningful, which is to say, detachable from the audacious project of reaching a zero point where reason and nonreason meet. Having been detached from this project, the Cogito can then be attached to a philosophical program in which reason reassures itself of its own rationality by means of "a deductive system" and "with reference to God *and* a certain memory" (*WD*, 58). Once the Cogito is interned in such a system, it no longer "wanders" (*WD*, 59): it ceases to roam from one context to another, none of these contexts being *its* context, the one with reference to which its meaning can in principle be determined. Derrida wonders about this wandering, and this wondering takes the form of an astonishingly untimely proposal: according to Derrida, it is time to distinguish thought from language. For the moment of the Cogito's internment is the very event of its articulation, which is, however, the one and only event available to the historical record, regardless of how this record, as a certain form of memory, is conceived. Derrida does not propose some other clandestine or shadowy event prior to the one into which an historian can inquire; rather, he asks whether now is the time to renew the distinction between thought and language, the latter being available to a public archive, whereas the former is not.[9]

But the term *thought* here is tentative; that to which it refers is not something outside history, still less to a modification of the *res cogitans* but is only a *tactical* point in both senses of the word: a strategic move and rhythmic movement. According to Derrida, the rhythm of philosophical history takes its tact from the interplay between thought and speech, which is to say: the interplay between – not the dialectical mediation of – frightening projects and reassuring communications. While bringing attention to the "pathetic"[10] dimension of this rhythm, Derrida insists that his effort to rescue something of the classical distinction between thought and language does not aim to resurrect *philosophia perennis* but, on the contrary, seeks to account for the enabling condition of history or, in other words, for historicity. Derrida thus lays down something like a Credo – not in order to establish a creed but to mark the tentativeness of his thought, especially his proposal for detaching thought from language:

> I believe that historicity in general would be impossible without the history of philosophy, and I believe that the latter would be impossible if we possessed only hyperbole, on the one hand, or, on the other, only determined historical structures ... The historicity proper to philosophy is located and constituted in the transition, the dialogue between hyperbole and finite structure ... that is, in the place where, or rather at the moment when, the Cogito and all that it symbolizes (madness, derangement, hyperbole, etc. ...) pronounce, reassure themselves, and fail, necessarily forgetting themselves until their reactivation, their reawakening in another speaking of the excess that will also later become another decline and another crisis. (*WD*, 60–61)

Derrida may be primarily concerned with the "historicity proper to philosophy" in his confrontation with Foucault's history of madness; but an account of the historicity of philosophy is of no particular importance unless it yields an account of historicity in general. And his exposition of the Cogito does – at least in part. For, as Derrida emphasizes, it is not one event among others; it is not even *an* event within an identifiable context. The Cogito cannot even be called an event within the history of philosophy, although *The Meditations* is, of course, such an event. The Cogito is a name for that which makes it impossible for any historical context to be closed, even in principle: no context can be so completely determined and fully saturated that it thereby excludes the possibility of "thought" – the possibility, in other words, not only that utterances mean something other than what they are said to mean but that utterances mean precisely nothing, that they are "mad" utterances and therefore not utterances, strictly speaking, but, as Derrida underscores, *silences* or, to use Foucault's phrase, "the absence of work." The internment of nonreason in articulate sentences can never be complete, for articulation can always *also* be entangled in, or a matter of, thought. This is the lesson of Descartes's "I think," its audacious pedagogy, and it is the reason Derrida turns toward it – rather than toward the discourses and practices of internment, say – for an account of historicity in general.

In his reading of *The History of Madness* Derrida employs no term with greater insistence than *silence*. The meaning of silence cannot be determined according to its context, nor can any effort of contextualization determine whether silence is in fact meaningful. Derrida goes so far as to invoke the questionable category of life in an effort to make this overburdened term – who among the successors of Hegel has not made silence into the supreme philosophical theme? – accomplish its tactical task. Silence is supposed to mark the opening of historicity:

> if madness in general, beyond any factitious and determined historical structure, is the absence of work, then madness is indeed, essentially and generally, silence, stifled speech, within a caesura and a wound that *break open* [*entament*] life as *historicity in general*. Not a determined silence, imposed at one given moment rather than at any other, but a silence essentially linked to an act of force, a prohibition that opens history and speech. *In general*. (*WD*, 54)

Responding to the question, "what remains of the opening of history?" Derrida can be said to echo the last words of Hamlet, who knew something about madness at the inception of the classical age: the rest (of this opening) is silence. But Derridas account of "silence . . . *within* a caesura and wound" leaves room for certain ambiguities, as does the term *silence* itself. Not only is this term given over to an inarticulate pathos; it is not itself the cause – however this be understood – of the wound to life; rather, it is only a remnant of the violent act of force that opens history in both senses of the word. Silence, in other words, is not a force in its own right. The term *silence* allows Derrida to formulate in a concise manner the aporia of Foucault's history of madness, but it does not give him a chance to account for something he emphasizes near the end of his essay: the Cogito must be capable of being repeated or, as he would later say, "iterated." Without the possibility of an altering repetition, there can be no philosophical history and indeed no history at all. An indeterminate silence can be neither altered nor repeated: it can only be extended. No version of historicism, even Foucault's, can make room for such silence; but by countering *every* version of historicism, Derrida tends to leave something like a "negative rationalism" intact, as silence assumes the role previously reserved for reason: "[to] bear and haunt language" (*WD*, 54).[11] The last word on the "zero point" – itself a questionable term[12] – relative to which historical events and structures appear as such cannot be *silence*. In "Cogito and the History of Madness" Derrida lays out the limit to historicism and calls it "thought," but in order to prevent this exercise from turning into a negative rationalism, he must describe these limits in more precise terms, and there is no better place to turn for such a description than toward a history of reason that aims to overcome the opposition between historicism and rationalism as it repeats – or, as Edmund Husserl would say, "reawakens" – the Cartesian Cogito.

THE HISTORY OF REASON

Derrida concludes "Cogito and the History of Madness" by aligning Foucault's "archeology" with Husserl's late reflections on the history of reason. Both projects are concerned with "crises of reason." Whereas Foucault presents the crisis of reason in the classical age, Husserl seeks to account for the general pattern of perils to which reason exposes itself as it loses the sense of its origin, forgets its destination, and thus becomes "menaced by its own security" (*WD*, 62). Derrida's early writings, especially his extensive commentary on Husserl's posthumously published fragment "The Origin of Geometry," leaves no doubt that Husserl's inquiries into the history of reason develop out of his early efforts to establish phenomenology as a "rigorous science." Such a science cannot rest content with the description of the constitution of the things that appear to consciousness, as all "naive" attitudes toward the world, including the belief in its reality, are suspended; it must inquire into their genesis. Of particular importance in this regard are the "things" upon which the sciences depend and whose sense, according to Husserl, have been forgotten: the ideal objects of mathematics.[13] And the way to re-discover the sense of these "things" is to return them to their original context: the all-encompassing context Husserl calls the "life world." Derrida *could have* chosen to accompany Husserl on this path toward the life world; more exactly, he could have followed Trân Duc Thao – a successor to Husserl whom Derrida admires as he does few others[14] – and interpreted Husserl's fragmentary reflections on the origin of geometry as an indication that Husserl himself began to recognize that phenomenology must henceforth undertake more inclusive, more extensive, less idealist, and more materialist inquiries into the life world as the universal "infrastructure"[15] within which the meaning of every act, event, object can alone be determined.

But something in Husserl's inquiries into the history of reason leads Derrida to wonder less about the necessity than the possibility of the mode of inquiry Trân Duc Thao proposed and in part pursued. For the history of reason cannot escape a recurrent paradox: reason is historical only under the condition that its "products" detach themselves from empirical history. Derrida's meticulous reading of "The Origin of Geometry" gravitates toward various versions of this paradox, one of which runs: "a sense [*sens*] has entered into history only if it has become an absolute object, that is, an ideal object, which, paradoxically, must have broken all the moorings that secured it to the empirical ground of history."[16] Phenomenological inquiry encounters this paradox as it responds to an unconditional historical imperative: historicize reason without falling prey to historicism and resolve the crisis in which reason finds itself as the ever-expanding discoveries of the modern "European"[17] sciences continue to cover up the sense of the scientific enterprise as such.

Husserl does not denounce historical relativism so that he can revive a philosophical tradition according to which the conditions for the possibility of undertaking rational inquiry are understood to be preserved in a *topos ouranios* (heavenly place) and thus removed from history. On the contrary, as Derrida underscores from the beginning of his analysis of "The Origin of Geometry," phenomenology distinguishes itself from classical metaphysics on precisely this point: any assumed, presupposed, or postulated condition for the activation of reason, including the existence of a Platonic realm of ideas, must be rejected as "technicist and objectivist irresponsibility" (*O*, 26). In order to respond to the demand of phenomenology for absolute responsibility to – and for – appearances as they show themselves, Husserl therefore undertakes a "return inquiry" (*Rückfrage*) into the origin of the original scientific project. The value of geometry as an example – at once particular and universal – is directly linked to its originality. The ideal objects of the geometry must have been created at a specific, if nevertheless unspecifiable moment, and the question that phenomenology poses is: under what conditions? The inquiry into the origin of these ideal objects does not seek out facts about the first geometricians; indeed, the inquiry is less concerned with the history of a particular discipline than with historicity as such, and Husserl chooses to concentrate on the example of geometry precisely because "ideal objects, 'the higher forms of reason's *products*,' [Husserl] . . . assure the possibility of historicity, i.e., the always intersubjective consciousness of history" (*O*, 29). Without ideal objects, it would be impossible to experience the *same* things over time, and unless this happens there can be no history in either sense of the term. If, moreover, the origin of first science is indeed exemplary, then an answer to the question of its possibility can issue into a response to the question: how is reason historical? And if, finally, history in general does depend on the "higher forms of reason's products," like those of geometry, then the response to this last question gives direction to the one Derrida encounters in Foucault: how is history possible?

Husserl has a provisional response to the last question, and this response, for Derrida, orients every step of his "return inquiry." It makes no sense to speak of historical experience unless it is contrasted with something else, more exactly, "hallucination (and imagination in general)" (*O*, 46). One constitutive element of historicity is the invariable givenness, datedness, or more exactly, "datability" of an occurrence. Something – an event or a structure – can be considered historical, however, only under the condition that it participate in a broad assemblage of intersubjective connections: "language, tradition, community, and so forth" (*O*, 110). And this assemblage, which is "precomprehended" in every historical experience, is another constitutive element of historicity. No experience of history is possible unless subjectivity, having grasped these elements, "goes outside of itself" (*O*, 63) and encounters or constitutes an object: "The conditions of Objectivity are the conditions of historicity itself" (*O*, 64). Whereas Foucault links the possibility of history to "the necessity of madness," Husserl ties it to the necessity of absolute objectivity. For only absolutely "objective" or "unbound" objects guarantee the unity of history, which is to say, assures all speakers, regardless of time or place, that the same phenomena will always have been under discussion over a potentially indefinite extent of time and across a potentially indefinite expanse of space. Only objects that are at once fully enmeshed in the intersubjective connections of "language, tradition, community" *and yet* are entirely "unbound" from *particular* languages, traditions, and communities can claim objectivity in the strong sense, and these objects are the ones in view of which questions concerning history in general can be raised.

The unbinding of ideal objects from empirical history, which first occurs at – and *as* – the origin of geometry, can take place only if they are able to exceed both the spheres of any individual consciousness and any given culture. To represent the ability of unbound idealities to remain outside these spheres in terms of some extra-mundane realm and to affirm that they inhabit a *topos ouranios* is, according to Husserl, irresponsible: such a realm is always only postulated; it is never given. Husserl therefore has to search for something that serves the same function; otherwise, he would succumb to historicism and be forced to admit that all objects are bound to particular languages, traditions, and communities after all. This "something" must allow for an emancipation of idealities from their entrapment within an individual consciousness and its particular cultures – without, however, making this emancipation into a flight toward some mythical realm "beyond" both consciousness and culture. Near the center of his commentary on "The Origin of Geometry" Derrida identifies the almost inadvertent result of Husserl's search. *Writing* is the replacement for the *topos ouranios*:

> Husserl insists that truth is not fully objective, i.e. ideal, intelligible for everyone and indefinitely perdurable, as long as it cannot be said *and* written . . . Undoubtedly, truth never keeps the ideal Objectivity or identity of any of its particular de facto linguistic incarnations; and compared to all linguistic factuality it remains "free." But this freedom is only possible precisely from the *moment* truth can in general be said or written, i.e., *on the condition* that this *can* be done. Paradoxically, the graphic possibility permits the ultimate freeing of ideality. (*O*, 90)

Truth is bound to be written, and the history of reason is a history of its "products" being inscribed, forgotten, and reawoken. Husserl thus comes across the peculiar function of writing: it does not simply make up for a lack but makes up for something that was never there in the first place – the *topos ouranios*, realm of ideas, or "plain of truth."[18] By affirming the nonexistence of any transhistorical realm of ideas, phenomenology distinguishes itself from classical metaphysics; by nevertheless conceiving of writing as a replacement for *something missing*, it guarantees that its inquiries will remain within the "closure of metaphysics."[19]

Speech allows unbound idealities to exceed the sphere of any individual consciousness, but writing grants them a further freedom by liberating them from the event of their articulation. Because of this "graphic possibility" ideal objects can indefinitely wander away from the context in which they were created. Only this wandering lets these objects be objects in the strong sense. Yet the possibility of indefinite wandering exposes reason to a crisis: meaning could be forgotten and truth disappear. This is the risk of all idealization, and accounting for this risk is "the most difficult problem posed by the 'Origin' and all of Husserl's philosophy of history" (*O*, 93). In an essay on "genesis and structure" in phenomenology Derrida summarizes the complex arguments with which he addressed this problem in his earlier commentary:

> "The Origin of Geometry" describes the necessity of the exposition of reason in a worldly inscription. An exposition indispensable to the constitution of truth and the ideality of objects, but which is also the danger to meaning from what is outside the sign. In the moment of writing, the sign can always "empty" itself, take flight from awakening, from "reactivation," and may remain forever closed and mute. As with Cournot, here writing is the "critical epoch." (*WD*, 166)

An indefinite "taking flight" *would be* the fate of reason's "higher products," including the ideal objects of geometry, if reason were not from
its inception teleological; if, therefore, its end and purpose were not the
rediscovery and recovery of its origin. But history can then have no other
subject than meaning, and meaning must be recovered *after all* – after,
that is, the dangerous epoch of writing. An inquiry into the history of
geometry, for example, could never begin if it did not take the telos of
this history – "the sense [of geometry] as we now know it" $(O, 50)$ – for its
starting point; otherwise it could never be sure that the *same* things were
experienced under the same *names* over an indefinite extent of time and
across an indefinite expanse of space. And if the history of geometry is
exemplary, this is true of the history of reason in particular and history as
such: whatever happens, the danger to meaning will have been arrested
after all.

Mute and forever closed signs, by contrast, fall outside history in both
senses of the term. The an-historical character of such signs cannot,
however, be confused with the immunity from history that classical metaphysics attributes to the ideal objects of geometry.[20] They are not only *not*
ideas inhabiting a supersensible realm, they cannot even be understood
as signs *of* something: an idea or an object. And all signs are *potentially* so:
forever closed and mute. Such signs – if they can be said to exist – are
more akin to "wild singularity" and "stark fact" $(O, 151)$ than to any
of the endless variety of intentional objects and acts available to phenomenological research. The problem posed by the possibility that signs
might take an endless flight from reawakening requires modes of inquiry
other than those sanctioned by the phenomenological idea of evidence.
Derrida associates these other modes of inquiry with "empiricism or
nonphilosophy" $(O, 93)$,[21] and near the end of his study he proposes
an "ontology (in the non-Husserlian sense)" $(O, 151)$ that would "complement" phenomenology; but in any case the questions posed cannot
presuppose that the "object" in question will have been able to respond
to the inquiry and reveal its meaning after all.

The moment of writing has the same function in Derrida's analyses of
Husserl as the Cogito plays in his reading of Foucault: it names a "zero
point" where "meaning and nonmeaning come together in their common origin" $(WD, 56)$. Derrida seeks names for this "originary" space–
time in his commentary on "The Origin of Geometry" for the same
reason that he does so in *The History of Madness*: so that he can respond
to the question "how is history possible?" The writings of Husserl and
Foucault indicate the direction of this response: history is possible on

the condition that meaning – and therefore a secure distinction between reason and nonreason – be endangered and that this danger be arrested after all. The Cogito, for Derrida, endangers meaning only to be arrested by its linguistic articulation. By contrast, writing arrests meaning so that, paradoxically, it can wander away from its origin. Not only does writing have the capacity to bind intentional objects of all kinds, especially the unbound idealities of the sciences; it can also intern utterly boundless "thoughts" – "thoughts" so boundless that they cannot even be said to be thoughts *about* something. If it is true, moreover, that "the conditions of Objectivity are the conditions of historicity itself" (*O*, 64), then these "thoughts" must be considered an-historical in a sense unknown to classical metaphysics: they are, as Derrida writes at the conclusion of *Speech and Phenomenon*, "unheard-of" (*SP*, 102). Being unheard-of is not quite the same as being silent; the signs of nonobjective or objectless "thoughts" are "mute" and "closed." Conversely, the muteness of any sign that takes flight from reawakening may be the sign of its excessiveness: it overshoots "the world as the totality of what I can think in general" (*WD*, 56). Such signs do not belong to history as long as history consists in the covering up and recovery of meaning. And it remains a question whether history can consist of anything else. In the course of explicating "the strange dialogue of speech and silence" (*WD*, 133), Derrida underscores the questionable character of this question: the concept of history "is difficult, if not impossible, to lift [*enlever*] from its teleological or eschatological horizon" (*WD*, 148).[22]

Mute and forever closed signs – Derrida will later speak of "cinders"[23] – endanger history in both senses of the term: no historical inquiry can account for them, and they cannot be said to exist or occur in the same manner as identifiable events or recognizable objects. It is even questionable whether there can be such signs, especially if existence is understood as the appearance of something to a consciousness that can assure itself of its own existence; and it is equally questionable whether a discourse about these signs can do anything but betray them – by making them, for instance, into signs of absolutely unbounded "thought" or "thought" bound for no discernible destination. The danger posed by forever closed and mute signs cannot be arrested; indeed, every form of arrestation – the articulation of a word, the formalization of a thought, the institution of a rule, the installment of a new method, the invention of a new system of organization – is *also* a danger, for each one makes up for a lack and is, to this extent, another mode and moment of writing. Arresting the danger to meaning only exacerbates the danger, and each exacerbation gives rise to new versions of arrestation, which, in turn, exacerbate the danger even further, *ad infinitum*: the "cure" for the potential muteness of signs consists in the production of more signs, each of which is potentially mute as well. If history is possible only on the condition that meaning be endangered and that this danger be arrested after all, then the possibility of forever closed and mute signs – and once again, all signs harbor this possibility – means that history is *potentially impossible*. When Derrida asks about the possibility of history in his reading of *The History of Madness* or when he poses a closely related question at the close of his commentary on "The Origin of Geometry" – "Is there, and why is there, any historical factuality?" (*O*, 150) – he does not expect answers; but the questions he proposes do not presuppose that history is possible and that there is, strictly speaking, any *historical* factuality.

Nothing is perhaps more daring in Derrida's early writings than this reluctance to affirm that history is possible and that the philosophy of history – true to the tradition of transcendental argumentation inaugurated by Kant – need only ask about the conditions of its possibility. An understanding of history that would allow for the possibility of forever closed and mute signs not only must put itself into question; it must also make room for an expanded concept of writing, on the one hand, and a contracted "point" that cannot be said to belong to any specific historical context or structure, on the other. In Derrida's hands, therefore, the concept of writing expands to include everything that makes up for a lack, even if – or especially when – the "things" writing replaces have never existed in the first place; and a place is opened up for an ahistorical "point" that, far from representing the ahistorical perspective of pure reason, cannot be properly conceptualized as a point, position, or thesis at all.

If, however, the ahistorical is called "thought" and this word – against all of Derrida's warnings – is still understood in terms of representation, signification, and idealization, then the idea of history that emerges from Derrida's early work gives off the air of idealism, if not the aroma of gnosticism: thought is supposed to exceed the world, and worldly events appear as thought's repeated internment. Such interpretations of Derrida's writings, which he encountered in more or less vociferous forms as soon as they were widely discussed,[24] doubtless ignores the letter of his text, especially his often-repeated insistence that "thought," a tactical term, cannot be conceived as the modifications of a *res cogitans* and that the ahistorical must be understood in "a sense radically opposed to that of classical philosophy" (*WD*, 308); but Derrida nevertheless runs the risk of having his writings mistaken for idealism for a very precise reason: only by expanding the concept of writing and by making room for something – neither an object nor a concept – that "'is' . . . in a necessarily but newly ahistorical sense 'older' than presence and the system of truth, older than 'history'" (*SP*, 103) does he have a chance of approaching the goal that, according to Trân Duc Thao, Husserl began to envisage as he inquired into the origin of geometry: the goal of lifting the idea of history from its teleological horizon.

THE ELEMENTS OF HISTORICITY AT ODDS

Derrida hesitates, however, to claim that a new – and this time materialist – concept of history will emerge once the concept of history is finally lifted from its teleological horizon. Not only is it possible for materialist concepts of history to preserve teleological horizons; as long as materialism is primarily a matter of dispelling illusions, casting away phantoms, and forging a path to real objects, materialist concepts of history are grounded in the same principle that underlies and gives direction to Husserl's inquiries into the history of reason: "The conditions of Objectivity are the conditions of historicity itself" (*O*, 64). Derrida, by contrast, does not go along with this "self-evident" identification of the conditions of historicity with the conditions of objectivity. Near the opening of *Of Grammatology* (1967), he rehearses the argument of his commentary on "The Origin of Geometry" and, instead, presents "the graphic possibility" (*O*, 90) as the enabling condition of history in both senses of the term: "[H]istoricity itself is linked to the possibility of writing; to the possibility of writing in general . . . Before being the object of a history – of an historical science – writing opens the field of history – of historical becoming."[25]

Of Grammatology, as an inquiry into the history of writing, like Foucault's investigation of the history of madness, cannot be simply historical. And like Husserl's "return inquiry" into the origin of geometry, Derrida's investigation must pose questions that positive historiography is "obliged to suppress" (*G*, 28): "A history of the possibility of history that would no longer be an archeology, a philosophy of history, or a history of philosophy?" (*G*, 27–28). In response to this question, *Of Grammatology* does not attempt to elaborate a "meta-philosophy" of history that would also be a history of "meta-philosophy" – an historical account, for instance, of the philosophy of philosophy as it was conceived from Hegel and Nietzsche to Freud and Heidegger. Nor does *Of Grammatology* model itself on one of the principal texts it analyzes – Rousseau's "Essay on the Origin of Language"[26] – and seek to identify, reawaken, or reconstruct the events that make history possible. *Of Grammatology* does not do any of these things, not only because it cannot in fact pinpoint the origin of writing, which, of course, it cannot, but above all because Derrida claims no right to do so: he does not presume to know what the terms through which the word *writing* has been generally defined – especially the words *language* and *sign* – mean. Derrida, in other words, does not follow Foucault's procedure, which, even if it is meant to disturb the self-certainty of reason, is nevertheless sure that it knows what has been under discussion all along: "everything transpires as if Foucault *knew* what 'madness' means" (*WD*, 41). And Derrida does not follow Husserl's procedure, which, although it recognizes that the telos of all phenomenological research, like that of reason in general, is an infinitely removed "pole" or Idea in the Kantian sense, nevertheless demands that every "return inquiry" into the genesis of something take its point of departure from the sense of that thing "as we now know it" (*O*, 50). On this point Foucault and Husserl agree: the history of what we call "madness" will be a history of madness (even if it is an erroneous one), the history of what we call "geometry" a history of geometry (even if it is a misguided one).

Far from affirming – or simply denying – that we know what the term *sign* means and indeed know it well enough that a universal "science of the human" can be developed in its name, Derrida insists on its elusiveness: "The 'formal essence' of the sign can be determined only in terms of presence. One cannot get around that response, except by challenging the very form of the question and beginning to think that the sign is that ill-named thing" (*G*, 18–19). *Of Grammatology* does not withhold its consent in response to a skeptical impulse, a feeling that old words have somehow failed us and that we must return to experience and formulate a new empiricism – or new historicism – if we are ever going to regain semantic control. Only by refusing to affirm that it precomprehends one of the principal terms through which it undertakes its own "return inquiry" does *Of Grammatology* have a chance of lifting the concept of history from its teleological horizon. By calling the sign "that ill-named thing," Derrida challenges the basic requirement under which concepts of history generally operate: the requirement that, regardless of the crises, catastrophes, and interruptions to which history as a whole is subject, historical phenomena be recognizable and "discussable" – or capable of entering into "discursive practices" – as the *same* phenomenon over an indefinite extent of time or expanse of space.

In the course of his analyses Derrida then collects – and invents – terms that, like *madness*, defeat in advance the constitutive desire of historiographic inquiry to arrest any grave danger to meaning: "supplement," *pharmakon*, "hymen," *différance*, even "death," to name only a few.[27] Not only would any historical inquiry into one of these "things" encounter paradoxes analogous to the ones Derrida underscores in Foucault's *History of Madness*; these terms also challenge the requirement by which phenomena are understood to be historical in the first place. For no one can be sure that the "phenomena" to which they refer, if terms like *phenomenon* and *reference* are still relevant here, can be recognized and discussed as the same phenomenon over space and across time. For precisely the same reason, however, Derrida's inquiries can be understood to be historical in an eminent sense, especially when one of the constitutive elements of historicity – datedness[28] – is emphasized over another such element: the requirement that historical phenomena participate in those intersubjective connections of language, tradition, and community that make dates memorable, communicable, and representable. Those "things" of which Derrida writes could always be only matters of a single time and a single place, "wild singularities" (*O*, 151), dated in a radical manner, and for this reason available only by way of a testimony that, for its part, cannot ascertain the matters – disasters, monsters, and specters – about which it testifies.

For Derrida, then, the elements of historicity are at odds with one another: whatever is dated in a radical sense – and every *datum*, like every gift, is so dated – offers resistance to the broad assemblage of intersubjective connections that, by making things generally accessible, makes them dat*able* and thus historical in the first place. It is even possible to affirm that the specific force of Derrida's work from his earliest analyses onward consists in its ability to register the anhistorical – not preestablished – *dis*harmony among the elements of historicity. The manner in which he indicates the "out of jointness"[29] of both time in general and of "the times" in particular – which might be called "Derrida's method" – is to heighten, indeed to *hyperbolize* each of these elements *at the same time*. At its height, the assemblage of intersubjective connections would have to be absolutely universal: one language, universal communicability, a tradition to which everyone in principle and in fact belongs. And Derrida insists on the necessity of such universality: without it there could not even be a thought of justice. Every "date," by contrast, at *its* height would be so singularized that it would slip away from generality, retreat from what is generally called "language," and be accessible only in and as an entirely untranslatable, encrypted idiom – or in and as a "forever closed and mute" sign.

The matters toward which Derrida's writings gravitate are, in sum, those "things" that, far from repairing the breach among the elements of historicity, exacerbate it. As they register the breach in these elements, however, these "things" also announce, perform, or transform certain openings to historical configurations. Not only historical configurations, moreover, but geographical ones as well. In one of his later publications – the title of which, *L'Autre cap*,[30] is highly idiomatic – Derrida momentarily returns to an analysis of Husserl's "return inquiry" into the history of the universal and yet geographically specific European sciences. Derrida's inquiry into the "heading" of Europe does not follow Husserl, however, for it is not simply a philosophical or phenomenological inquiry into the conditions of the very mode of inquiry it exemplifies; rather, the questions it pursues occur in the midst of an intervention into the debate concerning Europe's "direction." The intervention – here as elsewhere in Derrida's writing – takes precedence over the inquiry, for, as an intervention, it breaks with certain conventions of inquiry and allows these conditions to be opened up in both senses of the phrase: "disclosed" and "split asunder." Derrida does not authorize his intervention on the basis of some position he represents, least of all that of universal humanity; nor, in reverse, does he undertake it for the sake – or for the salvation – of the particular phenomenon under inquiry, which, in the case of *L'Autre cap*, would be Europe or "its" sciences. Rather, the intervention takes place in response to another directive, direction, or "heading." The otherness of this "heading" not only is comprehensible in terms of those historically verifiable figures that have been forgotten, repressed, or suppressed in the course of European history; it must also be measured against whatever withdraws from the regime of figuration and declines to be represented as the other *of* Europe, including the dialectical other that grants Europe its identity. Those "things" for which there is no possible figure and which, for this reason, cannot be memorialized do not fall out of history; on the contrary, for Derrida, they are what makes history possible and what, in turn, makes it impossible to say, once and for all, whether or not grave dangers to meaning have been arrested and the possibility of history has been secured after all.

NOTES

1 See Plato, *Theatatus*, 155d; Aristotle, *Metaphysics*, 982b11-22. For a concise exposition of the relation between these two interpretations of the beginning

of philosophy, see Hannah Arendt, *The Life of the Mind* (New York: Harcourt Brace & Co., 1978), 114–15 and 142–43.

2 See Alexandre Kojève, *An Introduction to the Reading of Hegel*, trans. T. Nichols, Jr. (New York: Basic Books, 1969); and Jean-Paul Sartre, *Critique of Dialectical Reason*, trans. A. Smith (London: New Left Books, 1976).

3 See, for example, the concluding chapter to Claude Levi-Strauss's *Savage Mind* (Chicago: University of Chicago Press, 1966).

4 Jacques Derrida, "Force and Signification," in *Writing and Difference*, trans. A. Bass (Chicago: University of Chicago Press, 1978), 4; hereafter, *WD*. Emphasis is always Derrida's own; translations are often modified.

5 G. W. F. Hegel, *Philosophy of History*, trans. C. Friedrich (New York: Dover, 1956), 60. Derrida quotes this passage in one of his early essays, "Violence and Metaphysics" (*WD*, 114).

6 Michel Foucault, *Folie et déraison: Histoire de la folie à l'âge classique* (Paris: Plon, 1961); partially translated as *Madness and Civilization: A History of Insanity in the Age of Reason*, trans. Richard Howard (New York: Pantheon, 1965). I will refer to Foucault's book as *The History of Madness*.

7 Derrida's essay was originally delivered as a lecture (in 1963) at which Foucault was present. In an appendix to the 1972 edition of *The History of Madness* Foucault counters Derrida's reading of the Cogito by emphasizing that Descartes presents his "first philosophy" as a "meditation," that is, as a specific and historically bound mode of "spiritual" practice; see Michel Foucault, "My Body, This Paper, This Fire," trans. G. Bennington, *Oxford Literary Review* 4, 1 (Autumn, 1979): 9–28. Foucault launches an assault on Derrida near the end of his article without responding to any of the more general questions concerning the possibility of history posed by "Cogito and the History of Madness." In a much later lecture on *The History of Madness*, Derrida refers to the controversy unleashed by "Cogito and the History of Madness" while paying particular attention to the shifting figurations of Freudian psychoanalysis in Foucault's work; but, like Foucault, he leaves aside many of the questions he raises in his earlier essay; see Jacques Derrida, "'To Do Justice to Freud': The History of Madness in the Age of Psychoanalysis," in Derrida, *Resistances of Psychoanalysis*, trans. P. Kamuf, P.-A. Brault, and M. Naas (Stanford: Stanford University Press, 1998), 70–118.

8 See Foucault, "My Body, This Paper, This Fire," 27.

9 This proposal makes its way into an early footnote in "Cogito and the History of Madness" (*WD*, 308), and it serves as one of the motifs by which Derrida distinguishes his project from Levinas's: "One would then have to ask whether it is any longer possible to identify thought and language as Levinas seeks to do" (*WD*, 148).

10 Derrida's exposition of the pathos of thought perhaps owes something to the famous thesis Heidegger proposes in *Kant and the Problem of Metaphysics*: that Kant "shrank" from his insight into the abyssal foundation of reason; see Martin Heidegger, *Kant and the Problem of Metaphysics*, trans. R. Taft (Bloomington: Indiana University Press, 1990), 110–17.

11 Besides *thought* and *silence*, the other term Derrida emphasizes in "Cogito and the History of Madness" is *negativity*: "it could be demonstrated that as Foucault intends it, if not as intended by the historical current he is studying, the concept of madness overlaps everything that can be put under the rubric of negativity" (*WD*, 41).

12 Derrida undertakes a critique of points and punctuality in various later texts: see, for example, the concluding remarks to "La Parole Soufflée" (*WD*, 194–95); and especially *"Ousia* and *Grammé*: Note on a Note on Being and Time," in *Margins of Philosophy*, trans. A. Bass (Chicago: University of Chicago Press, 1982), 31–67; hereafter *MP*.

13 Derrida concentrates for the most part on Husserl's inquiry into origin of geometry, but he also touches on his investigations into arithmetic, especially Husserl's attempt to account for its genesis in the early "psychologistic" *Philosophie der Arithmetik: Psychologische und logische Untersuchungen* (Leipzig: Kröner, 1891); see the opening section of Derrida's "'Genesis and Structure' and Phenomenology" (*WD*, 155–60).

14 See Trân Duc Thao, *Phenomenology and Dialectical Materialism*, trans. D. Herman and D. Morano (Boston: Reidel, 1986), esp. 124–30: "the passage from the sensible to the intelligible can be correctly described only by the analysis of the *technical* and *economic* forms of this production [of the conditions of human existence]. This is, moreover, what Husserl obscurely presaged when, in a famous passage of *The Origin of Geometry*, he sought to found geometrical truth on human praxis" (125). In Derrida's remarks in "The Time of a Thesis: Punctuations," he indicates that Trân Duc Thao's work "pointed to a task, a difficulty, and no doubt to an impasse" ("The Time of a Thesis," trans. K. McLaughlin, in *Philosophy in France Today*, ed. A. Montefiore [Cambridge: Cambridge University Press, 1983], 38). Derrida also briefly discusses Trân Duc Thao's "miscarried endeavor" in *Moscou aller-retour* (Paris: Éditions de l'Aube, 1995), 77; for similar remarks, see "'The Almost Nothing of the Unpresentable,'" *Points . . . : Interviews, 1974–1994*, ed. Elisabeth Weber (Stanford: Stanford University Press, 1995), 78.

15 Trân Duc Thao, of course, borrows this term from Marxian discourse: the goal of his inquiry is to uncover "the real *infrastructure* which founds the ideal *superstructures* in their historical emergence and in their truth value" (*Phenomenology and Dialectical Materialism*, xxii). Derrida occasionally follows Trân Duc Thao by interpreting the phenomenological enterprise in terms of the relationship between the infra- and super-structure; see, for example, "Form and Meaning: A Note on the Phenomenology of Language" (*MP*, esp. 171–72). Without mentioning Trân Duc Thao's precedent, Rodolphe Gasché presents Derrida's deconstruction as an excavation of an "infrastructure"; see R. Gasché, *The Tain of the Mirror* (Cambridge, MA: Harvard University Press, 1986).

16 Jacques Derrida, *Edmund Husserl's "Origin of Geometry": An Introduction*, trans. John P. Leavey, Jr. (Stony Brook, NY: Nicolas Hays, 1978), 64; hereafter,

O. Derrida's reading of "The Origin of Geometry" is unusually demanding; and it draws on the idiosyncratic vocabulary Husserl developed over the course of four decades of phenomenological inquiry. In this chapter I try to keep this vocabulary to a minimum – without, I hope, betraying the thought of either Husserl or Derrida.

17 Husserl defines the sciences in terms of a particular geographical location, "Europe." For Derrida's analyses of this specificity, see the final remarks of this chapter.

18 Plato, *The Phaedrus*, 248b; see Jacques Derrida, "Plato's Pharmacy," in *Dissemination*, trans. B. Johnson (Chicago: University of Chicago Press, 1981), 166–67; hereafter, *D*.

19 Jacques Derrida, *Speech and Phenomenon*, trans. D. Allison (Evanston: Northwestern University Press, 1973), 102; hereafter *SP*. *Speech and Phenomenon* investigates Husserl's exposition of writing (under the rubric of "indication") as a replacement for something that never existed in the first place, but this "something" is not an independent world of ideal objects on whose basis the universality of the sciences are secured but, rather, the self-presence of the subject speaking with itself (and hence doing without the "indicative" function of language).

20 Instead of using the term *ahistorical*, which would suggest an eternal immunity from history, Derrida generally uses the adjective *an-historical* ["*an-historique*"], which implies a certain neutrality with respect to the distinction between the historical and the nonhistorical. Not all of Derrida's translators have respected this distinction.

21 Derrida often insists upon the necessity of a certain "empiricism and nonphilosophy" as the point of departure for a philosophical inquiry that does not wish to remain within what he calls the "closure of metaphysics." As he writes in "Outwork," "The breakthrough toward radical otherness (with respect to the philosophical concept – of the concept) always takes, *within philosophy*, the form of an *a posteriori* or an empiricism" (*D*, 33).

22 The term on which Derrida draws to describe a "difficult, if not impossible" task – *enlever* ["lifting;" "removing"] – is clearly related to the Hegelian term for the speculative operation as such, namely *Aufhebung* (which Derrida also discusses in "Violence and Metaphysics," *WD*, 113–14), but *enlever* does not have one sense of *aufheben*: it does not mean "preserve."

23 See especially Jacques Derrida, *Cinders*, trans. N. Lukacher (Lincoln: University of Nebraska Press, 1991). *Cendres* ["cinders"] are at the *centre* ["center"] of Derrida's writings from his earliest writings onward.

24 See, for example, the papers of a conference held at Cluny in April 1970; *Littérature et idéologies, Colloque de Cluny II*, F. Cohen *et al.*, eds. (Paris: La Nouvelle Critique, 1971). Derrida responds to the contention expressed by various participants that his writings amount to "idealism" in *Positions*, trans. A. Bass (Chicago: University of Chicago Press, 1981), 48–56; hereafter, *P*. See also Derrida's exposition of a sentence in *Of Grammatology* in which he states that "in a certain sense, 'thought' means nothing" (*P*, 49).

25 Jacques Derrida, *Of Grammatology*, trans. G. Spivak (Baltimore: Johns Hopkins University Press, 1976), 27; hereafter, *G*.

26 Paul de Man analyzes *Of Grammatology* from this perspective; see *Blindness and Insight* (Minneapolis: University of Minnesota Press, 1983), esp. 137.

27 For exemplary analyses of these terms see, respectively, "From/Of the Supplement to the Source" (*G*, 269–316); "Plato's Pharmacy" (*D*, 63–171); "The Double Science" (*D*, 172–285); "Différance" (*MP*, 1–28); and *Aporias*, trans. T. Dutoit (Stanford: Stanford University Press, 1993), esp. 46–51. The latter contains an analysis of Philippe Ariés, *Essais sur l'histoire de la mort en Occident du Moyen Age à nos jours* (Paris: Éditions Seuil, 1975).

28 On date and datability, see Derrida, "Shibboleth," in G. Hartman and S. Budick (eds.), *Midrash and Literature* (New Haven: Yale University Press, 1986), esp. 307–47; on the *datum* and gift, see Derrida, *Given Time: I, Counterfeit Money*, trans. Peggy Kamuf (Chicago: University of Chicago Press, 1992); *The Gift of Death*, trans. David Wills (Chicago: University of Chicago Press, 1995).

29 From its epigraph onward, Derrida reflects on Hamlet's famous announcement that "the time is out of joint" in *Specters of Marx: The State of Debt, the Work of Mourning, and the New International*, trans. Peggy Kamuf (New York: Routledge, 1994).

30 For Derrida's exposition of this phrase, see *The Other Heading*, trans. P.-A. Brault and M. Naas (Bloomington: Indiana University Press, 1992); 13–16.

FURTHER READING

Derrida, Jacques. *Aporias*. Trans. T. Dutoit. Stanford: Stanford University Press, 1993.

Archive Fever: A Freudian Impression. Trans. Eric Prenowitz. Chicago: University of Chicago Press, 1996.

Edmund Husserl's "Origin of Geometry": An Introduction. Trans. John P. Leavey, Jr. Stony Brook: Nicolas Hays, 1978.

"Force of Law: The 'Mystical Foundation of Authority.'" *Cardozo Law Review* 11 (1990): 919–1045.

"The Last Word of Racism." In *For Nelson Mandela*. Ed Jacques Derrida and Mustapha Tlili. New York: Seaver Books, 1987.

Monolingualism of the Other, or, The Prosthesis of Origin. Trans. Patrick Mensah. Stanford: Stanford University Press, 1998.

Moscou aller-retour. Paris: Éditions de l'Aube, 1995.

Of Grammatology. Trans. G. Spivak. Baltimore: Johns Hopkins University Press, 1976.

The Other Heading. Trans. P.-A. Brault and M. Naas. Bloomington: Indiana University Press, 1992.

Politics of Friendship. Trans. George Collins. New York: Verso, 1997.

Points . . . : Interviews, 1974–1994. Ed. Elisabeth Weber, trans. Peggy Kamuf *et al.* Stanford: Stanford University Press, 1995. See especially "Of a Certain Collège International de Philosophie Still to Come" (109–14) and "Once Again from the Top: Of the Right to Philosophy" (327–38).

Positions. Trans. Alan Bass. Chicago: University of Chicago Press, 1981.

Specters of Marx. Trans. Peggy Kamuf. New York: Routledge, 1994.

Writing and Difference. Trans. Alan Bass. Chicago: University of Chicago Press, 1978. See especially the essays "Cogito and the History of Madness" (31–63), "Violence and Metaphysics" (79–152), and "'Genesis and Structure' and Phenomenology" (154–68).

CHAPTER 12

Derrida and psychoanalysis: desistantial psychoanalysis

René Major

1. DERRIDA AND PSYCHOANALYSIS

In a text written at the beginning of the 1990s, Jacques Derrida pressingly raises the following question: "Will we forget psychoanalysis?" He is indeed concerned with the symptoms of forgetting already at work in philosophical and in public opinion in general, not to mention what – also in the order of forgetting – can be observed in the psychoanalytic field itself and in its institutions:

A worry about what I'd call, vaguely, free-floatingly (but the thing itself is vague, it lives on being free-floating, without a fixed contour), the climate of opinion, the philosophical climate of opinion, the one we live in and the one which can give rise to philosophy's weather reports. And what do the reports of this philosophical *doxa* tell us? That, among many philosophers and a certain "public opinion" (another vague and free-floating instance), psychoanalysis is no longer in fashion, having been excessively in fashion in the 60's and 70's, when it had pushed philosophy far away from the centre, obliging philosophical discourse to reckon with a logic of the unconscious, at the risk of allowing its most basic certainties to be dislodged, at the risk of suffering the expropriation of its ground, its axioms, its norms and its language, in short of everything philosophers used to consider as philosophical reason, philosophical decision itself, at the risk, then, of suffering the expropriation of what – this reason very often associated with the consciousness of the subject or the ego, with freedom, autonomy – of what seemed also to guarantee the exercise of an authentic philosophical responsibility.[1]

The decentering of consciousness carried out by Freud – consciousness is no longer master in its own house, it is largely submitted to obscure forces which it ignores – and the necessity that the history of reason itself be reinterpreted became genuinely significant in France, and later in Latin and Anglo-Saxon countries, only with the teachings of Lacan, who introduced this problematic in the literary and philosophical worlds. These worlds were seriously affected by it up to the point where one began to speak of the "end of philosophy." Some, among whom Derrida – and for him most obviously and eminently – were already no longer thinking without psychoanalysis, while ceaselessly requiring of it that it "render reason." Others were applying themselves to forget this troubling calling into question while attempting to restore a thought which was taking no account of Freudian advances. Let us continue reading:

> What has happened, in the philosophical climate of opinion, if I may take the risk of characterizing it grossly and macroscopically, is that after a moment of intimidated anxiety, some philosophers have got a grip on themselves again. And today, in the climate of opinion, people are starting to behave as though it was nothing at all, as though nothing had happened, as though taking into account the event of psychoanalysis, a logic of the unconscious, of "unconscious concepts," even, were no longer *de rigueur*, no longer even had a place in something like a history of reason: as if one could calmly continue the good old discourse of the Enlightenment, return to Kant, call us back to the ethical or juridical or political responsibility of the subject by restoring the authority of consciousness, of the ego, of the reflexive cogito, of an "I think" without pain or paradox; as if, in this moment of philosophical restoration that is in the air – for what is on the agenda, the agenda's moral agenda, is a sort of shameful, botched restoration – as if it were a matter of flattening the supposed demands of reason into a discourse that is purely communicative, informational, smooth; as though, finally, it were again legitimate to accuse of obscurity or irrationalism anyone who complicates things a little by wondering about the reason of reason, about the history of the principle of reason or about the event – perhaps a traumatic one – constituted by something like psychoanalysis in reason's relation to itself. (ibid.)

Psychoanalysis is what Derrida never forgets. He is bound to it, as to his mother tongue, by an originary, which does not mean univocal, bond. The one and the other resist him, just as he resists the one and the other. As with the mother tongue, the relation to the unconscious, which psychoanalysis brings into play, always remains both foreign and familiar. There is no relation to the unconscious which is not a tensed relation, one of resistance. But resistance is neither forgetting, nor negation. The unconscious can be approached only through resistance, as resistance is to psychoanalysis what air is to Kant's dove. It is impossible to fly without the resistance of air.

As Geoffrey Bennington notes, the relations which Derrida's thought entertains with psychoanalysis are original on several accounts. They are not only original in the sense in which they are properly his own [*propres à lui*], but also inasmuch as the relations which his work entertains with Freud or Lacan's thought are singular with respect to the relations this very same work entertains with other thinkers. Finally, they are so inasmuch as Derrida's relations to Freud are originary, at the origin, from the outset; there would be, there is no Derrida without Freud.[2]

In return – and I shall mostly insist on this – the paths opened up by Derridean readings of Freud and Lacan's work have become ones which psychoanalysis cannot forget or foreclose, unless it forget itself.

From the early deconstruction of logocentrism and the early analyses of the repression of writing as a mode of constitution of Western knowledge since Plato, Derrida finds a powerful ally in Freud. In spite of the fact that Freudian concepts belong to the history of metaphysics, and that they are forged right at the level [à même] of the linguistic matter which he inherits, Freud diverts and subverts their meaning. Such is the case, for example, with the numerous traditional oppositions. The unconscious is no longer simply outside consciousness. It lives as a parasite to consciousness. Pleasure is no longer quite plainly the opposite of displeasure. It can be experienced or felt as pain and pain as satisfaction. The subject seeks and finds itself in the object which is not, in itself, its opposite. There is no pure present in relation to the past. The past is present in the present and the present always already past. The origin is already delayed, the delay is therefore originary.

The Freudian concept of Nachträglichkeit, deferred action or afterwardness, which calls into question the metaphysical concept of "presence to self," is essential to the Derridean thought of the trace, of the deferred, of différance. This debt is explicitly acknowledged in "Freud and the Scene of Writing":

That the present in general is not primal but, rather, reconstituted, that it is not the absolute, wholly living form which constitutes experience, that there is no purity of the living present – such is the theme, formidable for metaphysics, which Freud, in a conceptual scheme unequal to the thing itself, would have us pursue. *This pursuit is doubtless the only one which is exhausted neither within metaphysics nor within science.* [my emphasis][3]

Derridean "différance" is not the delay which a consciousness grants itself or the adjournment of an act. It is originary in the sense in which it erases the myth of a present origin. Since Freud, memory is represented through differences of breaches [frayages] and there is no pure breaching without difference. The Freudian Verspätung, the à-retardement, is irreducible not only in the inscription of subjective traces, but also in the history of culture and of the peoples, as Moses and Monotheism shows.[4] Psychical writing is such an originary production that writing in a literal sense [*sens propre*] is but a metaphor of it: "The unconscious text is already a weave of pure traces, differences in which meaning and force are united – a text nowhere present, consisting of archives which are *always already* transcriptions" (*FSW*, 211). Derrida always conceives of the possibility of writing, of the one which is considered to be the most conscious and effective one in the world "in terms of the labor of the writing which circulated like psychical energy between the unconscious and the conscious" (ibid., 212).

From the Freudian scene of the dream, Derrida retains two things which he never abandons: 1) the connivance between so-called phonetic writing and the *logos* dominated by the principle of non-contradiction, which a certain psychoanalysis and a certain linguistics renew; 2) the unstable frontier between the non-phonetic space of writing (even in "phonetic" writing) and the space of the scene of dreams. Hence, linkings which do not obey the linearity of logical time are possible. Derrida relies on Freud's appeal to the pictogram, to the rebus, to the hieroglyph, to non-phonetic writing in general, for explaining the strange logico-temporal relations of the dream, when he has to take issue with Jacques Lacan's phonologocentrism in his commentary of Edgar Poe's "The Purloined Letter." The general writing of dreams puts speech in its place: "It is with a graphematics still to come, rather than with a linguistics dominated by an ancient phonologism, that psychoanalysis sees itself as destined to collaborate" (ibid., 220), and this, following what Freud literally recommends in "The Claims of Psychoanalysis to Scientific Interest" (1913):

[For] in what follows "speech" must be understood not merely to mean the expression of thought in words but to include the speech of gesture and every other method, such, for instance, as writing... it is even more appropriate to compare dreams with a system of writing than with a language. In fact, the interpretation of dreams is completely analogous to the decipherment of an ancient pictographic script such as Egyptian hieroglyphs... The ambiguity of various elements of dreams finds a parallel in these ancient systems of writing.[5]

Derrida focuses on the three analogies of writing Freud develops for explaining the functioning of the psychical apparatus in his *Notes upon a Mystic-Writing Pad*: 1) the keeping [*mise en réserve*] and the indefinite preservation of traces as well as an always ever-ready receptive surface; 2) the possibility of the erasure of the traces on a first layer – perception-consciousness [Pcpt.-Cs.] – assimilated to the celluloid sheet of the Writing Pad, does in no way prevent the persistence of the traces on the wax, which is compared to the unconscious; 3) the temporality of writing: "temporality as spacing will be not only the horizontal discontinuity of a chain of signs, but also will be writing as *the interruption and restoration* of contact between the various depths of psychical levels: the remarkably heterogeneous temporal fabric of psychical work itself" [my emphasis] (ibid., 225). As in the Mystic Pad, writing is erased each time the close contact between the paper receiving the excitation and the wax pad retaining the impression is interrupted.

Derrida notes that in making a scene of writing, Freud will have let the scene be redoubled, repeated, and exposed in the scene [on the stage]. All of Derrida's writings, his thought of writing, indeed the concept of *arche-trace* and of the erasure of the origin, bear the trace of his reading of Freud. Everything will have begun in duplication, in iterability. Meaning is always ambiguous, multiple and disseminated. This is, long before structuralism in psychoanalysis existed, the first elements of a critique of it, that is to say, of a critique of the primacy, indeed of the imperialism of the signifier and of the symbolic order as they were developed by Lacan.

From the study of the metaphoricity of writing for giving an account of the functioning of the psychical apparatus and from his discussion of Freud's Writing Pad as a technical model for representing memory externally as an internal archivization, Derrida was anticipating on the new printing, reproductive, formalizing, and archivizing techniques, by supposing that the machine itself might begin increasingly to resemble memory. Henceforth, would the psychical apparatus be "better represented" or "affected differently" by so many new prostheses of the so-called live memory?[6] Derrida comes back to this question twenty-eight years later and notes that "the technical structure of the *archiving* archive also determines the structure of the *archivable* content even in its very coming into existence and in its relationship to the future" (*AF*, 17). Now, psychoanalysis – its theory, its practice, its institution – is wholly a science of the archive and of the proper name, of a logic of hypomnesis which explains the lacunas of memory, of what archivizes memory by transforming it, or anarchivizes, erases, and destroys it; it is also the science of its own history, of that of its founder, of the relation between private (or secret) documents and the elaboration of its theory and of everything which, in a subterranean manner, can enlighten its appearance in the world.

One finds the principle of the so-called "originary" delay and the notions of "imprint, pre-impression and of pre-inscription" again in the thought of *desistance*, which, since Derrida, I consider to be a central concept for psychoanalysis. Indeed "something began before me, the one who undergoes the experience. I'm late. If I insist upon remaining the subject of this experience, it would have to be as a prescribed, pre-inscribed subject, marked in advance by the imprint of the ineluctable that constitutes this subject without belonging to it."[7] It is thus a matter of *a constitutive desistance of the subject* which destines the demand for meaning or for truth to the question of its own finality. *Desistance* redoubles or disinstalls everything which secures reason, without however falling into unreason "against which Platonic onto-ideology, or even Heidegger's interpretation of it, is established" (D, p. 24). The logic proper to *desistance* leads to the destabilization of the subject, to its disidentification from every position in *estance*, from all determinations of the subject by the ego. This does not mean that the subject "desists itself" ("to desist" does not allow a reflexive construction in English which it requires in French) but rather that *it* desists without "desisting *itself.*" For Derrida, the thought of *desistance* is one of the most demanding thoughts of responsibility.

To think responsibility on the basis of the *desistance* of the subject from all determinations arising from the identifications that constitute their mask is also to think responsibility from the unconscious, which ignores the difference between the virtual and the actual, between intention and action. It is to extend responsibility – that to which the subject must answer – well beyond the data of consciousness, to which Right and Morals usually refer. It is to open the field of the subject's responsibility to what preceding generations bequeath us and to what is transmitted by a transgenerational memory. It is also to render the ethical act of nomination ineluctable.[8]

While maintaining a possible recourse to the archive, to what is id-iomatically inscribed inside or outside us, to what is both offered and subtracted from translation, psychoanalysis always attempts to come back to the live origin of the traces which the archive loses by keeping them in a multiplicity of places. There would be no drive [*poussée*] to preservation without, in the opposite direction, a drive to destruction, which itself belongs to the process of archivization. And if the authority of the principle which renews the law of the archive, its institution, its domiciliation is deconstructed by Freud, a patriarchal logic, also entirely Freudian, renews its institutionalizing strategy. For Derrida, "The possibility of the archiving trace, this simple *possibility*, can only divide the uniqueness. Separating the impression from the imprint" (*AF*, 100). One of the lessons Derrida draws from Freud, and it is not the least important one, is that "contradiction . . . modulates and conditions the very forma-tion of the concept of the archive and of the concept in general – right where they bear the contradiction" (ibid., 90). Psychoanalytic language no longer understands the Unconscious from the standpoint of experience, of meaning and of presence, as Husserl did, but conceives of the Unconscious by removing it from what it makes possible, and by giving access "to what conditions the phenomenality of proceeding from an a-semantic instance."9 Translation henceforth operates within the same language by de-signifying and re-signifying concepts. For psychoanalysis this means: its "own" concepts, indeed the proper names which mark its history.

In his reading of *Beyond the Pleasure Principle*,10 Derrida indicates in what way "Freud advanced only by suspending, without any possibility of stopping, all the theses at which his successors or heirs, his readers in general, would have liked to see him stop. That reading was also an interpretation of what links speculation on the name, the proper name, or family names to science, particularly to the theory and the institution of psychoanalysis."11 That is to say, of what links the speculative to the specular, to the mirror which reflects the scene which the text describes. This reading will have left a strong impression on Derrida:

I wish to speak of the *impression left* by Freud, by the event which carries this family name, the nearly unforgettable and incontestable, undeniable *impression* (even and above all for those who deny it) that Sigmund Freud will have *made* on anyone, after him, who speaks *of him* or speaks *to him*, and who must then, accepting it or not, knowing it or not, be thus marked: in his or her culture and discipline, whatever it may be, in particular philosophy, medicine, psychiatry, and more precisely here, because we are speaking of memory and of archive, the history of texts and of discourses, political history, legal history, the history of ideas or of culture, the history of religion and religion itself, the history of the institutional and scientific project called psychoanalysis. Not to mention the history of history, the history of historiography. In any given discipline, one can no longer, one should no longer be able to, thus one no longer has the right or the means to claim to speak of this without having been marked in advance, in one way or another, by this Freudian impression. It is impossible and illegitimate to do so without having integrated, well or badly, in an important way or not, recognizing it or denying it, what is here called the *Freudian impression*. If one is under the impression that it is possible not to take this into account, forgetting it, effacing it, crossing it out, or objecting to it, one has already confirmed, we could even say countersigned (thus archived), a "repression" or a "suppression." (*AF*, 31)

In no way does Derridean deconstruction repress the Freudian inheritance. By a hyperanalytical necessity, it prolongs it by calling into question the desire or the fantasy of rejoining the originary, the irreducible, the indivisible. Concurrent with the two motifs of any analysis, the *archaeological* motif of the return to the old, which governs repetition and its alteration, and the *philolytic* motif of the disassociative unbinding, of the decomposition of unities, of the deconstitution of sediments, deconstruction maintains the analytic exigency of the always possible unbinding as the very condition of possibility of binding in general:

> What is called "deconstruction" undeniably obeys an *analytic* exigency, at once critical and analytic . . . The question of divisibility is one of the most powerful instruments of formalization for what is called deconstruction. If, in an absurd hypothesis, there were one and only one deconstruction, a sole *thesis* of "Deconstruction," it would pose divisibility: différance as divisibility.[12]

We are here touching upon the heart of the theoretical disagreement between Derrida and Lacan, the consequences of which for the psychoanalytic practice, theory and institution I shall briefly indicate.[13] This field is hardly explored and is one against which psychoanalysis still strongly resists. Let us recall that the analytic supplement [*supplément d'analyse*] required by "deconstruction" does not go without a certain emphatic homage to Lacan, of which I quote only an extract:

> Whether one is talking about philosophy, psychoanalysis, or theory in general, what the flat-footed restoration underway attempts to recover, disavow, or censor is the fact that nothing of that which managed to transform the space of thought in the last decades would have been possible without some coming to terms *with* Lacan, without the Lacanian provocation, however one receives it or discusses it.[14]

2. PSYCHOANALYSIS WITH DERRIDA

In the second part of this chapter, I shall attempt to show how several clinical, theoretical, and institutional aspects of psychoanalysis can be reconsidered, revised and modified by Derrida's reading of some major psychoanalytic texts, such as Jacques Lacan's seminar on Edgar Allen Poe's "The Purloined Letter." When transposed onto Lacan's other texts, that is, onto the development of the psychoanalytic corpus, these deconstructive readings put into question fundamental psychoanalytic concepts, such as, for example, transference and the place of the analyst in interpretation, the function of the signifier and of the letter, their destination and their "destinerrance" (their wandering destination), the status of truth and of the effects of truth, etc. Such a rereading has implications for the practice and the theory of psychoanalysis, as well as for the history of the psychoanalytic movement. The analogies that are woven between the development of a theory and that of the socio-institutional context of psychoanalysis shall be evident. All this adds a new dimension to psychoanalytic thought, which can henceforth be called "desistential." In the same way as Derrida is unthinkable without psychoanalysis, psychoanalysis has become unthinkable without Derrida. That is not to say that there is such a thing as "Derridean psychoanalysis," as some people either think or fear. Psychoanalysis is at the frontier of all research (literary, philosophical, but also biological, genetic, etc.). It recognizes its numerous debts, but it does not need to be marked by a proper name, even if the function of the proper name occupies a central place in it.

Since the 1960s, then, Derrida has interrogated numerous motifs governing both psychoanalytic and philosophical discourses. These motifs, to mention only a few, are called phonocentrism, logocentrism, phallocentrism, "full speech" as truth, the transcendentalism of the signifier, the circular return of the letter *missing from its "proper" place* (I shall come back to this), the neutralizing exclusion of the narrator from the scene of the narrative, etc. Now, these motifs are also those which, at the same time, confidently construct Lacan's theoretical, clinical and institutional movement of a "return to Freud," which is as powerfully articulated as it is dogmatically asserted. These motifs are indeed found in the *Écrits* (1966) and, exemplarily, in the opening text of this collection, which plays an organizing role independently from the date of its publication and that of the articles included in the collection.[15] This text, "Seminar on 'The Purloined Letter'," provides a reading of Edgar Poe's tale "The Purloined Letter," on the basis of the Freudian notion of "repetition automatism" which, for Lacan who finds support in Saussurean linguistics, becomes "the insistence of the signifying chain." Hence, Lacan's aphorism which concludes his commentary: "Thus it is that what the 'purloined letter,' nay, the 'letter in sufferance,' means is that a letter always arrives at its destination" ("Seminar," 53). This conclusion is possible only in so far as the "letter," which is for Lacan the place of the materiality of the signifier, cannot be divided. Now, this "indivisibility" of the letter corresponds, according to Derrida, to the ideal identity of the letter, to its "idealization," to which one can always object that a letter is divisible, can arrive or not at its destination. This affects the logic of the event, the thought of singularity, the dissemination of the unique beyond the logic of castration, etc.

In order to limit my development, I shall concentrate here on how the neutralizing exclusion of the narrator in Lacan's reading of Poe's tale, which is echoed in the exclusion of the interpreter in "The Direction of the Treatment and the Principle of its Power" (a contemporary text to the "Seminar" which is formalized according to the same model), brings about an identification with one of the protagonists of the scene.[16] We shall see that this identification acts as a resistance to the *desistance of the subject* which alone is likely to situate the interpretation outside the scene where it can otherwise only but be expected and agreed upon by the analysand and the analyst. In this way, we shall see that what closes such a reading of Poe's tale by locking it up is nothing less than a historical scene, contemporary to the writing of the "Seminar" and "The Direction of the Treatment," which evades this very reading.

In order to follow these developments, let us recall Poe's "The Purloined Letter." Two scenes generally leave the reader with a vivid memory of them. The first is played out in the royal boudoir in the presence of the Queen and the King. The Queen has received a compromising letter which she conceals from the eyes of the King through a simple gesture of turning it over on the table. Enter Minister D—, who perceives the discomfort of the Queen and who, while he keeps up chatter about affairs of State, takes a similar letter out of his pocket and makes as if to read it before letting it fall onto the desk. All he then has to do, while continuing the conversation, is to pick up not his own letter, but the other, while the Queen is watching, prevented from stepping in so as not to attract the attention of the King right alongside her. The second scene takes place in the Minister's study. While there on his first visit, the lynx eye of Dupin is drawn to a ticket which seems to have been abandoned in a card-rack hanging under the mantelpiece. From that moment on, his mind is made up. He deliberately leaves behind his snuff-box so he can return the next day to retrieve it. Armed in his turn with a counterfeit and having set up a street incident to bring the Minister to the window at the right moment, Dupin, like the Minister in the first scene, substitutes one letter for the other before taking leave of his host in the normal way.

In the "Seminar," these two scenes are designated as two primal scenes, the second one being the repetition of the first. But Derrida reminds us that the two triangular scenes that Lacan discusses are narrated within the totality of the narrative structure. The scene which takes place in the royal apartments is recounted by the Prefect when he visits Dupin in the presence of the narrator and the second by Dupin, telling the narrator after the Prefect's departure. Several consequences follow from the exclusion, not to say the foreclusion, of the narrator in Lacan's reading, notably – as far as what interests me here is concerned – that of bringing about the identification of the analyst with Dupin's position. The place proper to the letter in sufferance (and of the being in sufferance) is the one where Dupin and the psychoanalyst expect to find it: "In which respect Dupin shows himself quite the equal of the psychoanalyst when it comes to success." Or else, "do we not in fact feel concerned with good reason when for Dupin what is perhaps at stake is his withdrawal from the symbolic circuit of the letter – we who become the emissaries of all the purloined letters which at least for a time remain in sufferance with us in transference" ("Seminar," 48). But why should the analyst just as well not identify himself with the narrator, who occupies the much more neutral position of hearing the narrative, for Dupin has a revenge to take on the Minister? Why should he not identify with the Prefect? Another reading can easily show that, by going to Dupin, the Prefect knew that the letter was already there or, if it were to be found, could not but be found there, since for him, to search the honorable detective or to exert any kind of pressure in the presence of the narrator is of course out of the question. He could only intimate that he was ready to pay the price for it. The same could be said of the Minister D—, Dupin's brother. It is not the fact that the letter has been left exposed, as one pretends to believe, which makes it the best hiding place for the good sleuth. The Minister has left clues which might be indecipherable for anyone else other than Dupin. One knows that the stolen letter bears the Duc de S's seal, which is small and red, and that the writing of the superscription addressed to the Queen is bold and masculine. Now, the writing on the letter Dupin notices in the Minister's office is tiny and feminine, the seal large and black and marked with the cipher D. A woman, whom Dupin cannot but know and who owns the Minister's seal, will thus have lent her support to the returning of the letter, of the same one, by invaginating it like a glove in order to divide it [*la rendre double*], to make it bear inverted signs on the inside and on the outside. Why should the reader, the interpreter, the analyst not still identify with the Queen, to whom the letter is returned in the end, to whom the letter returns by erasing itself?

Why should the analyst, if one really insists on retaining the analogy, not traverse the chain of identifications with each of the protagonists of the scene, who, in their turn, by escaping each of these identifications, will have been emissaries of the letter; by putting himself, without desisting *himself*, in *desistance* from the one or the other, from the one and the other, as far as it is possible to do the impossible? For the identification always has an end, a *telos*. Here, through the identification of the analyst with Dupin, the "Seminar" aims to make Poe's letter – its decipherment – return to Lacan, by dethroning Marie Bonaparte's too hermeneutical interpretation, which Lacan nevertheless partly takes up again on his own account. The "Seminar" also aims to make Freud's very letter return to the same Lacan, that is, Freud's letter, which prefaces the Princess's book devoted to Poe, but also, by establishing the insistence of the signifying chain, the letter of the repetition automatism, the letter, then, of the resistance *of* the unconscious *to* the unconscious, which, beyond pleasure, governs the most determining effects for the subject.

Poe's tale which, together with "The Murders in the Rue Morgue" and "The Mystery of Marie Rogêt," makes up a sort of trilogy, does not only authorize a series of abyssal readings [*lectures en abyme*], none of which can dominate the others, or allow an analogical reading with the unfolding of an analysis, but it also stages characters which are closely related to events of real life that are taking place at the time of their writing. Can one find analogies with such a model in Lacan's "Seminar"? If such were the case, Lacan's identification with the analyst Dupin would be overdetermined. The author of the "Seminar" tells us that "Dupin, *from the place he now occupies*, cannot help feeling a rage manifestly feminine" (51). A curious remark that is echoed in the "explosion of feeling" which the author shows towards a lady who remains unknown in the "Seminar." She emerges on the occasion of Baudelaire's inexact translation, pointed out by the Princess, concerning the place where the letter exactly lies: Baudelaire indeed erroneously translates "*just beneath the middle of the mantelpiece*" into "above the mantelpiece" (47). This question is of considerable importance if one expects the place where the phallus-letter is supposedly *missing from its place* to be precisely indicated: between the "cheeks" [*jambages*] of the fireplace. But, visibly yielding to anger, the author states that this question "may be abandoned to the inferences of those whose profession is grilling" and even adds in note, "and even to the cook herself" (47).

This scene of writing made of Marie Bonaparte in the "Seminar" is duplicated in "The Direction of the Treatment" in another scene made of Sacha Nacht (Lacan's rival in the 1953 institutional fights) concerning the latter's work entitled *La Psychanalyse d'aujourd'hui*. It might be useful to recall, in passing, that in this work the identification of the analysand with the analyst is promoted as the criterion of the end of analysis. Here is an "intersubjective triad" – a triad comparable to the one formed by the Queen, the Minister and Dupin – terribly heated by a circulation of letters, by broken alliances and by an institutional scission. A letter dated 14 July 1953 from Lacan to Loewenstein (who was *both* Lacan's and Nacht's analyst, and Princess Bonaparte's friend) enlightens, two years before the "Seminar," the historical scene of legacy at issue, still the scene of the inherited letter, of the very letter of the inheritance. After having painted a picture of the state of play of psychoanalysis in France to Loewenstein, who is exiled in the United States and has now become influential within the IPA (International Psychoanalytic Association), Lacan turns to the analysis of motivations. Let us follow the insistence of the signifying chain and the logic of the *quart exclu*: "To give you an analysis of what impels things, I must do justice to Nacht in conceding that he has neither vacillated nor flagged in the pursuit of his scheme [*dessein*]."[17] *Dessein* is the message-word, taken from the citation from Crébillon: "*Un dessein si funeste / S'il n'est digne d'Atrée, est digne de Thyeste*" [So baleful a plan, / If unworthy of Atreus, is worthy of Thyestes][18] which Dupin leaves as a signature on the substitute letter left to the Minister. It is also the lapsus object-word that Lacan transforms into destiny [*destin*] when he quotes "*Un destin si funeste*," two times out of three. The design which Lacan attributes to Nacht is worthy of Thyestes and of the Minister, for "if he has grouped around him the majority of our old colleagues, it is due to a constancy in his policy which would be worthy of respect if it had not been the result of equally unchanging but implacably unscrupulous methods" (*LS*). For Lacan, Nacht is thus an "unprincipled man," as it is said of the Minister. But, as the Minister for Dupin, he is also a brother: "My wife made him welcome and, in the house of my brother-in-law, Masson the painter, he was received with a hospitality that made it possible for him to remarry in the cordial atmosphere of a small Provençal village" (ibid.). And further on: "My confidence in him, it must be said, was rock solid" (ibid.). This was still before the explosion of their friendly ferocity. A lady, and not just anyone, the legatee of the Freudian letter, is at the heart of their falling out:

> Unfortunately for us, opposition took root in an unstable situation. Nacht, sure of his success, thought he could rid himself of the Princess: he dismissed her from our Counsels by refusing to welcome her. To be sure, it is reasonable to consider the actions of this person to have always been inauspicious in our group. The social prestige she brought with her can only warp relations there, the prestige she gains from her closeness to Freud means she is listened to with a patience which passes for approval, the respect one must show for an old lady requires a tolerance for her opinions which demoralizes the younger ones, in whose eyes we appear to be in a ridiculous position of subjection. (ibid.)

Nonetheless, the Princess still remains Lacan's ally: "The help of the Princess, whose character you are well acquainted with, has *brought matters to a head* but has, I am sorry to say, served to crystallize a cell around Nacht" [my emphasis] (ibid.). And then, with the entrance of the lady from Vienna: "I was the extremely unwilling witness of the Princess's astounding telephone calls to Anna Freud, in which she described our adversaries as gangsters" (ibid.). Then came the switching of alliances that followed Lacan's drawing up of the principles on which an Institute of Psychoanalysis should be run:

Simply failing to mention both the Princess and her honorary functions was sufficient to decide everything. In a meeting that she had asked for . . . she concluded a treaty with Nacht whose terms were only revealed by what then happened: the *secret pact* [my emphasis] was, after four months, to be sealed by a session uniquely devoted to giving the Princess the prize for her good and loyal services. (ibid.)

In connection with this, one should reread an enigmatic passage from the "Seminar" held two years later: "It is here that the origin of that horror betrays itself, and he who experiences it has no need to declare himself (in a most unexpected manner) 'a partisan of the lady' in order to reveal it to us: it is known that ladies detest calling principles into question, for their charms owe much to the mystery of the signifier." The letter, let us recall, is the materiality of the signifier. The final lines of Lacan's letter reveal a man confronted with despicable schemes, confident about the contribution he thinks he is currently making to the conception of analytic experience. The word *destiny* flows naturally from his pen: "Whatever happens, you should know that you will encounter here a man more convinced of his duties and his destiny" (*LS*).

The analogy between the events of real life, a sequence of unfathomable readings and a theory of the "analytic cure" is perhaps most "analogous" with the writing of Edgar Poe. "There are ideal series of events which run parallel with the real ones" reads the inscription at the beginning of "The Mystery of Marie Roget."[19] This citation from Novalis adds that these events "rarely coincide," but the narrator goes out of his way to emphasize the coincidences: "The extraordinary details which I am now called upon to make public, will be found to form, as regards sequence of time, the primary branch of a series of scarcely intelligible *coincidences* [Poe's emphasis]" (*The Mystery*, 143). And "The Murders in the Rue Morgue" suggests, for anyone interested in enigmas, rebus and in hieroglyphs, to reduce the totality of pieces down to *four kings* with each of the pieces having their double, just like Dupin, the narrator and the reader redouble themselves, just as the letter circulates with its interior and exterior faces.

In the example that follows, which is even more closely related to analytic practice, it is once more the identification with one of the protagonists in a scene of inheritance of thought that reveals the blind spot of the interpretation or the fixation to a demand for meaning.

In "The Direction of the Treatment," Lacan takes up again from Ernst Kris, one of the analysts of the famous *troïka* – Hartman, Kris and Loewenstein – whose names remain attached to *Ego Psychology*, the example called *The Man with the Cold Brains*. At issue is an American academic who cannot publish his research because he believes that he is guilty of plagiarism. His analyst, who aims to link this resistance to the analyst's own interpretation of patient defenses, seizes the opportunity of using some work that the patient has just completed, in which the latter claims that he repeats the ideas found in someone else's work, to assess the situation. The analyst discovers that the patient has apparently done nothing more than is normal practice in the field, indeed that it is he alone, the patient, who accuses the author of having said what he wants to say, even that the author might in fact have repeatedly taken over the patient's own ideas. In brief, since the situation is reversed through reality-testing, the patient, after analytic sessions, begins to wander along in the neighboring streets in order to scrutinize restaurant menus in search of his favorite dish: cold brains. The so-called reality-testing will only have displaced the compulsion by making it look as if only existing in the brain of the analyst: "It's not that your patient doesn't steal that is important here. It's that . . . steals nothing."[20] This pertinent remark does not, however, wear down the point where *something* [*ça*] resists and which has once again something to do with identification. This time, it has something to do with the identification of "Dupin's equal," not with the patient believing himself to be a plagiarist, or with his reluctantly behaviorist analyst, but with the real or imaginary plagiarized. A note from Lacan cannot help but say it: "In the United States, where Kris has achieved success, publication makes news and teaching like mine should stake its claim to priority each week against the pillage that it cannot fail to attract" (ibid., 280).

The impression of strange familiarity uneasily bears the division [*partition*] of the same and the effects of the double, and more precisely, of the uncanny inherent in the *Bewusstsein* (being *known* for having always been "already seen" [*déjà vu*]) and to consciousness taking itself for the object of its own [*propre*] "reflection." For Freud, the phenomenon of consciousness lies in the doubling of an agency by itself: "But it is only this latter, material, offensive as it is to the criticism of the ego, which may be incorporated in the idea of a double. There are also all the unfulfilled but possible futures . . . and all our suppressed acts of volition which nourish in us the illusion of Free Will."[21] The experience of an exterior gaze on the so-called "self," which is redoubled through its passage to the "inside," implies the *desistance* of this gaze from the object which lends it assistance. This experience frightens reason, it is its risk and its chance. Its risk, for the meeting with the double, this double, which the subject calls to daylight, always confronts one to the other as wholly other and to one's death. It is its chance of not being liberated by anyone else but "oneself"[22] and of dying of one's own death.

Lacan has not failed to represent to himself, on the most spectral mode, such an experience. It should attract, as a hypothesis, a hypothesis of the school, the attention of the "candidates in training":

Let us imagine what would take place in a patient who saw in his analyst an exact replica of himself. Everyone feels that the excess of aggressive tension would set up such an obstacle to the manifestation of the transference that its useful effect could only be brought about extremely slowly, and this is what sometimes happens in the analysis of prospective analysts. To take an extreme case, experienced in the form of strangeness proper to the apprehensions of the *double*, this situation would set up an uncontrollable anxiety on the part of the analysand.[23]

The problematic of the double goes hand in hand with the division of the letter. It is in this respect that it prevents one from conceiving of a circular trajectory from send-off to destination. If the trajectory is possible it is nevertheless not guaranteed. Indeed, the double – notably in the analytic transference – redoubles the circuit of the letter from start. The send-off is split [*dédoublé*] and turned back – *to the starting point* – and the divided letters, crisscrossing in their trajectories, constantly intercept each other's messages. This is also what takes any demand for meaning back to its own finality.

These few indications aimed to draw attention to the impact of Derridean deconstruction on the analytic practice, theory and institution. Derridean deconstruction, which is not identifiable with any system, pursues indefinitely, or hyperanalytically, the analysis of the effects of the assignation of a place, of the subjection to a thought and of the fixation to the imaginary properties of a proper name.

NOTES

1 Jacques Derrida, "Let us not Forget – Psychoanalysis," *Oxford Literary Review*
  12, nos. 1–2, *Psychoanalysis and Literature* (1990), nos. 3–4. This citation is taken
  from Derrida's introduction to my paper "Reason From the Unconscious,"
  which I delivered on 16 December 1988 at the Sorbonne in Paris, on the
  occasion of the Forum "Thinking at Present," organized by the Collège
  international de philosophie.

2 I here follow closely Geoffrey Bennington's remarks in his paper entitled
  "Circanalyse (La chose même)" delivered at the Colloque de Cerisy in July
  1996 (forthcoming Paris: Aubier).

3 Jacques Derrida, "Freud and the Scene of Writing," in *Writing and Differ-*
  ence, trans., with an Introduction and Additional Notes, A. Bass (Chicago:
  University of Chicago Press, 1978), 212; hereafter, *FSW*.

4 See S. Freud, *Moses and Monotheism, Three Essays* in *The Standard Edition of the*
  Complete Psychological Works [SE], vol. XXIII (London: Hogarth Press and the
  Institute of Psychoanalysis, 1958), 129–30.

5 SE, vol. XIII, 176–7.

6 Jacques Derrida, *Archive Fever: A Freudian Impression*, trans. E. Prenowitz
  (Chicago: University of Chicago Press, 1995), 32; hereafter, *AF*.

7 "Desistance" in Philippe Lacoue-Labarthe, *Typography: Mimesis, Philosophy,*
  Politics, trans. C. Fynsk (Cambridge, MA: Harvard University Press, 1989).
  "Desistance" (hereafter, D) is Derrida's introduction to an English collection
  of essays by Philippe Lacoue-Labarthe who uses recurrently the verb *désister*
  and the substantive *désistement*. Derrida's essay begins by addressing the problems of translation which these terms are bound to raise, in particular as far
  as, in its juridical sense, the verb *désister* requires the reflexive construction
  [*se désister*] which does not exist in English. In his discussion – destined for
  an English readership – of Lacoue-Labarthe's concepts of *désistement* and of
  désister, Derrida introduces the term "désistance," but warns that it cannot
  be translated without further precautions as "desistance." For an elaboration
  of the divergent and "very different syntactic possibilities" of "desistance"
  and "désistance," see "Desistance," 1–5. In this translation, "désistance" is
  translated as *desistance*. The italics should suffice to signal that precautions
  must be taken around this term.

8 In "Géopsychanalyse" (in *Psyché: inventions de l'autre* [Paris: Galilée, 1987]),
  Derrida elaborates on the way in which the psychoanalytic institution
  has been able to archivize the unnameable and how psychoanalysis
  could contribute to another thought of the ethical, the juridical, and the
  political.

9 Jacques Derrida, "Me-Psychoanalysis: An Introduction to the Translation of
  'The Shell and the Kernel' by Nicolas Abraham," trans. R. Klein, *Diacritics*
  (1979), 7.

10 Jacques Derrida, *The Post Card: From Socrates to Freud and Beyond*, trans. with an
   Introduction and Additional Notes, A. Bass (Chicago: University of Chicago
   Press, 1987).

11 Jacques Derrida, "For the Love of Lacan," in *Resistances of Psychoanalysis*, trans. P. Kamuf, P.-A. Brault, and M. Naas (Stanford: Stanford University Press, 1998), 41.

12 Derrida, "*Resistances*," in *Resistances of Psychoanalysis*, 27–33.

13 I shall return later, without being able to develop them at length, to certain theses elaborated in R. Major, *Derrida avec Lacan: Analyse désistentielle* (Paris: Champs Flammarion, 2001).

14 "For the Love of Lacan," 46.

15 Jacques Lacan, "Seminar on *The Purloined Letter*," trans. J. Mehlman in J. P. Muller and W. J. Richardson, eds., *The Purloined Poe: Lacan, Derrida and Psychoanalytic Reading* (Baltimore: Johns Hopkins University Press, 1988), 28–54. See also Jacques Lacan, *The Seminar, Book II: The Ego in Freud's Theory and in Psychoanalytic Technique, 1954–55*, trans. Sylvana Tomaselli, with notes by J. Forrester (Cambridge: Cambridge University Press, 1988).

16 For a more detailed and meticulous analysis, I refer the reader to "La Parabole de la lettre" in *Derrida avec Lacan* [partially translated by J. Forrester as "The Parable of The Purloined Letter," *Stanford Literature Review* (Spring–Fall 1991), 67–102]. For Derrida's reading of Lacan's "Seminar on *The Purloined Letter*," see "Le Facteur de la vérité" in *The Post Card*.

17 *La Scission de 1953*. Documents edited by J.-A. Miller (with Lacan's consent) (*Ornicar?* 1976), 120–32. (hereafter, as *LS*). [Translated by J. Forrester in "The Parable of the Purloined Letter."]

18 Thomas O. Mabbott, "Text of 'The Purloined Letter' with Notes," in J. P. Muller and W. J. Richardson, eds., *The Purloined Poe*, 27.

19 E. A. Poe, *Selected Tales* (Oxford: Oxford University Press, 1980), 142.

20 Jacques Lacan, "The Direction of the Treatment and the Principle of its Power" in *Écrits, A Selection*, trans. A. Sheridan (London: Tavistock Publications, 1977), 239.

21 "The Uncanny," *SE*, vol. XVII, 236.

22 Allusion to one of La Rochefoucauld's sentences concerning *l'amour-propre*.

23 Jacques Lacan, "Aggressivity in Psychoanalysis," in *Écrits, A Selection*.

FURTHER READING

Derrida, Jacques. "Freud and the Scene of Writing." In *Writing and Difference*. Trans. A. Bass. Chicago: University of Chicago Press, 1978. [*L'Écriture et la différence*. Paris: Éditions du Seuil, 1967.]

The Post Card: From Socrates to Freud and Beyond. Trans. A. Bass. Chicago: University of Chicago Press, 1987. [*La Carte postale: De Socrate à Freud et au-delà*. Paris: Flammarion, 1980.]

"Me-Psychoanalysis: An Introduction to the Translation of 'The Shell and the Kernel' by Nicolas Abraham." Trans. R. Klein, *Diacritics* (1979) ["moi-La psychanalyse." In *Psyché: inventions de l'autre*. Paris: Galilée, 1987.]

"Desistance." In Philippe Lacoue-Labarthe, *Typography: Mimesis, Philosophy, Politics.* Trans. C. Fynsk. Cambridge, MA: Harvard University Press, 1989. ["Désistance." In *Psyché: inventions de l'autre.* Paris: Galilée, 1987.]

"Let us not Forget – Psychoanalysis." *The Oxford Literary Review* 12, 1–2, *Psychoanalysis and Literature* (1990).

Archive Fever: A Freudian Impression. Trans. E. Prenowitz. Chicago: University of Chicago Press, 1995. [*Mal d'Archive.* Paris: Galilée, 1995.]

"For the Love of Lacan"; "Resistances" in *Resistances of Psychoanalysis.* Trans. P. Kamuf, P.-A. Brault, M. Naas. Stanford: Stanford University Press, 1998. ["Pour l'amour de Lacan"; "Résistances" in *Résistances de la psychanalyse.* Paris: Galilée, 1996.]

Freud, Sigmund. *Moses and Monotheism, Three Essays in The Standard Edition of the Complete Psychological Works.* Vol. XXIII. London: The Hogarth Press and the Institute of Psychoanalysis, 1958.

"The Claims of Psycho-Analysis to Scientific Interest." *SE.* Vol. XIII.

"The Uncanny." *SE.* Vol. XVII.

Lacan, Jacques. *The Seminar, Book II: The Ego in Freud's Theory and in Psychoanalytic Technique, 1954–55.* Trans. Sylvana Tomaselli, with notes by J. Forrester. Cambridge: Cambridge University Press, 1988.

"Seminar on *The Purloined Letter.*" Trans. J. Mehlman. In J. P. Muller and W. J. Richardson, eds., *The Purloined Poe: Lacan, Derrida, and Psychoanalytic Reading.* Baltimore: Johns Hopkins University Press, 1988. ["Séminaire sur 'La Lettre volée'" in *Écrits.* Paris: Éditions du Seuil, 1966.]

"The Direction of the Treatment and the Principle of its Power"; "Aggressivity in Psychoanalysis." In *Écrits, A Selection.* Trans. A. Sheridan. London: Tavistock Publications, 1977. ["La Direction de la cure et les principes de son pouvoir"; "L'agressivité en psychanalyse." In *Écrits.* Paris: Éditions du Seuil, 1966.]

La Scission de 1953. Documents edited by J.-A. Miller (with Lacan's consent), 1976.

Mabbott, Thomas O. "Text of 'The Purloined Letter' with Notes." In J. P. Muller and W. J. Richardson, eds., *The Purloined Poe* (Baltimore: Johns Hopkins University Press, 1988).

Major, René. *Derrida avec Lacan: Analyse désistentielle.* Paris: Éditions Mentha, 1991. "La Parabole de la lettre." In R. Major, *Derrida avec Lacan: Analyse désistentielle.* Paris: Champs Flammarion, 2001. [Partially trans. J. Forrester as "The Parable of the Purloined Letter," *Stanford Literature Review* (Spring–Fall 1991).]

Poe, Edgar Allan. *Selected Tales.* Oxford: Oxford University Press, 1980.

Glossary

David Wills

The terms listed below, numbered in order of appearance, are italicized in the discussion that follows. The numbers are repeated in parentheses within the text in order to facilitate consultation. Each term is followed by the title of one representative work by Derrida in which extended discussion of the term can be found:

38. MOURNING (*Memoirs*)
24. NAME (PROPER) (*Glas*)
44. PARASITE ("The Law of Genre," *Glyph* 7)
22. PARERGON (*The Truth in Painting*)
3. PHARMAKON ("Plato's Pharmacy" in *Dissemination*)
16. POSTCARD (*The Post Card*)
33. PROMISE ("How to Avoid Speaking" in *Languages of the Unsayable*)
26. RE-MARK ("The Law of Genre," *Glyph* 7)
39. RESPONSIBILITY (*The Gift of Death*)
23. SIGNATURE (*Signsponge*)
7. SPACING (*Of Grammatology*)
36. SPECTRALITY (*Specters of Marx*)
1. SUBJECTILE ("Forcener le subjectile" in Paule Thévenin and Jacques Derrida, *The Secret Art of Antonin Artaud*)
13. SUPPLEMENT (*Of Grammatology*)
25. TECHNÉ ("Freud and the Scene of Writing" in *Writing and Difference*)
9. TEXT (*Of Grammatology*)
10. TRACE (*Of Grammatology*)
5. UMBRELLA (*Spurs*)
27. UNDECIDABILITY ("Force of Law" in *Deconstruction and the Possibility of Justice*)
34. VIENS ("Pas" in *Parages*)
43. WITNESSING ("Demeure" in *The Instant of My Death/Demeure*)
8. WRITING (*Of Grammatology*)

There are compelling reasons for refraining from any attempt to construct a glossary adequate to Derrida's ideas, especially one that claims to define a list of terms in a few words like a series of dictionary entries. The first difficulty arises from the proliferation of terms that could easily be included in such a series, making selection, or at least circumscription of the corpus especially hazardous, and necessarily arbitrary. Certain terms such as *subjectile* (1), to take the single example of a rare French word for the painted surface used by Artaud and picked up by Derrida in order to analyze the problematic of visual representation in the former's drawings, have in general remained within the local context of their original usage. One could develop a list of a score or so of similar terms in Derrida's voluminous writings. Others, such as *hymen* (2), which Mallarmé's syntactical and semantic torsions allow to be read as both a membrane and the marriage that implies the breaking of that membrane, or *pharmakon* (3), the remedy that Plato "confuses" with a poison, originally occurred in specific contexts, but have, as it were, sufficiently entered the Derridean lexicon to be repeated in other contexts. All these terms either occur in the work of the writer, philosopher, or visual artist under discussion, or suggest themselves to the analysis by virtue of their function as *hinge*s (4) or articulations that hold together elements of an argument or system while at the same time revealing the points at which that same system risks coming apart. The terms just mentioned are not, of course, restricted to abstract nouns. In many cases objects such as the *umbrella* (5), which can appear open or closed, protective or offensive, female or male, are made to function as types of conceptual configuration that raise similar questions concerning their own status, form, or function.

Still other terms have, for better or worse, become catchwords that Derrida himself elaborates upon, reluctantly or willingly returns to, or indeed replaces with another term, from one piece of writing to the next. Here we could mention the neologism *différance* (6) which began its career in a discussion of Husserl's difficulty in describing speech that was spoken and at the same time heard by its speaker. Derrida returned to it often in his early, and not so early work, playing on the differentiation operative in its written but not its spoken form to refer to the (at least on one level) imperceptible impetus – always at work, already in the beginning, as a delay or *spacing* (7) if nothing else – within a supposed intact system of sameness, and that gives rise to difference in any form.

The second difficulty thus derives from Derrida's repeated insistence that the words he appears to privilege mean no one thing in and of themselves, but take their sense from inscription within a chain of like terms and cannot be isolated from those contexts in which they appear. Often Derrida will gloss a word, like *writing* (8), the form of language that philosophy has consistently demoted to a position as poor cousin of speech but that he demonstrates as having the same structural constitution as speech, and that thus figures as the *text* (9), *trace* (10) or *cinder* (11) that stands in for the impossible or lost origin while at the same time being the *mark* (12) of every enunciation whatsoever, with a shorter or longer list of other terms – such as those just employed – that he wants to use somewhat synonymously. The dictionary, neologisms, and the accidents of etymological associations have always been, somewhat in the tradition of Heidegger, a resource for his reworkings of philosophical formulations, and any dictionary must be understood to be in constant revision, having *supplements* (13) added that complement and at the same time supplant already existing senses.

Furthermore, since Derrida's work involves a critique of *logocentrism* (14), or the will to singularity and truth, and repression of disruptive differences, that in his view characterize Western thinking in general, it would be contradictory for him to insist on a single sense for any of these terms. But that is less a strategy on his part, he would argue, than a simple consequence of the fact that no element of language can reduce to a single undivided sense. At the very least it is spoken and heard, and in the space between those two operations, even when they are supposed to take place within the same head, occurs the whole gamut of effects ranging from perfect comprehension to utter misunderstanding, falsehood, and capricious fabulation. Derrida insists that all those effects are coextensive, and indeed issue from the same "origin," and that even if we must make distinctions among them if we are to understand one another at all, the distinctions we make are as impossible as they are necessary for there is no identifiable point at which comprehension ends and misunderstanding begins. At the same time as it represents a form of communication, language is thus also a *dissemination* (15), a scattering of meaning throughout an inexhaustible context. In the case of the letter, or more precisely the *postcard* (16), another example of a "conceptual object" that Derrida has developed at length, what he calls its *adestination* (17) (in French, *la destination* and *l'adestination*, like *différence* and *différance*, have the same pronunciation) means that however carefully it is addressed, the fact of that address in no way guarantees its arrival. Arrival of the message at its address, or addressee, is at the mercy of the complicated and uncontrollable series of relays comprising the postal system, and even when it does arrive, whatever has occurred during its transmission means that arrival is neither the end of the story nor the whole story.

The idea that a message goes astray even as it is being delivered is therefore built into the linguistic system as a fact of every utterance, and cannot be considered an accident. It can also be explained as a function of *iterability* (18), whereby the units composing an utterance issue from the speaker's mouth or writer's pen not as unique speech acts or a private language but as repeatable elements, as it were citations, to be employed by another user in a different context and thus in a more or less different sense. Since the *borders* (19) of a given context are impossible to define, without for all that ceasing to be necessary if language is to avoid dissolving into complete indeterminacy of meaning, Derrida's analyses often concentrate upon the *economy* (20) (cf. Gk. *oikos*, house – economics always begins with home economics) by means of which what is proper or interior – to a word, a system, an argument, a philosophy – attempts, and ultimately fails to distinguish itself from whatever threatens its integrity from the exterior. It is to be expected that meaning becomes unsettled in the *margins* (21) or in those areas of articulation where one field seeks to delineate and define itself with respect to another, often making for more productive analyses. Such mechanisms of discomposure are especially explicit in the framings of visual representations, as Derrida has shown in his reading of Kant's use of the term *parergon* (22) in the Third Critique, where the word for forms of ornamentation that surround the work of art, literally the *hors d'oeuvre*, refers seemingly indiscriminately to a frame, clothing on a statue, and a palace column, revealing Kant's difficulty in separating inside from outside, a difficulty that might be said to extend to his construction of the principles of reason and judgment in general. A *signature* (23) on a painting is another case in point: it isn't part of the field of graphic representation, except where a painter like Gauguin makes of it a visual motif; yet it does, in fact, belong to that field, composed of brushstrokes that are of the same matter as the painting itself. Whereas it centers or anchors the meaning of the painting by returning it to the source or creator it is deemed to have issued from, at the same time it disrupts it, introducing an "external" heterogeneity that repeats, within the frame and on the surface of the painting, the problematic of distinguishing between inside and outside.

A signature is not only a case of writing within the field of painting, and of course it is used much more widely than that example suggests. But even when it appears, as it were homogeneously, within the field of writing itself, on a check or as the name of the author on the cover of a book, it continues to represent a peculiarly heterogeneous figuration of the *proper name* (24). On the one hand it represents what we would want to express as our purest selfhood – inimitable, idiosyncratic, ours and nobody else's – on the other hand it refers to a more general system of naming as well as to complex institutional forms, tying us to laws (of copyright, of patronymy, of torts and contracts, of the land) over which we have little control. In order to function it must, like any utterance, be repeatable, and therefore at a certain point it begins to function more like a common noun.

It also begins to function more like a machine. Repeatability introduces the technological, what Derrida often refers to by its Greek root, *techné* (25), into the first and most insignificant mark – for even that can be divided, and should more properly be called a *re-mark* (26) – thus calling into question the status of a supposed prior and intact naturality. The technological is the harbinger of death, of the lifeless machine, leading philosophers and our culture to be haunted by the malignant and almost mechanical effects of even memory and writing, the one binding us to a past that appears to repeat itself, the other continuing to function, on its own, after its author is dead.

Given all that, rather than a traditional glossary, what might be required in order to fairly represent the range of Derrida's ideas is something like the databank that Geoff Bennington devises in his "Derridabase" (Bennington and Derrida, *Jacques Derrida*, Chicago, University of Chicago Press, 1993), and the interested reader is referred to that reasoned and extensive discussion for further details and references. On the other hand, explaining something in more detail in no way guarantees less ambiguity. One of the paradoxes of language that Derrida has pointed out is that whereas fewer words create doubt about meaning and call for more words to explain them, the addition of more words serves only to compound the disseminative effect.

Because there is no simple way out of the quandaries Derrida describes, his insistence that we confront the *undecidability* (27) that derives from the absence of a controlling center for meaning, and from the necessary yet impossible task of delimiting the boundaries of its context, has often been interpreted as either nihilism or quietism. The opposite is in fact the case: far from preventing decision, undecidability is necessary if decision is to take place. Without the structure of undecidability, by means of which a quandary presents itself and more than one alternative is offered, there can be no decision and what we call decision is simply the result of a program. Derrida's concentration on the logical impasse is thus driven by the productive force of such *aporias* (28), and for all the negative formulations of many of the terms being described here – neither this nor that, neither sensible nor intelligible, neither positive nor negative, neither inside nor outside, neither superior nor inferior, neither active nor passive, neither present nor absent – they are nevertheless to be understood as affirmative.

Affirmation (29) does not, however, come in the form of a constative utterance, for once again, within that perspective nothing would have happened at all outside of a programmed and predictable repetition. By the same token, it is not a matter of making a proclamation, of simply saying "yes," once and once only. Like the signature and in the manner of Nietzsche's eternal return, affirmation is always at least double, to be conceived of as opening the possibility of (differential) repetition. In these terms the idea of the *event* (30) itself, as singular occurrence, must submit to the force of a certain *invention* (31) that, if there were such a thing – and that remains a question and a hypothesis – would surprise, disrupt and even disable whatever occurs. Drawing on the ambivalences of the German language in Heidegger's formulation – *es gibt (das) Sein*, where *es gibt* translates as "there is" but also means "there/it gives" – he reconfigures the event in terms of the structure of the *gift* (32), as that which can only occur if it somehow manages to escape from the economy of an exchange, of debt and repayment. From that point of view it *cannot* simply occur, since even the simple recognition of a gift indebts the donee, as is demonstrated by the complicated modes and registers, from effusion to silence, of the thank you. Just as invention, to be truly invention, would have to be completely unrecognizable, so the gift, to be a true gift, would have to pass unperceived into the hands of its donee.

If invention and the gift were to occur, they would occur for Derrida with the performative force of a *promise* (33). The promise repeats the structure of the gift for, though it opens the possibility of whatever is deemed to come to pass – if the event were assured of coming to pass there would be no need of a promise – it in no way guarantees it. Akin to the promise is the invitation or call of the familiar imperative *"viens"* (34) ("come"), that is developed from Blanchot and that relates to a type of apocalyptic or *messianic* (35) invocation (the term is repeated throughout a passage of the Revelation of St. John). Derrida wants it to be understood without the eschatological overtones of those references and, as if in order to avoid such overtones, to reinforce the idea of repetition and to further preempt any simple "presentness" that might be ascribed to the event, he similarly refers to *spectrality* (36), suggesting a *"haunt*ology" that would problematize the phenomenological and ontological status of what can be known, occur or exist. And, as if in counterpoint to the negative theology that his ideas at this point run parallel to or even intersect with, he more than once takes as his analytical model or pretext the *khôra* (37) of Plato's *Timaeus*.

The context of spectrality is also that of *mourning* (38), something in play since the first spacing or structure of loss that inaugurated language, making every utterance a type of obituary. More specifically, however, mourning, as the experience within oneself of unassimilable loss coming from outside opens the dimension of relations to the other. It therefore marks what has been referred to as an ethical turn in Derrida's writings, with (not unqualified) reference often being made to Levinas. Even invention, not something one can create, for that would rob it of its surprise, is said to come from the other. What is called for in each case is some form of response, however fraught with contradiction such responses might be, and it is on that basis that one might begin to speak of *responsibility* (39), in terms of an answering for oneself before the other and answering the call of the other. Again, this is less a matter of declaring one's standpoint or predetermined position and more a matter of letting the other come, what Derrida also refers to as *hospitality* (40), where the guest (Lat. *hostis*) can be either friend or enemy. Neither does it mean passivity or acquiescence, but the, as it were, existentially desperate situation of an asymmetrical relationship giving rise to an impossible demand – such as when Abraham was called upon to sacrifice Isaac – coming from the other who is recognized as wholly or utterly other, yet still urgently expects a response. For Derrida it is only out of such an extreme situation, requiring what amounts to a fiduciary link to the other if not an act of *faith* (41), that any ethics can begin to be developed. Or indeed any *justice* (42), which cannot be the application of a law but involves each time the madness of an impossibility – absolute recognition of the other, invention, irreducible undecidability.

The form of discourse associated with giving an account of oneself before the other, and indeed before the law, is testimony or *witnessing* (43). It calls for the actual presence of the same witness at the event being recounted and at the moment of the testimony. In so doing, it structurally divides the very (fully present) moment that it relies upon, not just between past event and moment of testimony, but also by virtue of an opposition between a singular witness who saw *what no one else saw*, and one who recounts it as if *anybody else* in the same situation would also have seen it. The witness is also expected to be able to repeat the same facts without variation any number of times, and such iterability introduces into this supposed singularly human event the structure of the technological – something courts are currently wrestling with. Finally, a truthful account is only possible to the extent that false witness is also possible, and so witnessing opens the possibility of the very fiction that it seeks to discount.

In these more recent emphases of Derrida's thinking (Derrida dates them however to 1972, and ideas such as the gift and sacrifice are already explicit in the 1974 *Glas*), one thus encounters the same logic of the aporia that was elaborated upon in his earliest analyses, whereby an utterance, discourse, or concept, in expressing or defining itself, is found to (over)extend and *parasite* (44) itself with differences that, however necessary and insignificant they might at first appear to be, lead into the impasses and self-disqualification that constitute an experience of the impossible. That, however much it be the condition of possibility of utterance in general, should lead one to renounce summarizing Derrida's thinking by means of a list of terms comprising a glossary.

Index